THE ENCYCLOPEDIA OF
THE CAT

This is a Dempsey Parr Book.
Dempsey Parr is an imprint of Parragon.

DEMPSEY PARR

Queen Street House,
4 Queen Street,
Bath BA1 1HE

Copyright © Parragon 1999

ISBN 1-84084-505-8

Produced for Parragon Books by
Foundry Design & Production, a part of
The Foundry Creative Media Company Ltd,
Crabtree Hall, Crabtree Lane,
Fulham, London SW6 6TY

Special thanks to Polly Willis and Dave Jones

Printed and bound in Italy

THE ENCYCLOPEDIA OF
THE CAT

MICHAEL POLLARD

DP

DEMPSEY
PARR

Contents

How to Use this Book

This book contains a number of important features:

- **Seven chapters of detailed information** on all aspects of owning and looking after a cat, the history of cats and their place in the human world. Photographs, illustrations, informative captions and 'cat-fact' boxes provide extra detail on every page.
- **Descriptions of 44 cat breeds.** Listing longhair and shorthair varieties and a unique section containing information on rare and new breeds.
- **'Breed Information' boxes** covering alternative name, body shapes and permissible colour variations within the breed.
- **The reference section** provides a reading list, useful contacts including addresses of international cat fancy associations, a glossary of vital feline terms and an extensive index.

KEY TO SYMBOLS

The three symbols used throughout the breed sections of the encyclopedia provide the reader with extra information at a glance:

 The size of a cat, being small, medium or large

 Maintenance required for the coat, ranging from one brush for little care to 4 brushes for high maintenance

   The amount of exercise required by the cat ranging from a sitting cat for little or no exercise, a walking cat for moderate exercise to a running cat for active breeds

Introduction

Opposite
This majestic animal is not only king of the jungle but now, also, the preferred British pet.

Top
Cats have been household companions for centuries, this Egyptian statue dates back to 600 BC.

THE RELATIONSHIP between cats and the human race goes back at least 4,000 years, and although this partnership has had its ups and downs over the course of history it has never been stronger than it is today. There are 7.6 million cats in Britain alone, and in 1998 it was announced that for the first time cats had overtaken dogs as Britain's favourite pets. This possibly reflects the fact that, in busy turn of the century lifestyles, cats are easier to care for than dogs and less demanding of time and space. Whatever the reason, today's world seems to favour cats as pets.

It is always interesting and rewarding to know and understand more about your pets, and that is the main purpose of this book. It is written by a cat-lover who has owned cats for over 30 years and knows that however much you find out about cats they always retain the ability to surprise you. Perhaps this is one of their appealing characteristics — that we never quite know our cats in the same way as we know our dogs or our best friends. As Sir Walter Scott wrote: 'Cats are a mysterious kind of folk. There is more passing in their minds than we are aware of.'

There are two notes of caution for the reader, one concerning the section on breeds and the other the section on feline health.

In a book of this size it has been necessary to summarise the descriptions of ideal specimens of individual breeds, and indeed the ideals vary from one country to another. Readers who are interested in detailed information on the show standards relevant to their country should refer to the appropriate breed club or cat fancy organisation.

On feline ailments, details are given of the most common problems which owners may meet. But it cannot be emphasised too strongly that the scope for do-it-yourself treatment of cats' diseases is very limited, and if there is any doubt at all about a cat's health, veterinary help should be sought. In cases of emergency, animal welfare organisations can either offer help themselves or point the owner in the right direction.

A World of Cats

ONE IN FIVE British and North American homes have at least one cat as a member of the family. There are more than six million pet cats in Britain and five times that number in the United States. North Americans have for some time owned more cats than dogs, and in 1998 it was announced that in Britain, too, cats had taken the lead among household pets. In some other countries, cat ownership is even more widespread. In France and Australia, for example, the proportion is nearer one in every three homes.

CAT FACT:
Several domestic cats have been known to live for well over 30 years. Similarly, wild cats kept in zoos often live for much longer than usual.

THE NON-PEDIGREE CAT

MOST OF THESE cats are non-pedigree. That is, they do not belong to any of the pure breeds recognised by national organisations of cat lovers. They are popularly known in Britain as moggies, and elsewhere, unflatteringly, as alley cats. A typical pet cat is the result of generations of casual crossbreeding, although it may well have some of the characteristics of an established breed. There is nothing to suggest that non-pedigree cats are in any way inferior to their more upmarket cousins. Indeed, some evidence points the other way. Heredity has probably weeded out the weaker specimens of non-pedigrees, whereas intensive breeding and genetic manipulation can cause health problems. An extreme example of this is the Peke-faced Persian, which is not recognised in Britain but is popular in North America. Breeding to shorten the nose to give the flat-faced Peke look has resulted in breathing problems, blockage of the tear ducts and incorrect mouth closure causing eating difficulties.

THE PEDIGREE CAT

IT HAS BEEN estimated that about one in 15 domestic cats has a pedigree, which gives a pedigree population of about 400,000 cats in Britain and over 1.5 million in the United States. To qualify as a pedigree animal, a cat needs to have a 'family tree' stretching back through four or more generations of registered parents, grandparents, and so on, all of

Bottom left
Non-pedigree cats, such as this tabby, make up the majority of pet cats.

Bottom right
Excessive breeding, to create desirable features, has weakened certain pedigree breeds.

the same breed, and it needs to be registered itself with the appropriate governing and registration body. By contrast, most pet cats are lucky if even their parents can be identified for certain.

The Governing Council of the Cat Fancy, Britain's sole registration body, recognises over 100 breeds. The situation in the United States is more complicated, because there are several registration organisations which do not agree on the accepted and approved breeds. An added factor is that many breeds recognised as distinct in Britain are regarded as mere varieties of major breeds in the United States, while some breeds recognised there are not accepted in Britain.

THE WORKING CAT

IN ADDITION TO pet cats, every country has populations of farm cats living free-ranging and independent lives and kept for their rodent catching ability. In Britain, over 90 per cent of farms have at least one working cat. Although most working cats live on farms, some carry out their duties in factories and public buildings and there are still a few ships' cats, though far fewer than in the days of sail.

THE FERAL CAT

IN ADDITION, THERE is the population of feral cats living as best they can on what they can find in town or country. Ferals are cats, or the descendants of cats, that at one time have been domesticated at least to

some extent. The feral population includes strays, cats that have been abandoned by their owners, factory cats made redundant by closures, and of course their grown-up kittens. Some will have been feral for generations, others will be newcomers to the twilight feral world. In towns and cities, feral cats are to be found round dockyards, abandoned industrial sites, rubbish dumps, markets and similar environments. Buildings with warm central heating ducts, such as hospitals and large apartment blocks, also provide attractive homes for ferals. It is estimated that there may be more than 1.5 million working and feral cats in Britain, and three or four times that number in North America.

NATIONS OF CAT LOVERS

ALL THESE STATISTICS of the cat population have several things to tell us about cats and their relationship with the human race. First, that although cats are essentially independent creatures equipped with excellent tools for survival in their hunting skills, they have built up a historical bond with humans based partly on their usefulness as destroyers of vermin and partly on their love of companionship. Second, that even when deprived of human support (although some feral colonies are regularly fed and looked after by kindly human friends) cats can survive and breed successfully. Third, the success of feral colonies shows that cats are equally adept at social life among their own kind as they are as the pampered and protected pets of adoring owners.

> **CAT FACT:**
> So far there has not been any recent extinction of a wild cat species, but several sub-species of lion, tiger and jaguar have now disappeared from our planet.

Top left
This farm cat is an adept hunter.

Bottom left and right
Although Britain proclaims itself to be a nation of cat lovers there continues to be a need for refuge homes for abandoned cats.

Cats in the Human World

CATS MAKE REWARDING and loving pets. While in many ways they are solitary creatures, often seeming to prefer their own company, what is certain is that cats need and value companionship. Their early months as kittens are full of strongly bonding experiences and this need for similar bonding persists in the domestic cat.

LIVING WITH HUMANS

CATS OWE THEIR friendship with humans to two qualities. First, they are opportunists, which drove them to attach themselves to human settlements in the first place. You have only to watch a cat on the prowl, even a well-fed one, to see how its senses are alert to anything that may be of advantage – a scuttling mouse, a new bird's nest, some new feature in the garden that could be a new vantage point. Second, cats are adaptable, which has allowed them to come to terms with domestic life and all the gradations between being a cat in the wild and a cat by the hearth.

Cats have adapted as easily to shipboard life – it was only in 1975 that, on health grounds, cats were banned from British naval ships at sea – as to life in a new colony (as was the experience of the Mayflower cat and its successors) or even a continent where cats were previously unknown, as was the case of settlers'

cats taken to Australia. Unfortunately, it must be added, the adaptability of cats has made them useful subjects for laboratory experiments, though thankfully the tide of public opinion is turning against this misuse of animals.

INDOORS OR OUTDOORS?

ALTHOUGH THEY ARE best suited to a combined indoor and outdoor life, housebound cats can live perfectly contented lives provided that they have plenty of companionship, a well-balanced diet, affection and opportunities to exercise their chasing and climbing skills. The downside of keeping a cat indoors is that if it should escape it will be less able to cope with the hazards of the outside world, especially road traffic, and may have to fight its way into territory occupied by other cats.

THEIR OWN MASTERS

CATS ALWAYS PRESERVE their own dignity and reserve and, unlike dogs, are not particularly eager to please their owners. They can rarely be taught to do tricks, not because they are less intelligent than dogs but because they simply do not see the point. If they want to master a particular skill, such as stretching up to operate a door latch to let themselves in out of the cold, they will do so because the reward is immediate and personal. Whether their owner thinks it is cute or clever is irrelevant. Play is of course a different matter, and even quite elderly cats will enjoy a hunting game with a catnip mouse or similar toy.

Bottom left
This domesticated cat waits for its prey. It continues to hunt – a survival instinct – although it has food at home.

Bottom right
A pampered cat enjoys the luxuries of home.

A striking characteristic of cats is how, having experienced the human world, they have added their understanding of it to their instinct for survival. A lost dog will tend to roam until it drops of exhaustion, whereas long before crisis point is reached a lost cat will seek the source of warmth and food it has learned is available – human habitation. Many a stray or lost cat has found a new home simply by persistence in appealing to the good nature of a welcoming household, or even of a reluctant one which nevertheless could not turn a needy cat away.

Some cats, indeed, take this confidence in finding a comfortable billet to extremes, and if they are upset at home take off in the certainty that there is grass just as green on the other side of the hill.

MEMBERS OF THE FAMILY

ALTHOUGH CATS ARE creatures of routine, and would therefore prefer things to go on as they have known them, they do not exhibit faithfulness in the canine sense. There are no feline equivalents of Greyfriars Bobby. It is incredibly rare to hear of cats pining after their dead owners, or even of cats waking their owners up because the house is burning down. Cats are pragmatic. They know that, for them, the most important thing is to go on living. If cats could laugh, they would find the story of Greyfriars Bobby amusing and pathetic. In a house fire, they would be the first out of the window.

This is not to say that they do not love, or something like love, their owners and favoured members of the family. Samuel Johnson's cat Hodge probably gained as much pleasure from the attentions of Dr Johnson as the doctor did from the attentions of Hodge. Perhaps the truth is that cats live for the moment whereas dogs live in hope of the future. The future for a cat might be uncertain. However placid and confident a cat might seem, it is never far away from the realities of the wild world where it might have to fight its corner against rival cats and find its own food and secure sleeping place.

Top left
If hungry, cats will find a way to feed themselves.

Bottom right
This statue commemorates Hodge, Samuel Johnson's favourite pet.

Anatomy and Senses of the Cat

I N THE CAT, evolution has produced a highly developed machine for hunting based on its skeleton of 245 bones compared with the human skeleton's 206. The difference is accounted for mainly by the larger number of bones making up the cat's vertebral column or spine and extending in almost all breeds into its tail.

UNIFORM STRUCTURE

UNLIKE DOGS, in which physical characteristics have been suppressed or bred out to suit individual breeds for specific purposes such as endurance in sheepdogs or speed in greyhounds, cats retain the same basic features of their skeletons across all breeds except for one or two oddities like the Manx and the Japanese Bobtail. Again, compared with dogs, cats develop physically within a fairly restricted range, from about

CAT FACT:
The original 'black panther' is the black form of the leopard. Melanism is most common in leopards, so they were once thought of as a separate species – the panther.

Above right

The skeleton of the cat has 245 bones, 40 more than the human skeleton. The structure of strong yet light bones enables the cat's highly developed muscular system to support an agile, precisely controlled mode of movement.

Right

The dominance of the jaws is the significant feature of the cat's skull. The prominent dagger-like teeth hold and kill prey, and tear flesh from it, while the molars and premolars grind the flesh into smaller pieces for swallowing.

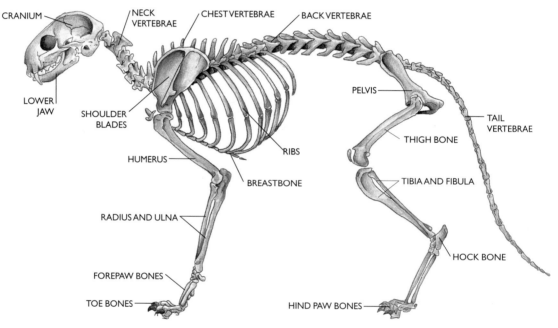

CRANIUM · NECK VERTEBRAE · CHEST VERTEBRAE · BACK VERTEBRAE · LOWER JAW · SHOULDER BLADES · HUMERUS · RIBS · BREASTBONE · PELVIS · TAIL VERTEBRAE · THIGH BONE · TIBIA AND FIBULA · RADIUS AND ULNA · FOREPAW BONES · TOE BONES · HOCK BONE · HIND PAW BONES

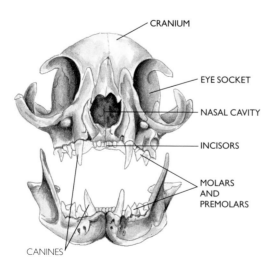

CRANIUM · EYE SOCKET · NASAL CAVITY · INCISORS · MOLARS AND PREMOLARS · CANINES

3.5–7 kg (8–15 lb) in the case of entire (uncastrated) males and from 2.5–4.5 kg (5.5–10 lb) for females. The average cat measures about 30 cm (12 in) at the shoulder and about 80 cm (31 in) from head to tail. Putting it another way, all domesticated cats are basically cat shaped and cat sized, whereas dogs come in all shapes and sizes.

Nonetheless, within the general cat shape there are distinctions of body type or conformation. The cat world defines three types. The cobby cat is short

and compact with a short, round head, a flat face, wide shoulders and hindquarters, and short legs. The British Shorthair and the Persian are typical cobby breeds. The muscular type, such as the Cornish or Devon Rex, has a less rounded head with medium legs, shoulders and hindquarters. The lithe type, the Siamese for example, has a long, wedge shaped head, long thin legs and narrow shoulders and hindquarters.

FLEXIBLE AND AGILE

PERHAPS THE MOST obvious feature of a cat's skeleton is the flexibility of its spine. This is due to the relatively loose connection between the vertebrae or spinal sections, which are separated, as in humans, by discs. Such flexibility enables the cat to rest comfortably in a wide variety of poses, to stretch and jump prodigiously, and to bring its head round to wash almost all of its body. The spine is attached to the skull and runs down the body to the tip of the tail. Flexibility continues through the tail, enabling the cat to manipulate its tail in a variety of 'language' gestures and also to use it as a balance when climbing or walking along a narrow fence or wall.

When a cat is active, the keys to its mobility are the connections from the spine to the scapulae (shoulder blades) and pelvis or hips.

There is no true collar-bone as in the human skeleton. The small triangular scapulae are at the sides of the chest rather than at the back as in humans. This is an aid to such familiar feline activities as climbing, walking along narrow fences and negotiating a way through horizontally or vertically narrow spaces. The scapulae are connected directly to the upper bones of the front legs, the humeri (singular, humerus), by the first joints, giving great flexibility of movement and allowing for long strides. The effect of this is seen at its best when a cat takes a flying leap with its front legs stretched out in line with its body or makes a pounce on its prey. Similarly, the upper bones of the rear legs, the femurs, have ball and socket joints connecting them with the pelvis which give a high degree of mobility in the chase.

DESIGNED FOR HUNTING

CATS, LIKE DOGS, are digitigrade – that is, they walk on their toes, compared with the plantigrade or flat-footed movement of humans. This posture suits a hunting animal, lengthening the stride and increasing speed since only a small area of the feet is on the ground at any one time. The cat's strong, powerfully muscled back legs do most of the work, providing the necessary push for forward movement and spring for jumping. But the front leg muscles notably come into their own when the cat hauls itself up a tree or fence.

Although capable of considerable power, the cat's limbs can also, when necessary, move with great sensitivity. A cat stalking its prey will often remain completely immobile for considerable periods. It may even 'freeze' in mid-stalk, with one front paw raised, and remain like that until the moment has come to strike. To acquire similar skills in the hunt, dogs have to be trained. One has only to compare an untrained dog and a cat on the hunt to see the difference between hopeful blundering on the one hand and highly developed skill on the other. But then dogs are great chasers, which cats are not. Incapable of sustained speed, cats rely on patience, surprise and deadly accuracy when it comes to the kill.

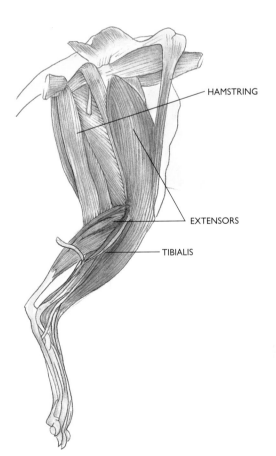

HAMSTRING

EXTENSORS

TIBIALIS

Top
A flexible spine gives cats an agility which makes them excellent climbers.

Bottom left
The muscles of a cat's hind leg, designed to give the cat powerful forward movement which cannot, however, be maintained for long periods. They perform most effectively in short, sharp chases and encounters.

Claws and Teeth

THE CLAWS – five on the front paws, four on the back – are a cat's hunting weapons, designed for efficient stalking as well as for the kill. Its paws end in sensitive, hairless pads which, when the cat is walking normally or relaxed, conceal the sheathed or retracted claws.

CAT FACT:
Thanks to their very powerful hind legs and flexible spine, cats are noted for their ability to leap long distances, often as much as six times their entire length.

THE CLAWS

THE CLAWS ARE unsheathed when the cat is climbing, moving quickly across ground, making a kill and sometimes, as some owners know to their cost, if it is annoyed. For this last reason, children should be taught to approach cats – even cats they know – with care and respect. Some cats are apt to unsheathe their claws in pleasure, while a small minority lack the sheathing mechanism owing to a genetic defect.

SHEATHING CLAWS

ALL MEMBERS OF the cat family, excepting only the cheetah, are able to sheath and unsheathe their claws at will. By far the fastest cat, and indeed the fastest animal on earth, the cheetah needs its claws out to maintain the speed on which it relies, rather than stealth, in the hunt.

The sheathing mechanism itself consists of an elastic ligament linking the last two toe bones, which are connected by tendons to the leg muscles. When

Top
A cat's forepaw. The toe pads correspond to the fingertips in human beings and the metocarpal pad to the base of the hand. The carpal corresponds to the wrist. The pads are sensitive to pressure and temperature and contain glands which enable the cat to leave behind scent marks.

Bottom left
Elastic ligaments linking the two end bones of a cat's paws enables it to sheathe its claws. To unsheath them, the strong tendons on the underside of the paw contract, pushing the claw out.

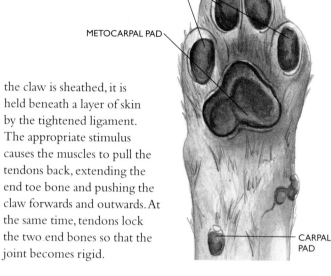

TOE PADS

METOCARPAL PAD

CARPAL PAD

the claw is sheathed, it is held beneath a layer of skin by the tightened ligament. The appropriate stimulus causes the muscles to pull the tendons back, extending the end toe bone and pushing the claw forwards and outwards. At the same time, tendons lock the two end bones so that the joint becomes rigid.

SHARP CLAWS

KEEPING THE CLAWS sharp is instinctive behaviour. Cats allowed to roam freely outside will sharpen their claws on a tree or fence post, often returning to the same one day after day. Cats kept indoors will instinctively find an object for the purpose, and if furniture and carpets are not to be damaged a scratching pad or post must be provided and the cat must be trained to use it. It is fruitless to try to discourage an indoor cat from scratching furniture without providing an alternative. The outdoor cat will normally keep its claws in trim without the owner resorting to clipping them, but indoor cats may need this attention occasionally. It is not an easy task and is best left to an expert.

Many American vets carry out de-clawing operations on the front paws of cats which live entirely indoors. This practice is not generally approved of elsewhere, and most cat fancy organisations ban de-clawed cats from shows. Outside the United States, the majority veterinary opinion is that de-clawing is cruel, disfiguring and unnatural, depriving the cat of a psychologically important tool. It must be added that if a de-

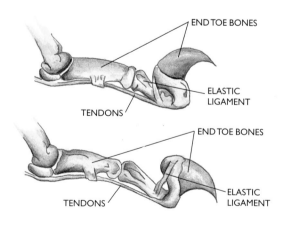

END TOE BONES

ELASTIC LIGAMENT

TENDONS

END TOE BONES

TENDONS

ELASTIC LIGAMENT

are six incisors in each jaw. These play a part in ripping and tearing food. When a cat eats canned cat food, it has no need to use the canines and will often gulp the food straight back. Hard, dry food, however, is transferred to the carnassial teeth to be crunched before swallowing.

Cats allowed outdoors will usually find enough natural prey to exercise their teeth and gums and keep them in good order. Owners of indoor cats need to give enough variety in the diet to provide this exercise, for which canned foods are not adequate on their own.

The cat's tongue also has a role in feeding. Its rough abrasive surface is used for rasping and softening food and licking the meat from bones. When drinking, the tongue forms a spoonlike shape to collect a few laps of liquid before swallowing. The tongue is also the cat's main self-grooming tool.

CAT FACT:
Cats are able to 'always' land on their feet because they have a very flexible spine, enabling them to orient their bodies aided by a balancing organ in their inner ears.

clawed cat escapes it is a virtual sentence of death since it cannot hunt effectively, defend itself in fights or escape from its enemies.

Although the claws are excellent tools for climbing upwards, they are less helpful when the cat wants to come down because they curve backwards and cannot provide a grip. This is the reason for the undignified slithering, followed by a swift turn and a forward jump, which is the cat's typical mode of descent. Cats' prowess at climbing upwards and their relative hopelessness in the descent have caused many an owner some anxious waits, and many a fire brigade a frustrating outing.

TOOLS FOR EATING

CATS IN THE WILD, and domestic cats allowed to hunt, feed by tearing pieces of flesh from their prey and swallowing them whole.

The food is not chewed, but digested entirely in the stomach. Most prominent among the cat's 30 teeth (kittens have four fewer) are the four long canines set below the nose and above the chin which are used for killing and holding prey and for tearing the flesh. Behind the canines are sets of carnassial teeth top and bottom, 14 in all, whose function is to cut meat into suitably sized pieces for swallowing. Between the canines

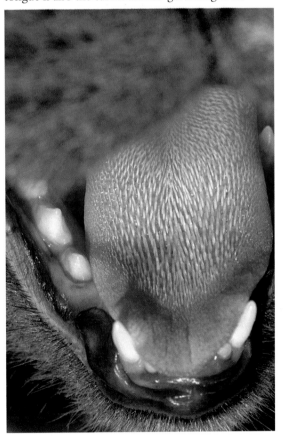

Top
Outdoor cats will find natural alternatives to keep their claws sharp.

Bottom right
This close-up of a cat's tongue reveals the rough surface.

Bottom left
Cats have four long canine teeth which are used to kill and hold its prey.

Opposite, bottom right
Domestic cats need to scratch to keep their claws sharp; a scratch post is an ideal alternative to furniture

Skin and Coat

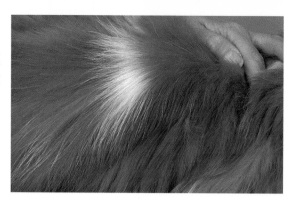

Bottom right
Devon Rexes have an unusual coat giving the breed a rough appearance.

Top right
Guard hairs can be seen on this Persian.

Bottom left
This drawing illustrates the different hair types that make up a cat's coat.

THE CAT'S FUR

CATS' COATS are their most admired feature and the main basis for the identification of breeds. But beautiful as it usually is, a cat's coat is also strictly functional. It provides a barrier between the cat and its environment, protecting it from injury, heat, cold, wind and rain. For the owner, the appearance of the coat is a good general guide to the cat's health.

A CAT'S FUR may contain up to 200 hairs per square millimetre, or 130,000 per square inch. Except in a few breeds such as the Rexes where the structure is entirely different, the coat is made up of three different kinds of hair. The guard or primary hairs form the coarse outer layer. These are about twice as numerous on the back and sides than on the chest and abdomen. They are rooted in individual follicles or pits in the skin and through them are connected with the nervous system. The guard hairs thus respond to anger, fear, cold and the excitement of the chase by standing upright, giving the cat an aggressive, 'fluffed up' appearance. They also respond to the flow of air and so form part of the cat's sensory system.

Interspersed with the guard hairs are more bristly awn hairs which have thickened tips. These grow from their follicles in clusters. Below the guard and awn hairs is the soft down hair which forms an insulating layer for the skin. The erection of the guard hairs in cold weather provides the extra insulation which cats need since, unlike dogs, they have no protective layer of fat.

THE HAIR OF THE CAT

THE HAIR OF the coat, like human hair, is constantly growing, dying and renewing itself. In long-haired cats the moulting process is continuous all year round, but in shorthairs it is most noticeable in spring when the thick winter coat is shed. This pattern is less obvious with shorthairs which are kept indoors in centrally heated homes.

The hair follicles have a secondary purpose which is essential to feline health. They secrete sebum, an oily substance which spreads along the hairs and gives it its shine. Sebum also contains a natural steroid, cholesterol, which is converted by sunlight to vitamin D. Cats obtain part of their supplies of this essential nutrient from fish oil and animal fats, which are present in commercial cat foods, but the action of sunlight on the skin provides an important additional source.

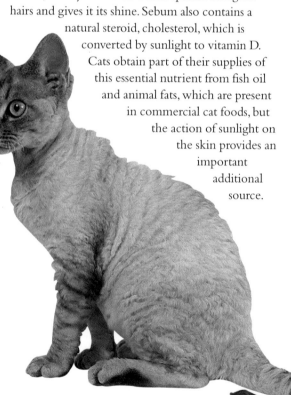

The hair follicles also contain sweat glands. The main function of these is to produce scent which is used to mark territory and, in unneutered cats, to make sexual signals. They are most prominent on the chin and ears and at the base of the tail. The cat's coat prevents it from losing heat effectively by sweating,

The hairs of the coat are rooted in the inner layer, the dermis. The outer layer, the epidermis, is mainly protective. The cells which make up the epidermis are constantly dying and being renewed, the dead cells either dropping away through the coat or being removed during grooming.

On the nose and feet, the epidermis is up to 75 times thicker than on the rest of the body, yet it is extremely sensitive to pressure and temperature. There are sweat glands only on the feet. Unlike a dog, a cat cannot lose heat through its nose pad, any dampness on the skin here coming from the mucous membranes inside the nose.

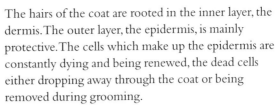

and the only glands that correspond to human sweat glands are on the hairless skin of the paws, which becomes damp in extreme heat or fright. If a cat makes wet footprints, or pants heavily, it is usually a sign of overheating and action should be taken to cool it down. Normally, cats regulate their temperature by the evaporation of saliva in grooming.

On certain parts of the body, the hairs are modified for specific purposes. The most obvious example is the facial whiskers or vibrissae, which are ultra-sensitive and used as a width gauge, to test environmental conditions and, in different positions, to express emotions. There are also sensitive vibrissae on the back of the forelegs which probably help the cat to move silently over unknown territory.

THE CAT'S SKIN

THE STRIKING FEATURE of a cat's skin is its looseness, particularly on the back of the neck, which can sometimes be so pronounced that the cat almost seems to be able to turn round inside it. This is an aid to heat loss, helps to prevent serious injury during fights, and helps the cat to perform its acrobatic feats of jumping and falling. The skin is in two layers.

Top
A cat's coat is kept healthy-looking not only from essential oils but also from sunlight.

Middle
Moulting is less obvious in cats that are kept indoors.

Left
Whiskers are hairs that have been modified for a different purpose. Cats use these hairs to balance and to judge distances.

A Cat's Life

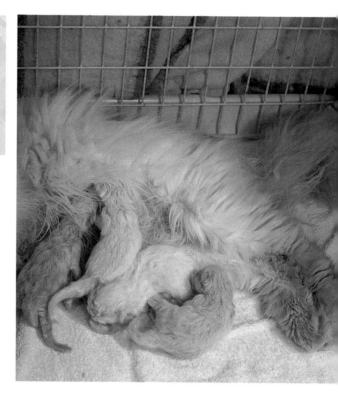

LIFE EXPECTANCY

THE LIFE EXPECTANCY of a typical domestic cat is from 12–15 years, although many survive to late teenage, a few live into their twenties, and ages of 34 and even 43 are on record. Domestic cats are more fortunate in this respect than their feral cousins, whose typical lifespan is about half as long. Accidents, poisoning, exposure, viral epidemics, dog fights, poor diet and human intervention all take their toll on cats living rough.

> **CAT FACT:**
> The whiskers of a cat are devices for indirectly feeling the immediate environment. When something touches a whisker it is sensed by special cells surrounding its root.

A CAT IS FOR LIFE

IT IS OFTEN said that, among domestic cats, neutered males and spayed females tend to live longer but this may be due less to medical reasons than to the fact that neutered and spayed cats tend to roam less and so are less vulnerable to accidents. In general, cats live longer if they enjoy happy and stable lives in homes where they are cared for, played with and loved.

The relative longevity of cats is a factor to be taken into account when acquiring one, especially if it is a kitten, in a society where cats last longer than many marriages. When the excited nine-year-old with her first kitten has grown up and left home, who will take on the responsibility? Who will care for the cat if its elderly owner dies? Does the owner's lifestyle or career involve frequent moves or spells away from home? Too many unwanted cats are unceremoniously dumped or abandoned, only the fortunate few finding new homes or sanctuary in an animal shelter, for such questions to be taken lightly.

THE YOUNG CAT

KITTENS ARE BORN in litters of between two and six but more usually three or four. At birth they are blind and without teeth. After about a week their eyes open – all kittens' eyes are blue – and a week or so later the kitten begins to use its eyes as well as its sense of smell to find its way about. It is now equipped to explore its immediate surroundings.

At this stage the mother starts to train her kittens, hauling them back if they stray too far or get lost, teaching them to play, and combining fierce protection with total care. This is a very rapid stage in the kittens' development.

At about three weeks they start to play, encouraged by the mother's flicking of her tail as a plaything. Mock fights and chases follow, chaser and chased often abruptly exchanging

Top
A Persian suckling her young litter; their eyes will open at about one week.

Bottom left
Unfortunately, many cats are abandoned to fend for themselves, consequently their life expectancy will be reduced.

Bottom right
All kittens have blue eyes.

roles in mid-game. This looks like fun, and it is, but more importantly it is preparation for adult life as the kitten psychologically expects it to be. The fact that it may never have to catch prey for food or fight with a neighbour's cat is irrelevant. Play serves a deeper emotional need, and kittens which have been orphaned and miss out on play in their young lives usually grow up to be fearful or aggressive cats.

INDEPENDENT LIVES

BY THREE MONTHS kittens are fully weaned and ready for independent lives although they will continue to enjoy the company of their siblings and, to the delight of young owners, still appear very

kittenish despite being already equipped with the essential skills they will need in life. The adult teeth appear at 4–6 months, and by 12 months the kitten is fully grown. From about six months, females are sexually mature, and males follow a month or so later.

From this, it can be seen that the first year of a kitten's life corresponds with about the first 15 of a human child's. The next five or so equate with the prime of a human life, and by six years a cat is approaching middle age. By eight, there may be definite signs of slowing down, although some cats retain their sprightliness, eagerness to hunt and young mode of life for much longer. The class structure of British shows organised under Governing Council of the Cat Fancy rules echoes this progression. Cats

between 9–15 months are called 'Adolescents'. 'Juniors' are under, and 'Seniors' over two years of age. Cats seven years and older are known as 'Veterans'.

THE OLD CAT

FROM THE AGE OF NINE, a cat may be regarded as old. It may lose interest in hunting, or take on only the least challenging prey. Sight and hearing may become less acute, and the cat may be more ready to seek home comforts such as a warm fire or a soft cushion.

Obvious physical signs of age include the greying of the muzzle, cloudiness in the eyes, a dulled coat, slackening of the skin and more prominent hips and spine. But cats are remarkably adaptable, even to the loss of clear sight and hearing. From 12 years on, a cat should be regarded as elderly, although some – like some humans – defy nature, and anno domini, and continue to lead active lives until they die.

Top
This short-haired tabby is in its prime; males are sexually mature from around seven months.

Middle
Cats are born without teeth; this kitten shows his new set.

Bottom
This elderly cat shows few physical signs of age such as a greying coat and a prominent spine.

Sight

CONTRARY TO POPULAR belief, cats cannot see in total darkness, but in dim light their vision is about half as good again as that of the average clear-sighted human being. As nocturnal hunters by nature, this ability is extremely valuable to them. Almost everything about a cat's eyes has to do with the cat's instinct as a hunter.

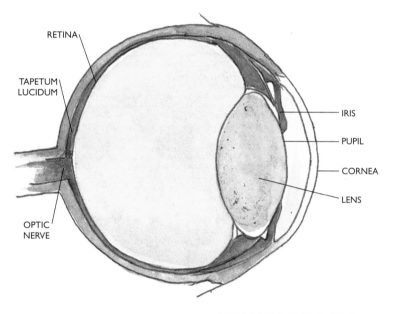

RETINA

TAPETUM LUCIDUM

IRIS

PUPIL

CORNEA

LENS

OPTIC NERVE

REMARKABLE VISION

First, the position of a cat's eyes are set well forward on the head and aim straight forward for an optimum three-dimensional image. Looking straight ahead, there are 120° of binocular vision, with another 80°

Above

A cat's eyes are remarkably adept at adjusting to different light conditions since the ability to detect movement and judge distances is essential to a hunting animal. The flexibility of the iris and the light-reflecting tapitum lucidum are key features.

on each side – a remarkable total of 280°. Ligaments inside the eye enable the lens to move to focus on objects some distance away or on something closer at hand, though in fact cats' eyes are not good at close-up work. They work best with objects between 2–6 m (7–20 ft) away.

The cat's ability to see in dim light is due partly to the flexibility of the muscles controlling the iris, the membrane that opens and closes to reveal more or less of the pupil. In bright light – for example, when a cat is in direct sunlight – the iris reduces the pupil to a mere slit, protecting the inner eye from light damage but retaining vision. At night, however, the iris muscles work in reverse, expanding the opening to as much as 12 mm (O.5 in). This allows more light to pass through to the retina at the back of the eye, thereby increasing the amount of information passed to the brain.

SEEING IN THE DARK

AT THIS POINT another distinctive feature of the cat's eye comes into play. This is the tapetum lucidum, a reflective layer on the surface of the retina which increases the sensitivity of the retina and enhances the received image. It is the *tapetum lucidum* that produces the startling reflection of cats' eyes caught in a torch beam or a car's headlights, and it is this effect, of course, which has been copied by road engineers for highway markings. The *tapetum lucidum* is, incidentally, not exclusive to the cat family. It is present in many other nocturnal animals. But although the real cat's eye can gather in a great deal of information in poor light, it is not very detailed information.

Nocturnal vision is fuzzy and without detail. For the cat, this does not particularly matter, because what it is mainly interested in is the movement of possible prey, which it can easily detect especially when assisted by the senses of smell and hearing.

DISTINCTIVE CATS' EYES

ANOTHER DISTINCTIVE feature of the cat's eye is the haw, a third eyelid arranged to flick diagonally across the cornea or surface membrane of the eyeball. This flicks continually when the eyes are open, but if a cat is seriously ill it will often show 'haws up', that is with the haws immobile across the corneas – sometimes so far across that the cat is temporarily blinded. In normal health the haws help, with the true eyelids, to lubricate the cornea.

The ability of a cat to 'stare its owner out' is well known, and it seems that a cat can stare fixedly at an object for an inordinate length of time. It is often seen when a cat is staring out of the window, perhaps at birds or windblown leaves in the garden. This is part of the hunting instinct. Be sure that under these circumstances no movement within the cat's field of vision will go unnoticed, and if it were in the open air the cat would already be planning to spring and pounce.

Siamese cats may be subject to a genetic fault which produces double vision instead of the usual stereoscopic image. The cat's attempts to correct this result in the characteristic Siamese squint.

SEEING IN COLOUR

EXPERT OPINION IS divided over the extent to which cats can see colours. Certainly they have nothing like the colour perception of humans, but it is equally certain that they have some means of distinguishing some colours, as many owners can testify. One school of thought is that they can distinguish between red, blue and white, but green, yellow and white all look grey. It may be that as movement is the dominant factor in a cat's use of its sight, colour is not all that important.

Strangely enough, cats' eyes, or rather their irises, can come in a wide range of colours, including red, blue, green and gold. These have no particular relevance to the cat's ability to see, but in the cat fancy they assume some importance as only specific eye colours are permissible for certain breeds and coat colours.

CAT FACT:
Most cats display camouflage markings or colouration on their coats. Whether stripes, spots or plain colour, they help the cat to blend in with its background while hunting.

Top
A Malaysian Flat-headed cat shows its reflector eyes, the tapetum lucidum.

Bottom left
The haw, or third eye.

Bottom right
This Siamese is correcting the double vision, a breed characteristic, and in doing so squints.

Opposite, bottom
The iris of a cat's eye is able to expand and retract depending on the amount of light available.

Sound

H OWEVER BADLY CATS' colour vision may compare with that of humans, there is no doubt that their hearing is far better. The effectiveness of the ears depends on their ability to receive sounds and interpret them in the brain. The cat's ear flaps or pinnae are each equipped with more than a dozen muscles which enable them to turn through 180° and focus on a distant sound. This helps not only to detect sound but also to locate its position and range. The mechanism of the cat's ear responds to vibrations from about 30 kHz, or 30 cycles per second, the same lower limit as in humans.

Top

A cat's ears are able to rotate through 180°, an advantage that enables it to hear and locate its prey.

Bottom left

Sound reaches the cat's ear via the ear-drum, whose vibrations are amplified by the hammer-and-anvil action of the ossicles. They then pass to the cochlea, which contains sense organs which send nerve signals to the brain. The system of semi-circular canals at the top transmits signals concerned with balance.

Bottom right

A cat's sensory life is very different to our own, they can hear the squeaks of mice and differentiate between sounds centimetres apart.

SHARP EARS

THE CAT'S HIGHER limit, however, is far higher: about 65 kHz (65,000 cycles per second) compared with the human's 20 kHz, a difference of more than two octaves. In effect, this means that a cat lives in a different sound world from us, a world in which the high-pitched squeaks of mice and other small creatures are part of everyday experience. The sometimes inaudible squeaks of young kittens enables their mother to find them if they have got lost.

This excellent hearing in the higher registers explains why, as a general rule, cats respond more readily to womens' and childrens' voices than to mens'. It also explains why cats sometimes sit up and pay attention to

— CANALS

— COCHLEA

— OSSICLES

— EAR-DRUM

noises that their owners have not heard. The popular myths about 'psychic' cats which can detect disturbances long before they become evident to humans probably also originate with the cat's superior hearing. This almost certainly accounts for the regularity with which cats turn up at the gate to meet their owners returning home by car. A particular car's sound 'signature', as far as the cat is concerned, is probably high in the upper registers, beyond human discrimination.

Another feature of a cat's hearing is its ability to locate the position of sounds very accurately. From a distance of about 1 m (3.28 ft) it can discriminate between two sources of sound only 8 cm (3 in) apart. The brain is able to detect the time delay in the arrival of the two separate sound signals. This is another hunting skill, enabling the cat to locate and track its prey.

THE QUIET LIFE

QUITE LITERALLY, CATS like a quiet life. They are disturbed by loud noises, which is why clapping the hands and saying 'No!' loudly is such an effective ploy in training. A cat sharing a home with a dog will often retreat if the dog barks loudly, not because it is frightened but because it simply does not like the noise. For the same reason, a cat will often walk away from noisy children. Domestically, the ideal home background for most cats is to be among people who are talking casually and quietly, with quiet radio or television sound in the background. Indeed, most cats left alone appreciate the sound of a radio tuned low. Perhaps, with their better hearing in the upper octaves, they can get more out of the programmes than we do.

HEARING IN THE OLDER CAT

DEAFNESS IS AN ailment to which some cats are prone, especially in old age. While it is not true, as is often said, that all white cats are deaf, the problem is certainly associated with whites, especially blue-eyed whites to the extent that in odd-eyed cats the deafness is often on the same side as the blue eye. It can affect one or both ears and is incurable. Although hearing is so important to a cat, deafness does not in fact seem to be a great disadvantage if it has been deaf from birth. Presumably the other senses work overtime in compensation. Deafness does, however, affect the mothering skill of a queen, who cannot hear the high-pitched cries for food or help of her young kittens, and for this reason among others, breeding from deaf females is to be discouraged. Cases have been reported of kittens who were born deaf suddenly acquiring their hearing at maturity and, not surprisingly, having difficulty in adjusting to their new world of sound.

Deafness in old age comes on gradually and is usually associated with other symptoms of ageing. Persistent shaking of the head or scratching at the pinnae may be an indication of some ear infection, or may be the cat's expression of puzzlement at its declining hearing. There is nothing to be done about deafness in old age but the cat's life can be made easier by making sure that it is not suddenly startled and by always approaching it in vision.

The ears, or rather the pinnae, have another function entirely divorced from hearing. They are important elements in the cat's body language. In association with other organs, they react to fear, stress, contentment, confrontation, anger and other similar emotions.

CAT FACT:
Cats are so well designed for recovering from falls that they are far more likely to injure their lower jaws rather than hurting their backs or legs as they land.

Top
White cats that are odd eyed are often deaf in the side of the blue eye.

Bottom
Deafness can sometimes be detected in older cats by a puzzled expression.

23

Smell, Taste and Touch

THE FIRST THING most cats do when offered food is to smell it. Only if the offering passes this test will it be eaten. The sense of smell is highly developed in cats; in fact, it is probably the most important of their senses. The cat's nasal cavity contains about 200 million olfactory or scent cells, compared with about half of that number in humans. Most owners will have been surprised by the acuteness of even young kittens to detect interesting odours such as a pack of bacon or liver brought back from shopping or the opening of a can of sardines or tuna.

SMELL

AS THE CAT'S natural diet is carnivorous, vegetable smells in general (except for catnip and valerian, mentioned later) excite little interest, although a cat may learn, for example, to associate the smell of onions with the presence of liver if this is a common meal in the home. Cats also use scent to detect prey, to identify other cats' territories, to explore and evaluate their environment generally and in their sex lives.

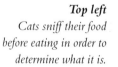

Top left
Cats sniff their food before eating in order to determine what it is.

Top right
The variety of smells found in the outside world are ordered by the cat to construct a scent map.

Bottom
This cat is scenting the air, perhaps to determine if this territory has already been marked.

DEVELOPING A SENSE OF SMELL

KITTENS' SENSE OF smell develops early. Their first experience of it is when they become aware of the smell of their mother and the nest. If they are moved, or their mother decides to move them, to a new nest, they show signs of distress until the mother rejoins them and settles them down, reassuring them by her smell that they are safe again. Even at this stage, at a few days old, their sense of smell is highly discriminatory. For example, it guides each kitten to one specific nipple from which the mother feeds it.

As with the other senses, the sense of smell develops rapidly in kittens to a high level. As they roam from the nest, they quickly pick up the smell 'language' of the wider world around them.

CREATING A SCENT MAP

WHEN A KITTEN finally leaves the nest to make a base of its own, it creates its own familiar world of smells, and when a cat ventures outside it again enlarges its scenting experience. It will leave its scent marks by rubbing its head or flank on pieces of furniture, trees and posts in the garden, its owner, other people and pets in the household and on other cats it meets in the wider world. These activities can be likened to the cat's drawing a 'scent map' of its environment. But more than this, the cat's sense of smell brings it information from outside.

For example, if its owner visits friends who have cats, they will absorb 'scent information' about the visitor's cat. When the owner returns home, the cat will receive information about the cats which have

animals but not in humans or dogs. This is a narrow passage leading from the roof of the mouth to a small receptacle above the upper jaw lined with sensory cells. When a cat detects an unusual or particularly interesting scent it opens its mouth, catches the scent on its tongue and flicks it back to the Jacobson's organ, from which it is transmitted to the brain. In doing so, the cat takes a distinctive stance, stretching its neck, opening its mouth, wrinkling its nose and curling back its upper lip. This gesture is called 'flehmening'. Flehmening is commonest among entire toms when they scent females on heat, but can also be triggered by other smells, particularly by the smell of catnip.

Catnip or catmint, *Nepeta cataria*, is a weed of the temperate regions of Europe and North America with purple-spotted white flowers. It is the scented leaves, however, which are particularly attractive to most cats, including members of wild cat species. Sniffing or chewing the leaves, rubbing against them or rolling in them produces a drug-like trance, or even phantom chases lasting for a few seconds. As quickly as this state begins, the cat snaps out of it and resumes its normal behaviour. This is a quite harmless biochemical reaction to the essence given off by the plant, and cats' sensory pleasures can be enhanced by planting the shrub in the garden – it is easy to grow – or even keeping it as a house plant. Another plant, also common in northern Europe and North America, which attracts similar attention from cats is valerian, *Valeriana officinalis*, with white or pinkish flowers. Interestingly, oil extracted from the dried root of valerian was formerly used medicinally in the treatment of hysteria, and in sixteenth-century Europe as a perfume.

been visited. With our relatively poor sense of smell, we can have little idea of the world of scents in which a cat lives. But the common human experience of catching a waft of scent – the particular mix of flower scents in a garden, the smell of the sea, the fragrance worn by a particular person, for example – that can 'take you back' to some half forgotten time years ago can perhaps give us some idea of how cats build up comprehensive 'information banks' of scents which stay with them throughout their lives. But it seems that the 'scent memory' which is only an occasional experience in humans is part of a cat's everyday life.

SENSITIVE SENSE OF SMELL

CATS' ABILITY TO detect and identify scents is enhanced by a special feature, the vomero-nasal or Jacobson's organ, which is present in some other

CAT FACT:
Whiskers are used to assess the dimensions of spaces in the dark. They also supply the cat with added information when prey is caught and too close to look at.

Top
With its nose raised and eyes closed the cat concentrates on scenting.

Bottom
This kitten is playing with its catnip mouse.

TASTE

THE SENSE OF taste is closely related to smell, and probably more closely related in cats than in most other mammals. This may explain why the cat's first reaction to food is to smell it, and why some cats exhibit such strong preferences for one kind of food over another. Why they should suddenly go off familiar food and even, to their owners' dismay, go on hunger strike until something more to their liking is provided is less explicable.

The taste-buds are located along the front, sides and back of a cat's tongue. Uniquely among mammals, members of the cat family do not seem to respond to sweet tastes and have a low tolerance of sugars in their diet, resulting in diarrhoea. This makes the cat's legendary liking for milk something of a mystery. Although most will drink it, its lactose or 'milk sugar' content makes water the preferred choice of drink from the point of view of the digestion. cats' low tolerance of sugar means that children should be discouraged from offering them sweets in the belief that they are giving them a treat.

As with humans, any congestion or blockage of the cat's nasal passages results in a loss of appetite which may be tempted only by strong-smelling foods such as grilled liver, canned sardines or canned tuna. The last seems particularly highly regarded by cats – so much so that some owners avoid offering it under any circumstances for fear that from then on the cat will eat nothing else.

CAT FACT:

Lynx use hairy feet to walk on snow by spreading their weight. Interestingly, sand cats use the same adaptation to help them walk on desert sand dunes.

TOUCH

ALTHOUGH CATS ARE well equipped with organs which are stimulated by touch, this sense seems to be less well-developed than the others. Perhaps this is because it is less vital to the instinctive need to hunt. The tongue, nose and paws, in that order, are the most sensitive parts of a cat's body, as can be seen when a cat will gently nuzzle unfamiliar food as well as smelling it, and when unfamiliar objects are patted with the forepaws by way of initial investigation.

When the cat is in motion, receptors in its paws also relay information to the brain about the texture of different surfaces, the temperature of a surface, and angles and inclines. This information enables it to move in the most favourable and effective fashion across the ground. It is thought also that the paws can detect minute vibrations in the ground, which would account for some of the stories about cats' ability to react to events such as earthquakes before the human senses can detect them.

Top left
Taste-buds can be seen on this cat's tongue, its rough surface should also be noted.

Bottom right
Water should always be provided, it is also preferable to milk.

Centre right
Cats can be fussy eaters and go off their favourite food seemingly without reason.

SENSITIVE TO THE TOUCH

THE FACIAL WHISKERS, or *vibrissae*, are also highly sensitive. Their value in navigation is indicated by the fact that cats which have damaged or lost their whiskers, perhaps in a fight, move about with far less assurance, while cats with particularly fine, spreading sets of whiskers often explore with supreme confidence.

The follicles of the cat's coat too respond to touch. This accounts for the pleasure that cats take in being stroked and the protests if the strokes are not to their liking. The enjoyment of being stroked is acquired when kittens are groomed by their mother. Sensors in the skin also inform the cat of warmth and cold. They enable it to find a warm place to sleep, while cold stimulates erection of the coat hairs to increase insulation. The skin sensors react too to the flow of air. Owners who are brave enough to bath their cats and use a hair-drier afterwards know that the coat is extremely sensitive to too strong an air current. In general cats dislike windy weather and will tend to hurry for a sheltered spot. However, in autumn the desire to get out of the wind has to compete with the excitement of chasing windblown leaves.

Oddly, cats seem to be relatively insensitive to high surface temperatures. Humans start to feel pain at about 44°C (112°F) whereas the threshold for cats is about 52°C (126°F). This explains why cats will often sleep closer to a fire than would be comfortable for humans, and will sometimes even burn their fur. But the nose pad is sensitive to cold, which is why a cat will often bury its nose in its tail fur for optimum warmth and comfort.

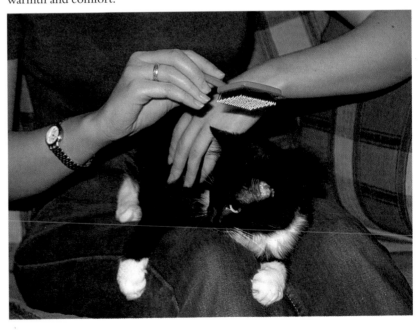

Movement and Balance

THE QUALITY OF a cat's movement is summed up in two words: graceful and precise. Whether walking calmly from one warm spot to another, taking a businesslike trot round their territories or caught up in the fury and excitement of the chase, cats use their muscles with superb economy, efficiency and elegance. The key to their success as hunters is a combination of finely honed senses of hearing, sight and smell which locate and identify their prey with a body conformation that allows for careful and purposeful or rapid and accurate movement according to the needs of the moment.

REMARKABLE AGILITY

FURTHERMORE, THE ABILITY to change almost instantly from a quiet, watchful mode to readiness to pounce is characteristic of the whole cat family and is evidence of the keenly balanced sensory world in which the cat lives. The feline brain's governance of the body is so secure that even if a cat loses a limb in an accident it will, after recovery, usually adapt quickly to its changed circumstances. Although its movements will necessarily be more restricted than before it will usually acquire enough mobility to follow something closely resembling its former mode of life.

In normal walking, a cat puts forward its right foreleg first, followed by its left hindleg, left foreleg and right hindleg, each foot placed in front of the other in a straight line. In a trot, the intervals between these movements decreases so that the opposite forelegs and hindlegs move at the same time. When the trot turns into a gallop, both powerful hindlegs thrust forward at the same time, leaving the forelegs to take the cat's weight in turn and giving a characteristic bounce to the hindquarters. During this change of speed, if the cat means business, the claws are unsheathed ready for instant use. The one flaw in the cat's movement equipment, however, is its inability to sustain a gallop for long.

Top
As this cat runs it uses its strong back legs to power it forward.

Bottom
Cats walk with their right foreleg leading.

At the same time, a safe haven high up from the ground is the best place to watch for potential enemies to arrive or go away. In the home, a cat will often take refuge on top of a cupboard or in some similar refuge if, for example, a strange dog arrives. The flexibility of the cat's spine is another useful attribute if it is chased or threatened, enabling it to wriggle through small openings or escape into inaccessible corners.

Coming down from a climb is more difficult and usually less elegant than going up. The claws point in the wrong direction for a graceful descent, and usually the cat will lower itself backwards in stages until it is near enough to the ground to turn round make a final forward leap. Most of the time, cats seem well able to judge whether they will be able to get down from a climb, and when they are caught out high in a tree or some other tricky spot it is usually because they have taken flight in panic without heed for the consequences, or have been caught up in the thrill of a chase. In general, however, after a bit of experience cats usually have a sensible appreciation of what is and is not possible, and they are not inclined to pursue a chase that looks like having only a slim chance of success.

This is a feature that extends right across the cat family, with the sole exception of the cheetah which although by no means a long-distance runner can do an impressive sprint. From the tiger to the tiniest Asian wild cat, the other cats' mode of hunting is by patience and stealth, not speed. Whether chasing prey or escaping from a threat, a cat will always choose to jump or climb rather than run. This will usually put it at an advantage in relation to either hunter or hunted.

JUMPING AND CLIMBING

CATS CAN JUMP up to five or six times their own height, having first measured the distance by eye, and often seem to enjoy climbing simply for fun. Climbing also enables cats to take up their favourite position of looking down on the passing scene. A cat at a vantage point such as a flat roof overlooking a garden will find enough activity to interest it for a considerable period. cats' climbing behaviour is strongly linked with their survival instinct. Few animals likely to be enemies have anything like the same climbing skills.

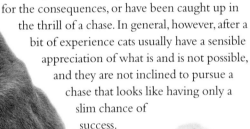

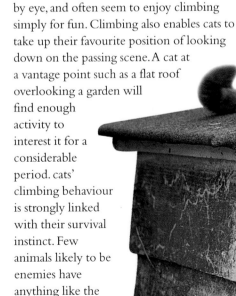

Top
Jumping gives cats an advantage over their prey, cats prefer to stalk as they are unable to sustain a chase.

Bottom
The domestic cat usually climbs to view the surrounding area or for enjoyment, in the wild, however, a cat may be escaping to safety.

CRASH LANDINGS

DESPITE CATS' JUMPING skills and the care they usually take to gauge height and distance before making an unfamiliar leap, they can and do make mistakes. A leap upwards to a ledge or a table-top can end in an undignified scramble with the back legs and a desperate heave with the front if the distance has been misjudged. It is then that the observer can see just how powerful the front claws and hind legs are as the cat hauls itself up. If it fails, it will twist to one side and jump down, looking crestfallen. An ambitious jump down from a difficult surface – typically, a steeply pitched roof – can result in a heavy landing, followed by a vigorous shaking and licking of the paws. Cats do not like to make mistakes, and even less to have been seen to make mistakes, and after such an incident go to some trouble to restore their dignity. A good wash – a displacement activity which cats often employ to cover disappointment, stress or disapproval – is often their remedy.

Top left
This cat is an adept jumper.

Top right
These illustrations show a cat rolling over in mid-air and landing on its feet in order to prevent hurting itself.

Bottom
Cat demonstrating how a tail facilitates its walk along a narrow fence.

LANDING ON ITS FEET

OF ALL THE CAT'S athletic skills, its ability to right itself in a fall is one of the most remarkable. It is due to an organ called the vestibular apparatus, which is particularly well developed in cats, and is located in the inner ear. This monitors all head movements and relates them to the position of the other parts of the body, so that the cat always has complete spatial awareness. It consists of a series of linked chambers and canals containing fluid and lined with millions of microscopic hairs linked to nerve endings connected to the brain. An alteration in the position of the head causes the fluid to move and the hairs move in the current, signalling the change to the brain's information centre. Any sudden change in the relation of head to body triggers reflex responses to correct any imbalance.

When a cat falls, the vestibular apparatus sends impulses to the brain which results in the neck muscles positioning the head horizontally. The cat can then twist from this fixed point so that it will land on its feet with its back arched to provide a shock-absorber. Kittens are born with this self-righting reflex, and it can be seen in operation as soon as young kittens start to tumble and play with their mother and with each other.

THE TAIL AS A TOOL

THE TAIL IS a vital tool in many of the movements in a cat's life. It acts as a balance in negotiating a narrow fence or wall, or taking up position on a post. In the self-righting action described above, it again operates as a balance to ensure a feet first landing. The tail can even be used as a rudder to trim the direction of a jump down into a confined space.

cat is able to learn from experience and apply a skill acquired through one experience to a new situation. It will even persevere in applying knowledge to the novel situation until it succeeds. Thus, a cat that has had a painful or upsetting fall is unlikely to risk trying the same manoeuvre again. This is learning from experience.

Examples of applying knowledge to new situations include the trick that many cats master of opening a door-latch, or at least rattling it to be let in, drinking from a dripping tap and retrieving an object, if it is interesting enough, from an inaccessible place. The last example often sees the cat exhibiting perseverance, trying the retrieval with different paws and from different angles. Most cats, however, are only driven to these activities out of self-interest. They are not much interested in pleasing their owners with tricks, displaying an independence which can sometimes appear perverse.

LIGHTNING REACTIONS

ALL THE CAT'S physical activities are governed by a network of over 500 muscles which are themselves driven by a highly developed information centre in the brain. This processes information extremely speedily, enabling the cat to react equally fast to stimuli such as the smell or sight of prey and to emergencies such as a sudden slip or fall. In a kitten, the brain progresses quickly and is fully developed within five or six months. During this time, it receives from its mother and siblings the stimulation which enables it to acquire and refine its muscular skills as well as experiences in the use of its organs of sight, smell, hearing and touch which will themselves initiate muscular activity.

THE BRAIN

THE CAT'S BRAIN weighs between 20–30 g (less than 1 oz), but the proportion of brain weight to body weight is larger than in most mammals other than apes or humans. The part of the brain that controls movement and balance is the cerebellum, which like the area of the brain dealing with the sense of smell is large and well developed in the cat. It is relevant to the exercise of movement and balance that the

Top left
Cat judging height to which it will jump.

Top right
This cat has learnt that scratching by the door will encourage its owners to let it out.

Bottom
A curious cat looking into a bottle garden.

Instinct and Learning

L IKE ALL ANIMALS, cats are born with certain instincts which are common across the species. They are by nature nocturnal, predatory, territorial, cautious and, unlike dogs which are pack animals, essentially solitary when it comes to the hunt. Some of these instincts are modified by domestication, but they are never lost, which perhaps helps to explain why stray and feral cats have a better survival rate than dogs in similar circumstances, even though it is far lower than that of stay-at-home cats. However pampered and protected a pet cat may be, it retains its strong survival instinct based on its keen senses, rapid reactions and good hunting skills.

CAT FACT:

Cats have lost their equivalent of the big toe completely. This is because the hind legs are used solely for running and jumping, so a dew claw might cause injury.

EARLY INSTINCTS

THE FIRST INSTINCT evident in the newborn kitten is the instinct to suck. It must take food from its mother within a few hours of birth, or it will die. Apart from nutrition, in the first milk the queen passes on antibodies that give her kittens protection from disease. The mother guides her kittens by lying on her side and nuzzling them towards her nipples, but what they do when they get there is a matter of instinctive behaviour. Occasionally a queen may reject a particular kitten, and this is a sign that she has detected something wrong with it – although a vet's opinion should be sought.

Centre right
This cat has been taught to cover its faeces, an important survival lesson in the wild.

Bottom left
Instinct tells new born kittens to suck, the mother will also help them by guiding them to her nipples.

Bottom right
A mother berates her kitten.

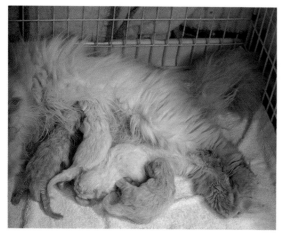

The months of kittenhood between two and six are a period of intense learning, when the mother imparts to her young the techniques needed for survival. She starts by weaning them off her milk so that they are encouraged to eat other food, and owners who see this process for the first time may be surprised by the determination and even harshness that a queen can show at this time. She teaches them to smell and whisker food before they eat it. As they become stronger and more viable, she teaches them to hunt, tempting them at first with morsels of her own hunting trophies.

THE ART OF CLEANLINESS

SIMILARLY, THE MOTHER teaches her kittens to take over the cleaning duties that at first she does for them, and will usually teach them to use a litter tray and cover their faeces. This is a survival ploy, hampering predators in following the cat's trail. Above all, the mother provides a

home base for her kittens. If they get lost, they will utter plaintive and repeated cries until she finds and retrieves them by carrying them home by the scruff of the neck. There is conclusive evidence that kittens which miss out on all this early education grow up to be dysfunctional and often aggressive. Such a cat might misinterpret an attempt to stroke it as an attack and unsheathe all its claws, be resistant to grooming, or be unable to relate to other pets or people in the household.

THE QUEEN AND HER KITTENS

THE EXCEPTIONALLY attentive mothering of the first weeks of a kitten's life creates a strong bond between the queen and her young, and if mother and kittens are kept together this bond continues and intensifies. Even into adult life the queen will continue to bring them choice scraps of food, indulge in mock hunts and generally repeat her early mothering behaviour. Despite this, the separation of the kittens at the usual age of 10–12 weeks seems to cause the queen little distress, and if mother and kittens are reintroduced at a later stage they will not usually recognise each other and may even fight. It seems likely that the original bond is based on the communal smell of the family nest, and that kittens which are separated soon acquire alien smells from their new surroundings which break the bond.

THE TERRITORIAL INSTINCT

ALL MEMBERS OF the cat family are territorial creatures by instinct. Feline territories have been the subject of a great deal of biological study, from which it has emerged that the size of a cat's territory depends on its lifestyle, the availability of food (or, in the case of suburban cats, the number of neighbouring homes offering tasty titbits) and, with unneutered toms, the number of available queens. It is enough to say here that a cat's natural territory is made up of two parts. Surrounding its base – its favourite sleeping place and immediate home territory – is the home range, which will be vigorously defended from strange cats, especially by

females. Beyond the home range, and linked to it by paths, is the hunting range, which will be visited less often. Generally, a male cat will have a home range about 10 times the size of the female's, sometimes as much as 40 ha (100 acres) in area.

These details refer to feral and farm cats, which exist in conditions very close to the wild. The territorial instinct of the domestic cat is of course greatly modified. If it is allowed to roam outside, its home range will usually be the garden or yard and its hunting range will include perhaps a couple of neighbouring gardens.

These areas will be scent-marked with the glands on the head and at the base of the tail, and also

sprayed with urine. The home range will be patrolled regularly and defended either by fighting or – more usually – by 'staring out' rival cats. In areas such as suburban gardens where there is a large cat population, the available spaces and paths between them will be carefully divided up, and there may even be separate time-slots for different cats. This can cause disputes if a cat rising unusually early ventures into another's slot.

> **CAT FACT:**
> Scratching objects serves to sharpen claws rather than blunt them because cats' claws are able to shed layers leaving them with new and pristine needle-pointed tips.

Top
This Persian marks its territory by spraying.

Bottom
Scent can be picked up from various surfaces, this Somali smells a rock.

largely on the quality of the light, which is why the time-slot factor in territorial behaviour mentioned above can work so successfully. A cat used to being fussed and admired by passing schoolchildren, for example, will make sure that it is in the appropriate place on the front garden wall at the right time twice every day. (In school holidays it may well hang about looking bewildered).

Once the key points of the daily routine have been established, the domestic cat will spend much of the rest of the time sleeping. The amount of sleeping a cat does varies, but it is typically 16–18 hours a day. Wild cats are of course nocturnal hunters, sleeping in the hours of daylight. Domestic cats have, apparently willingly, modified this habit, although cats let out at night revert to the nocturnal pattern. Kittens and older cats sleep most. The pattern of sleep varies in domestic cats according to the habits of its home. For example, if everyone is out at work or school all day, the cat will sleep for most of that time. But if it finds a particularly warm and comfortable spot, a cat will not resist sleep at any time, especially if it has just eaten and performed its after-meals wash.

CAT FACT:
Apart from the element of surprise, cats prefer to attack from behind so that their claws work efficiently as the prey attempts to flee away from the cat.

Top
Renowned for their propensity to sleep, cats spend on average 16-18 hours a day sleeping.

Bottom
Indoor cats usually have a favourite sleeping place, often a warm area with familiar smells, within the earshot of the family.

THE INDOOR TERRITORY

IN CATS KEPT INDOORS permanently, territorial behaviour is modified even more, but is still vestigially there. Within the house, the cat will have a number of sleeping places, some of them apparently chosen quite arbitrarily. (One possible clue for the choice is the position of underfloor central heating pipes). The indoor cat will also choose some observation points on window-sills and other strategic places, from which it can keep an eye on its theoretical hunting territory. The territorial instinct goes further than defending the home range against intruders. If you move the furniture, or introduce a new shed or garden seat within an outdoor cat's home range, the change will be thoroughly investigated and scent-marked.

CREATURES OF HABIT

CATS ARE NATURAL conservatives. They like things to stay the same, and they like things to happen at the same time every day. They do not like surprises. They very quickly learn the routines of a new home: when and where to expect food and drink, where the warm spots are, when and where the sun shines through the window on to a convenient ledge, what time the children come home from school and they can expect some play, what are the signals that the family is going to bed, and so on. Cats have an extraordinarily good sense of time, based

If a peacefully sleeping cat is a symbol of contentment, so is a gently purring one. Purring is instinctive, and it is the first sound that a kitten hears since most queens purr loudly and continuously throughout the process of giving birth. Its meaning is as mysterious as its source. It cannot be said to be communication in the usual sense, and in any case cats have other means of communicating vocally. Although purrs may vary from a faint sigh to a full-throated rumble, they seem to be inadvertent, with no relation to anything other than general contentment. As for how the purr is produced, biologists disagree. Some attribute it to resonances in the skull caused by disturbances in the bloodstream, but the more common explanation is that it is produced by two so-called 'false vocal cords', two membranes behind the true vocal cords. The fact that the purr can be felt at its strongest with a finger laid across the throat gives credence to the second theory.

> **CAT FACT:**
> Excluding the margay, cats have to climb down trees backwards because they need to use their claws for gripping the bark. Otherwise they would plummet to the ground.

CAT-NAPPING

IN PERIODS OF deep sleep, which last for a few minutes interspersed with long periods of lighter sleep, cats may show movements which suggest that they are dreaming. The ears may twitch, the legs and tail quiver and the whiskers flex. Human dreams, leave alone cats', are mystery enough, but it seems likely that during these periods cats are reprising previous hunting experiences or anticipating future ones.

Top
Cats are natural sun worshipers, they often find a place in the sun to sleep.

Bottom
This 'lappy' cat enjoys the body heat of its owner.

Grooming

ALL MEMBERS OF the cat family are fastidious by nature. Even leopards, which kill their prey with great ferocity and much bloodthirstiness, take great care not to soil their coats with blood. Some domestic cats can seem obsessively fastidious at times.

EARLY GROOMING

BEING GROOMED IS the newly born kitten's first experience, even before its first feed, so it is not surprising that the experience becomes fundamental

throughout its life. As each kitten is born, its mother licks it clean, which also stimulates the kitten's first breath. From then on until they are about three weeks old, the mother grooms her kittens at least once a day, and licking them is her way of awakening them for another feed. There is also a good deal of occasional grooming and nuzzling as the queen and her litter snuggle together. By about three weeks, the kittens begin to groom themselves and each other, and even after another three weeks, when they are proficient, they continue mutual grooming sessions with their siblings and their mother.

If the kittens stay together, this may continue throughout adult life, and two adult cats living amicably together will also groom each other. Most cats will 'groom' their owners, reinforcing the bond between creatures sharing a common territory, and cats will groom a friendly and familiar dog in the same spirit.

But it is self-grooming which is central to a cat's personal life. It is evidently a source of pleasure – perhaps a reminder of the comforts of kittenhood – as well as a matter of hygiene. It is also a dietary need, because sebum secreted in the follicles and spreading up the hair is a valuable source of vitamin D.

THE ART OF GROOMING

THE HOOKED BARBS on a cat's tongue, which also enable it to rasp at food, are its main grooming tools. The cat's flexible spine enables it to reach almost every part of its body in one way or another. Grooming typically begins with the scratching of the neck and perhaps the head and ears with a hind leg. The cat will then methodically clean its flanks, back,

Top left
Mutual grooming is a method of bonding between mother and kittens and, as here, adult cats.

Top right
Self-grooming is fundamental to a cat's mental and physical well-being. It ensures a supply of vitamin D, cleanliness and it relieves stress.

Bottom
Adult cats who share the same home will often reciprocate grooming.

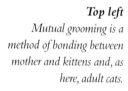

deposited on the coat. Another function of grooming is as a displacement activity to help the cat recover from stress. A cat will often groom itself after an awkward fall, for example, or after a confrontation with a strange cat. It has been suggested that this could be an automatic response to a rise in body temperature caused by fear or embarrassment. Certainly, cats will often indulge in a prolonged session of grooming after an exciting chase or a strenuous game. If the game has been with humans, this is a signal to end it and let the cat calm down.

tail and underparts. The paws, fore and aft, follow. Now it is time for the head and ears, cleaned with a saliva-dampened forepaw. The teeth and claws may be used to tease out pieces of mud, plant seeds or other debris from the coat and between the toes. At the end of the sequence, the cat may return to any part that seems to need more attention. A difficult spot on the coat, such as some sticky substance, may call for repeated attention. Some such taints, tar or paint for example, can be dangerous if ingested and should be removed by the owner, with a little surgical spirit, washed off well afterwards.

A NECESSARY PROCESS

GROOMING REMOVES loose hair and parasites from the coat. The loose hair is ingested and normally brought up harmlessly in the form of a hairball. But self-grooming is not a substitute for the owner's attention, particularly in the case of the long-haired breeds whose tongues cannot cope effectively with the length and density of hair.

In hot weather, grooming is the main method by which a cat cools itself by evaporation of the saliva

GETTING OUT OF THE HABIT

SOME CATS ARE more devoted groomers than others, and generally they become less fastidious as they grow older. They may have physical difficulty in the process of washing their paws to clean the ears, for example, and the ears of older cats should be inspected regularly for mites and other parasites.

Although cats vary widely in their grooming habits, a sudden change in an individual's routine may be a warning sign, especially if associated with loss of appetite. Lack of attention to grooming is a frequent response to illness, but a cat under undue stress may also take to unusually excessive grooming. However, this can be prompted by other disturbances such as the prolonged absence of someone from home, a loud domestic quarrel or even the rearrangement of furniture. A useful test for reluctant groomers is to spread a little cold melted butter on the coat, which no healthy cat can resist.

Top left
A cat uses its teeth to remove dirt from between its toes.

Top right
When grooming follows play, it is a sign that the cat wants to rest.

Bottom
Owners should continue to groom their cat even if their pet is fastidious, grooming can reveal parasites which the cat cannot remove.

The Curiosity of Cats

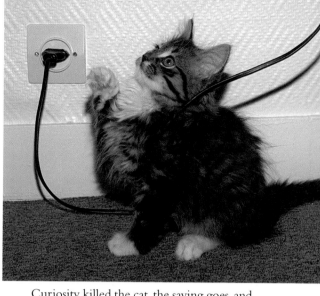

THE PROVERBIAL CURIOSITY of cats is a reality. It is evidence of high intelligence, because it shows that cats have good memories and are capable of interpreting information. It is based on their instinct for survival and their need to know as much as possible about their environment, including anything that might be a threat or offer the chance of a hunt.

AN INQUISITIVE NATURE

CATS DO NOT voluntarily change their territories – although change may be forced upon them by the

hierarchical structure of feral communities – and aim to know them intimately. They are cautious about changes within their territory, so that any novelty, from a pile of builders' sand or even garden tools left lying about to some major change like a fallen tree, will be investigated and probably scent-marked. Sheds or cars left open will attract the curious cat and are always worth investigating if a cat goes missing.

Curiosity killed the cat, the saying goes, and cats' inquisitiveness can certainly land them in dangerous situations. It starts early in kittenhood. Almost as soon as they can scramble about at 2–3 weeks, kittens start to explore their environment, and mother cats keep a watchful eye – or rather a scentful nose – on their young to keep them out of trouble and drag them back to safety. Curiosity can often be a stronger driving force than the caution that would ensure a way out of difficulties. This is particularly true of kittens and younger cats. The mature cat will have built up a wealth of experience of what is or is not possible, but the younger animal lacks this.

Even so, curiosity can overcome even the most mature and sensible cat. In a cat-friendly house and garden the dangers can be minimised by, for example, covering water-butts securely, covering open pipes and drains, storing poisons away carefully, securing garden sheds and stopping up any inviting-looking cat sized gaps and holes. Some house plants are poisonous to cats and should be avoided, and everyone in the house should be trained to shut

Top left
Garden poisons should be stored out of a cat's reach as even sheds can become their playground.

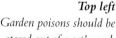

Top right
Kittens are more likely to put themselves in danger than adult cats as they are more curious and playful.

Bottom
Although cats generally hate water this one's curiosity has enticed him onto a water-butt.

cupboard doors. Unused chimneys are best blocked up, especially when a kitten or new cat is introduced to the house. As a cat grows older, at about eight years, it begins to care less about the curiosities of life and more about the certainties, such as warmth, comfort, and the regularity of meals.

TERRITORIAL PATROLS

AS THE CURIOUS cat patrols its territory, it absorbs information through its senses, mainly its sense of smell. A cat new to the area may have left scent markings. There may be new nests of birds or mice. A variety of other animals may have left their scent on the cat's patch. Each of these must be sampled and considered. At the same time, there will be old, familiar smells which give the cat reassurance.

A housebound cat will express its curiosity by finding a window-sill or other spot from which it can observe the world outside. The movements of birds, cats, other animals and humans will be watched very closely even though they can have

little or no effect on the cat's security or offer the prospect of hunting. Anything new in the house, such as an empty box or basket, will be investigated. If a cat's curiosity reveals that something is about to happen that it does not like – the appearance of its travelling basket might herald a visit to the vet, for example – it may well hide.

A SENSE OF PRIVACY

ALONGSIDE ITS CURIOSITY, a cat is not keen if any other creature is inquisitive about its own life. While it is not quite true – of domestic cats, at any rate – that cats 'keep themselves to themselves', they do retain a degree of privacy. They like to see without being seen, as when they lie low, observing, in undergrowth. The cat family's experts in this are, of course the big cats, whose coats are so adapted to their habitats that it is possible to pass within 6 m (20 ft) of a leopard or tiger without knowing it is there. Cats become extremely offended if another animal intrudes when they are feeding or using the litter tray. And however sociable they are, they like to hunt and patrol their territory on their own. It is said with some truth that you never quite get to know a cat in the same way as you do a dog.

Top
Cats' excellent senses allow them to hear and smell things about which they may be curious.

Bottom left
Windowsills are a favourite lookout post.

Bottom right
This cat sniffs the undergrowth for signs of intruders.

CAT FACT:
In cats the equivalent of the thumb is known as the dew claw. It is raised above the ground on the inside of the front leg and is used as a hook for holding prey down during the kill.

Felix the Hunter

I N THE NATURAL world, hunting is the major waking activity in cats' lives. Farm cats, perhaps understandably given their opportunities, are the champions among hunters. One English farm cat called Mickey is said to have caught 1,000 mice each year of his 23 year life. Not many cats would have the longevity or the stamina to approach that record, but a survey of British farmers showed that 88 per cent thought their cats did a good job in keeping down rats and mice.

HUNTING INSTINCTS REMAIN

TRADITIONALLY, FARMERS HAVE let their cats go hungry to encourage them to hunt, although a farm cat that relates to the farm as a source of food and warmth is more likely to hunt in the immediate vicinity and will, therefore, be of more practical use than if it is driven out to the woods and fields to find enough to eat.

The reality of the domesticated cat's life is that it does not need to hunt in order to survive. None the less, the hunting instinct persists and indeed needs to be satisfied in some way if the cat is to live a full, contented life.

Kittens are taught to hunt by their mothers. In the wild, where whatever the queen can catch is the only source of food for her and her new family, there is pressure on her to encourage the kittens to do their own hunting once they are able. The very rapid development of hunting skills even in domestic litters is no doubt an echo of the urgency of the task in the wild. There is only a limited amount of time to get

through the teaching process before the kittens' intake is more than a solitary hunter can provide for. By 4–5 months the kitten, in the natural world, must be able to fend for itself, so there is no time to waste.

TRAINED HUNTERS

SO THE DOMESTIC queen, like her wild cousin, trains her kittens from an early age, starting by twitching her own tail as a tempting plaything. She will encourage them to carry out mock kills on any suitable object to hand, and to rough and tumble among themselves in mimicry of hunting behaviour. In the wild, she will eventually take them on hunting trips, helping them to locate and if necessary to kill the victims. In the setting of the nest, hunting will continue as a game. It needs to be continued as a game by the owner, in as many ingenious ways as can be devised, if the young cat is not to become bored. Interestingly, domestic kittens which for some reason have not had a hunting education from their mothers grow up to be either uninterested in hunting or very bad at it, and consequently are easily bored and may even become zombie-like. It is as if they have been robbed of their main purpose in life.

Compared with the hunting methods of dogs, those of cats are economical, methodical and effective. The most notable difference between the two is the extent to which cats conserve their energy for the last stages of the hunt. Dogs, other than

---

CAT FACT:
Cats have tongues covered in sharp hair-like points called *papillae*. They are used to scrape blood and flesh from bones, and for raking their fur while cleaning themselves.

Top
Cheetahs rely on a short burst of speed to catch their prey, this cub will need to learn from its mother to be able to fend for itself.

Middle
Mock kills are enjoyable and educational for kittens.

Bottom
The first stage of the kill is locating the prey.

CAT FACT:
Purring is most obviously used to express pleasure, but cats are known to purr when they are ill or injured, suggesting that it comforts them during times of stress.

trained hunting dogs, tend to charge about wildly and often unrealistically, without much consideration of whether the quarry is worth the effort. cats' hunting techniques, by contrast, are more single-minded and meticulous.

GOING IN FOR THE KILL

THE HUNT CAN be divided into three stages: locating the prey, stalking it, and the kill. A cat alerted to the possibility of prey will take up observation for a considerable period of time, its senses of sight, smell and hearing all working overtime. When the victim

has been selected, stalking begins. The cat moves forward with its belly close to the ground, ears pricked forward, eyes wide, totally concentrated on the prey. If the target is moving, this attitude may be broken and taken up again and again until the cat judges that it is in the right position for the pounce. The body quivers and the hind legs tread the ground silently. Then, when the timing and position are right, the cat springs with its front paws extended, usually keeping its hind legs firmly on the ground.

As many owners will have seen, this is the trickiest moment of the hunt. A mouse or a small bird may slip through the paws, especially if the cat is not an expert hunter. A literal game of cat and mouse will

then follow. Sometimes the cat is confident enough to allow the victim to slip away so as to add to the excitement of the occasion.

Finally comes the kill. The ideal kill is a bite with the canine teeth on the nape of the neck, severing the spinal cord, but this does not always work first time. It may only disable the victim, which then becomes a plaything before finally being despatched. Larger prey such as rats or rabbits may have to be leaped on and attacked by the front paws before they are beaten into submission. Cats almost always exercise proper caution about the size and strength of a potential victim. For example, most will take on a young or diseased rabbit but not a fully grown healthy one, whose legs pack a powerful and painful kick. Rats in particular are treated with respect, because they can inflict nasty bites even in their death throes. Despite this, an unnamed female tabby on the staff of a London greyhound stadium is said to have caught 12,500 rats in a six year tour of duty.

Top
This cat is observing the prey before it makes its move.

Bottom left
While stalking the cat keeps its stomach low to the ground and ears pricked forward.

Bottom right
Cats often bring their kill home, they should not be scolded as it is a present to be shared with the owner.

HUNTING STYLES

FERAL AND WILD cats eat their victims quickly, without pausing. Domestic cats tend to take more time, pausing now and again to look round, perhaps because they are not under the same pressure. Eating a mouse, a cat will start at the head, biting it off at the neck, passing it to the carnassial teeth and then swallowing it more or less whole. The top half of the body follows. Then the usual technique is to work forwards from a hind leg to the victim's abdomen. Some cats eat the lot, while others leave the gall bladder, small intestine and other parts of the digestive system. If fur and skin are swallowed, they are regurgitated later.

Dead prey, or parts of it, are often carried back to the home area. The origin of this habit is probably to share the prey with other kittens in the nest, and an owner assumes the 'other kitten' role. Another post-

hunting activity which many owners find disturbing is the habit of playing with dead prey, as if re-living the hunting and killing experience, by repeatedly tossing it in the air, pouncing and rolling on it, and hiding and rediscovering it.

In spite of the cat's finely tuned and frequently practised hunting skills, many chases are unsuccessful.

Top
Cats in the wild, such as this lion, are forced to eat their kill immediately because of the threat of scavengers and other cats.

Bottom
Cat playing with prey.

It has been estimated that as many as 90 per cent of chased birds may escape, and over 75 per cent of mice. These observations were made of farm cats, so they are not a reflection of laziness or inexperience.

LOCATING THE NEXT MEAL

WELL FED DOMESTIC cats usually seem to be as keen on hunting as cats which prey for food. There seems to be a deep-seated philosophy in the cat family generally that 'you never know where the next meal's coming from'. Large cats such as lions and tigers often eat beyond their immediate needs until they are sated and have to go and sleep it off. Domestic cats which are good hunters will go on catching prey tirelessly, even if they do not eat their victims. Indeed, not all prey are killed to be eaten. Some creatures such as shrews and moles are hunted and killed despite the fact that the cat knows from experience they are not good to eat, but many edible species such as mice are ignored after the kill and the end game. Most cats, however, make an exception for birds, which are regarded as delicacies and consumed with relish, usually leaving only a small heap of feathers to tell the tale.

CATS AND BIRDS

THE SUPPOSED DECIMATION of garden birds by cats is one of the crosses that has to be borne by owners who allow their pets outside, and unfortunately it provides an argument for anti-cat bird lovers which can hardly be gainsaid when there is a sad heap of feathers lying on the path. In truth, the toll of adult birds is not as heavy as is often claimed. With their wild field of vision, their shrill warning systems, their willingness to 'dive-bomb' marauding cats and above all their ability to escape into the sky, adult birds are well able to take care of themselves. Small birds are also adept at 'playing dead' and then seizing a chance to escape. It is really only as regards fledglings that cats stand guilty of serious damage, though even here many birds, such as blackbirds, defend their young by relentless alarm calls and repeated diving at the enemy. It makes sense, of course, if you have both cats and birds in your garden, to feed and water the birds at a cat-proof bird table.

HUNTING AND THE HOUSEBOUND CAT

HUNTING IS SO integral to a cat's life that owners of housebound cats need to compensate by providing substitute activities such as extended sessions of chasing games. A variety of sophisticated and expensive toys can be bought from pet stores, but table-tennis balls, screws of paper jerked along on a string, lengths of string (for supervised play) and similar everyday objects will provide just as much fun and exercise.

Top
Cats are not proficient bird killers.

Bottom
Toys are an excellent alternative to hunting.

Cat Psychology

A DOMESTIC CAT'S relationship with its owner and the owner's family and any other pets is complex. It is made up of impulses which are derived from a cat's life in the wild combined with others which are driven by its willingness to adapt to domestic life. It is a trade-off. The domestic cat exchanges its freedoms – to hunt at will, to choose its own territory, to mate when it feels like it – for the undeniable advantages of shelter, warmth, and a ready supply of food. There is clearly a potential for inner conflict in this situation, and perhaps it is surprising that conflict comes to the surface so rarely and in so few individual cats' lives.

PERSONAL SPACE

QUEENS ARE ALMOST invariably good mothers and provide for their kittens an environment of care, warmth and comfort. The taste for comfort is

implanted young and persists throughout the cat's life, reflected in its liking for a place in the sun, a warm rug in front of the fire, a favourite cushion or its owner's bed. In addition, the cat needs its own personal space, a distance of about 50 cm (18 in) around its body, where it feels itself totally in control, choosing what goes on there and who or what should be admitted to it. This is where it will retreat if stressed,

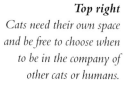

Top right
Cats need their own space and be free to choose when to be in the company of other cats or humans.

Bottom
Whether a cat can sit on the furniture or enter particular rooms must be decided upon from the beginning and adhered to.

and for this reason this home base should be in a quiet part of the house where it can rest or sleep, or quietly observe the passing scene, without being disturbed. If there is more than one cat in a household, the personal space should be large enough for two, or each cat should have its own Overcrowding in itself causes stress.

As for the cat's other favoured places, everyone in the household must agree on where the cat may or may not sleep or sit, and on what is or is not regarded as acceptable behaviour. It is as confusing and stressful to cats as it is to children if one member of the family permits something which another prohibits. To a cat, if one bed is permitted territory there is no apparent reason why another should not be, especially if it happens to be in a warmer or sunnier room, and some people may welcome a cat lying on their toes through the night while others dislike it. Probably the best solution, for reasons of hygiene apart from anything else, is to make all bedrooms no go areas for cats.

CATS IN COMPANY

A SIMILAR DIFFICULTY can arise if a visitor who does not like cats comes to call. The innocent caller sits in a chair on which the cat is accustomed to jump up to be stroked. The cat jumps, the visitor is appalled, and the cat is hauled off, not surprisingly confused. But

while some cats demand cuddles and attention others want no more than to sit in the same room with people. Children should be warned to back off if a cat seems not to want their attention.

ROUTINE AND SECURITY

CATS ENJOY HAVING an environment which they know and in which they feel secure. Their sense of time is a source of security, provided the household routine is not upset. Minor changes such as moving furniture around, or major ones like the introduction of a new baby or another pet, can be very disturbing – even for a well established cat. When faced with this kind of stress, or indeed any unusual behaviour among the humans in the household, cats tend to hide or even disappear for good.

New cat owners are often surprised by the way in which their cats seem to sense impending changes such as moving house or going on holiday. This is sometimes attributed to a feline 'sixth sense' but the truth is far more mundane. A cat's life is so firmly rooted in the here and now that it is constantly on the alert for changes. In the wild, such changes in its circumstances could mean real threats such as the appearance of a rival cat that would have to be fought off and might be a challenge to food supplies. For cats, a change is not as good as a rest.

cats have rights too, especially in their own homes, and all the owner can do to put things right is to offer the cat a cuddle in another chair. It is unfortunately true that cats have an uncanny knack of wanting to make friends with anti-cat people.

Some cats, on the other hand, seem to go to some lengths to preserve an air of aloofness and stand-offishness with everyone, but this does not necessarily mean that they do not quietly enjoy company. Most cats will seek it, often at particular times such as in the evening when things at home are relaxed. Yet they preserve their independence, and

CAT FACT:
The claws of a cat are actually properly termed protractible as opposed to retractable. This is because muscles are required to stick them out, but they pull back automatically.

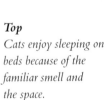

Top
Cats enjoy sleeping on beds because of the familiar smell and the space.

Bottom
Cats sometimes feel secure sleeping underneath furniture, especially if they want to be alone.

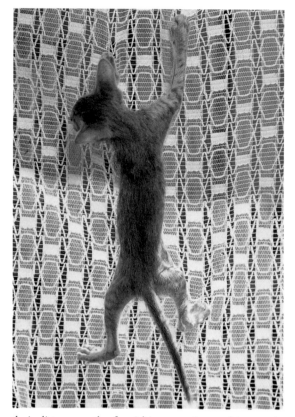

As a result, strange noises upstairs as suitcases are assembled, the appearance of removal mens' boxes, unexpected comings and goings, unfamiliar smells as clothes are packed, are all noted and, although of course they cannot be interpreted in detail, all add up to a sense of insecurity. Owners also sometimes fail to take account of a cat's good memory, which explains why the mere appearance of the travelling basket can make it dive for cover. The basket might mean a visit to the vet or a spell in the cattery.

Any of these happenings might involve a journey by car, which some cats dislike intensely and none seem to take as calmly as dogs. This is perhaps not surprising if one thinks of how dogs and cats live in the wild: dogs in roaming packs, cats almost entirely on their own patch. To put a cat in a car is to deprive it of all the sights, sounds and smells of its familiar environment and replace them with what is, for cats, an unwanted degree of noise and the smells of petrol and oil.

CATS AND HUMANS

IT IS NOT ENTIRELY frivolous to suggest that whereas pet dogs tend to regard themselves as humans and part of the human pack, the owner being the pack leader, cats regard the humans in the household as other cats. In many ways they behave towards people as they would towards other kittens in the nest, 'grooming' them, snuggling up with them and communicating with them in the ways that they would use with other cats. The owner of a placid cat may not realise the extent to which it is taking cues from sounds, scents and visually observable behaviour of the people of the house, even though its reactions are muted.

Owners who live alone may face a particular problem in that their cats become too dependent on their company, especially if they have been obtained as kittens and are confined to the house all the time. All the cat's bonding emotions are concentrated on one person. This, compounded by boredom, can lead to extreme distress when the owner goes out. The cat may run and hide, refusing to eat or use its litter tray until the owner returns. Some cats may work out

their distress on the furnishings, tearing cushions and curtains and scratching furniture. These difficulties can be avoided if an owner living alone takes on two kittens from the same litter who, given a selection of toys, will amuse each other. Two kittens are really very little more trouble than one, and the companionship will offer each of them a more interesting life.

Top left
Cats may associate travelling baskets with bad memories, such as a trip to the vet or a cattery.

Top right
Kittens need to be amused, if not they can destroy furnishings.

Bottom
A second cat can offer companionship to relieve the boredom of a cat that is often left on its own.

THE OUTSIDE CAT

CATS ALLOWED OUTSIDE perhaps have the best of all feline worlds. While keeping their safe, warm base at home, they are able to approximate more closely to their natural mode of life. They can stake out and maintain a territory, do a little hunting, choose a selection of outdoor sleeping places suitable for all angles of the sun, and even, if they are allowed to, revert to a nocturnal lifestyle. They become less dependent on their owners and can get their exercise more naturally. The downside of this is of course the outdoor cat's vulnerability to accidents and fights and, not uncommonly, its sudden decision to desert the owning family and set up house with another one for no particular reason. Even if it does not go as far as this, roaming cats quite often develop human networks, calling at each house regularly for a cuddle or a titbit, of which the owner is unaware. This echoes territorial behaviour among wild cats, which will visit a number of sites on their patch where food or shelter is available.

THE ART OF MANNERS

ONE OF THE problems of taking on a stray or a cat from an unknown background is that it may never, as a kitten, have learned the rudiments of social behaviour. A good mother will curb a kitten's over-aggressiveness with a sound pat, but will also encourage harmless and constructive play, as well as settling down with her litter for quiet times of warmth and contentment. A cat that has not had these experiences loses out as severely as a child without a loving family and is subject to similar disturbances in later life – inability to adjust to others, bursts of aggression or simple bad behaviour. This is a sound argument for buying a grown cat only from a known source and for observing the queen with her kittens before taking any on.

Top
A sunny ledge or seat overlooking the cat's territory from where it can hunt is a prime position.

Bottom
One danger for an outdoors cat is its attraction to cars.

Cat language

CATS BRING TO domestic life the whole repertoire of body, facial and vocal language that their wild and feral cousins use, the main difference being that domestic cats have a larger range of vocal expressions. This is probably because they have observed from experience that vocal sounds are important in the human world and achieve a more immediate response.

VOCAL COMMUNICATION

BODY LANGUAGE AND scent tell cats about each other, but they are not effective for communicating with humans. So a cat will make a particular sound if it wants to be fed and another if it wants to be let out, situations that would not occur in the wild or

Top right
White cat showing displeasure by bearing its teeth, this may be followed by a hiss.

Top left
Siamese are the most vocal breed.

feral world. Some cats – especially Siamese – develop a range of miaow variations for specific circumstances which can rate as primitive forms of conversation with their owners. However, cats rarely achieve the same level of understanding with their owners as dogs. This does not mean that dogs are more intelligent; it means only that cats tend to limit their vocal expressions to those which produce desired results whereas dogs are more positively eager to please.

A FELINE VOCABULARY?

OVER 50 YEARS ago an American psychologist, Mildred Moelk, identified 16 different meaningful sounds in the cat's audible vocabulary, discounting the purr which is a reflex action. She analysed these sounds closely and divided them into three groups. She identified murmurs made with the mouth closed, 'miaow' sounds made by starting with the mouth open and gradually closing it, and the more urgent and loudest sounds made with the open mouth.

Some of these sounds, such as the male and female calls used in mating or the growls, snarls and shrieks of a full-blooded cat fight, may never be uttered by a spayed or neutered domestic cat. But most owners come to recognise a repertoire of a handful of sounds which can be said to be specific communications between cat and owner, or cat and cat. They are also likely to hear, on occasion, the more generalised howl of anger or pain and the half-hissed frustrated stutter when, for example, the cat is teased by a bird.

EVERYDAY EXPRESSIONS

PROBABLY THE MOST familiar and delightful vocal expression among domestic cats is the bird-like chirrup of greeting that most cats give their owners and members of the family when either comes home, often accompanied by a lift of the tail, arching of the back and a bounce with the front paws. This is similar to the sound used by friendly cats meeting each other on neutral territory in a feral colony. It is confirmation that cats regard their owners and the family as members of the same 'colony' even though this is made up of different animals.

Another familiar sound is the 'see me' call, a more long drawn out vocalisation typically used when a cat is waiting by the door to be let out. This or a shorter miaow may be used if the cat wants to be fed. These different sounds do not, of course, 'mean' anything in the same sense as words in human language have specific meanings. They are merely the sounds that the cat has learned by experience produce the desired results. If growling at the door resulted in its being opened, the cat would use that signal instead – except that growling is reserved, in cats, for displeasure. Queens growl at their kittens if their play becomes too boisterous, they feed too greedily or stray too far from the nest, so it has a special significance in the cat's life. So does the hiss, a sound which is rather higher up the cats' 'Richter Scale' and is more urgent and threatening. A cat's hiss is a warning for even its owner to take care – something has made the cat extremely cross. After the hiss, the next step up the scale is spitting.

EARLY VOCALISATION

THE FIRST VOCAL language that kittens learn, or are born with, is the distress call, which immediately alerts the mother and results in attention or feeding. Their vocabulary gradually increases until at about three months they are vocalising freely with an extended repertoire. The more they interplay with their siblings, the greater their range. In adult cats vocalisation varies considerably, Siamese being the champion 'talkers'. Naturally, the more a cat is spoken to regularly, using the same phrases and tone of voice each time, the more communicative it will become. It aids the response if all members of the family use the same phrases and tone.

Top
This cat is displaying a friendly greeting towards its owner; rubbing its body against their legs; raising its tail; and arching its back.

Bottom
Cats recognise their names from an early age, this owner is calling her cat to be fed.

BODY LANGUAGE

IN CAT TO CAT communication, body language is more significant than vocal expression. The cat's body language involves movements of the ears, whiskers, hair, spine, legs and tail. Some experts claim to have distinguished nine different facial expressions and 16 body and tail postures. These can be used in a variety of permutations to express subtleties of meaning – or to put it more accurately, of reactions to events – only partly accessible to humans.

Aggression is signalled by the raising of the tail, with the hair fluffed out and the tail waving slightly. The facial whiskers bristle forward, the ears are erect but curled slightly backwards, and the pupils narrow to slits. The angrier the cat becomes, the more its ears go back and its whiskers forward. If it is going to move in to the attack, the ears swivel even more and the tail waves more briskly.

ON THE DEFENSIVE

A CAT ON THE defensive lays its ears flat, pointing sideways. Its coat and whiskers bristle, it arches its back, and its mouth opens slightly ready for a growl or snarl, to hiss or to spit. To indicate submission, the cat cringes, the coat subsides, the whiskers droop, the tail falls low and thumps and the pupils dilate.

A challenge between two strange cats exhibits the whole range of aggressive and defensive stances. The encounter usually begins with a prolonged

Top left
An archetypal display of aggressive body language is an arched back, flat ears and raised hair.

Top right
Circling one another before one cat decides to attack is typical in cat fights.

Bottom right
Pleasure can be read from this cat's half-closed eyes.

session of staring, after which one cat will put up the challenge by sniffing at its rival's tail and growling. This forces the second cat on to the defensive. If the aggressor continues to advance, the defender may give up and back off, leaving its rival to strut confidently away. Alternatively, it may decide to stand its corner and take on an aggressive pose. This is the cue for real trouble. One cat will launch an attack, whereupon the other will roll onto its back and bring its paws up, claws unsheathed, to defend itself. This is now a full-blown cat fight of the kind that occasionally splits the night sky apart. It will continue until one or other of the cats decides that it has had enough and seeks a chance to scramble away. When both cats are a safe distance apart they will settle down for a thorough wash. But matters have probably not been settled for good. There will most likely be a return bout on another day.

INSTINCTIVE LANGUAGE

FIGHTING TALK APART, cats also have gestures which spring from the life of the nest and which they use with their owners. For example, movement of the ears back and down, perhaps combined with a pat from a velvetted paw, is an invitation to play. A contented cat keeps its ears pricked – they spring up surprisingly strongly if they are stroked – and its eyes half-closed, settling down on its hocks and wriggling into a comfortable position.

Just as we can interpret some feline movements, so of course our cats interpret ours. If its owner is sitting comfortably watching television, a cat knows from experience that this is a good time to jump up and settle down to be stroked. The cat knows where its food dish is kept, and a move towards it will perhaps produce a chirrup of anticipation or rubbing round the owner's legs. Similarly, your cat will have registered the signs of your going out, going to bed, getting ready for the children to come home from school, and so on.

In a class of its own among cats' body language is the 'lordosis' position adopted by unspayed females on heat, indicating their readiness to mate. The front

end goes down and the rear up with the tail held to one side, and the queen treads with her hind feet. All this may be accompanied by bouts of rolling, brushing against people and objects, and repeated cries. If the queen is not mated, this behaviour will continue for 3–5 days and, in some breeds (notably Siamese), considerably longer. In unspayed kittens, lordosis begins at about 6–7 months.

SCENT COMMUNICATION

BEYOND VOCAL AND body language is another form of communication which cats use between themselves and for their own information – the language of scent. Two cats meeting each other will gently touch noses and heads, sniffing at each other's scent glands. If they are very friendly, they rub each other's bodies. A cat patrolling its territory will frequently pause to check on its own scent markings and those of others on posts, trees, fences and shrubs. Sharpening of the claws leaves scent markings on the object used which are of particular significance since cats are choosy about where they sharpen their claws and usually remain faithful to selected places.

The instinctive form of communication through scent is translated into domestic life when a cat rubs against its owner's legs or scent-marks its owner's feet with its head. In turn, this activity gives the cat information about its owner, who may notice that certain shower gel or soap fragrances are particularly attractive to their pets. Spraying is another aspect of scent-marking, a less pleasing one unless it can be successfully discouraged indoors.

Top right
Two amiable cats greet one another, they familiarise themselves through smelling each other.

Top left
This cat illustrates the 'lordosis' position, a sign that this female is on heat.

Bottom
In sharpening its claws this cat leaves its scent mark on this tree.

Owning a Cat

CATS HAVE A reputation as easy and relatively inexpensive pets to keep. Nevertheless they do need a certain amount of basic equipment, food, shelter and a share of loving attention. Although many cats can appear aloof and independent, in a domestic setting they depend heavily on the company of humans even if they do not make this obvious.

A MEMBER OF THE FAMILY
MANY ARE HAPPY merely to add their presence to the home, while others want to take a more active part, demanding play, cuddles and occasional 'conversations'.

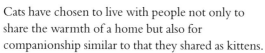

Cats have chosen to live with people not only to share the warmth of a home but also for companionship similar to that they shared as kittens.

Cats depend on their owners for shelter, food, affection and good health. This means that someone in the house – and it is best to decide from the outset exactly who – will have to devote some time to the cat each day, feeding, attending to the litter tray, grooming and providing company. At the same time,

everyone should agree about having a cat. It should have no enemies in the house. It is important to remember that the cat will be part of your life for many years – typically up to 12 or more if you start with a kitten, and maybe a good deal longer.

QUESTIONS TO BE ASKED
A FUNDAMENTAL QUESTION is whether your family's lifestyle is such as to accommodate the addition of a cat. The ideal home for a cat is one where there is a regular pattern to the day; cats like, and have a psychological need for routine. At the other extreme, a household where people are in or out at unpredictable times and the house is empty for long periods is highly unsuitable for a cat. Most cats will adapt to being left alone during the working day, especially if they are allowed to go out at will or are provided with some toys and a good lookout post on, say, a window-sill, but they like to be able to predict when someone will come home, a skill which they rapidly acquire. No one who is frequently away overnight should own a cat unless reliable arrangements can be made for feeding and care.

Consideration also needs to be given to what will happen when the family goes away on holiday. Regrettably, too many cats are left to fend for themselves when their owners are away. The ideal solution is for a friend or relation to take on caring duties, preferably in the cat's own home. Boarding

Top
Time should be put aside to play and talk to your cat; kittens, especially, require attention.

Bottom left
Everyone in the family should agree to a new pet so that it is made welcome.

a cat indicates that it has had enough play and wants a nap, it should be left alone. Above all, they should be taught about the danger of cat's claws. These can be unsheathed not only when the cat is angry, but often in the excitement of play. Children should be warned to take particular care to keep their faces out of range.

There must also be a set of basic (and consistent) rules about where the cat is and is not allowed to go – for example, not in the kitchen, not on tables or work surfaces, not in bedrooms, and so on.

OTHER PETS

INTRODUCING A CAT into a household where there are already other pets can raise difficulties, but these can usually be avoided if the owner is sensitive

catteries are an acceptable alternative, but they are expensive and cats do not adapt to kennel life with the ease of dogs. Many of the problems of the owner's absence are lessened if there are two cats in the home. They will entertain and provide company for each other and are less likely to exhibit symptoms of disturbance such as spraying or damaging furniture and furnishings. The ideal two-cat household consists of two kittens from the same litter.

to the feelings of the senior resident and distributes attention evenly. An incoming cat will in any case take a little time to adjust to its new home, and will generally work out its own relationships. It is important that it is provided with a secure place of its own where it can retreat if the attentions of the rival pet become too pressing.

CHILDREN AND CATS

IT IS NOT A good idea to introduce a kitten into a home where there are very young children. A cat already in residence when a baby arrives is a different matter. Provided it feels it is still getting some attention, it will usually adjust easily to the situation. But young children new to cats need to be taught some basic rules of cat handling. They should learn, for example, that a cat should always be approached from the front, never from the back or from above. They must understand that when

Top
Although catteries provide warm, safe accommodation for cats while the owner is away, they are not a long-term solution.

Bottom
This kitten and puppy have been introduced to the household at a similar time, thus avoiding rivalry.

Choosing a Cat

PEOPLE CHOOSE CATS in a variety of ways. Sometimes, it can be said that cats choose people. Many a stray or abandoned cat has found temporary shelter with a well-disposed family and then settled down to become part of the household. The reverse is also true. Some cats, especially if disturbed by the arrival of another pet or a new baby, or by having to move house, go off to find another more settled home. In such ways the domestic cat demonstrates its dependence and independence at the same time.

fail to settle in its new home. In the absence of a detailed contract, the owner should come away with at least the kitten's registration certificate, a transfer form (which entitles the new owner to show the cat) and written confirmation of any conditions that have been agreed between the original and new owners.

Breeders also sell kittens, sometimes without a pedigree certificate, that have 'faults' which disqualify them for show but are perfectly healthy and acceptable as domestic pets. The term 'pet quality' is sometimes used for these. They are often sold neutered or with the condition that they will be neutered within a stated period of time.

The names of reputable breeders can be obtained from cat fancy organisations, individual breed clubs and the cat fancy press. Vets should be able to recommend local breeders, and also often know of healthy non-pedigree cats needing good homes. It should be noted that not all breeding catteries are necessarily registered with a cat fancy organisation and so are not, in that sense, 'approved.'

BUYING A PEDIGREE

MORE CONVENTIONAL WAYS of acquiring a cat range from newspaper small ads and cards in shop windows to buying from a pedigree breeder. The latter is of course vital if the owner is planning to show the cat as a pedigree animal. The regulations governing the issue of pedigree certificates vary in detail from country to country, and even between the various organisations within the United States, but generally they require that at least four generations of a kitten's antecedents should be traceable and named. It is important to note, however, that a pedigree certificate is in itself no guide to the kitten's quality as a potential show cat, or to its health.

On acquiring a pedigree cat, the new owner may be asked to sign a contract specifying, among other things, the circumstances in which breeding may take place; for example, outcrossing may be prohibited with certain breeds. The contract may also oblige the original owner to take the kitten back if, within a specified period, it should fall seriously ill or

Top left
All kittens are endearing but it is vital to choose one with a dry coat and clear eyes.

Top right
Kittens should be at least 10 weeks old, and preferably 12 weeks, before they are found new homes.

Bottom
Cat being neutered; one of the few but necessary expenses in owning a cat.

RESCUE CATS

ANIMAL SHELTERS AND welfare organisations are another source for both kittens and mature cats. Many of the latter will have already experienced family life, but others may have been through

traumatic episodes. While no reputable organisation will offer a cat which it does not feel has a good chance of settling in as a domestic pet, some disturbed cats may need to be handled with care and may, for example, not settle into a home where there are other animals or young children. Before releasing a cat, most voluntary organisations will want to send an inspector to the potential new home who will ask

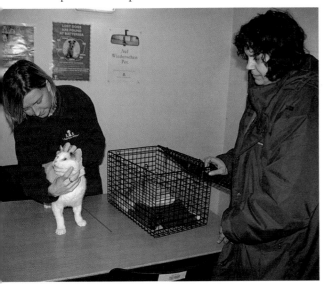

questions about, for example, how often and for how long the house is left empty. Some of these questions may seem intrusive, but organisations which have rescued a cat from an unsatisfactory life naturally do not want to run the risk of sending it to another one.

Street markets are definitely not the place to buy any pet, and most vets would advise against buying from pet stores, where feline diseases are often endemic. Care should also be taken when buying from newspaper and shop window ads, although inspection of the original home and, in the case of kittens, the rest of the litter is usually a good indicator of the background from which the cat comes.

WHAT TO LOOK OUT FOR

IT IS PROBABLY best not to take children along when choosing a cat, or at any rate not to be swayed by their views. The pathetic-looking animal clearly in need of a good home is unlikely to be the best choice. It is a good idea for a new cat owner to take

along someone with some knowledge of cats – not necessarily an expert, but someone familiar with the way a healthy cat should look. Any animal with sore or weeping eyes, a runny nose or a dull or matted coat should be avoided. Kittens should be at least 10 weeks old, and preferably 12, before being taken from their mothers. Almost all kittens look appealing, but the best choice is likely to be the most lively and friendly of the litter. It should come up to investigate an outstretched hand and, after a pause, respond to stroking and allow itself to be picked up. This provides an opportunity for closer inspection. There should be no runniness about the eyes, nose or mouth, the ears should be clear and the coat should be clean and feel dry.

The decision to acquire a cat should not be made 'blind'. The owner and the family should have some idea about what kind of cat is wanted. In the event, the choice is often more a matter of personal taste than of practical considerations.

Top
Rescue centres are an ideal place to find a cat.

Middle
It is important that a vet ensures the health of any cat you choose before you take it home.

Bottom
If people are out the the home during the day then it may be worth considering getting two kittens as they will keep one another company.

MALE OR FEMALE?

SINCE ALL CATS except those kept for breeding should be neutered, there is very little difference between male and female cats, in terms of behaviour, health or longevity. Males tend to be bigger, but that neutered males become fat and lazy is a myth.

PEDIGREE OR NON-PEDIGREE?

HERE AGAIN, THE choice is insignificant in terms of the cat as a household pet. Many non-pedigree cats are as handsome and attractive as their pedigree cousins, and there is no difference in their health, sociability or suitability for domestic life. The only consideration, in choosing a pedigree cat, might be the degree of vocalisation and activity exhibited by some breeds and the need of others for a quiet life or constant company. These traits are mentioned where appropriate in the notes on various breeds.

KITTEN OR MATURE CAT?

Top left
This non-pedigree cat is no less beautiful than its pedigree cousins.

Top right
Long-haired cats do require more time for grooming.

Bottom
Children often enjoy and benefit from seeing a kitten grow into a cat.

PERHAPS A LITTLE more thought is needed here. A mature cat may have more difficulty in adjusting to new surroundings, although this is by no means inevitable. Even if it is intended that the cat should eventually be able to go outside, it should be kept

indoors for a period until it has made its adjustments or it may try to return to its old home. It is very rewarding for children to watch a kitten grow up, and a kitten is more easily trainable and will adjust more quickly to its new home.

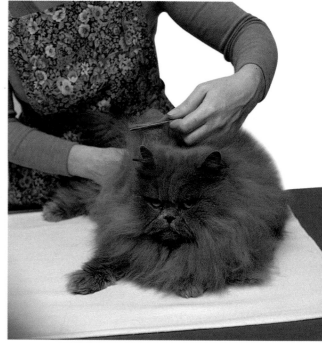

LONGHAIR OR SHORTHAIR?

THIS IS THE remaining area of choice. Here, there is a practical pointer. Longhairs do moult more heavily than shorthairs, their coats are often finer, and they are more inclined to harbour dust and mites. This may be a consideration if anyone in the family suffers from asthma, hay fever or eczema. Of course, if these conditions are severe they may rule out the presence of a cat, and a doctor's advice should be sought.

HEALTH REQUIREMENTS

IT IS IMPORTANT that anyone acquiring a kitten should find out whether it has been vaccinated against the most dangerous feline diseases such as 'cat flu', and, in countries where it is appropriate (which do not include Britain), against rabies. Kittens may be vaccinated from the age of about two months and from then on through the adult cat's life are usually given annual booster injections. Responsible vendors and breeders will provide documentation if vaccination has already been done, often in the form of a card which notes the dates of vaccination and of the next booster. On acquiring an adult cat, such information is unlikely to be available and the vet's advice should be taken.

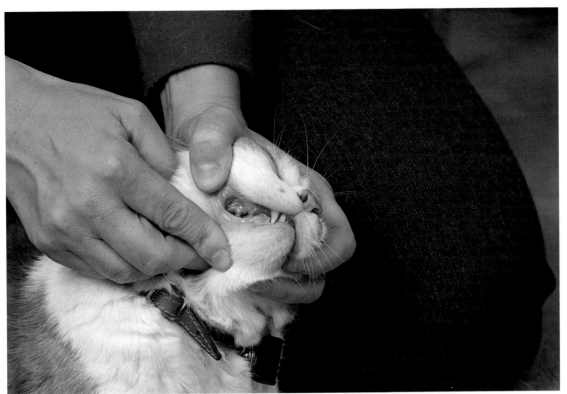

It is sensible, in any case, to have a vet look over any cat or kitten before you make a final decision to purchase. This is equally true whether acquiring a cat from a neighbour or from a registered breeder. In the case of adult cats whose age is uncertain, the vet can make an educated estimate by inspecting its teeth.

NEUTERING

MALE CATS REACH sexual maturity at 6–8 months, and females about two months earlier. By this time, they should have been neutered unless it is intended to breed from them. When in oestrus, a female is noisy, moody and may spray urine. A male will spray, giving rise to a particularly noisome smell, and may behave aggressively. Neutering not only removes these problems and reduces the possibility of unwanted litters, but also tends to make cats more home-loving and less inclined to wander. It is a myth that neutered cats are less keen and able hunters; the hunting instinct in cats is quite distinct from their sexual nature. Another myth is that females should be allowed one litter before they are spayed. There is no evidence that this benefits them either medically or psychologically. Vets generally discount stories about neutered cats being more prone to urinary and other disorders;

in fact, statistics show that neutered cats live longer than others, although this may be due to their lesser tendency to stray rather than any specific medical benefit from neutering.

The operation is normally performed before a cat reaches sexual maturity. For both males and females, it lasts only a few minutes and is followed by a few days' quiet convalescence, usually in the owner's home. Mature cats may also be neutered with equal ease.

Top
A vet is able to age a cat by looking at its teeth.

Bottom
Male cats tend to be bigger than females.

57

The Cat's New Home

THE EQUIPMENT NEEDED for cats is fairly minimal and need not be expensive, with one exception. This is a purpose-built basket or other secure carrying container which will be needed to take the cat to the vet, to a boarding kennels or on holiday. Never be tempted to carry a cat loose in a car. It is a recipe for disaster, whether this is damage to the interior trim or dangerous distraction for the driver.

Pet bed or cardboard box, the sleeping quarters will act as your cat's home base, a place of safety to which it can retreat. It is best placed out of the traffic of the house, but within sight and sound of family activities, warm and out of draughts. But it is quite likely that once it gets used to its new home, a cat will find its own favourite sleeping place, for example on the carpet over an underfloor central heating pipe or close to a convenient radiator.

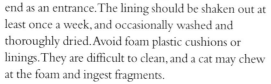

BEDDING

OTHER BASICS ARE inexpensive or free. You can, of course, pay handsomely for a fancy pet bed and bedding, but a box about the size of a wine case, with some newspaper at the bottom and an old piece of towel or blanket, or even an old sweater, on top, will make any cat happy. A space can be cut in one end as an entrance. The lining should be shaken out at least once a week, and occasionally washed and thoroughly dried. Avoid foam plastic cushions or linings. They are difficult to clean, and a cat may chew at the foam and ingest fragments.

PRACTICAL REQUIREMENTS

APART FROM THE BED, you will need a food dish, a water bowl, a litter tray and a collar with an identification tag. Cats dislike poking their muzzles into deep, bowl shaped containers, so choose wide, fairly shallow-sided dishes heavy enough not to be knocked over or to slide around. There is nothing wrong with the traditional saucer, although this may result in spillages. A washable mat under the food and water bowls is useful. Water should always be available and changed at regular intervals.

COLLARS AND IDENTIFICATION

THE COLLAR SHOULD be elasticated or have an elastic section so that the cat can wriggle free if it gets caught in a tree, for example. Even if it is intended that the cat should live an indoor life, there is absolutely no way of guaranteeing, even in the most

Top left
Cats' dislike of carrying baskets is more reason to ensure that they are safely contained and cannot escape.

Bottom
Cats may reject a sleeping box in favour of a warm place such as an airing cupboard or windowsill in the sun.

plenty of clever and relatively inexpensive toys, but in fact a cat will get just as much pleasure out of rolled-up sheets of paper, table-tennis balls, the cores of toilet rolls and kitchen towels, and similar objects. Check that they cannot be torn apart and swallowed; chewed-up paper can't do much harm, but ingested plastic could be fatal. For more adventurous play, most cats will enjoy a tunnel made out of corrugated cardboard and just big enough for them to clamber through. If you want to spend the money and have the room, you can of course buy a whole adventure playground for your cat, but it is not necessary and there is always the possibility, even likelihood, that the cat will find its own pleasures among your furniture and ignore your expensive plaything.

> **CAT FACT:**
> Aelurus, an Egyptian cat god, represented the moon. This was because of the nocturnal habits of the cat, and the elliptical moon-like shape of cat pupils.

careful household, that it will not escape, so indoor cats as well as outdoor roamers should have some form of identification. This could be attached to the collar either on an engraved disc or a cylinder containing a rolled-up slip. These should give the cat's name and the name and address or telephone number of the owner. It is as well to have a collar and identification tag in reserve, because cats have a habit of losing them frequently.

As collars can be lost, or removed if a cat is stolen, many owners have their cats micro-chipped, providing a permanent, tamper-proof form of identification. A rice-grain sized chip, bearing a special code which can be cross-referenced with the owner's identity, is painlessly inserted just under the skin at the scruff of the cat's neck. Then, when a special scanner is passed over the cat, the code number can be 'read'. You can obtain information and have the procedure performed at your veterinary surgery.

OTHER EQUIPMENT

THE OTHER REQUIREMENTS are a soft grooming brush, a steel comb and some toys. Pet stores have

Cats dislike change, and during the first few days in a new home they are likely to be nervous. They will often find a quiet, dark hiding place, perhaps behind a chair or under a bed, in which to rest and adjust to their changed surroundings. Unsafe hiding places such as chimneys or other hazardous openings should be securely blocked, and windows, cupboards, drawers and wardrobes should be kept shut. Other pets and children should be kept out of the way, or at least at a distance, until the cat chooses to emerge and mix with the rest of the family.

The first priority for a new cat is bonding. Once any initial nervousness has passed, it is important to spend time with it every day, talking quietly and using its name. Cats vary in their willingness to be stroked and cuddled, and you should use the first few days as an opportunity to discover your new cat's preferences.

Top
For families which are out all day, catflaps are ideal to enable the cat access to the garden.

Middle
These cats have found a hiding place away from the bustle of the family.

Bottom
Sometimes the cheapest toys are often the favourite.

Kitten Care

U NLESS FOR SOME extraordinary reason, such as that the mother has died or a kitten has somehow become separated from its litter, an owner will normally take on a new kitten when it is between 10–12 weeks old. It will have been weaned on to solid food by its mother, and also house-trained, although in the upset of the move it may temporarily forget its toilet training and need to be reminded.

ADJUSTING TO A NEW HOME

NEVERTHELESS, EVERY ASPECT of its new life will be new and potentially frightening. It may not be used to the food it is offered. The sounds and smells of its new home will be unfamiliar. It will not understand what has become of its mother and siblings. Every certainty of its short life has been whisked away and replaced by a range of uncertainties. The familiar world of the nest has turned into an alien environment dominated by large, incomprehensible humans.

All this, not surprisingly, may produce symptoms that can be worrying if you are not prepared for them. The lively, affectionate kitten that was purchased may seem to have turned into a nervous, timid introvert. It may go to ground in some hidey-hole and refuse to come out. If this happens, there is only one thing

Top
This kitten, at 11 weeks old, is ready to be re-homed.

Middle
At two weeks old this kitten is still completely dependent on its mother.

Bottom
A bed should be made available for a newly homed kitten, but it should not be forced to sleep there.

to do – bide your time. Keep children and other pets out of the way, and try to avoid sudden or loud noises. Make sure that food and water and a prepared bed are available, for they may eventually tempt the kitten out. If the kitten settles down for a thorough wash, this is an encouraging sign that it is adjusting to its new home, but let it take its own time.

If there are other pets in the home, it is best to separate the new kitten's feeding and sleeping places. Otherwise, it may be too frightened to eat or the others may steal its food, and it may be too nervous to sleep. Later, when everyone is used to each other, the feeding and sleeping places can be brought together although each animal should always have its own food and water dishes and its own bed. Often, as they grow more accustomed to their new life, kittens will snuggle up with the other pets. Two kittens from the same litter, bought at the same time, will happily sleep with each other from the start. It is what they have been used to.

when they wish, and this should be the rule in the home. Children should be warned that even kittens are liable to lash out if some attention annoys them or they become overtired. As the kitten grows, its periods of sleep will grow shorter and its appetite for play keener, but everyone must be patient.

HANDLE WITH CARE

KITTENS ARE VERY fragile, and must be handled with great care. They should never be squeezed, because their bones are still delicate and easily damaged. They should not be picked up by the scruff of the neck. It is true that this is what their mothers do when they are small, but the correct method for a kitten old enough to leave its mother is to slide one hand underneath its middle and support it with the other hand on the neck or shoulders. The underneath hand can then be transferred so that the kitten is sitting on it. If it struggles to get away, always lower it to within an easy jump to the floor.

Like babies, kittens need a great deal of sleep and, to children excited by the prospect of a new pet to play with, they may seem disappointingly inactive. In the nest, queens indulge in short periods of play with their kittens, allowing them to stop and rest

Top
The kitten's dish should not have high sides but be clean and kept in the same place.

Bottom left
These two kittens are from the same litter and are accustomed to sleeping with one another.

Bottom right
The correct way of holding a kitten.

CAT FACT:
Although cats have a relatively poor sense of smell compared with dogs, for example, they do rely on scent to communicate with one another.

FEEDING

ALTHOUGH THE NEW kitten should be fully weaned, it still needs an intake of milky food to replace that of its mother's, especially for the calcium content which contributes to the formation of strong bones and teeth. You can buy special kitten milk substitutes.

At 12 weeks the kitten should be eating a good quality kitten growth formula diet which provides all the nutrients required to build a fit, healthy kitten. Feeding guides vary from brand to brand and between dry and canned food, so feed according to the guide on the label, adjusting if your vet advises. Bear in mind that a kitten's stomach is very small, and the kitten will only be able to manage a small amount of food at a time. This means that kittens tend to 'graze feed', eating little and often.

From the start, however, a variety of flavours should be offered so that the kitten does not grow up to be a fussy eater. Food and kitten milk should never be given straight from the refrigerator. It should be taken out in advance and allowed to reach room temperature.

SOLID FOOD

AS THE KITTEN grows, the number of milky feeds should be decreased so that by six months it is feeding entirely on solid food in two meals per day, morning and evening. At the same time, the amounts per meal should be gradually increased.

As kittens become increasingly active, their energy needs will increase, but the best guide to the amount to feed is the kitten's own appetite. If it clears its dish, try giving a little more next time; conversely, if some food is left, cut the next meal down slightly. Left over tinned food should be removed and thrown away to prevent spoiling or contamination by flies, so if your kitten is unable to

take in enough to sustain its appetite when eating a tinned food, see if it will eat a dried version, which can be left out to 'graze' on later.

By about 10 months, kittens will be eating adult size meals and can be introduced to a wider range of foods.

INDOORS OR OUTDOORS?

AS KITTENS GROW and adjust to their new home they become ever more playful, active and adventurous, and a source of great entertainment. At about eight or nine months the decision must be taken on whether they are to spend their lives indoors or to be allowed outside. If the latter, some training is required.

A kitten which has spent the first few months of its life indoors, and is then allowed out, is released into an exciting new world of sights, sounds and smells which may go to its head. More hazardously, it may find itself invading the established territory of a neighbour and be scared away. The key is to allow it out initially only for short periods, preferably before

meals, and to accompany it round the garden calling its name frequently, keeping an eye open for any other cats in the vicinity. It is a good idea to have some fragments of a delicious-smelling food, such as

CAT FACT:
Catgut, formerly used in the stringing of musical instruments and sports rackets, was not obtained from cats at all, in fact it was made from the dried gut of sheep.

Top
Kittens prefer to eat little and often, they should, however, have their own bowl.

Middle
These Abyssinian kittens are exploring the new and exciting outside world.

Bottom
Kittens may stumble across the territory of an adult cat.

GROOMING

GROOMING IS AN important element in the bonding of kittens to their owners, especially in the early days when they miss the attention of their mothers, although it is hardly necessary from the point of view of hygiene. Gentle brushing with the hand and with a soft brush, while the owner makes conversation, will accustom the kitten to the pleasures of human companionship and help to form a happy, trusting relationship that will last for the cat's lifetime. Grooming time also provides an opportunity, as with adult cats, to carry out a general check on the condition of the coat, skin, ears, eyes and so on.

canned sardines or tuna, to entice the kitten back if it strays too far. Some owners prefer these initial excursions to be made on a makeshift lead.

Soon, the kitten will begin to scent-mark its territory by rubbing its head and flanks against trees and fence posts. In this way, it establishes its 'map' of the territory for future reference, and also makes its presence known to other cats that may be passing through. Once this stage has been reached, the periods outside may be gradually increased, but it is advisable to keep eyes and ears alert for signs of confrontation with other cats, and eventually to recall the kitten and feed it at once, implanting the idea that home is where the food is. The next stage, if you have a cat door, is to train the kitten to use it, and to remind yourself to check that it is bolted, with the cat inside, at night.

Young kittens are particularly prone to ear mite infestation, which they often bring with them from their nests. The first symptom is dark brown wax inside the ear canal. Ear mites multiply rapidly and cause intense irritation, pain, and sometimes irrational behaviour. Veterinary attention is essential if an infestation is suspected. But health problems in kittens are rare. By the time they reach their new owners they have passed through the most vulnerable period of their lives and, rather like young adolescent children, are generally at the peak of good health.

Top
Cats need to be taught to use a catflap, the idea may scare them at first.

Middle
This young kitten will soon bond with its owner through this grooming process.

Bottom
Two healthy Somali kittens.

63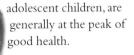

Training your Cat

I T IS SOMETIMES said that cats are difficult, if not impossible, to train. While this is an exaggeration, it is certainly true that they do not respond to training with the same willingness and even enthusiasm as dogs. As a pack animal, a dog instinctively responds to its owner, whom it recognises as the pack leader and whose approval it seeks.

It is necessary to train cats to do a number of desirable things, such as to come when called, and to avoid doing some undesirable things, like scratching the furniture. Each training task should be tackled separately and approached with patience and plenty of time.

TOILET TRAINING

KITTENS ARE USUALLY given toilet training by their mothers, but they may forget it in the excitement of moving to a new home, and the litter tray may be unfamiliar. A little reinforcement will usually soon restore good manners. The kitten should be stood with its front paws in the

THE RIGHT APPROACH

CATS LACK THIS inherent desire to please. They are more pragmatic, taking a particular course of action only if they can perceive an advantage to themselves. This means that the training of cats must be largely reward-based. What it emphatically does not mean is that cats are not intelligent. They have sometimes quite phenomenal memories for people and places, and they very quickly learn the routines of their home so that they know, for example, when the children are due home from school or when it is time for people to get up in the morning. Reward and memory are the keys to training cats. Cats in the wild know this very well. When they teach their kittens to hunt and kill, they repeat their demonstrations over and over again, rewarding good performances with titbits from the victim.

Top
Girl teaching cat to use litter tray by moving its front paws in the litter.

Middle
Kittens can be trained to know which areas they are forbidden to go in.

Bottom
Cats will use the litter tray with caution at first.

COMING WHEN CALLED

IT WILL SAVE a considerable amount of time and frustration if you train your cat to come when called, especially if it is allowed outside, although some are notoriously resistant to the idea. Its name should be constantly used, especially when putting down food. Everyone in the house who is likely to want to call the cat in should take part in this programme so that it gets used to responding to different voices and intonations. The instruction 'come' should then be introduced together with its name. The next stage is to call the cat between mealtimes, rewarding obedience with a cuddle and a titbit. For cats who are allowed outside, a call must be developed which will carry a reasonable distance. An alternative is to train the cat to respond to the tapping of the food dish with a spoon or even the ringing of a bell.

litter tray, and the owner should hold its paws and move them gently forwards and backwards to show it how to move the litter about. Cats instinctively cover their urine and faeces, and the idea should not take long to click. Always reward for success with strokes, words of praise and perhaps a small titbit. The litter should be changed immediately and the tray cleaned, so that the kitten comes to expect a clean place to use.

DAMAGE TO FURNITURE

AN UNTRAINED CAT can play havoc with a well-furnished room, spraying and scratching upholstery and curtains and sharpening its claws on table and chair legs. One of the advantages of having cats neutered is that it inhibits spraying, though most cats will indulge from time to time, especially if they feel that their territory is threatened. So moving furniture around, the arrival of a new pet and any similar change in the home may cue an uncharacteristic outburst of spraying.

Cats allowed outside will generally spray there and not in the house.

Top right
Outdoor cats are unlikely to spray indoors.

Bottom
Kittens love to climb curtains but can be taught not to.

CAT FACT:
Wild cat species have litters ranging from one to seven offspring. Although each species has a typical litter size, the number can be affected by availability of milk in the mother.

DETERRENTS

THERE IS NO point in remonstrating with the cat after the event, but if it is caught spraying a loud 'No!', clapping the hands or the rattling of a newspaper or piece of foil should act as a deterrent. Spraying that takes place in the owner's absence is more of a problem, but effective cat deterrents, which give off smells disagreeable to cats but not to humans, are available from pet shops. A cheaper alternative, obtainable from pharmacists, is oil of citronella, which is pungent though not disagreeable to humans and should be used sparingly – a mere drop or two wiped on appropriate surfaces with a tissue.

Repellents are also useful in deterring cats from scratching furniture and carpets, but a more effective and permanent solution is to provide a scratching post and train your cat to use it.

Sharpening the claws – the cat's major tools for hunting and survival – is an instinctive activity, and no cat can be trained not to do it. Cats can, however, be trained to do it in an appropriate and acceptable place. Scratching posts can be bought from pet shops but can also be run up by any person competent with a hammer and nails. It should be between 60–90 cm (1–2 ft) tall, with a firm base. Raw soft wood is best for the upright, preferably covered with bark. Some owners cover the post with carpet, but this will need to be replaced fairly often and should not be the same as any carpet used in the house or the cat may be confused. Carpet or cork squares which can be fixed to the wall are also available. Show the cat how to use whatever device is provided by standing it close and making scratching movements with its front paws against the surface. Again, reward success.

Even cats allowed outdoors will sometimes want to scratch when they are at home, if only to sharpen their claws. (Scratching outside also has territorial significance.)

FORBIDDEN TERRITORY

IT IS ESSENTIAL to develop a means of deterring the cat from undesirable activities such as lying on 'forbidden' items of furniture, jumping up to the meal table or kitchen surfaces or playing with electric flex. Again, a sharp 'No!' or the rattling of a newspaper may be sufficient. Alternatively, firmly but kindly remove the cat from the scene of the offence. It is important that all members of the family observe the same rules, or the cat will be confused. There should be a consistent policy about which parts of the house are 'out of bounds.' But a cat's life should not be too

full of prohibitions. Cats enjoy an armchair as much as humans, and it is possible to work out compromises such as an old blanket or even a special cushion to keep hair off the upholstery. Remember too that a cat may choose certain places because they are out of draughts or afford a good view of the garden.

USING A CAT DOOR

CATS UNFAMILIAR with a cat door will need to be trained to use one. They should first be shown from each side how the flap can be made to swing to and fro with a paw, and encouraged to go through the hole while the flap is left open, in return for a titbit and lavish praise. This can be repeated with the opening gradually decreased until finally the cat itself is doing all the work. At this stage, training can be turned into a game by feeding a scrap of paper on the end of a string through to the cat's side and jerking the paper through. Remember to demonstrate and reinforce the use of the flap in both directions.

COMING IN

IT IS USEFUL to train cats allowed outside but without access to a cat door to give a signal, such as tapping on the kitchen window, when they want to come in. Some will of course learn this kind of behaviour for themselves, and some even teach themselves to open doors with lever-type handles. Others can be taught by demonstration, together with the usual praise and reward for success.

WALKING ON A LEASH

SOME CITIES IN the United States require cats allowed outside to be on a leash, and in these places, if the cat is to have any kind of outdoor exercise, training a cat to walk on a leash is essential. Some pedigree breeds, such as Siamese, respond to this particularly well, but most cats, while accepting the leash, will tend to wander. It is a good idea to walk a cat just before a meal, so that this becomes the

reward on returning home. The cat should be fitted with a light harness, preferably with elastic inserts, and training should begin by letting the leash trail on the ground. Then hold the leash and gradually introduce the idea of control, starting with a short period and increasing the length of time each day. The first walks should be in quiet surroundings, perhaps in a park, and when the cat is used to being walked it can be introduced to streets and traffic. However, do not expect a cat ever to walk to heel as obediently as a dog.

CATS AND GARDENS

A CAT LOVER who is also a gardener will often find these two interests in conflict, and cats can also be a source of friction with garden-loving neighbours. It is certainly very irritating if a cat decides to choose your prize flower-bed as its lavatory, and even more annoying if it is not even your cat. A water-pistol, aimed into the air so that it rains on the cat, is a useful discouragement which, if it is used often enough, can become a permanent deterrent. Cat repellents in crystal form are available, and are disagreeable enough to make a permanent impression on some cats but they will usually need to be renewed regularly. Two non-chemical solutions are to plant shrubs which cats find pleasant, such as catmint (*Nepeta cataria*) or valerian (*Valeriana officinalis*), in areas which it is preferred that they should use, and rue (*Ruta graveolens*) in 'keep off' areas.

Top
This cat is adept at using its door.

Bottom
Although cats can be taught to walk on a leash they will, invariably, stop to smell the surroundings.

Feeding your Cat

CATS ARE NATURAL carnivores. In the wild, their diet consists almost entirely of animal prey, and centuries of domestication have not changed this basic need. A cat's body system requires certain amino-acids and other nutrients which it can derive only from animal protein, and also fat.

THE NATURAL HUNTER

ITS METABOLISM IS unable, unlike many other mammals, to create these essentials from other kinds of food, and it needs direct input. Consequently, cats need a high proportion of protein in their food – about twice as much as dogs – and at least one-third of their diet should consist of animal protein. A good feline diet is rich in fat, which the cat's digestive system is equipped to cope with easily.

Top right
Canned foods provide a domestic cat with a balanced diet.

Top left
Like all members of the cat family the Cheetah is a carnivore, this one feeds on a Springbok.

Bottom
Owner calling her cat for food by hitting a fork against the side of the dish.

REGULAR MEALTIMES

CATS ARE CREATURES of habit, and they prefer regular mealtimes in a familiar feeding place where they can eat undisturbed, preferably twice a day. The usual practice is to give a light meal in the morning and a larger one in the evening, but the cat's appetite is the best guide here. In the case of canned or fresh food, the entire day's ration should not be put out at one time, because what is left over will become stale and vulnerable to contamination by flies. Left-overs should be taken away when the cat has finished and the food bowl cleaned ready for the next meal.

CANNED FOOD

THANKS TO THE pet food industry, most domestic cats are given a better diet today than at any time in their long history. No more than 40 years ago, a cat was expected to survive on the family's table scraps together with an occasional saucer of milk. Today, by far the most convenient and balanced diet is provided by a good quality complete cat food which will contain an appropriate proportion of fat and protein. It will also contain 'built-in' mineral and vitamin supplements. Check the label to see that it provides a 'complete' diet, and avoid cheaper brands which replace some, sometimes most, of the protein with cereal filler and chemical flavouring.

So-called 'speciality' or 'gourmet' foods can be given as an occasional treat (although cats may not necessarily appreciate what they are being given), but they may not be as well balanced or nutritionally complete as good quality regular brands. Do not be tempted on grounds of economy to feed a cat canned dog food. This is less rich in animal protein, which is why it is generally cheaper, and contains added cereal and vegetables. Opened cans of food should be kept in the refrigerator but taken out about half an hour before feeding time to reach room temperature.

THE RIGHT BRAND

WHILE SOME CATS remain faithful to particular flavours of a favourite brand of food all their lives, others are notoriously fickle and will suddenly refuse to eat. Fortunately (manufacturers being wise to this) brands come in a variety of flavours and it is not usually hard to find one that suits. But for this reason it is as well, especially with a new cat, not to buy too far in advance. A cat that is fussy about its food is a nuisance, and kittens should be encouraged, as soon as they are weaned, to eat a variety of types and flavours.

It is a mistake to go on feeding the same brand and flavour in the assurance that it will be eaten; the kitten may grow

up to refuse anything else. But it is not so easy to encourage mature cats to be more adventurous in their diet. They can be extremely stubborn, and refuse to eat at all until their favourite food is restored. Rest assured that your cat will not allow itself to starve, and carry on putting out fresh supplies of the despised food. It will be a battle of wills, but you have a fair chance of winning.

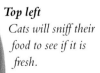

Top left
Cats will sniff their food to see if it is fresh.

Bottom
Cats prefer their food to be served at room temperature.

DRY FOOD

BRANDED DRY AND semi-moist cat foods have a number of advantages, but there are also some caveats. In favour, they keep well in the dish and so the cat's whole daily requirement may be put out at once. This is a distinct advantage for owners who are away from home all day. Also, these foods exercise the cat's teeth and gums, replacing the exercise that cats in the wild obtain from dealing with whole prey, and help to keep the teeth free from tartar. Against this, even the semi-moist types contain only a small proportion of liquid which must be supplemented with a lot of additional water, either added to the food or given separately. Owners should check that sufficient water is being drunk, and if this is not so this kind of food should be used sparingly, varied with canned food. In the past, dry foods have been associated with bladder and kidney problems, but today's food have been formulated to avoid this. However, elderly cats or cats with urinary system problems may require special diets, prescribed by the vet, which are especially easy on their kidneys.

Top
Dry foods prevent tartar build up on cats' teeth.

Bottom right
Automatic food and water feeders.

Bottom left
Tinned and dry food is often the cheapest, easiest and most nutritional cat food.

HOME-COOKED FOOD

SOME CAT OWNERS feel, quite erroneously, that giving their pets manufactured food is a soft option,

and go to great lengths to provide fresh, home-made food. This is not notably cheaper if a properly balanced diet is to be provided, it takes a good deal of trouble and time, and the diet will need to be supplemented by vitamin and mineral preparations. For example, a cat fed on a home-prepared fish or meat diet will need an additional source of calcium, thiamin and taurine, and regular doses of cod liver oil for vitamins A and D, while ensuring that overdoses of nutrients do not occur.

An occasional treat of meat or fish, however, is a different matter – provided it is truly occasional and does not come to be regarded by the cat as its everyday right! Offering a small portion of the normal food, slightly warmed to release the aroma, is a good way of persuading a cat to eat after an operation or any kind of shock. Treats such as minced beef, chicken, boned fish (fresh, frozen or canned) and liver would probably not harm a healthy cat, but they are not recommended by vets.

NUTRITIONAL REQUIREMENTS

AS A GENERAL guide, a fit healthy adult cat requires 31 per cent protein, 41 per cent fat and 28 per cent carbohydrate in its diet, but remember that

information on pet food labels is not usually on a 'dry matter' basis, and the conversion calculations are not easy. Also, growing kittens and elderly cats require different proportions of these nutrients. The best solution is to buy a good quality commercial complete diet, appropriate for your cat's life-stage, and ask your vet for advice if necessary.

If part of the food put out is regularly left, adjust accordingly until the right amount has been gauged. Unlike dogs, many cats like to eat slowly and some will leave food expecting to return to it later.

WATER INTAKE

A TYPICAL CAT'S water requirement is about 200 ml (7 fl oz) a day (though this will vary greatly, depending on the cat's diet). In the wild, most of this comes from its freshly killed prey, which contains about 70 per cent water. Some of the domestic cat's water needs will come from its food, especially if it eats canned products, but fresh water should always be available and a close watch kept on how much is drunk. If the cat consistently drains its dish, and medical causes such as diabetes and hyperthyroidism have been ruled out by your vet, additional warm water can be poured over its food to boost the water intake, as too small a water intake can lead to urinary disorders.

LOSS OF APPETITE

IN THE WILD, cats tend to have an uneven pattern of feeding, gorging when they have the opportunity and then sleeping it off, so a sudden and temporary lack of interest in food need not worry the domestic cat owner. A cat that is 'off its food' may indeed be ill, but it is quite likely that the cause is more mundane, especially if the cat roams out of doors. Most outdoor cats supplement their diet with prey given the chance, and some develop supplementary feeding stations at the houses of kindly neighbours.

Changes in routine – even minor ones such as the return of children to school after the holidays – can also affect a cat's appetite. Another possibility is that the cat has been disturbed while it was feeding, perhaps by another pet. For cats, feeding is not a social activity and they like to be undisturbed. But if the loss of appetite persists beyond a day or two, and the cat continues to resist known favourites such as sardines or liver, a veterinary check is advisable.

TITBITS

MEALTIMES APART, a variety of titbits can be given as a reward for good behaviour in training or simply as a treat. A wide variety of cat treats are available commercially, and these are healthier and safer than offering fresh meat or fish. However, the oil from cans of sardines is also welcome, poured over a few small pieces of bread. Children should however be restrained from giving cats sweets or chocolate; in any case, as cats are not sweet-toothed, these will not be seen as treats.

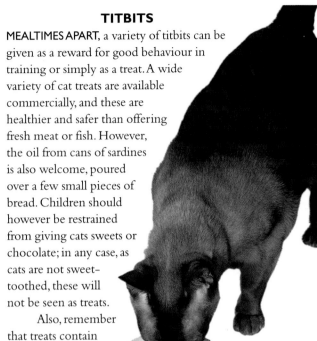

Also, remember that treats contain calories, and if you regularly give your cat treats, you should decrease the size of its meals accordingly. However, never be tempted to replace more than a very small proportion of your cat's regular food with treats, and consult your vet if your cat's weight seems to be increasing or decreasing significantly.

CAT FACT:
The Egyptian cat god Aelurus was so feared by worshippers that anyone who killed a cat was punished by death. Diana, the Roman goddess of hunting, angered the giants by taking a cat form.

Top left
It is important to have a fresh supply of water available.

Top right
Excessive drinking can be a sign of diabetes or hyperthyroidism.

Bottom
Elderly cats may need help or encouragement to eat.

Grooming your Cat

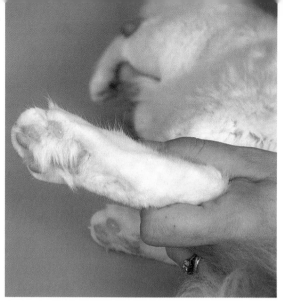

THE CLEANLINESS OF cats is one of their most attractive features as pets. But contrary to the popular myth, cats do not 'look after themselves', trained as kittens by their mothers, despite the amount of time they spend in self-grooming. There are three good reasons why a grooming session with the owner should be a regular part of every cat's routine.

The grooming described here is the sort that all cats should receive rather than the specialised grooming needed for show purposes. The only tools required are a brush with long, soft natural bristles – a baby brush is ideal – and a fine-toothed metal comb.

TECHNIQUE

KITTENS SHOULD BE groomed from their earliest days in the new home, and will soon become adjusted to it if the owner talks quietly and reassuringly while it is going on. With older cats, especially cats which have been strays or re-homed from a cat sanctuary, adjustment may be more difficult. Gentleness, patience, determination and a 'softly softly' approach is the key to success.

The cat should be stood on a newspaper to catch any dead fleas, debris or stray hairs, and held gently with one arm to prevent rolling and keep the

BONDING EXPERIENCE

FIRST, IT IS AN important element in bonding, and for almost all cats is – or becomes with usage – an enjoyable experience. It echoes the caring attention experienced from its mother in the cat's early kittenhood. Second, it removes dead hair from the coat which might otherwise end up as a hairball in the cat's stomach or intestine. This is particularly important with longhairs. Third, it provides an opportunity for a regular check on the condition of the coat, ears, eyes, nose and paws. Grooming is particularly important in spring and early summer, when most cats (excepting breeds such as the Rex and Sphynx) shed their old coats, often in tufts. For the houseproud, regular grooming will go a long way towards preventing deposits of hair on carpets and furniture.

Top
Paws should be inspected while grooming.

Middle
Although cats clean themselves it is important that the owner continues to groom.

Bottom
Combing should be in the direction of the hair, going towards the tail.

front paws under control. The newspaper should be carefully folded inwards and disposed of afterwards. The coat should be combed lightly and then brushed slowly and gently with a soft brush, working down the body towards the tail and down the hind legs. With shorthairs, this need take only a few minutes. Longhairs require more attention.

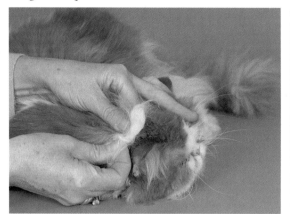

First, any mats or tangles should be teased out with the fingers or a comb, taking care not to pull at the skin. Slightly dampening the hair can make this easier. Tangles are particularly common under the chin and between the front legs. If they cannot be teased out they should be carefully cut out with scissors. Then the coat can be brushed, lifting the brush sharply at the end of each stroke so that the ends stand free. Be warned that most cats dislike attention paid to their tails and hind quarters generally, and should be held firmly.

THINGS TO LOOK OUT FOR

A WATCH SHOULD be kept for any stains – particularly tar, paint or oil stains – on the coat. These can be softened with cooking oil before being swabbed away with a little surgical spirit. This must be kept away from the eyes, nose and mouth and used very sparingly. Cats can become intoxicated with the fumes and exhibit the symptoms of human drunkenness which, although they pass off after a few minutes, are best avoided.

Routine checks should ensure that the eyes are clear, with no discharge, and the ear flaps are clean. Any debris can be removed from the ear flaps with cotton wool, but the ear canal itself must not be probed. If possible, the cat should become accustomed to having its mouth examined to check the condition of the gums and teeth. The index finger and thumb of one hand should be placed in the corners of the mouth while the other hand gently

draws the lower jaw down. This is not easy and will result in protests, but care of the teeth in a young cat will prevent problems in middle and old age. If there is any sign of discolouration on the teeth, or the gums look inflamed, veterinary advice is needed. The condition of the cat's skin can be checked, before brushing, by lifting the hair in a few places with the fine-toothed comb.

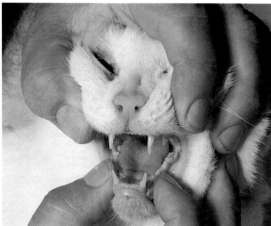

Choose a time for grooming when the cat is relaxed and comfortable. When it is over, a session of play will reinforce grooming as an enjoyable experience. For shorthairs, one session of grooming a week is sufficient, but longhairs need attention every three days or so, particularly in the moulting season.

Top left
Owner eases a matt from her Persian.

Top right
How to open a cat's mouth.

Bottom
The ear lobe should not be entered, but the owner should clean the outside.

Travelling with a Cat

ALMOST ALL CATS will, at some time, have to travel, if only to the vet's surgery. Once the journey is under way, many will settle down, even if in a somewhat grumpy mood, but preparing for the journey can be a nightmare. The minute that the travelling basket or carrier appears, most cats will go to ground, dig their claws into the carpet, and protest at being moved.

PREPARING TO TRAVEL

This is no doubt because most cats' experience of travel will have been to the vet's, where they may have memories of being pulled around, inspected and subjected to various indignities, all the while in a world of alien sounds and smells. The best advice that can be given is to keep the basket out of sight until the last moment, try to behave in an everyday way, and make a swoop on the cat when it is time to go. Putting a cat in its travelling basket is ideally a job for two – one to handle the cat and the other to fasten the door once it is inside.

CAT FACT:
The idiom to 'not let the cat out of the bag' comes from an old market trick where a cat was substituted for a piglet in a sack following a barter.

Top
This is an excellent travelling carrier as it is made of plastic and wire so is easily disinfected and allows for ventilation.

Bottom
If the cat is injured it should be wrapped in a towel securely and taken to a vet.

EQUIPMENT

AS MENTIONED ON earlier, a purpose-made travelling carrier is essential. The only exception is if the cat is very ill or immobile owing to an accident. In these cases it is best wrapped in a blanket and held securely by the owner or a passenger. Do not be tempted to use one of the cardboard carriers sold in pet shops, or to try to economise with a grocery box from the supermarket. Any self-respecting cat can claw its way through corrugated cardboard in a matter of minutes. The ideal carrier is made of plastic-coated wire, which can be cleaned and disinfected thoroughly after use (an especially important consideration if it has been used to transport a sick cat). Some cats feel more secure in the darkness provided by a carrier with closed-in sides. The bottom should be lined with lining paper or kitchen towels to absorb urine or vomit.

THE JOURNEY

IF GOING BY CAR, the cat should travel with the passengers and never in the boot. If there is a spare pair of hands, these can hold the carrier steady on the rear seat. (A bin-bag under the carrier will prevent any seepage of urine or vomit). The carrier should not be placed on the floor of the car, where there is often intense vibration and noise.

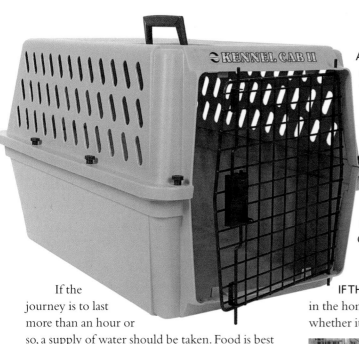

QUARANTINE

AS A GENERAL RULE, sending a cat unaccompanied is to inflict severe trauma, but occasionally it cannot be avoided. For example, if a cat is brought into Britain from abroad it will normally travel unaccompanied from its point of departure to the quarantine kennels in Britain. The carrier's requirements should be ascertained well in advance, and arrangements must be made for the cat to be met at the destination airport. Quarantine kennels normally see to this.

BOARDING KENNELS

IF THE FAMILY is planning a self-catering holiday in the home country, the question often arises whether it is better to take the cat or make other

arrangements. Unless the holiday is to be an extended one, it is probably less stressful for the cat either to put it into boarding kennels or, better still, arrange for it to be looked after at home by friends or relatives. There is also the risk that, in the stress of moving to unfamiliar surroundings, the cat may go missing or meet with unfamiliar hazards.

The same advice applies to moving house, which is stressful enough anyway without running the risk of losing the cat at the crucial moment. It can then be introduced to the new home when things are stable and there is time to settle the cat in.

If the journey is to last more than an hour or so, a supply of water should be taken. Food is best avoided because of the risk of motion sickness. Care should be taken in summer that the car does not become too hot; ensure a flow of fresh air. Cats should never be left in cars unattended, even if this means that the family has to forego a meal en route and settle for sandwiches instead.

If a journey has to be made by public transport, you should check beforehand whether cats are acceptable as passengers and under what conditions. A secure container is always a requirement. Airlines usually require cats (as with other pets) to be carried in the pressurised and heated section of the cargo hold, in a container which they have specified. Some railway companies also regard pets as luggage to be carried in the luggage compartment.

Top
This carrying basket may be preferable for some cats as it is covered.

Middle
This trip to boarding kennels could mean that the cat will associate the basket with its stay there.

Bottom
Cats should not be transported in the boot of a car.

The Indoor Cat

THE PROS AND cons of keeping a cat indoors or letting it roam outside at will are hotly contested by vets and cat lovers alike. In the United States, except in farming areas, majority opinion seems to favour the indoor life whereas many Europeans would tend to let cats, except for pedigree and breeding animals, roam free. In some situations, such as high-rise apartments, there is of course no option, and in some United States cities local bye-laws require that cats should be allowed out only on a leash.

OUTDOOR DANGERS

TRAFFIC POSES THE main danger to outdoor cats; about 5,000 cats a year are found dead on the streets of Baltimore, Maryland, a city with a human population of about 750,000. No doubt many of these road casualties are ferals or strays, but even so it is a grim statistic. It would drop considerably if owners of outdoor cats brought them in at night.

Other hazards can be discounted as major threats to outdoor cats. In particular, there is the myth of gangs roaming the streets looking for cats to capture and sell on to medical laboratories. The unsavoury truth is that medical laboratories are well supplied with animals bred for the purpose by cat-farmers.

KEEPING THE CAT INSIDE

IT IS GENERALLY agreed that if a cat is to be confined indoors it should not be allowed to experience freedom. If it has known nothing else it will accept the indoor life, although this may not prevent it from trying to escape. But to

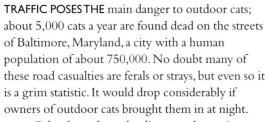

confine a mature cat which has previously been allowed to wander is unreasonable, except in the case of an elderly cat with declining powers which shows no great interest in going out. The problem of a change in the cat's lifestyle may arise if an owner's age or circumstances dictate a move from a house to an apartment, or to a sheltered housing scheme where cats are not welcome. For people who find themselves in this situation, it is kinder to find a new home for the cat where it can still lead an outdoor life and to start afresh with a kitten – or, better still, two – which can be habituated to living indoors. Note, however, that some leases and rental agreements place restrictions on the keeping of pets or on the number permitted.

It has to be said that as wandering and hunting are firmly entrenched in a cat's nature, the indoor life is unnatural, and care must be taken to provide alternative stimuli to give the cat's life some interest and variety. Failure to do this leads to boredom and stress which may be expressed in aggressive behaviour, overeating or failure to use the litter tray. We may keep pets to enhance our own lives, but we owe it to them to let them enjoy their own.

Top left
If an adult cat is used to an outdoor life then to keep it inside is difficult and unfair on the cat.

Bottom
Elderly cats often tire of going out and may prefer a life inside.

persuaded to look in round the middle of the day to check that all is well and offer a few moments' conversation and petting. A radio left playing quietly may also help to relieve a cat's sense of isolation.

EXERCISE

THE INDOOR CAT must be provided with opportunities for exercise and be given extra encouragement to play games. Large, strong cardboard boxes (provided they have not been used to pack hazardous substances such as household bleach), tubes of cardboard and corrugated paper and postal tubes with the plastic ends removed will all provide welcome diversions. Indoor 'climbing trees' can be obtained from pet shops. Catnip mice and similar toys will remind the cat of its hunting skills. An old slipper makes a welcome toy. Some kind of scratching post is essential.

HOME ALONE

IT IS DOUBTFUL whether a lone housebound cat can enjoy a reasonably contented life if its home is deserted by people during the working day. It has been suggested by some authorities that a cat's life is one of perpetual kittenhood, in which it needs the companionship of the nest all its days. It sometimes comes as a surprise to new cat owners to find that although a domestic cat may spend up to three-quarters of the day sleeping it requires company and activity for the rest of the time.

The problem of providing daytime company can be solved by having two cats or even by providing the companionship of a sympathetic dog, which the cat gets along with. It helps, too, if a friend or neighbour – perhaps a reliable teenager – can be

Top
This multi-purpose toy and scratch post keeps these two cats entertained.

Bottom left
Dogs sometimes make good companions for cats.

Bottom right
Resourcefulness is required to entertain cats cheaply.

OUTSIDE VISTA

EVEN IF IT is not allowed outside, the cat should be able to observe the outside world. If a ready-made vantage point such as a wide window-sill is not available, a firm shelf can be fitted at window-sill

height from which the cat can see out. If there is a choice, select a window where the midday sun does not pour through and where outside activity is most likely to be observed. Although the sight of a housebound cat staring, apparently wistfully, at the outside world may present a sad spectacle, the cat will in fact find a great deal of interest in the movement of birds, leaves, people and even passing traffic.

THE ESCAPEE

SPECIAL CARE NEEDS to be taken over doors and windows. Remember that if an indoor cat escapes it is very unlikely to be able to survive outside, being less adept in the techniques of survival and also, in winter, being unaccustomed to outdoor temperatures. It will also be completely unused to traffic. Cats can show remarkable ingenuity, and it is not enough simply to leave fanlight windows slightly open without securing them with a lock. The same applies to sash windows. One possibility is to make or buy a removable frame covered with small-gauge plastic-covered metal mesh which can be fitted securely over a partially open window. It may be necessary to fit an extra internal door inside the main door to make sure that people can come and go easily without letting the cat out.

CAT FACT:
The adage that cats have nine lives is derived from their remarkable agility in escaping injury from falls and their knack of fleeing from packs of dogs.

Top
This cat benefits from a clear view of the world outside.

Centre
Indoor cats should have fresh grass made available for eating.

Bottom
Cats can find escape routes in a variety of places.

HAZARDS

IF ONE OR MORE cats are to be left alone indoors for any length of time, scrupulous care must be taken to shut cupboards, especially in the kitchen where they may contain hazardous substances, and to block chimneys. Electric flexes should be tidied up and secured so that they do not offer a temptation as playthings. There should be one or two fairly large surfaces free of ornaments and available as resting places. Bedding should be shaken out each day.

REQUIREMENTS

MOST CATS OCCASIONALLY eat grass, and a pot or tray of growing grass should be provided for indoor cats. This can be grown from seed at home or bought ready-sown from pet shops. However, many house plants such as all forms of ivy are poisonous to cats and they should either be made inaccessible or discarded.

If a cat is to be left during the day, the owner should follow a routine before leaving home. The litter tray should have been cleaned and refilled. A dish of fresh water should be put down. A few pieces of dry food may be left in the food dish, but the morning feed should have been given and any remains cleared away before the owner leaves. Windows and cupboard doors should be checked.

There is always a risk that an indoor cat will not get enough exercise to burn off its energy intake, and will

consequently become obese. This implies that closer attention than usual should be paid to its diet, and in particular that the supply of titbits should be strictly controlled. The standard test as to whether a cat is overweight is to feel for the ribs. If they are not evident, the cat is probably obese and its food intake should be regulated. Do not be tempted to devise your own slimming diet for your cat – ask your vet for advice on a plan and the many special low-calorie diets available for cats.

ALTERNATIVES

EVEN IF THE owner does not want a cat to roam freely, there are alternatives to a completely indoor life. One is to train the cat to walk on a leash, which will certainly give it more exercise and a welcome addition to the daily routine. Another is to build or buy an outside run with mesh sides and roof on a stout frame. This is undoubtedly the best solution for owners of pedigree cats who do not want to expose them to outdoor risks but aim to give them the best practicable life.

Even a small run, say 2 x 1 m (6.5 ft x 3.3 ft), will greatly enhance an indoor cat's lifestyle. Ideally, there should be a litter tray, or a removable and cleanable area of soft earth or sand for use as a litter tray, a patch of grass and a hard concrete or paved area. A tree for climbing and claw sharpening, shelves, and toys such as a stout rope suspended from the roof will add to the amenities. The run should be sited carefully out of winds and the midday sun. A covered area should be provided to give shelter from strong sunlight and rain. It would be perfect if the cat could reach the run from the house through a cat door. An alternative to the self-contained run is to build out a wire mesh extension from a garden shed.

CAT FACT:

Feral domestic cats will live in social groups if food is plentiful enough to prevent them from having to confront or fight one another too often.

Top
If a cat cannot go out to go to toilet then a litter tray is essential.

Top
Obesity is an issue that owners should consider when deciding whether to let their cat out.

Bottom
This Birman benefits from an outside run to exercise in.

The Outdoor Cat

THERE IS NO doubt that a cat that is allowed to roam freely out of doors but also has a warm, secure home to come back to has the best of both worlds. It can still practise its instinctive stalking and hunting skills, but does not have to face the constant challenge of survival which is the lot of the feral or wild cat.

the greatest danger (as with children) is in suburban streets lined with parked cars which obscure the view. Conversely, country cats are often at risk because of the relative rarity of traffic so that they do not perceive it as a danger.

Other risks include the possibility of fights, although serious cat fights are relatively rare if cats have been neutered. As well as the risk of injury, there is also the danger of contracting diseases such as feline leukaemia and FIV, through blood and/or saliva.

However, most confrontations between cats are of the 'shot across the bows' variety and end when the point has been made. Curious cats do get themselves locked inside neighbours' sheds and garages, but rarely. Serious straying is also fairly rare. Cats generally have a good sense of where they are in relation to home and are unlikely to venture out of their range unless frightened or seen off by a rival cat. If this happens, they may become disorientated and, lacking familiar landmarks and scent marks, wander hopelessly.

HAZARDS

There are, of course, dangers in the outside world. The main one is road traffic. Yet it is surprising, considering the number of cats roaming the streets, that the toll of casualties is not higher than it is. Urban cats do seem to develop road sense. It is a common sight to see a sensible cat looking both ways on a busy road and then scurrying across. Probably

NOCTURNAL DANGERS

THE CATS MOST at risk are those that are turned out at night. No doubt this practice stems from the fact that cats are nocturnal by nature, but in fact most wild cats hunt at dawn and dusk. Any domestic cat will enjoy a hunt at these times, but that is no reason to shut it out all night. It is fairly easy to establish the habit of coming in for the night when called, especially if the evening meal is delayed until then. Cat doors should be secured at night. It is not unknown for cats which have been shut out from their own homes to seek shelter and food in a neighbour's house, possibly resulting in a noisy confrontation downstairs in the small hours!

POINTS TO CONSIDER

TWO POSSIBLE disadvantages of letting a cat outside should be mentioned here. One is hostility from neighbours. Some people are paranoid about cats, especially

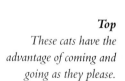

Top
These cats have the advantage of coming and going as they please.

Bottom
The warm engine and wheels of a car can be enticing to curious cats, but are obviously a danger.

neighbours to spread on their flower-beds, or give them freedom to deter your cat from their garden with a well aimed water-pistol. Bird lovers are harder to satisfy, except perhaps by pointing out that successful bird hunts are relatively rare. Some owners claim to have trained their cats not to go after birds, but these claims seem unlikely. The noise and movement of birds are so deeply entrenched in a cat's instincts that to make them of no interest would mean starting evolution all over again.

if they are keen gardeners or bird lovers. There is also the occasional ailurophobe, a person with an obsessive fear of cats. The best that can be hoped for here is negotiation. You might, for instance, offer to buy some cat-repellent crystals for your gardening

The other problem is the cat's delivery to your door, or even your hearth rug, of hunting 'trophies'. Although this is, in fact, a compliment to you (the cat wants you to share in its good luck), disposing of the remains, perhaps still half alive, of some poor mouse or bird can be challenging. It is possible at least to train cats to leave their offerings outside the door by removing them there with lavish words of praise and a titbit. Protesting at each new presentation is pointless and confusing for the cat, which only meant well.

Top
A white Persian hoping to get lucky.

Top right
A Somali cat stalking its prey.

Bottom
Two tabby Siamese enjoy exploring their back garden.

81

TERRITORIES

THE KEY ELEMENT in an outdoor cat's life is its territory. This will vary in size according to sex (even neutered males have far larger territories than females) and depending on the density of the cat population. In a heavily populated suburb it may amount to no more than the owner's garden and a couple of gardens on either side, and even these may have to be shared with other cats.

It may also include a number of access paths between adjacent territories claimed by other cats. These seem to have the status of 'no cat's land'. A cat which would not tolerate an interloper on its actual territory will allow one to pass along an adjacent access path without protest. In the country, territories are larger and may include rabbit warrens, farmyards, cornfields and outlying farm buildings.

Cats establish their territories by spraying urine (a practice which is not confined to unneutered cats), scent-marking with the glands on their heads and flanks, and scratching posts and trees with their claws. Territories have a time as well as a spatial dimension. A given area may be patrolled by one group of cats in the morning and another in the evening. A cat let out unusually early one morning can find itself trespassing on another cat's time-slot.

Top left
A cat exploring its territory.

Bottom left
Cats' territory in rural areas can be vast; with a variety of favourite places, such as on neighbours' roofs.

Bottom right
This cat marks its territory by scratching.

In the country, a male's territory can encompass the whole of a small village. Unless you make a deliberate effort to find out, you may never discover the extent of your cat's range. Many an owner of a cat that has died has received enquiries from neighbours some distance away who had been used to regular visits. A typical territory will include a number of sleeping places such as flat garage roofs and car roofs for sunny days, shady shrubs, and so on; observation posts in trees or on roofs; hunting grounds such as the foundations of a garden shed which may harbour mice underneath; and perhaps supplementary feeding stations at other people's houses.

A NEW HOME

ON MOVING TO a new home, cats should be kept indoors for a few days until they have overcome the stress of the move and have realised that, although in new surroundings, the life of the family is going on much as before. Then it is time to introduce the cat to its new outside world, having first ensured that it has a reliable form of identification such as a collar and tag or a microchip.

Folklore is full of stories of cats that, once let out, immediately make tracks for their old homes, giving rise to the theory that places mean more to cats than people. While some of these stories are doubtless true, most cats which feel reassured about their owners' affection will overcome the stress of moving and stay faithful; cats seek comfort above all. It is therefore extremely unlikely that your cat, let out for the first time into your new garden, will make a run for it. Some owners, however, adopt defensive stratagems which, even if they are unnecessary, do no harm. One is to loop a piece of string through the cat's collar and take it for a walk round the garden, beating the bounds. Another old wives' tale is the country custom of buttering the cat's paws. The theory here is that it will be able to find its way back by retracing its buttery footsteps. In fact, by the time it has done a circuit of the garden it will have made its own scent marks which will guide it home.

DEFENDING ITS TERRITORY

THERE ARE NOT many urban or suburban areas which do not form part of some cat's territory. Although domestic cats are not such aggressive defenders of their territories as wild cats, probably because their food needs are taken care of in any case, a newcomer will have to fight its way in against physical and psychological resistance. As far as the immediate garden is concerned, you can help your cat here by being seen frequently in its company in the garden and

evidently approving of its presence. This will to some extent establish its bona fides in the eyes of other cats, and will also give your own cat confidence. There will almost certainly be confrontation none the less. This may range from long sessions of 'staring out' to full-scale fights, although these are rare and invariably sound worse than they are.

THE MISSING CAT

DESPITE ALL YOUR precautions and care, it may unfortunately happen that your cat goes missing. You have called repeatedly and it does not return. You have searched the vicinity without result. What next?

The first rule is not to panic. Cats are quite capable of disappearing for up to 72 hours and then walking in expecting their next meal as if nothing has happened. Obvious first steps are to call the police and local animal shelters to see if there have been any reports of stray cats or accident victims. Sometimes shops will allow you to place a notice in their window. Your cat may somehow have lost its identity tag and simply been 'adopted' as a stray by another family. It is worth letting local vets know; a conscientious person who takes in a stray is likely to take it along to the vet for a check-up.

It is also worth thinking back over any visitors who may have called at the house, including builders and other tradesmen. Some cats are drawn to explore vans with open doors.

Top
Meeting on neutral ground, these cats smell each other in an amicable way.

Bottom
This cat displays a collar with bell and identity tube.

83

Creatures of Habit

ADAPTABLE AS DOMESTIC cats generally are, they have willingly traded in some of their independence in return for the comforts that home life can give. People have pets to enhance their lives, but it must be remembered that pets have their needs too. These pages are about some aspects of cat ownership that need to be considered before embarking on it.

CAT FACT:
Cats are now officially the most popular pet, by numbers, in the world. It is indicative of the modern city lifestyle that people find cats easier to keep than dogs.

ROUTINE

CATS ARE CREATURES of habit. In the wild, they follow a daily and nightly routine which is dictated by the quality of light. They patrol their territories in a systematic way, stopping at selected places to rest or observe the scene. They are very sensitive to changes in their environment which may mean disturbance or danger.

The taste for routine persists in domesticated cats. They like today to be like yesterday and tomorrow to be like today. This applies not only to feeding times but also to times for play and rest, times to be cuddled and stroked, times to be groomed and times to be let out or called in. They are sensitive to time and quickly learn when it is time for food, for the family to get up, for children to leave for and return from school, and for people to settle down in the evening. They are also sensitive to any unusual activities in the home such as preparations for moving house or going on holiday and the absence of familiar members of the family. Events of this kind can cause stress which may be expressed in lack of appetite, hiding away or even disappearing from home. They can be reassured by being given extra attention and affection at such times.

Of course, you cannot be expected to let the life of your household revolve round your cat, but you should, whenever possible, take into account its need for the security of routine and familiarity.

Another aspect of routine is consistency in the way that you and your family treat your cat. It is confusing if it is all right to sleep in an armchair one day but not the next, or if one member of the family turns the cat out of a room when the others do not. Most cats are willing to accept restrictions on where they can go, but they cannot be expected to observe rules that are not consistent.

Top
This cat has learnt that it is allowed to sleep on a particular chair.

Centre
Hiding is sometimes the result of stress or change.

Bottom
Petting your cat should be incorporated into its daily routine.

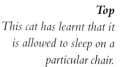 84

Top left
During kittenhood the cat will gain experience and learn many lessons. A second cat will, however, enrich its life further.

Top right
Play can consist of mock-hunts or fights with its owner.

Bottom
These two cats have made the linen basket their bed.

for a friend, neighbour or relative to feed your cat and spend a little time each day with it if you go away. This is preferable to, and cheaper than, making use of a boarding cattery, excellent though the best of these are.

COMPANIONSHIP

ALTHOUGH CATS LIVE largely solitary lives in the wild as adults, their early months as kittens are full of strongly bonding experiences as they feed from their mothers, learn from them, and play with their siblings. The need for similar bonding seems to persist in the domestic cat, and indeed some veterinarians have suggested that domestication is a kind of arrested kittenhood in which the cat never quite grows up.

What is certain is that cats need and value companionship. This may mean no more than merely being in the same room as the rest of the family, or it could mean sitting on the owner's desk or lap or on the bed (not to be encouraged, especially with children). Or it may mean more active companionship such as play, mock-hunting games or a rousing mock fight with the owner's fingers. Companionship also means 'conversations.' The more you talk to your cat, the more it will respond.

A cat left in an empty house all day will have a happier and more interesting life if it has a companion. After a certain amount of stand-offishness, neutered cats of the same sex normally settle down together even if one is introduced later. The ideal answer is to buy two kittens from the same litter, which will already have bonded.

A cat should never be left unattended overnight or turned out to fend for itself. If possible, try to arrange

A HOME BASE

ALTHOUGH WILD CATS are more often predators than victims, their kittens are extremely vulnerable and it is probably from their mothers that cats learn to be cautious. The nest represents safety. A domestic cat needs a centre to its world, whether this is a cardboard box or an expensive basket. Ideally, the base should be within sight and sound of family activities but out of draughts and away from loud noises and sudden movements. In practice, most cats will, if they do not like the base offered to them, choose one of their own.

> **CAT FACT:**
> The largest domestic breed of cat is called the Ragdoll, with males weighing in at between 7–9 kg (15–20 lb). Ragdolls are said to be immune to pain but this is not true.

Cats will often make themselves scarce if there is too much noise or sudden movement round them. Conversely, they like the murmur of voices, and a radio quietly tuned to a speech station provides the illusion of company if they are to be left alone for any length of time.

RESPECT

ONE OF THE MOST appealing characteristics of cats is their dignity. While many dogs will do anything for a laugh, humour does not seem to figure in a cat's psychological make-up. A cat that misjudges a jump and ends up in an undignified heap on the floor is usually very put out, and will often retire to comfort itself with a self-grooming session. Never laugh in such circumstances. Nor should you try to teach a cat party tricks, although some may acquire one or two of their own, or dress it up. Impress upon young children that the cat is not a plaything but a member of the household.

FREEDOM

IN THE WILD, cats are free to define and mark their own territories, exercise themselves, choose their own feeding times and move about at will. Inevitably, domestication restricts that freedom, but it also does away with the freedom to be hungry, cold or wet and for most cats this seems a fair exchange. One of the first things you have to decide as a new cat owner is whether your cat will be housebound or allowed outside.

Undoubtedly, a cat allowed outside has a more natural and interesting life, but this must be weighed against the dangers from traffic, fights with other animals, picking up diseases or parasites from other cats, getting lost and other hazards. On the other hand, housebound cats are more likely to spray indoors, scratch the furniture and become overweight through lack of exercise. It is a choice only you can decide, with one proviso. If you take on an adult cat, it should continue to live the kind of life it is used to. It is cruel to confine to the house a cat which has previously had the freedom to roam outdoors, and equally it is dangerous to let loose a cat which has not learned to live with outside hazards.

PEACE AND QUIET

CATS SPEND UP TO three-quarters of their day sleeping, preferably in a warm cosy spot but not necessarily or always in the home base. Cats allowed outside will, like their wild cousins, choose a number of sleeping-places for different times of the day – perhaps under a shrub through the heat of midday, on a flat roof to catch the afternoon sun, and so on. Similarly, a housebound cat will often 'follow the sun' from room to room. Domestic cats adjust their sleeping pattern to suit the routine of the household. For example, if the family is out all day, they will spend most of this time sleeping and be ready to socialise (and eat) when someone comes home. Like humans, cats like to sleep undisturbed. If children or other pets prevent them, they are understandably likely to lash out.

Top
This cat has found itself a warm spot under a chair.

Bottom
This tabby is awake and ready to play, knowing that its owners will soon return home.

THE COST OF A CAT

ONLY ONE ESSENTIAL item of cat equipment – the travelling basket or carrier – is expensive, and this can often be found second-hand. (Clean it before use with a cat-friendly disinfectant). Non-pedigree cats

or kittens can often be obtained free from friends or neighbours, with care, or from animal shelters for the price of a small donation. If you want a pedigree cat of show quality, of course, you must expect to pay a considerable amount of money, and if you commit yourself to showing the expense of travelling, entering and special veterinary attention is quite high.

The running costs of the ordinary domestic cat are, however, modest. A week's food supply will cost about the same as a bottle of cheap supermarket wine. It makes sense to buy a good, balanced brand even if it costs a little more, because you are then unlikely to have to

supplement it with extra vitamins and minerals. The only other expenses you will have to worry about are veterinary fees, which are quite costly but cannot be avoided if only for such occasions as the annual booster injections and general health check, and boarding cattery fees if cheaper alternative arrangements cannot be made for holidays. The fact that cats are the favourite pets of older people on limited incomes is an indication that the cost of owning a cat is not high.

CARE

A FINAL WORD. Your cat is entirely dependant upon you to look after its health, welfare and happiness, and it has a right to a share of your attention and time. If you cannot give it that, then cat-owning is not for you.

CAT FACT

Cats have large pupils to let as much light in as possible at night. A pet cat's eyes are only slightly smaller than ours, yet it can see six times better than a human in the dark.

Top left
A bored cat, or one that is kept indoors without a scratching post, can damage furniture.

Centre left
A cat at the Battersea Dogs Home waiting to be re-homed.

Top right
This boy ensures he has a happy kitten.

A Healthy Cat

CATS ARE ROBUST and healthy by nature, and most domestic cats will meet a vet during their lives only for routine check-ups and vaccinations, and possibly neutering. Domestication removes at a stroke many of the hazards of a wild cat or feral's life – exposure to the weather, shortage of food, the attacks of predators and the infections and parasites which are endemic in wild and feral communities.

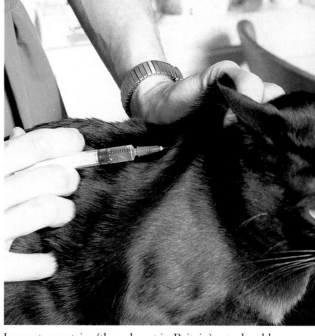

CAT FACT:
Cats have very good navigational abilities, because they may have to wander considerable distances in order to find animals to hunt, before returning home.

In most countries (though not in Britain) cats should also be protected against rabies.

Kittens may be vaccinated from the age of around two months. A kitten bought from a reputable breeder will be already partially or fully protected and should come with a vaccination certificate. From then on, annual boosters are recommended, and this provides an occasion for a general veterinary check-up. Boarding catteries will refuse cats which do not have up-to-date written evidence of vaccination, which is also required for all cats entered in shows.

KEYS TO GOOD HEALTH

NEVER THE LESS, even the most pampered domestic cat is vulnerable, like all living creatures, to attack by disease organisms of varying degrees of severity ranging from a minor cold to life-threatening infections.

There are however some simple steps owners can take to enhance a cat's chances of a healthy life.

Top left
Outdoor cats are especially prone to infection through fighting with other cats.

Top
Vaccinations are essential if the owner wants to have a healthy cat.

Bottom
Kittens can be vaccinated from two months.

Vaccinations: The first is vaccination against some of the more common feline diseases. These are feline infectious enteritis (FIE), respiratory viral infection ('cat flu') and feline leukaemia virus (FeLV).

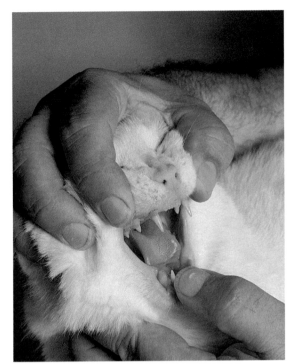

Hygiene: The third key to a healthy life is scrupulous hygiene. Litter trays should be removed after use and, as necessary, either thoroughly cleaned or the soiled litter scooped out and replaced. At least once a week, the tray should be emptied and disinfected using a cat-friendly disinfectant which can be obtained from pet stores. There is a bonus in adhering strictly to this procedure.

Diet: The fourth element in good feline health is a well-balanced diet. This is provided in the wild by freshly killed prey, and good commercial cat foods replicate the elements of the natural diet with added vitamins and nutrients where necessary. Most owners understand this, but it is sometimes forgotten that an adequate intake of water is essential to a cat's good health, and

indeed some cats tend to ignore their water bowls. This situation can be remedied by adding hot water to regular feeds (creating its own 'gravy') then, after it has cooled, offering it to the cat. Few cat owners are able to resist giving their pets an occasional treat, but these should be given sparingly.

Weekly Check: The second general preventive measure is a weekly check which can conveniently be combined with grooming (remembering, of course, that longhairs require more frequent grooming than this). The coat should be inspected for the presence of parasites by 'opening' it with a comb. There should be no discharge from the eyes, ears or nose, and the anal area should be clean. Check the paws of a cat that goes outside for soreness, cracking or splinters. The mouth should be pink and the teeth white. Kittens can be trained to accept having their teeth cleaned, but a mature cat unused to this is best dealt with by a vet. The best instrument to use is a cotton wool bud or a cat toothbrush (available from vets and some pet shops), with a special 'cat toothpaste'.

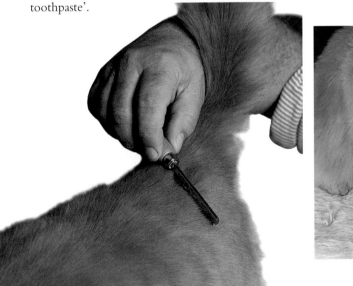

Top
This cat is having its teeth and gums checked for inflammation and general health.

Top right
Litter tray covers should also be disinfected.

Bottom
Flea combs facilitate the removal of parasites.

which has happily been eating a particular canned food for months can suddenly go off it. A useful test is to put down some especially attractive food such as sardines in oil – just once. You may have strayed into a psychological battleground, and if you have established that the loss of appetite is due more to cussedness than illness you should return to a normal diet with the next meal. Otherwise, the cat might hold out for the more attractive food, which would not be a well balanced diet.

Other symptoms: Usually, loss of appetite due to illness will be accompanied by other symptoms such as unusual listlessness, bad temper, hiding away in unusual places in the house or, with a cat allowed outside, reluctance to go out. Again, it is a question of knowing your cat. However, with cats, fasting can lead to a serious condition called hepatic lipidosis, so if your cat refuses food for more than 24 hours, consult your vet.

Like most animals and indeed people, a cat's instinct if it is not feeling well is to go away into a quiet corner and sleep in the hope that the feeling will go away, and often, as with most minor human ailments, it does. The appearance of the 'haws', the third eyelids extending from the corner of the eyes, is often a symptom of illness. These may sometimes appear when a cat is dozing, but in normal awake mode they recede. The condition of the coat is another indicator.

If it is unusually 'open', with the hairs standing erect and rather apart, the cat may be struggling to regulate its body temperature. Other symptoms include difficulty in passing urine or faeces, drooling at the mouth, unusually noisy and copious drinking and the failure to self-groom after meals.

SYMPTOMS OF ILLNESS

Loss of appetite: is a fairly reliable symptom of illness, but it is also a matter of knowing your cat. Many cats are always ready for their meals and polish them off quickly, but others are slow or even reluctant eaters. If you have observed your cat's pattern of feeding, you will be able to detect any marked change, and this will be a warning signal. Of course – as with humans – lack of interest in food may be caused by factors other than illness. A cat allowed outside may have found some prey, or may even have been fed at another house. If there has been a territorial dispute or a fight with another cat, this may have produced stress which inhibits the appetite.

Within the home, stress factors such as the introduction of another pet, changes in the domestic routine or even moving the furniture may put the cat off its food for a day or so. Also, allowances must also be made for the infuriating fact that a cat

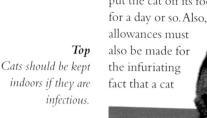

Sickness: One disturbing event that need not, on its own, cause too much alarm (although, to the uninitiated, it sounds very alarming) is an isolated incident of vomiting. Cats vomit with great ease, and usually very noisily, for a variety of reasons. This is the way they get rid of hairballs from the stomach. They may have eaten some prey that does not agree with them. They

Top
Cats should be kept indoors if they are infectious.

Bottom
The failure to self-groom is often an indicator of sickness.

may even simply have eaten too quickly. Food arrives in a cat's digestive system unmasticated (unchewed), and the system itself has to do all the work of breaking it down which, in most mammals including humans, is begun in the mouth. It can therefore easily become overloaded, which is why cats tend to pause during their meals. Of course, if vomiting persists it is a symptom of a more serious problem. Similarly, an isolated instance of diarrhoea or sneezing need not cause alarm, but if it persists it should be taken seriously.

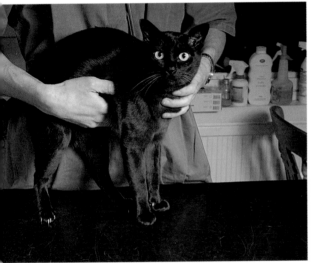

Spraying: Unaccustomed spraying in the house can also be a symptom of illness. It is certainly an indication of some disturbance in the cat's life which is causing stress, and if it persists a visit to the vet's is called for. If, after an examination, the cat seems physically fit the vet may refer the cat to an animal behaviourist, or even prescribe tranquillisers to temporarily reduce the stress.

CATS AND HUMAN HEALTH

STORIES APPEAR IN the press from time to time about infections that can pass from animals to humans and are known medically as zoonoses (pronounced zo-oh-no-sees). The good news for cat owners is that in the case of cats zoonoses are very few.

Rabies: The most serious is rabies, which occurs worldwide except in Australasia, Britain and a few other islands where controls are particularly strict. These places apart, vaccination is available for domestic pets, and often compulsory. Rabies is normally transmitted by a bite from an infected animal, and occurs in a wide range of wild animals such as foxes, raccoons, skunks, mongooses, bats and feral cats. It

passes from these to domestic pets. Once the disease enters the system, it is incurable. An agonising death is virtually certain but may take up to 10 days.

Toxoplasmosis: Less terrifying, but never the less potentially serious, is the risk of toxoplasmosis, from the Toxoplasma parasite which lives in the cat's gut and can be transmitted to humans from the faeces. Toxoplasmosis generally has no symptoms and if passed to humans normally goes unnoticed. However, it can cause congenital abnormalities in unborn babies, and medical advice is that pregnant women should avoid dealing with the cat's litter tray. It is always a sensible precaution for everyone to wear rubber or disposable gloves when carrying out this duty, and of course to wash their hands thoroughly afterwards.

Ringworm: One of the most common zoonoses is ringworm, a fungal disease of the skin and hair which can be passed on to humans by contact. Occasionally it is transmitted by cats which are carriers but exhibit no symptoms themselves. If it is suspected, the cat should be isolated immediately and taken to the vet. The risk of ringworm is one reason why washing the hands after handling a cat should be a strict rule.

Fleas: Fleas are an irritating but less serious problem. Cat fleas are only one of a number of species that can pass freely between cats, dogs and other animals, and to humans. Although they will not infest humans, they may bite. Serious infestation on a cat needs veterinary attention, but commercially available flea treatments specifically for cats are effective preventive measures.

Bites: Cats' saliva inevitably contains bacteria, and any cat bite that breaks the skin should be cleansed with antiseptic and covered. The same applies to any claw scratch. If the cut becomes swollen or painful it should receive medical attention. One very rare but serious result of a cat bite is a disease known as 'cat-scratch fever', which may need hospital treatment.

Top
Vet's advice should be sought if unusual symptoms persist, such as constant vomiting, diarrhoea or spraying.

Bottom
Flea dirt in Persian's coat.

Veterinary Care

I T IS AN IMPORTANT that routine trips to the vet become a part of your cat's life. Even the healthiest of cats will need to go to the vet on an annual basis for vaccinations and a general check up and your vet should be chosen with the same care as a doctor, with the aim that vet and cat will have a long term relationship.

WHEN TO CALL THE VET

SOME INFECTIOUS diseases of cats develop with startling rapidity, but many of the most common ones can be ruled out in a cat whose vaccinations are up to date. So, discounting these, the best guide is that if any symptoms persist for more than 24 hours veterinary help should be sought. Meanwhile, the cat should be kept indoors and under observation. For the average cat owner it is not particularly helpful (and the cat will hate it) to take a cat's temperature or check its pulse rate, and no medicines should be given without veterinary advice.

However, if at any time during the 24 hours you still feed worried, call your vet and ask their opinion on whether a visit to the surgery is necessary. It is important to be able to give the vet an account of the symptoms and their onset and timing, and it is useful to make a note of these as soon as you suspect anything is wrong, together with details of what the cat has eaten and done during the previous day or two – for example, whether it has been outside, brought back pieces of prey, and so on.

HEALTH CARE COSTS

VETS' FEES ARE a cost which must be taken into account when you are thinking of keeping a cat. It often comes as a shock to people who go to vets only occasionally to find how high the fees are, but they reflect the true cost of running a surgery, dispensing medicines, employing staff, using outside services such as pathological laboratories and, in Britain and some other countries, the obligation to provide a 24 hour emergency service either in person or through a locum. In addition, of course, the full unsubsidised price has to be paid for drugs and medicines. If the possibility of unexpected heavy vets' fees is a serious worry, you can take out insurance, but this will not cover the cost of routine attention, vaccinations, neutering and so on.

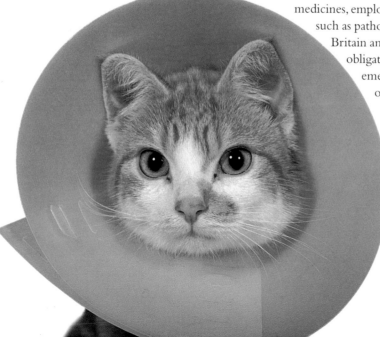

Top
Vet using a stethoscope during a general check-up.

Bottom
After an operation an Elizabethan collar is sometimes placed around the cat's neck to prevent it from pulling out the stitches.

CAT FACT:
The musical 'Cats', by Andrew Lloyd Webber, uses lyrics taken from T. S. Eliot's book of poems *Old Possum's Book of Practical Cats*, published in 1939.

If you have a choice, opt for a vet that specialises in small animals. If you have just moved to a new area, or have not kept a pet before, you could ask a local cat club, animal welfare organisation or cat sanctuary for the names of suitable vets. It makes sense, before committing yourself, to ask the vet about the scale of charges. These can vary considerably depending on the geographical location, the size of the practice and the facilities in the surgery.

EMERGENCIES

VETS WILL MAKE house calls in cases of emergency (which adds to the expense), but prefer to see their animal patients by appointment at the surgery where there are facilities for tests and treatment. They should always be prepared to discuss problems on the telephone, which is another advantage of having a vet who knows your cat. If it is likely that an operation will be necessary, you will be advised on how long before your visit you should keep the cat without food (usually 12 hours before surgery) and whether one or more overnight stays will be necessary. You should, of course, take the cat to the surgery in a secure container and not open this until you are in the consulting room.

CHOOSING A VET

IN LINE WITH the growth in responsible pet ownership, the veterinary service in most industrialised countries has improved greatly during the past 50 years. There are few suburban or even rural areas which are without a choice of practitioners, and some larger pet stores also provide veterinary services. A vet should be chosen with the same care as a doctor, with the aim that vet and cat will have a long-term relationship. The advantage of this is that a patient record will be kept at the surgery which may be helpful in future diagnosis and which will result in your receiving reminders when vaccinations and annual check-ups are due. As with a doctor, you should expect the vet to explain things to you in non-technical language and answer your questions. The surgery staff should be helpful and confident in handling animals. The premises should be clean and there should be operating facilities on site.

CAT FACT:
Puss in boots, from the fairy tale of Italian origin, is so called because he 'wore the boots' by cleverly securing a fortune and a royal partner for his humble owner.

Top
The cat should be carried to the vet in a secure cat basket.

Bottom
Confident handling by the vet will result in a quicker examination and cause less distress to the animal.

Feline Ailments

THE RESPIRATORY VIRAL infections ('cat flu'), feline infectious enteritis (FIE) and the feline leukaemia virus (FeLV) are the diseases we are able to vaccinate against and therefore protect our cats from. Fit, healthy cats from the age of nine weeks can be started on a two-injection course, boosted annually, from your veterinary surgeon – contact the surgery to find out exactly when to vaccinate your cat.

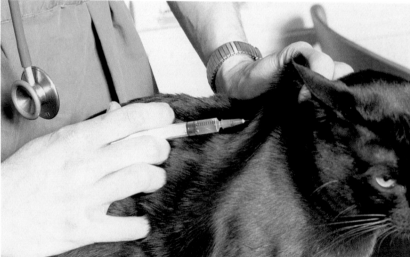

accompanied by sneezing and possibly conjunctivitis. If FVR is suspected, the cat should be isolated and the vet called at once. Survival is rare in kittens or elderly cats. Cats which do survive may suffer complications, including partial or total blindness, and will probably continue to be carriers of the disease, infectious to other cats.

The characteristic symptom of FCV is an ulcerated mouth, which may or may not be accompanied by symptoms similar to those of FVR, together with feverishness. The main danger of the disease arises from complications, which may include pneumonia. Again, veterinary help should be sought urgently.

RESPIRATORY VIRAL INFECTIONS

THESE ARE INFECTIONS of the nose and throat, termed the upper respiratory organs. They are caused by a number of different viruses, but the two most common are feline viral rhinotracheitis (FVR) and feline calcivirus (FCV). Both are highly infectious, especially where a number of cats are in close proximity as at shows and in boarding and breeding catteries. However, FVR and FCV are preventable by vaccination.

Symptoms of FVR include discharges of mucus from the eyes and nose, together with excessive salivation, loss of appetite and general disinterest in life. The incubation period varies from 2–10 days. The infected cat develops a fever which reaches its peak at about the fifth day and is

Top right
This cat show illustrates how easily infection could be passed from cats in such close proximity.

Top left
Vaccination can prevent cats from catching FVR.

Feline infectious enteritis (FIE): Also known as feline panleukopaenia, this is a disease which strikes suddenly and progresses quickly to death. If suspected, action must therefore be of the utmost urgency. Symptoms are diarrhoea, loss of appetite, the vomiting of bile and cries of pain if touched, followed by total collapse. FIE affects cats of all ages and those which do survive appear to have lifelong immunity.

However, vaccination against FIE in kittenhood, with annual boosters, is almost totally effective.

Feline leukaemia virus (FeLV): This is a highly infectious and incurable disease which is almost always fatal. It is transmitted by body fluids, such as blood and saliva, and is therefore most common in cats that roam and fight, or in breeding or boarding catteries or households with large numbers of cats. Kittens appear to be particularly vulnerable. Before a vaccine was developed in the 1980s, it was the scourge of cat breeders. A vaccine, with yearly boosters, is now available, though this is of no help at all if the cat already has the disease, and this has not yet been detected. A test is available, to prevent vaccination of already infected but undiagnosed cats.

The symptoms of FeLV include vomiting, diarrhoea, difficulty in breathing, fever and anaemia, but commonly the only sign of the disease

is gradual wasting over a long period, sometimes years. Diagnosis is by blood test, and if this is positive vets usually recommend isolating the cat to prevent spread of the disease to others, and treating the symptoms until it is judged kinder for the pet to be put to sleep.

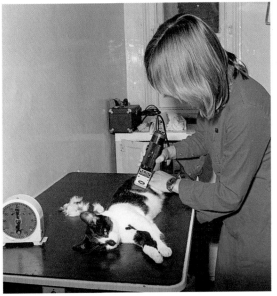

FIP and FIV: The two other major cat diseases are Feline Immunodeficiency Virus (FIV) and Feline Infectious Peritonitis (FIP), which are incurable. At present there is not a vaccine to prevent either disease, but by neutering cats not intended for breeding (therefore reducing the risk of confrontations and fights over territory boundaries), not allowing your cat access to obviously unhealthy cats and, for breeders to breed only from tested stock, the risks of infection are reduced. Cases of FIV and FIP are not as common as the other diseases mentioned above.

Top left
Young kittens are particularly susceptible to illness; their mother's milk will help protect them with her antibodies.

Top right
Female cat being shaved before her operation.

Bottom Left
Infections, such as FeLV, may be transmitted during a cat fight.

SKIN DISEASES

MANY SKIN PROBLEMS in cats are caused by parasites, and these are discussed later in this section. The most important disease of the skin is ringworm, which is doubly serious as it can be passed on by contact to humans and other animals, sometimes by cats which are merely carriers and do not exhibit symptoms themselves. Once established, it is extremely difficult to eradicate.

Ringworm: This is caused by a fungus which grows on the surface of the skin and in the hairs, and releases toxins deep into the skin which cause inflammation and itching. The hairs die and break, followed by the appearance of the circular bald, scaly patches on the head, ears, front paws and back which give the condition its name. Scratching at the irritation naturally worsens the condition. Surprisingly, the cat usually seems otherwise unaffected, showing no other form of distress or loss of appetite.

Ringworm is treated with lotions applied to the skin and/or tablets, but the key to clearing up an infection is rigorous attention to hygiene. The cat must be isolated from other animals and direct human contact avoided as much as possible. Bedding used in the period prior to infection should be disposed of and disposable bedding substituted. Disposable food and water bowls and a disposable litter tray should also be introduced and used until tests carried out by the vet indicate that the infection is over.

Dermatitis or eczema: Can arise from a number of causes and, as with humans, the difficult task of establishing the cause is more than half the battle. It takes the form of scaly patches on the skin, which may form into pustules and weep. In all cases the condition is worsened by scratching.

Contact dermatitis is caused by contact with allergenic substances. Detergents and other cleaning materials are the most common culprits.

DIGESTIVE AILMENTS

CONSTIPATION IS OFTEN a problem in longhaired or older cats. It can be the result of tumours in the gut, which are incurable, but is more likely to be due simply to the lack of muscle tone in the intestines, or a blockage cause by swallowed fur. An occasional attack of constipation can be treated at home by feeding a dose of oily food such as canned sardines in oil – or merely the oil itself – together with plenty of fluids. If the condition persists, the vet should be consulted.

The occasional attack of diarrhoea, if unaccompanied by other symptoms of illness, need cause no alarm. It is most likely to be the result of something the cat has eaten; only if the diarrhoea lasts for more than a day or so need the vet be consulted.

URINARY PROBLEMS

OLDER CATS IN particular are prone to bladder infections such as cystitis which result in frequent urination and sometimes blood in the urine. Bladder and kidney problems can also arise and symptoms include offensive breath, frequent urination or unsuccessful attempts to urinate and noticeably increased thirst.

As thirst can also be a sign of hyper-thyroidism (most common in older cats) and diabetes, a cat that starts to drink more should always be taken to the vet.

Top left
This Chinchilla is a beautiful, white, longhair.

Top right
This Persian blue, which has been shaved because of ringworm, is also a long hair like the Chinchilla.

Dealing with the immediate irritation is the easy part; tracing the source of the problem less so. It is a painstaking matter of going over everything that has happened in the cat's life over the past 10 days or so. Has there been a change of diet? Has a new type of domestic cleaner been used? Has the cat's bedding been washed, and if so, using what detergent or soap? Has there been any unusual stress in the cat's life? Has the cat had a new collar? It is worth checking whether other pets or anyone in the household have been similarly affected. Tracing the cause of dermatitis is notoriously difficult, in cats no less than in humans, but a process of elimination can sometimes provide the answer. Meanwhile, your vet may be able to solve the immediate problem with steroid creams.

A cat may, for example, rub itself against kitchen cupboards which have been washed with an allergenic cleaner, or its bedding may have been washed with an enzyme detergent. Allergic dermatitis is a response to certain specific foods. Solar dermatitis is rather like sunburn, and mainly affects white or partially white cats. Dermatitis may also result from parasitic infections (see below) and from stress.

The first priority with dermatitis is to prevent the cat from scratching and so turning minor skin blemishes into septic sores. Your vet can supply soothing powders or lotions which will relieve the irritation, but in extreme cases it may be necessary for the cat to wear an 'Elizabethan collar' until the skin heals.

Oil problems: Excessive oil from the sebaceous glands at the roots of the hairs may cause skin problems which, although not disturbing to the cat, are unsightly. One form of this condition is called stud tail, which causes greasy marks at the base of the tail. It is most common in unneutered males but can also occur in neuters. Another form is known as feline acne and appears as blackheads on the lips and chin. In each case, treatment is the same – frequent washing with cat shampoo and, under veterinary advice, special antiseptic cream. In extreme cases the vet may prescribe antibiotics.

CAT FACT:
The cat's cradle of the child's game with string, actually started life as cratch cradle, cratch being a corruption of crèche – French for manger or rack.

CAT FACT:
There is an opalescent gem often worn by those who believe in witchcraft, called Cat's eye. It is so called because it reflects a streak of light when polished .

Top left
Cat acne may appear around the lips and the chin.

Bottom left
White cats are particularly susceptible to sunburn.

Fleas: The cat flea is the most common parasite, and almost every cat will have fleas at some time in its life. Flea powders and collars help, but they are not 100 per cent effective. Cat fleas are dark brown, wingless insects about the size of a pinhead which bite the cat's skin and feed off its blood. The cat then scratches the bites which can create sores, and an allergy to flea saliva may cause a flea-allergic dermatitis.

If a flea-infested cat's coat is combed, live fleas may or may not be seen, but dead fleas and specks of flea excreta can be seen in the cat's coat. On discovering a flea outbreak, treatment of the cat itself is relatively simple. Flea powders, sprays and collars are available from pet shops, and more effective treatments in the form of pump-sprays (less frightening to the cat than aerosols), 'spot-on' drops applied to the back of the cat's neck, or even a vial of liquid given in food which prevents fleas which bite the cat from breeding, thereby halting the infestation. Instructions on the pack must be followed closely – never be tempted to use more than one treatment at once, as this can cause a fatal overdose.

Furnishings in the home also need to be sprayed with a special household flea treatment as the fleas on the cat are only the tip of the iceberg – flea eggs, larvae and pupae will be lurking in the carpets and the cat's bedding.

ABSCESSES

ABSCESSES ARE FORMED when a scratch, cut or bite which breaks the skin becomes infected and produces a swelling filled with pus. A minor abscess can be treated at home by applying a pad of cotton wool soaked in hot Epsom salt water, and applying gentle pressure to bring it to a head. Once the abscess has burst, keep the area scrupulously clean. If the abscess shows no sign of healing, you should visit the vet who may prescribe antibiotics.

EXTERNAL PARASITES

CATS CAN BECOME hosts to a range of parasites which live on their skin and coats. Some of these may be mere irritants, but others, unless eliminated, can give rise to allergies or even severe anaemia in kittens. Cats allowed outside are most at risk, but indoor cats are also vulnerable to some species.

Top

Vet giving cat antibiotics; he holds the cat's head and opens its mouth.

Centre

If fleas are discovered while grooming then furnishings and bedding will also have to be treated.

Bottom

Unfortunately, an outdoors cat will catch parasites from contact with other animals.

Mange: This is an unsightly and distressing skin condition transmitted by mites which live in the coat or on or under the skin. There are several species of these mites, but all produce similar effects ranging from minor flaking of the skin like dandruff to large, bald, scaly patches. As the different species respond to different treatments, the form of mange must first be identified by the vet.

also kill ticks once they have bitten, but by that time the cat may have scratched the tick off, perhaps leaving the jaws embedded in the skin, which could set up an infection.

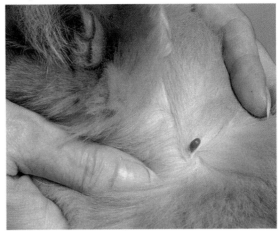

Ear Mites: A particularly troublesome and common parasite is the microscopic ear mite. Many cats play host to this parasite without any ill effects, but they can increase in number to the point where they set up inflammation in the ear canal, known to vets as otitis, and cause irritation. If the cat's weekly health check reveals the presence of dark brown wax in the ears, this is the likely reason, as it is if the cat persistently scratches its ears or shakes its head. Treatment is by ear drops obtainable from the vet, and possibly the use of an 'Elizabethan collar' to prevent scratching until the infestation is past.

Ticks: Cats may pick up ticks on their ears, neck and paws if allowed outside but ticks are not a common cat parasite. They are generally discovered in grooming because when they are engorged with the cat's blood they can be up to 1 cm (0.5 in) long. No attempt should be made to remove the tick without first applying a dab of surgical spirit. After a few seconds it can then be detached with tweezers or a special tick-remover, taking care that the whole insect is removed. Some anti-flea preparations are

Lice: These parasites are also a relative rarity in domestic cats, although ferals in poor physical condition often attract them. Although cat lice are specific to cats, they are similar to human headlice, and it is their whitish eggs, glued to the hair, which are the tell-tale sign. A serious infestation can be very debilitating, making the cat distressed, irritable and depressed. Treatment is by liquid or powdered insecticide, on the vet's guidance.

When the infestation has passed, your vet may advise you to feed a special diet to restore the cat's good health.

In North America, cats are vulnerable to infestations of botfly maggots which hatch from eggs laid in the coat. The eggs should usually be seen during grooming and are relatively easy to remove. If the maggots hatch, however, veterinary advice should be sought.

Top
A tick hidden in the coat of this Persian.

Bottom
Vet checking cat's ear for dark wax, this is often a sign of ear mites.

INTERNAL PARASITES

CATS ALLOWED OUTDOORS are particularly vulnerable to a number of internal parasites often picked up from prey. One of these is coccidiosis, caused by a protozoan, which results in foul-smelling motions.

Top
In outdoors cats prey is often the source of worms, especially mice.

Bottom
Kittens can get worms from their mother's milk.

With very few exceptions, cats' internal parasites are worms of various species which are extremely common in the feral and stray population but relatively rare in healthy, well fed domestic cats. It must be admitted that cats allowed outside are more likely to pick up worms by eating infected prey. Worms live in the cat's intestine and feed either on digested food or on the intestine wall. The eggs are then passed out of the body in the faeces, where they become a further source of infestation. Queens can pass on some species of worms to their kittens in their milk, with the result that the kittens start life debilitated and undernourished despite an apparently healthy appetite. They can be treated by the vet from the age of three weeks.

Worm problems can be avoided in two specific ways. One is the regular use of de-worming drugs. These can be obtained over the counter in pet shops, but it is safer to go to the vet, who will make a proper identification of the parasite before prescribing treatment. The other deterrent is scrupulous attention to hygiene when disposing of litter and cleaning the tray.

Roundworms: Also known as ascarids, Roundworms are the most common form. They are thick, white worms up to 10 cm (4 in) long which may be found in a cat's faeces. The eggs are often picked up from mice. Roundworms come under suspicion if a cat with a good appetite and no other apparent health problem nevertheless looks in poor condition, with a dull coat and possibly a pot belly.

Hookworms: These are bloodsuckers found in humid tropical climates though extremely rare in Britain and northern Europe. They may inflict such blood loss that the cat dies. Early symptoms include extreme weakness, anaemia, diarrhoea, and flecks of blood in the faeces.

Whipworms and threadworms: It is rare for a cat to contract these parasites in Britain. Both are small and may live in the cat's body without doing any harm or causing apparent distress, but serious infestations can lead to a steady wasting and general decline in health, accompanied by diarrhoea.

Tapeworms: Easily picked up when the cat is grooming and ingests infected fleas or lice, and from infected prey. Segments of tapeworms, resembling grains of rice, appear in the faeces. Tapeworms are not a serious health hazard unless the infestation is very heavy.

MEDICATION

NEVER GIVE MEDICATION to a cat except on the vet's advice. In particular, never give a cat aspirin or paracetamol which may be lethal to them. It may be necessary to pass this warning on to children who might, with the best of intentions and out of concern for their pet, make a fatal mistake.

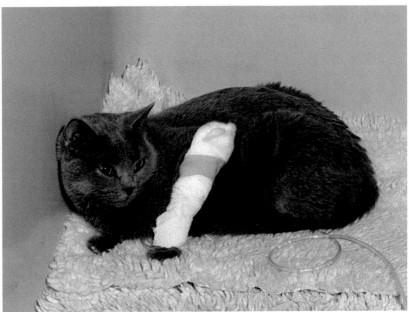

LOOKING AFTER A SICK CAT

IN CARING FOR A sick cat, if you apply the same principles as in looking after a sick child you will not go far wrong. The patient should be kept warm and comfortable, in a quiet part of the house, and allowed to sleep as much as it wants. If possible, the sick room should be within earshot of family activities, which will give the cat some reassurance. Young children and other pets should be kept out of the way, but some cats will like the company of a quietly tuned radio. In cases of serious illness, ask the vet's advice on what kind of food to provide. Otherwise, put down small quantities of known favourites and make sure there is plenty of water available. A sick cat should not be expected to go far to eat, drink, or use the litter tray.

Sick cats are prone to depression, which attacks the will to recover and live, so give as much time and attention to your cat as you can, with frequent visits, 'conversations', petting and, if the cat is up to it, gentle play. Bedding, food and water dishes, the litter tray and general surroundings must be kept scrupulously clean, but if disinfectants are used these must be of a kind which are safe for cats. Many common household disinfectants and antiseptics contain phenols, cresols and chloroxyphenols, which are derived from coal- or wood-tar and are highly poisonous to cats. It is safest to ask your vet or buy a cat-friendly disinfectant from a pet store, reading and following the instructions to the letter.

If a cat has suffered from an infectious disease or from external parasites, it may be necessary to dispose of all the bedding that has been used during its illness and convalescence. If this cannot be burned, it should be secured in a plastic bag and put out for the garbage collection. It is not worth risking re-infection by merely washing the bedding, which may not rid it of contamination. It is also advisable to replace any soft toys that the cat has used during its illness, and to sterilise any others in a suitable disinfectant.

> **CAT FACT:**
> 'The Owl and the Pussycat' was a limerick poem taken from Edward Lear's *Book of Nonsense*, published in 1846. Another famous literary cat.

Top left
This sick cat rests in a basket in a warm and quiet place at home.

Top right
A cat rests in this veterinary hospital with its broken leg.

Bottom
This kitten convalesces with a familiar toy, light play can relieve boredom it the pet is up to it.

Nine Lives

CATS ARE GREAT survivors, but their curiosity, and their habit of getting themselves into situations which they cannot easily escape from, make them accident-prone.

and this and the fact that they are not so nimble as they used to be, or as adept in judging speed and distance, makes the older cat particularly vulnerable to traffic accidents.

Most cats involved in traffic accidents are, perhaps mercifully, killed outright. The first priority for anyone coming across an injured cat is to remove it carefully to a place of safety, moving the cat as little as possible. The next step must be to seek veterinary help. In emergencies, contact an animal welfare organisation or the police. Apart from this, all the bystander can do is to treat for possible shock, by keeping the victim calm and warm. The cat should be wrapped in something warm, and no food or drink should be given. Passers-by or neighbours can be asked for a suitable container – an escape-proof cardboard box, for example – in which the cat can be transported to a vet. Remember that an injured cat is conscious and mobile, its instinct may be to lash out and escape and hide itself away, so it may have to be gently restrained. A note should be made of the name and address on any identity disc or tag so that the owner can be informed.

ROAD ACCIDENTS

THE MOST COMMON cause of serious injury to cats outside the home is road traffic. Although it is surprising how streetwise many urban and suburban cats become, large numbers are killed and injured on city roads each year. They are not immune even in the country, where owing to relatively light traffic a passing vehicle can take them by surprise. As cats get older the acuteness of their hearing falls off sharply,

Top
An acrobatic Siamese tests its nine lives.

Bottom right
Cats should be taken to the vet immediately after a road accident.

Bottom left
Cat hiding under a parked car.

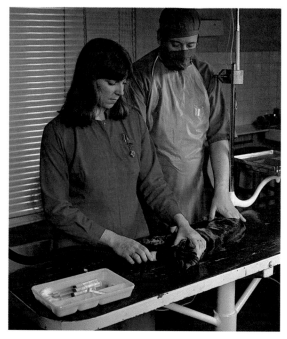

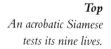

A cat which appears to have only minor injuries should never the less be taken to the vet for a check-up as there may be, for example, internal bleeding and the cat will almost certainly need further, veterinary treatment for shock.

FALLS

THE SAME GENERAL rules apply to cats injured in falls. An adult cat may survive a fall of up to about 6 m (20 ft) without injury, but a fall of any greater height is likely to result in more serious damage. It may also cause concussion, leading to partial or total loss of consciousness; treat as for shock. Even if the cat lands the right way up there may be damage to the front paws and head, but whether this is obvious or not, it is best to have a veterinary check. Meanwhile, wrap the cat in something warm and keep it calm.

ELECTRIC SHOCK

ELECTRIC CABLES ARE particularly attractive to kittens, which can bite through them and sustain electric burns to the mouth and paws. This is usually immediately fatal, but if a kitten or cat is found in these circumstances, dead or alive, the first step must be to isolate the current by removing the plug from the socket or switching off at the mains. If the cat is still alive, it should be treated for shock while the vet is called. The dangers of electricity are avoided by training a kitten from its earliest days in the house not to play with electric wires, which should as far as possible be secured with insulated staples and not be allowed to stray. Care should be taken to ensure that cats are not given playthings that in any way resemble electric cable.

HEAT STROKE

CATS ARE VULNERABLE to heat stroke, especially longhairs on a long car journey in summer. Remember that a travelling basket or carrier is a confined space with less ventilation than the open space of the car and less freedom for the cat to move. The symptoms of heat stroke are exceptionally rapid breathing, the appearance of the haws and a noticeable rise in temperature, and they can appear alarmingly quickly. Always have water, a dish and an old towel to hand on a long journey. At the first signs of distress, offer the cat a drink and then wrap it in a wet towel, paying particular attention to the head, though making sure it can breathe easily. If the symptoms persist, veterinary help should be sought however inconvenient this might be on a long journey. On recovery, there are usually no after-effects. Liability to heat stroke can be minimised by ensuring a flow of fresh air over the travelling basket or cage and keeping it in the shade. The car should be opened up or the basket placed outside at rest stops. A cat should never be left alone in a car, even if the window is left open.

Bottom

This kitten amuses itself with flex; cats can be trained not to play with electric cables.

Bottom

Long-hairs, such as this Birman right), are particularly susceptible to heat stroke.

> CAT FACT:
> Yawning in cats, as with other animals, draws oxygen into the lungs. It is not to awaken them though, but to assist in the digestion of a heavy meal while dozing.

Top
Through self-grooming cats may ingest poisonous substances that they have picked up on their coat.

Bottom
Cats are natural climbers, only very occasionally will they get stuck.

POISONS

CATS' DIGESTIVE SYSTEMS are ill-equipped to cope with poisons, but their curiosity and their liking for rodents which may themselves have been poisoned render them especially vulnerable. In the country, cats may come into contact, either directly or through prey, with herbicides and pesticides in gardens or on farmland. Many of these are based on petrochemical or coal-tar substances to which cats are particularly sensitive. Even common substances such as wet paint, creosote, turpentine and anti-freeze are seriously poisonous to cats and can result in convulsions leading to coma. They are generally taken in when a cat tries to clean its coat after brushing against a contaminated surface, or licked off the paws. This is an added argument for removing any stains from the coat and paws as soon as they are seen. Liquid substances can be washed off using a mild detergent such as washing-up liquid, taking care to swab down with plenty of fresh water afterwards. More resistant substances such as paint or tar should be softened with butter or cooking oil and then washed as before. If the cat may have been licking its coat, a vet should be consulted.

Unfortunately, in many cases a cat will exhibit symptoms of poisoning (vomiting, diarrhoea, staggering, compulsive licking of the coat, drooling and convulsions) when the cause is unknown. In all cases of suspected poisoning, treat for shock (see above) and phone the vet for immediate advice, before taking the cat to the veterinary surgery as soon as possible. It is unwise to attempt to administer any kind of emetic at home. Any information on what the poison might be will be helpful (the brand names of gardening chemicals, for example, will give the vet a clue), but many poisons have no specific antidote and the vet's first priority will be to stabilise the cat's system and keep it under observation.

TRAPPED!

A CAT TRAPPED on a roof or in a tree and rescued by the fire brigade always makes the headlines in the local paper, but it is not a common occurrence because cats are usually wise enough not to venture out of their depth. However, in the heat of the chase, particularly if it is the cat that is being chased, it can happen.

The first rule is not to panic – and certainly not to ring the fire brigade, which is absolutely the last resort. Most cats trapped high up will weigh up the situation and, perhaps after a few false starts, find their way down. This may even take a day or more. It is best to leave the cat alone, and unwatched, to sort out its own escape. Placing a dish of strong-smelling food within range, if possible, will provide an added incentive. When the cat returns, observe for symptoms of mild shock or injury which may result from the scramble to the ground.

SEVERE WOUNDS

IN THE CASE of severe wounds, bleeding should be stopped or slowed down by finger pressure. But do not spend too much time on first aid; the main priority is veterinary treatment. If you know the cause of the wound, tell the vet as he may advise antibiotics.

RESPIRATORY PROBLEMS

THE SMOKE FROM burning fat, even to the extent commonly experienced in the average kitchen, can be very distressing to cats and cause severe respiratory problems. The cat should be taken into the fresh air and may need treatment for shock. This is a good reason (there are many others, related to both hygiene and hazards) for making the kitchen out of bounds to cats if this is possible.

CAT FACT:
Cats can tell the difference between colours, but they rely on shape and movement while hunting, because they usually hunt in the very low light levels of night time.

MINOR WOUNDS

MOST CATS SUSTAIN minor wounds from time to time, often as a result of fights with dogs or other cats or when attacking prey. The ears, face and front paws are particularly vulnerable. Wounds should be inspected for any dirt or other matter that can be removed with cotton wool and then bathed in salt solution, 1 tsp to 0.5 litre (1 pint) of cooled, boiled water. Proprietary disinfectants should not be used as these may be harmful. Veterinary attention is not normally necessary unless the wound fails to heal or an abscess develops.

Top
Fighting can result in wounds, check to make sure they are superficial.

Bottom
If the wound is minor a salt solution should be applied with cotton wool.

Caring for the Elderly Cat

SIGNS OF AGEING

THE LIFE EXPECTANCY of a typical domestic cat is about 14 years, although many live much longer. There is evidence that neutered cats outlive unneutered ones and this may be because they tend to roam less and therefore get involved in fewer accidents rather than that neutering has a positive medical effect.

MOST CATS remain alert and playful until they are into their teens, but generally speaking the age of 10 can be equated to the human age of 60. This is of course not seriously old, but it does mean that, for example, reaction times may be slowing, sight and hearing may not be as acute, periods of intense activity are shorter and more time is spent sleeping. But having said that, some cats continue to hunt until the day they die.

At the age of about 10 it is advisable to increase the number of veterinary check-ups to two a year, and of course vaccinations must be kept up to date as ageing cats have a lower resistance to infectious diseases.

Top right
This elderly cat will typically spend more time sleeping than in its youth.

Bottom
Vets can tell the age of a cat by looking at its teeth.

The first signs of ageing are usually subtle changes in behaviour – less enthusiasm to go out especially in cold or wet weather, greater fondness for sleep and warmth, and a slackening of appetite. Play may become less boisterous and the cat may tire of it more quickly. Later, the coat may lose its lustre and richness, and grey hair may appear round the muzzle. Males tend to become more jowly.

Cats tend to lose weight rather than gain it in middle and old age, but some do become obese if they are overfed and do not exercise enough. It is important to encourage older cats to exercise if they show reluctance to do so, and in the case of cats allowed outside it must be remembered that they will probably spend less time there and indulge in less active hunting than in their younger days. It is hard to expect a cat which has been used to an outdoor life to give it up, but periods outside should be made shorter and suspended altogether in bad weather.

THE RIGHT DIET

A DIET HIGH IN easily digestible protein must be maintained in older cats, perhaps with vitamin and mineral supplements if advised by the vet. Do not feed supplements without this advice; too much of certain vitamins and minerals can be as harmful as too little. Some older cats seem to lose their staying power for the usual two meals, and it is worth trying to feed smaller portions three or four times a day. Cats should, however, maintain their enthusiasm for food, even if in smaller quantities. Watch carefully for any sign that the cat is having difficulty in eating. Mouth disorders are fairly common in ageing cats, in particular gingivitis – inflammation of the gums, usually as a result of poor dental health.

Loss of appetite may also be a symptom of kidney failure, which is one of the classic health problems of feline old age. Even more care must be taken than with younger cats that the older cat is having sufficient liquid intake, moistening the meal with water if not enough water is being taken up. A decline in bladder function is another common problem, and also possibly the loss of bowel control.

PHYSICAL PROBLEMS

FAILING SIGHT AND hearing do not seem to hamper cats too much provided that they are not symptoms of more serious problems. You may find that you have to speak more loudly or sharply to get your cat's attention, and serious deafness should mean an end to the outdoor life.

Ageing cats are subject, like humans, to benign and malignant cancers. These develop slowly, and often cannot be detected until it is too late for treatment and the cat is too old to withstand an operation. Cancers and other ailments will hasten the day when the decision must be made to ask the vet to put the cat down. This is never easy, especially if there are children involved, but there are two clinching questions. First, is the cat so ill or so old that life has become a burden to it? Second, is it better to have the cat put down humanely (it is a matter of instant sleep after the injection and death within half a minute) rather than run the risk of its wandering off, as is its natural instinct, to die slowly and possibly painfully? No true cat lover would have any doubt about the answers.

Top left
Elderly cats, such as this one, may resist play preferring a quieter life.

Bottom
This elderly cat looks unwell, it is listless and lacks energy.

107

Breeding from your Cat

BREEDING CATS IS a fascinating hobby, but it demands time, money and study. No one takes it up with the prospect of earning a living, but it can become a full-time occupation dominating the breeder's life. But professional breeding apart, it is possible that you might like your queen to produce just one litter before she is spayed.

CAT FACT
Sleeping and otherwise living a cat's life is typical of many cats because their diet allows them the time to relax between meals and it takes some digesting.

CHOOSING TO BREED

SOME OWNERS BELIEVE that this is only right – that the female should have the fulfilling experience of giving birth at least once – but vets generally discount the idea that this benefits the cat either physically or psychologically. Another possible reason for breeding a litter is to give children the educational experience of observing the process and caring for the kittens, but this could be obtained by asking a cat-breeding friend to allow them to watch a birth, and to be involved with the kittens afterwards.

What is certain is that before you embark on this adventure you should know that the surplus kittens can go to good homes. The first stage is therefore to ask around and get firm promises. On no account should kittens be offered to pet shops or to any other outlet which intends to sell them on.

Top left
A Somali queen with her kitten.

Top right
Although females can produce a litter all year round it is preferable that new born kittens benefit from the heat of the summer months.

Bottom
This Persian demonstrates that she is in oestrus; a raised tail, rolling and being overtly affectionate.

POINTS TO CONSIDER

BECAUSE OF THE anti-social spraying habits of the unneutered tom, it is not practical to set about breeding cats in the same way as with other small animals, by buying a pair and simply letting them mate. There are two choices. It is generally considered irresponsible to let your unspayed queen out and let her find, or be found by, her own mate in the rough-and-tumble of the outside world.

If you are more particular, or own a pedigree animal, you will want to take the queen to be mated by a stud cat. In this case it is important to choose a stud cat which is experienced. Queens, especially in their first sexual encounter, can be combative after the event and an experienced tom knows how to beat a swift retreat once the act is done. In practice, many owners of unspayed household queens have the situation thrust upon them by accidental, unplanned matings.

MATING INSTINCTS

FEMALES COME INTO oestrus ('on heat') at ages ranging from about four months to about 12. For ordinary domestic cats, six to

OESTRUS

ONCE OESTRUS IS established, it recurs at two-
or three-weekly intervals in spring and summer
and, in heated and lit indoor conditions, virtually
throughout the year. It lasts from 7–10 days.
Veterinary opinion is that queens should be first
mated at not younger than nine months but not
later than their third or fourth oestrus, but it is
advisable to have your vet check over your queen
before going ahead with mating. Because of the
regularity of the oestrus cycle, it is possible to
forecast the cat's next oestrus and to make
suitable arrangements (including agreement on
the fee) with the owner of the stud male. The
ideal is to aim for kittens to be born in spring or
early summer so that they and their mother can
benefit from warm conditions and sunny
weather at a time of relative weakness.

GOING TO STUD

QUEENS ARE USUALLY taken to stud on the
second or third day of oestrus when the stage of
rolling has been reached, and they normally stay
3–4 days. The first day is spent in a pen adjacent
to, but separated from, the tom by a wire partition. By
the second day both queen and tom are in a state of
arousal and are allowed together, whereupon they will
mate several times. Some pairs will keep their distance
when they are not actually mating, but others will curl
up and sleep together in the same box.

When the queen is collected, she must be kept
indoors in quiet conditions for a few days. She will
still be in oestrus and despite her experience may well
continue to display the symptoms. Certainly she will
still be attractive to toms and
her presence may even inspire
serenades at the windows.
Meanwhile, the owner has
some planning to do.
Assuming the mating has been
successful, the kittens will be
born in about 63 days' time.

Top
*All kittens should be
promised homes before the
queen is mated, if not it
may result in abandoned
cats.*

Bottom
*A cat foetus at about
eight weeks, shortly
before birth. It recieves
its nutrition from the
placenta via the
umbilical cord, while it
is protected from damage
by fluid inside the uterus
or womb. When the
kitten is born, this fluid,
together with the
placenta and umbilical
cord, will be ejected.*

eight months is typical. Oestrus brings on a style of
behaviour known as 'calling'. It typically includes
unusual demonstrations of affection, pacing the
room, rolling on the floor, anxiety to get out of the
house, cries which increase in intensity as oestrus
proceeds, and the adoption of the mating stance –
crouched down with the hind quarters raised and the
tail deflected – when the cat is stroked. In extreme
cases queens in oestrus may jump from windows or
plan a rush at the front door.

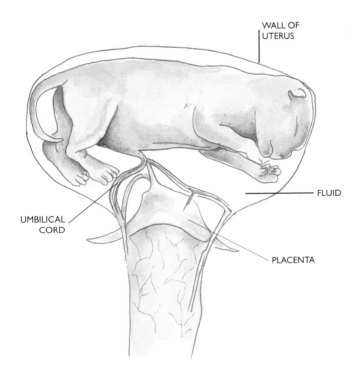

WALL OF
UTERUS

FLUID

UMBILICAL
CORD

PLACENTA

CAT FACT:
To 'become a cat's paw'
is to be manipulated.
There is a fable which
tells of a monkey which
uses the paw of a live
cat to drag roasted
chestnuts from a fire.

Pregnancy and Kittening

IT CANNOT BE emphasised too strongly that a pregnant queen is going through a completely normal phase of life and that the owner should approach it in a matter of fact, relaxed manner. Any anxiety will communicate itself to the cat. At the same time, fussing may make the queen feel too dependant on her owner, so that when it comes to mothering she will not carry out the duties of care for herself.

PREPARING THE QUEEN

IF SHE HAS been used to going outside, this may continue until at least the sixth week of pregnancy, and if she is an indoor cat normal play routines can be continued. Normal grooming practice should of course be maintained. Like human mothers, queens normally look in the peak of condition during pregnancy, and there is no need to take any special care of them except towards the end. Pregnancy is not an illness.

Top left
This pregnant Siamese is in the peak of condition.

Top right
A heavily pregnant queen; she should be discouraged from going outside to make a nest.

Bottom
The queen may find grooming more tiring and will be unable to clean all areas during the late stages of pregnancy.

THE STAGES OF PREGNANCY

THE FIRST SIGNS of pregnancy appear at about three weeks, when the nipples begin to become enlarged and pinkish in colour. The next oestrus would normally be due about this time, and its non-appearance will act as confirmation. There will as yet be no visible swelling of the abdomen, and nothing to feel, but if absolute confirmation of the pregnancy is needed the queen should be taken to the vet. This is, however, not necessary. At no time during the pregnancy should the owner, or anyone other than the vet, attempt to feel the kittens in the womb.

By the fourth week a slight swelling will be apparent in the abdomen, and swelling of the nipples will become increasingly evident. About this time, there will be an increase in appetite, and by the fifth

week this should be satisfied by changing to a growth formula advised by your vet. The appetite increases through the sixth week, by which time the queen will be obviously pregnant to even the most casual eye. She will now move with more care, avoiding stretching and twisting actions, and will probably not want to go out. It is however important that she should continue to exercise, and this is the time for a return to the gentle games of kittenhood with twists of paper on a string and catnip mice. Allow the cat to set the pace and call time when she has had enough. Small children should be kept away where possible and warned not to lift her or haul her about.

The seventh week marks a notable change in behaviour as the queen begins to show signs of excitement. This is the 'quickening' stage of pregnancy when the foetuses begin to move. The queen will roll and stretch, and start to search for a suitable nesting place. If she is not already confined to the house, she should be kept in now in case she decides to make a nest outside. Indoors, she may select an open drawer or cupboard, so these should be kept shut. Now is the time to prepare a kittening box.

REQUIREMENTS FOR THE BIRTH

SPECIALLY MADE BOXES are available from pet stores and some professional breeders use boxes made of wood or plastic, but a cardboard box of about wine case size is perfectly adequate and has the advantage that it can be disposed of and cheaply replaced when it gets soiled. Make sure that it has not been used to pack some harmful substance such as household bleach, and check that any staples or other fastenings are safely hammered down. The top flaps should be loosely folded over for privacy and a suitably sized hole cut in one end for access. A smaller hole cut in one side for observation during and after labour is also useful. Acquire one or more similar boxes to keep in reserve.

Newspaper should not be used for bedding because printing ink contains petrochemical solvents. Buy a roll or two of cheap lining paper from a wallpaper shop and crumple this up to form a soft bed. For real luxury it can be topped off with some

crumpled kitchen towels. The box should be sited in a warm, draught-free spot but within sound and preferably sight of household activities. The ideal temperature, which should be constant day and night, is 22°C (72°F). It is possible that the queen may reject the owner's choice of site and indicate her own preference, which should be followed – provided that the temperature and draught-free conditions can be maintained – unless it is impracticable. She may need to be shown how to use the kittening box by rustling the bedding and enticing her inside, showing her how to get in and out and demonstrating how the top flaps fold down to make a private, cosy nest.

Top
Queen washing her four-day-old kitten.

Bottom
A cardboard box is perfectly adequate as a kittening box and has the advantage that it can be disposed of and cheaply replaced when it gets soiled.

CARE OF THE QUEEN

FEEDING SHOULD NOW move to four times a day. Constipation sometimes occurs at this stage of pregnancy, and it can be eased by occasionally feeding oily fish such as sardines or tuna. Gentle grooming should be continued.

As the queen moves into the eighth week of pregnancy you should check the anal area daily as she may by now be too bulky to attend to her own cleaning. If necessary, sponge the area with mild soap and warm water and dry with tissues.

The nipples should also be checked, and if they are encrusted or dry a tiny smear of petroleum jelly should be applied.

At this time it is important to maintain the queen's interest in her kittening box or, even at this late stage, she may start looking for an alternative. Supplying it with a favourite toy can help. A sympathetic, helpful child can be a useful watchdog at this time, encouraging (but not pulling) the queen back if she strays. The signs of imminent birth are noticeable enlargement of the breasts and abdomen, usually affectionate behaviour towards the family, increased use of the litter tray and sometimes a lowering of the appetite. The last need cause no concern, but an effort should be made to maintain the queen's liquid intake.

PREPARING FOR THE BIRTH

AS THE TIME of birth approaches it is a good idea to confine the kittening box, litter tray and food dish within a temporary enclosure such as a child's play-pen, provided you can obtain access easily if necessary. Queens normally manage the birth of their kittens without fuss or human intervention, but you should have a number of items close to hand in case they are needed. These are: kitchen towels, cotton wool, a few hand towels, a cat-friendly disinfectant – ask your vet to recommend one – a hot water bottle, a supply of polythene bags and a plastic or metal bin

for disposal. If you have a good relationship with your vet, a warning that an urgent call might be necessary does no harm, but it is unlikely that you will need to follow it up.

LABOUR

LABOUR CAN BEGIN as early as 61 days or as late as 70 days after conception. In the case of accidental matings, of course, the date of conception will probably not be known and you should be prepared a few days in advance. It is essential that the owner is close at hand throughout labour and birth, to the extent if necessary of having a camp-bed in the kittening room.

The onset of labour is prefaced by restlessness accompanied by growls or rhythmic purring. This stage may persist for several hours, even up to 24 in some cases. The second stage is marked by the start of contractions, which at first may occur only every 30 minutes or at even longer intervals, gradually becoming more frequent until just before the birth of the first kitten they are occurring about every 30 seconds. They may be accompanied by further growling and repeated licking of the vaginal area to stimulate the birth.

Top
The pink, enlarged nipples are clearly visible on this pregnant Siamese.

Bottom
This non-pedigree cat is able to enter and leave the kittens' pen with ease.

At this point, some queens prefer to be on their own in the kittening box, in the dark, while others – particularly first-time mothers, who may be frightened or bewildered – need the presence and encouragement of their owners. Either way, you should stay close to the scene and prepare for a longish wait with the radio, television or a good book to while away the time, continually reassuring the queen of your presence. Children should be kept out of the way, and other pets confined to quarters as far away from the kittening room as possible.

BIRTH

THE FIRST KITTEN is normally born within 20 minutes of the onset of frequent contractions. The others – four is the typical size of a litter – may follow in rapid succession or at long intervals during which contractions stop. It is not uncommon, especially if the litter is large, for up to 24 hours to go by before labour is completed. In this case, the queen is likely to become exhausted and need nourishment to see her through the remaining births. She should be offered a small amount of favourite food.

Each kitten arrives, usually head first, in a membrane sac which the queen ruptures with her tongue. The queen's first action is to clean the kitten, licking away the fluid from the face and stimulating the kitten's first breath. The kitten cries and flexes its body, a sign that so far all is well. When the queen has finished licking it dry, she will bite the umbilical cord and usually eat it with the placenta and the remains of the birth sac. The kitten will then crawl towards its mother's body and find a nipple to suck. This normally stimulates the queen into maternal attentions.

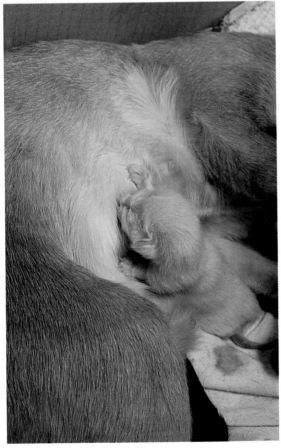

Top left
A Colourpoint queen with her kittens in the kittening box.

Top right
The mother often gives her new born kitten a helpful nudge towards her nipples.

Bottom left
New born Burmese cream kittens, their eyes are still closed, feel their way searching for their mother's nipples.

113

THE NEW-BORN KITTENS

IF KITTENS ARE born in rapid succession, the queen may not have time to deal with one properly before the next arrives. She will normally start the licking and cleaning-up process within a few seconds of the birth. If she delays and shows no sign of starting (which may be due to the distraction of another imminent birth or, in the case of a first-time mother, simple inexperience) you should clear the sac from the kitten's head, and leave the queen to come back to the kitten. If she shows no interest after 15 minutes, a vet should be called. If at all possible, try to avoid removing a newborn kitten from its mother, as she may reject it when you try to return it, which would necessitate foster- or hand-rearing.

Hand-rearing is a demanding and difficult task, and you should seek veterinary advice. It is possible that the vet will know of a possible foster-mother, which is an easier and more satisfactory alternative to hand-rearing. But bear in mind the comments made below about weak or sick kittens.

COMPLICATIONS

ALMOST EVERY BIRTH is as simple and uncomplicated as the procedure described on the previous page, but it is as well to know of the complications that can occur. As a general rule, you should interfere in the process only if there are obvious signs of difficulty or if the queen is in real distress. The natural activities during and after birth are an important element in the mutual bonding of queen and kittens and provide the best introduction of the kittens to the world.

It sometimes happens that in licking her vagina to stimulate the birth the queen ruptures the birth sac before it is expelled. This presents no problem if the kitten is emerging head first, and even in a breech birth (tail first) a few extra contractions and perhaps the bracing of the queen's hind legs against the wall of the kittening box or your hand will usually release the kitten. However, if one leg remains trapped inside the birth canal it may be more difficult for the queen to expel it, and she and the kitten may become exhausted in the process. If so, this is the time to call the vet or take the cat to the surgery urgently.

THE NEW FAMILY

WHEN ALL THE litter has been born, the queen will normally give herself a thorough wash and then settle down happily with her new family. She should be given clean bedding with a warm blanket uppermost, and if the kittening box itself has been soiled it should be replaced. Some queens like a large meal after giving birth, but most – especially if they have eaten the placentas – may not want to eat for a

Top
The natural processes after birth allows mother and kittens to bond.

Bottom
Hand-reared kittens, such as this one, need a lot of the owner's time and attention.

AFTER BIRTH CARE

QUEENS NORMALLY recover from giving birth within a few days and become preoccupied with feeding and cleaning their kittens and keeping them warm. Provided that the accustomed diet is balanced and rich in vitamins and minerals, it is best not to change it now in an attempt to make it even richer for the nursing queen. Diarrhoea could result. But if it appears that milk is in short supply or there are other signs of undernourishment the vet should be asked to recommend a suitable diet or supplements.

few hours. The queen will need little attention for a while, and will indeed hanker for peace and quiet, but you should check visually that all the kittens are healthy, none are deformed, and all are getting their fair share of milk. If a queen rejects one of her kittens, it is likely to be deformed, weak, or unviable in some other way, and a vet should be consulted. It is kindest to put down a kitten which, in the vet's judgement, has little or no chance of developing into a healthy cat.

> **CAT FACT:**
> Cats have predated humans ever since we started evolving in Africa. Fossil human skulls have been found bearing the puncture scars from cat incisor teeth.

> **CAT FACT:**
> Scientific research has shown that young cats learn the skills for hunting from their parents, but they instinctively know how to seize and kill their prey.

Top left
These two young kittens will spend most of their time sleeping.

Bottom
It is important that all the new born kittens have their share of milk.

Rearing Kittens

FOR THE FIRST three weeks of a kitten's life, it and its siblings receive their mother's total care: feeding, cleaning, grooming and comforting. Kittens are born blind and their ears are limp and folded over. The ears unfold and become erect at about two weeks. They open their eyes within 5–10 days, but it takes 2–3 days for the eyes to open fully.

CARING FOR THE QUEEN AND KITTENS

DURING THIS TIME there may be a discharge which should be wiped away carefully with a tissue soaked in warm water. All kittens' eyes are blue, and remain so for at least the first 12 weeks of life. In some breeds the adult eye colour does not fully develop until the cat is one year old.

FOOD SUPPLY

A WATCH SHOULD be kept in the early days to ensure that each kitten is getting its share of milk. Each kitten tends to favour one particular nipple, which it soon identifies by its own body smell, and if it is rejected will cry loudly. The reason for rejection may be that the nipple is sore, and the vet should be

Top left
All kittens have blue eyes until they reach about 12 weeks.

Bottom left
This kitten has just opened its eyes but its ears remain limp.

Bottom
On average kittens should gain their birth weight every week.

consulted, because the queen's distress may be caused by mastitis. As she has eight nipples, there should be enough to go round. To maintain a supply of high quality milk and also for the queen's own good health, four meals should be given each day while she is feeding her litter, and a supply of fresh water should also be on hand.

EARLY ROUTINE

KITTENS SPEND THEIR first few days alternately sleeping and feeding. Normal weights at birth are between 57–114 g (2–4 oz), and they should add about 15 g (0.5 oz) a day. As a rough guide, they should gain the equivalent of their birth weight each week. After a couple of days, giving time for the feeding routine to be set up and stabilised, the kittens should be inspected and if possible weighed daily. They should be lifted by placing one hand underneath and another lightly on the back of the neck, and must be held firmly enough to feel secure. A healthy, well fed kitten will feel firm and plump and should be clean about the face and hindquarters. From the first day, the queen will lick her kittens' anal area to stimulate defecation and urination,

and will clean up afterwards. She will also groom their faces, bodies and legs almost obsessively.

After a few days, the queen may decide on a move, and one by one carry her kittens by the scruff of the neck to a new location. This is common behaviour among wild cats and is inspired by the queen's desire to avoid attack by an observant predator which has been watching the nest. She can usually be deceived into thinking she has made a move by moving the position of the kittening box (making sure that it is still in a warm situation out of draughts) and changing the bedding, but a few unsoiled pieces of the old bedding should be left in place so that the nest retains its familiar smell.

AT TWO WEEKS

SOON AFTER THE age of two weeks the kittens will begin to crawl round the kittening box and may even venture outside, to be hauled back by their mother. If they move too far away before being noticed, they will wail for rescue and their mother will respond with a call and hurry to the scene. As they learn to walk, at about three weeks, they will venture further and their mother will let them do so, though she will keep a watchful eye and call or collect them if they go too far. The milk teeth begin to develop about this time, but this normally causes no problems. As they explore their surroundings, kittens tend to nuzzle and lick any unfamiliar surface or object, so polish, detergents and such products as bleach must be banned in the kittening room from the beginning.

CAT FACT:
One of the main reasons why most cat species prefer a solitary existence is that the available prey in a given area cannot support more individuals.

CAT FACT:
Dick Whittington's cat was in fact a special type of ship which he used for transporting coals from Newcastle to London during the fourteenth century.

Top
Young kittens should be handled with care and should not be taken from their mothers for long.

Bottom
Kittens, such as these, begin to crawl at around two weeks.

WEANING

AT FOUR WEEKS, when the kittens have a sense of balance, weaning can begin. This is a gradual process of replacing the mother's milk, first with milky and then with solid foods. Special milk for kittens is commercially available. It should be warmed to the appropriate temperature for the kitten's age (check the instructions on the packaging) and you can obtain a special feeding kit from your vet. Each kitten can then be introduced to its own feeding dish, which should be sited separately from the queen's dish or she may assume it contains extra rations for her.

The next stage, after 2–3 days, is to offer a little of a commercial weaning diet. Kittens' stomachs are small, so 'little and often' – four or even five meals a day – is the rule. Regarding the amount to feed, once more follow the packaging instructions. Kittens often have difficulty at first in picking up solid food, and it is easier for them if it is arranged in three or four small mounds. By about eight weeks the kitten should be encouraged to give up its mother's milk and be having a 'growth kitten formula' with water always available.

> **CAT FACT:**
> Cats will avoid taking unnecessary risks, because even slight injuries can lead to their death simply by rendering them unable to hunt effectively enough for survival.

TRAINING

WHILE SHE IS feeding her litter full time, the queen will continue to stimulate their defecation and urination and clean them up afterwards, and may even nudge them towards the litter tray and show them what to do. An experienced queen, but not often a first-time mother, may even complete toilet training. But once weaning begins she will lose interest, and the owner may have to finish the task. It is important at this stage to ensure that there is always clean litter available, cleaning and replenishing the tray after every usage.

VACCINATIONS

AS SOON AS the kittens are fully weaned they are ready to receive their first vaccinations. Your vet will advise on the exact timing. It is important that they are vaccinated before they have contact with any cats other than their mother and siblings. Until they are weaned they are protected by their mother's vaccination, if this is up to date, passed on through the milk, but this effect quickly fades.

STIMULATION

FROM ABOUT THREE weeks, kittens begin to play with each other. Their mock fights can look vicious and dangerous, but they are only in fun and are in any case well supervised by their mother who will remove an over-enthusiastic pugilist from the scene.

Top
Kitten grooming can begin from around four weeks, this will accustom the cat to being handled.

Bottom
These kittens are being weaned onto solid food.

From then on to the age of six months it should progress gradually to eating just two meals of ordinary commercial cat food or special commercial kitten food, but let its appetite be the guide to the frequency and size of meals offered. The kitten should be offered a variety of foods so that it does not become fixated on a particular flavour and set up a future as a fussy eater. It should be allowed some preferences, however, and there is no point in persisting with a food that is constantly refused.

responsibility to ensure that the kittens are going to a home where they will be loved and cared for.

In the case of pedigree kittens, they should already have been registered with the appropriate organisation (this can be done from the age of about six weeks) and the certificate should be handed over together with a form for registering the transfer of ownership. The owners of pedigree stud toms may have rights over the kittens sired by their cats, such as the choice of one of the litter; these will be noted in the stud contract and must be observed.

> **CAT FACT:**
> Cats only bury their faeces when they feel it might otherwise betray the whereabouts of their den (or house with domestic cats); otherwise it is left as a territorial scent mark.

Games are carried on with increasing accuracy and a widening repertoire of movements. Soon after this, the owner and family can begin to join in with simple and gentle games such as twitching twists of paper on a string or bowling a table tennis ball to be chased. The mother will often encourage her kittens by taking part herself.

It is important that this human contact, as well as picking up and cuddling, is continued as it is the key to happy domestication. The same applies to grooming. This is not really necessary with kittens except as an excuse for a weekly inspection, but experience of gentle grooming from an early age – say four weeks – will make it an undisturbing and enjoyable experience later on.

Kittens are usually nervous for the first few days in their new home, but they do not normally appear to suffer distress. The queen will, however, miss her kittens and should be given extra treats and comforts for a few days, although curiously enough she will not acknowledge them if she meets them again after a period of separation.

A NEW HOME

KITTENS SHOULD not be passed to another owner until they are at least 10 weeks old, and it is preferable to wait a couple of weeks longer. They should be reliably toilet-trained, partially or fully vaccinated and, on the vet's advice, de-wormed. There should be written evidence of veterinary attention, particularly of vaccinations, including the dates when booster injections are due. It is of course the owner's

Top left
Toys can be introduced to kittens to be used in mock fights or kills.

Top right
This mother teaches her kitten hunting skills.

Bottom
It is normal that a kitten is nervous in its new home.

In the Beginning

THE DOMESTIC CAT is one of 38 species of the cat family or *Felidae*. To trace their evolution, we have to travel back in time about 200 million years to when the first mammals – warm-blooded creatures that bear and suckle young – appeared on the earth. These were small creatures, no match for the larger egg-laying dinosaurs which then ruled the world. About 65 million years ago disaster overtook the dinosaurs. No one knows what kind of disaster it was, but a huge asteroid strike which raised a dust cloud that blotted out the light of the sun for many years is a likely answer. Whatever really happened, it was the end of the dinosaurs and mammals were left in the ascendant. From then on they grew in size, variety and numbers.

creatures but some of terrifying size which have been identified from fossilised remains. To judge from these fossil discoveries, one of the most successful miacid species – and certainly one you would not wish to meet on a dark prehistoric night – was Smilodon, the sabre-toothed cat with a mouth dominated by two canine teeth like tusks several centimetres long.

SMILODON

SMILODON FLOURISHED from about 35 million years ago. Unlike other tree-hunting miacids, it fed off the great herds of grazing animals which then roamed the continents. The oldest sabre-toothed cat remains found so far were in Derbyshire, England. They were 30,000 years old. Remains of sabre-toothed cats found in California have been carbon dated to only about 13,000 years ago, so Smilodon had a long reign.

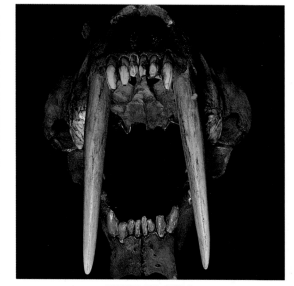

Bottom left
The mouth of the prehistoric Smiloden showing the long canine teeth.

Bottom right
Skull of the saber-toothed cat found in California.

THE MIACIDS

OF ALL THE mammals one group, the miacids, were among the most successful. They were adept hunters, using their intelligence to locate their prey and their ferocious claws to kill. Their teeth were designed to cut and tear at the flesh of their victims. About 40 million years ago, different groups of miacids began to develop, most of them small tree

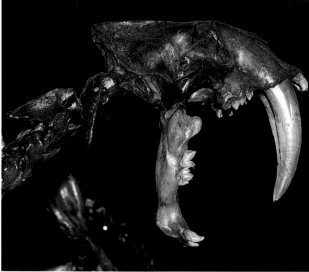

DINICTIS

BUT IT WAS another miacid descendant that led to today's Felidae species. These were the Dinictis species, smaller and faster creatures. By the time the great Ice Ages began about 3 million years ago, Dinictis species closely resembling modern small cats were evidently well established. The oldest fossils of these have been dated at about 12,000,000 years ago. The harsh conditions of the Ice Ages, killing off the grazing herds and making hunting more a matter of skill and intelligence, favoured them over larger species. As the Ice Ages came and went, cats even more like those of the historical world, large and small, began to develop, all descended from Dinictis and numbering about 100 species. Fossil evidence shows that these species well pre-dated the evolution of any creature resembling Homo sapiens.

SPREAD OF A SPECIES

THE PROCESS OF evolution described above began before the continents had yet reached their present geographical positions. At this stage the land masses which were to become the southern continents – South America, Antarctica and Australasia – had begun to break away from the northern mass consisting of North America, Europe, Asia and Africa. When the original cat species evolved, they were able to spread easily through the northern mass, crossing from Asia to North America (like the first American settlers) by the 'land bridge' across what is now the Bering Strait. There is fossil evidence that a variety of cats large and small made this crossing in prehistoric times, although the only modern species to inhabit both Asia and North America is the lynx. Antarctica and Australasia, however, were too isolated by this time for any cat species to reach them, and in Australasia evolution pursued its divergent course with the development of marsupials like the kangaroo and wallaby. To this day, the only Australian or New Zealand cats are descendants of felines introduced by settlers.

So by the time the first humans were developing in Asia and Africa, cats of various kinds were already established on the northern land mass. No doubt the larger cats found prey in the human settlements. Probably the smaller species found the scraps of meat thrown away by the hunting humans a useful and easily obtained addition to their diet. But while Homo sapiens was still living a roving life, hunting and gathering and later keeping herds of goats, his contact with the cat family must have been occasional and accidental. It was only when humans began to settle and till the soil to produce grain that the long relationship between cats and humans began.

Left
The Lynx is the only modern species to inhabit both North America and Asia.

Right
This Australian feral cat is a descendent of the cats brought to the country by European settlers.

The Evolution of the Domestic Cat

TODAY'S PET CATS have all evolved from three or possibly four of the wild Felidae species. The first domestic cats of which we have any physical evidence were those of Ancient Egypt, whose mummified remains were discovered by archaeologists at Beni Hasan in central Egypt in 1889.

THE EGYPTIAN CAT

THESE REMAINS DATED from about 2000 BC, when the worship of the cat had evidently become well established. The most common type found in Egypt was similar to the lightly tabby African wild cat, *Felis libyca*, which is native to areas bordering the Mediterranean. Not all the mummified cats were *Felis libyca*, however. There were also some examples of *Felis chaus*, the ring-tailed jungle cat which is another native of the Middle East.

If by 2000 BC the cat had achieved cult status, it must have arrived on the farms and in the cities of Ancient Egypt long before. Ancient Egyptian civilisation was based on the rich crops of grain, two and sometimes three harvests each year, grown on the annually flooded fertile land of the Nile valley and delta. By about 3000 BC Egypt was a united kingdom and its great days were about to begin. No doubt wild cats were attracted to Egyptian farms by the rich pickings of rats and mice to be found in the barns, and later to the cities where vast stocks of corn were stored in granaries. Famously adaptable, the cats would have become a permanent feature of Egyptian life, and from there the process of domestication, and eventually of deification, would have begun.

THE ORIGIN OF THE SPECIES

Top right
The cat was deified in Ancient Egypt.

Top left
A mummified cat from around 800 BC.

Bottom
The African wild cat, Felis libyca, *is the most similar cat to those which were mummified by Egyptians.*

IT WAS A remarkable find involving literally hundreds of thousands of mummified cats' bodies – possibly millions, for the majority of the bodies were ground up and either used locally as fertiliser or exported. Over 19 tonnes – representing, it is thought, some 180,000 cats – found their way to England where they were sold at an agricultural auction.

EUROPEAN WILD CAT

THE THIRD ANCESTOR of the modern cat is the European wild cat, *Felis silvestris*, with its distinctive, rounded, black-tipped tail. This is similar to the African wild cat, but rather stockier and with darker, more pronounced tabby markings which are possibly the result of its natural habitat in more temperate regions. How *Felis silvestris* came into the genetic picture can only be guessed at, but it was (and, apart from the British Isles still is) a common species in northern Europe and may well have infiltrated into farming

The domestic cat populations of south-east Asia were well established in early historical times, and it is possible that *Felis manul* – a fearless cat which would not have any doubts about approaching human settlements in search of food – interbred with the other ancestor species.

BECOMING DOMESTICATED

IT WOULD BE too much of a simplification, however, to suggest that these wild species simply adopted human hosts and thus automatically became domesticated. Many wild cats, large and small, hang around human settlements to take what they can, but they remain as implacably wild as when they were

settlements there in the same way as the African wild cat in Egypt. Another possibility is that Egyptian cats taken to Ancient Rome by traders, or possibly carried aboard ship as stowaways, spread northwards with the Roman legions and interbred with their European cousins. It is known that the Roman army took cats with them all over western Europe to protect their food supplies, and also that interbreeding between *libyca* and *silvestris* can be genetically successful.

ASIAN ANCESTORS

A POSSIBLE FOURTH ingredient in the 'mix' of the domestic cat is Pallas's cat, *Felis manul*. A native of central Asia, its hair is longer than that of the other three and it could have introduced a longhair gene into the mixture as the domestication of cats spread.

born. Domestic cats, by contrast, are born tame and are soon habituated to human company. Even feral cats, which either directly or by heredity have experienced human contact but may have become 'wild' in their behaviour, soon accustom themselves to human company as when, for example, they are fed by human friends.

Clearly some genetic changes must have taken place, in the many generations since the first time a wild cat approached a farm and found its barn full of mice, during which prolonged contact with humans (and the plentiful warmth, comfort and food available in human surroundings) has given the domestic cat a more placid – or more pragmatic – personality than its wild relatives. That gradual genetic change rather than mere habit was responsible for producing the domestic cat is shown by the fact that its brain is significantly smaller that that of the wild cat.

CAT FACT:
Cats have an immensely powerful bite because of the design of the skull which displays short mandibles combined with muscles stretching to the back of the head.

CAT FACT:
The most prolific man-eater on record managed to claim an estimated 436 human victims before being shot in 1907. She was known as the Champawat tigress.

Top
European wild cat kittens cannot be tamed even from this early age.

Centre
This wall painting of Egyptian ladies features a cat at their feet, suggesting its importance as a family member.

Bottom
The introduction of Pallas's cat to the evolution of the modern cat led to long-haired breeds.

Friends and Enemies

IT WAS ABOUT 8000 BC when people began to turn from the nomadic life of herdsmen and hunters to a pattern of living based on settlement and farming. The first settlements were in the Middle East. The arrival of the smaller wild cats at the edges of these settlements was one of many changes – a relatively minor one – that followed from this major shift in human behaviour. The settlements would have been a rich source of food for the feline visitors. Mice and rats were attracted in their millions to the primitive grain stores and to the middens, or rubbish dumps, on the village perimeters. Unlike wild dogs, which could be a nuisance, cats were not rivals for the humans' food supplies and posed no threat to the stock animals or to humans themselves.

ANCIENT EGYPTIAN RECORDS

CATS DO NOT appear among the cave paintings and other artefacts left behind by these early settlers. The art of the first civilisations seems to have favoured the larger mammals either as hunters or hunted, and sometimes herd animals are represented. It is not until we reach the civilisation of Ancient Egypt, round about 3000 BC, that cats appear as significant figures in people's lives.

Over about 1,000 years, the cat progressed in Ancient Egypt from a useful destroyer of vermin to a religious icon. It was also well respected and even venerated in the ancient civilisations of Greece, Rome, China and Japan, but evidently these peoples took to cats with less enthusiasm than the Egyptians.

MYSTICAL QUALITIES

BECAUSE OF THE evidence left behind, a great deal is known about the place of the cat in Ancient Egyptian culture. Cats came to have mystical qualities, perhaps associated

with their acute night vision. They also came to be valued household possessions, so much so that when a family's cat died the entire household went into mourning and the head of the house shaved off his eyebrows as a mark of grief. If an Egyptian house caught fire, the cat was the first thing to be saved from the flames. Farther up the social scale were the temple and royal cats, which were pampered in life and honoured in death by mummified burial.

FELINE IMAGES

ANCIENT EGYPTIAN ART was full of cat images in wall paintings, palace decorations, bronze and wooden figurines, jewellery and other artefacts. Some cats are shown in domestic settings – sitting at the feet of their owners, for example, or on a woman's lap – or in the hunting fields, where they seem to have been used to flush out wildfowl for the

hunters and perhaps to retrieve. But many art works associate cats with Bastet or Pasht, the goddess of fertility and femininity. The cult of Pasht (which is said by some to have given us the word 'puss') lasted for about 1,500 years, during which time it was forbidden by law to harm any cat in any way for fear of offending the goddess.

CAT WORSHIP

EGYPTIAN WORSHIP of cats became well-known outside Egypt and was seen as rather ridiculous. A probably apocryphal story was told of a battle between Egypt and Persia in 525 BC, in which the Persian commander stationed cats in his front line. The Egyptians refused to attack for fear of harming the cats, and so lost the battle. The story may be unlikely, but it makes a point about how the Egyptians' veneration of the cat was seen by the outside world.

Cat-worship apart, Egyptian art also featured cats in a humorous vein, in much the same way as modern greetings cards. Scraps of papyrus and limestone found at Ancient Egyptian sites

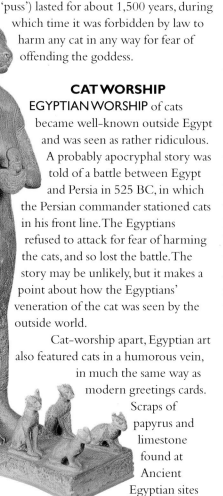

include cartoon-style drawings of cats in various unlikely roles. One is carrying a jar and a basket balanced across its shoulder on a pole. Another is herding a flock of ducks. In another, a cat sits at table, holding a fan and a napkin, with a large rat and is offering it a roasted goose. It is thought that these drawings may have been made as a pastime by masons employed in building royal tombs and temples. Whatever their origin, they show that cats were held in affection as well as veneration.

Egyptians forbade the export of cats, but Phoenician traders – the great entrepreneurs of the time – smuggled domestic cats abroad throughout the Mediterranean area. The Ancient Greeks identified cats with women and in particular with the goddess Venus. As Venus was the goddess of farming as well as of fertility, the cat's prowess as a vermin destroyer was perhaps responsible for this association. But the Greeks had nothing like the Egyptian veneration for cats – weasels, martens and polecats were also kept and trained to destroy vermin – and do not seem to have been adopted as household pets. The representation of cats in Ancient Greek art is relatively rare, and usually on coins.

Top
This Egyptian painting represents the intrinsic role that cats played in Egyptian daily life; here the cat aids farmers to fowl.

Bottom left
A bronze figure of the goddess Bastet from the 22nd Egyptian dynasty.

Bottom right
Statue of Bast, cat goddess of the city Bubastis.

beloved cat named Muezza, and on one occasion he is said to have cut off the sleeve of his robe rather than disturb Muezza's sleep. He also washed himself in water from which he had seen Muezza drink.

ASIAN CAT-LOVERS

MEANWHILE, CATS WERE finding a place in the lives of the people of Asia. House cats were kept in India from about the time of Christ, when there was a cat goddess associated with fertility. Cats had arrived in China about 1,000 years earlier. The Ancient Chinese could not quite make up their minds about them. Together with the snake, the cat was under a curse in Buddhism because they were traditionally the only two creatures that did not weep at Buddha's death. Cats somehow became associated in Chinese culture with poverty, perhaps because of the Buddhist association or because a prosperous, well managed farm should not need the help of cats to keep down vermin. But, strangely, popular belief had it that the way to avoid poverty was to put up a china figure of a cat on the outside of the house, and pictures of cats

ROMAN CATS

ANCIENT ROME TOOK a fairly practical attitude to cats, welcoming them as vermin controllers but lavishing no great affection on them. Although the goddess of liberty was sometimes shown with a cat at her feet, presumably a reference to the cat's free-ranging nature, most representations of cats in Roman art show them in workaday situations with no suggestion of reverence or mystical powers. A mosaic from Pompeii, for example, shows a tabby cat attacking a pigeon. The cat is presented realistically and not at all idealised. However, the value of cats as store watchmen was recognised by the Roman army, which carried cats with it through Gaul and eventually to Britain. Roman colonial families became enthusiastic pet owners (many kept larger cats as well as the domestic variety) and no doubt some of their cats strayed and interbred with *Felis silvestris*, the wild cat which was then common across the higher land of Britain and western Europe. When the Romans retreated to Rome in the fourth century AD they left their cats behind.

Top
Roman mosaic from c.
100 AD depicting a
cat and bird, and a duck
and fish.

Bottom
Cartoon illustrating the
superstition of the magic
Chinese cats guarding
the silkworms.

MOHAMMED AND HIS CAT

ISLAM SPREAD EASTWARDS through southern Asia and westwards along the North African coast following the death of Mohammed in AD 632. Cats had a special place in Islam, Mohammed had a

CATS AS VERMIN HUNTERS

CHRISTIANISATION IN western Europe and the establishment of religious houses meant that cats became highly valued as vermin hunters. Monasteries were at this time great centres of agriculture, where corn had to be stored for months before it could all be threshed and winnowed by hand, so having a few cats about the farmyard was a valuable asset. From the farmyard, cats moved into the monks' cells, and indeed cats were the only pets permitted to be kept by monks and nuns. The Lindisfarne Gospels and the Book of Kells, both dating from the eighth century, contain affectionate representations of cats among their illuminated pages.

Pangur Ban is just one of the monastery cats whose owner saluted him in a poem which appears in most anthologies of verse about animals. Followin this heyday, however, monastery cats were killed and their skins were used to trim and line clerical habits. Cat skins were the only skins allowed by canon law for this purpose.

indoors. It was from Ancient China, incidentally, that we first hear of bad luck resulting from seeing a black cat. This has proved perhaps the most enduring cat myth, with only the British believing the opposite.

In Japan, where cats were introduced from China in medieval times, the cat had a close economic relationship with the silk industry, whose farms were infested with mice. When it became fashionable about AD 1000 to keep house cats, farm cats are said to have fled in droves to more comfortable quarters, leaving the farms unattended. For several centuries, images of cats on the silk farm walls had to do duty as substitutes, but with the silk farmers (and the considerable trade and industry that depended on them) facing ruin, the Emperor finally ordered that the house cats should be released from their pampered existence and earn their keep back on the farms.

AMERICAN INDIAN MYTHOLOGY

AMERICAN INDIANS, perhaps because of their roving way of life, do not seem to have valued the cat as a domestic animal, but the wild cat's hunting skills were much admired. It makes an appearance in Pawnee tribal myth as one of the beasts appointed by Tirawa, the 'One Above' – together with the black bear, the wolf and the puma or mountain lion – to guard over the Evening Star.

> **CAT FACT:**
> The puma of the Americas, otherwise known as the mountain lion or cougar, is unusual in being the only 'small cat' species with circular pupils to its eyes.

> **CAT FACT:**
> The largest litters have been recorded in domestic breeds of cat. Burmese and Siamese cats can give birth to as many as 15 kittens in a single litter.

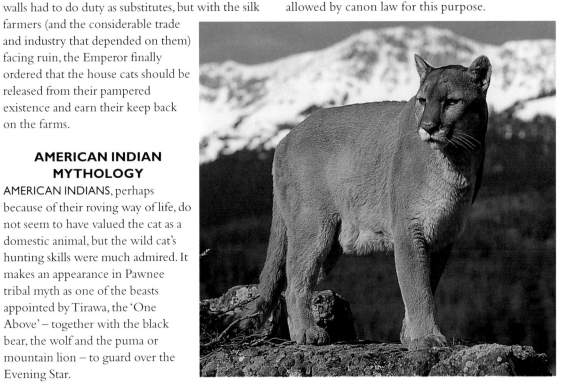

Top
Nineteenth-century, Japanese painting featuring an elderly lady running to defend her cat.

Bottom
The puma was highly regarded by North American Indians and figured in their mythology.

From Persecution to Popularity

IT IS NOT ENTIRELY clear how, from about the year 1400 onwards, the relationship in Europe between cats and humans began to go sour. Cats were welcome enough in the middle of the fourteenth century, when fleas living in the fur of black rats spread the Black Death along the caravan trade routes from China to Europe. In the widespread crop failures and starvation that followed, caused by the shortage of farm labour, the loss of crops to rodents was doubly serious and cats were front line troops in the fight to save grain from damage. Soon afterwards, however, and apparently quite suddenly, the cat became a creature to be feared, reviled – and killed.

THE ANTI-CAT MOVEMENT

THE CHRISTIAN CHURCH, both Catholic and later Protestant, seems to have played a major part in this. It is impossible today to see into the mind of medieval theologians, but a superstition arose, or was cultivated, that the form in which Satan often appeared on Earth was as a black cat. From there it was a mere step to associate cats with witches, Satan's earthly agents, as their 'familiars' or companions.

Two sources, both from legend, have been suggested as the core of this anti-cat movement. One, from Ancient Greece, concerns Hecate, the Greek goddess of magic arts and spells and haunter of graveyards. One of Hecate's servants was Galenthius, who had been turned into a cat and could conjure up the spirits of the dead. The other comes from Norse mythology. In Germany's Rhineland in the thirteenth century there was a revival of a pagan fertility cult based on Freya, the Norse goddess of love and fertility, whose chariot was drawn by two cats. Cats played a prominent role in the Freya cultists' rites.

> **CAT FACT:**
> Cats can hear the very high pitched noises used by rodents. These calls fall between 20–50 kHz; they are beyond human hearing and known as ultrasound.

Top
This painting illustrates the Norse myth of Freya who is shown here with a cat, two of which drew her chariot.

Bottom
The cat and satan have been aligned since medieval times.

medicines, and the fact that women thought to be witches were also likely to be peddling folk remedies did not help the cat's reputation.

By the beginning of the sixteenth century, the persecution of witches and their cats was in full swing. It was a case of an unholy alliance between the Church's teaching and popular superstition. Any elderly woman living alone (as many did because of the gap in longevity between men and women, bearing in mind that in those days anyone over about 40 was regarded as elderly) came under suspicion, especially if she had a pet cat and particularly if the cat was black. By association, cats even without witches became suspect. Lent became a season for the slaughter and sacrifice of cats. They were hanged in many parts of western Europe, and thrown on to bonfires or roasted in baskets on the end of long poles in various districts of France.

The wickedness of the cat could be invoked in the Protestant cause as easily as in the Catholic church. In John Foxe's *Book of Martyrs*, published in 1563 as an attack on the Roman Catholic church, a cat was shown hung in chains and dressed like a Roman priest.

Either of these stories seems a thin pretext for an all-out Christian attack on the cat, even when reinforced by the fact, often quoted, that there is no mention of cats in the Bible. (There is just one in the Apocrypha, in the *Letter of Jeremiah*). But cats became convenient, catch-all scapegoats and representatives of evil, particularly in relation to witchcraft. In the late fifteenth century, Pope Innocent VIII – a ferocious opponent of magicians, witches and the Freya cult – ordered that when witches were burned their cats should be burned also.

CAT–WITCH ASSOCIATION

THE LEGAL DEFINITION of a witch in England was 'a person who hath conference with the devil to consult with him or to do some act'. Witches could therefore be blamed for such catastrophes as floods, epidemics of disease, shipwrecks, fires, storms, accidents – the kinds of events that we describe today as 'acts of God'. Witches' cats were popularly supposed to be able to foretell these disasters, and witches were thought to be able to change into cats and back again up to nine times (perhaps the origin of the cat's proverbial 'nine lives'). They were also said to ride on cats to their meetings with the devil. Various organs of the cat's body were said to be used in witches' brews. They were also used in quack

CAT FACT:
When lions gather hairballs in their stomachs, they can accumulate mineral deposits over time, eventually becoming smooth and polished like black stones.

Top
Along with thousands of women, cats were burnt at the stake under the accusation of witchcraft.

Bottom
Popular mythology continues to associate cats with evil.

ELIZABETHAN PERSECUTION

IN 1566, DURING the reign of Queen Elizabeth I, aversion to cats reached new heights in England with the first of a series of witchcraft trials at Chelmsford in Essex. There were three accused: Elizabeth Francis, Agnes ('Mother') Waterhouse and her daughter Joan. They were said to have communicated with the Devil by means of a white spotted cat which they called Satan. Agnes Waterhouse was found guilty and executed together with her white cat. Over the next 20 years there were 150 witchcraft trials in one county of Essex, England, alone.

A witch tried at Windsor in 1579 confessed to owning a demon in the form of a black cat which she fed daily with bread and milk mixed with her own blood. In 1646 a woman told the jury that a witch had instructed her that if she wished someone to die she should utter a curse, prick her finger and give it to her cat to lick. A Scottish witch, Isobel Gowdie, told a trial in 1622 that she could change herself into a cat and back again at will, and she even quoted the curses she used. Magistrates and judges were only too ready to hear stories of cats jumping through open windows, lifting a door latch or carrying out any other natural cat-like activity and to attribute this to malevolent supernatural powers.

From time to time, cats were credited with more ambitious achievements. There was a legend at Leyland in Lancashire, England, that the stones of the church had been moved there from the village of Whittle, a few kilometres away. The devil, it was said, came every night in the form of a large cat to carry out this work stone by stone. Anyone who tried to interfere was sprung upon and throttled. Finally the builders decided to erect the church at the site the devil cat had chosen.

CATS AND VAMPIRES

PERHAPS ASSOCIATED WITH the link between cats and witchcraft, or possibly having a quite different origin in the Greek legend of Hecate, was the belief held widely in central Europe in the sixteenth and seventeenth centuries that cats could possess a corpse and turn the dead person into a vampire. Cats were kept out of rooms in which a corpse was laid out, and any cat that wandered in accidentally was chased and killed. In the original vampire legends the vampire not only sucked the blood of its victim but then injected it into a recently dead corpse, thus reviving it and claiming possession. The revived corpse was then equipped to do the devil's work. Until Bram Stoker published *Dracula* in 1897 there was no association between vampires and bats. Traditionally, vampires were either cats or wolves.

END OF THE PERSECUTION

AS THE SEVENTEENTH century came to a close, the obsession with witchcraft in the Church faded as mysteriously as it had begun. The last trial for witchcraft in England was in 1684, and in Scotland in 1722. The notorious witchcraft hysteria in Salem, Massachusetts, which resulted in 20 executions, took place in 1692, but it did not feature witches' cats. The North American view of cats seems to have been more benign than Europe's during this period, perhaps because the one or more cats which crossed the Atlantic with the Mayflower had done sterling work in protecting the settlers' food stores.

CAT FACT:

It has been shown in trials that man-eaters will sometimes not attack if a convincing mask is worn on the back of the head, because cats like to spring from behind, so are fooled.

Top
A cartoon of one of the Chelmsford witches with her cat.

Bottom
Book dating to 1619 describing the trials of supposed witches.

THE
WONDERFVL
DISCOVERIE OF THE
Witchcrafts of *Margaret* and *Phillip*
Flower, daughters of *Joan Flower* neere *Beuer*
Castle: executed at *Lincolne*, *March* 11. 1618.

Who were specially arraigned & condemned before
Sir *Henry Hobart*, and Sir *Edward Bromley*, Judges
of Assize, for confessing themselues actors in the destruction of *Henry*, Lord *Rosse*, with their damnable prac-
tises against others the Children of the Right
Honourable FRANCIS Earle of *Rutland*.

Together with the seuerall Examinations and Confessions of *Anne*
Baker, *Ioan Willimot*, and *Ellen Greene*, Witches in *Leicestershire*.

Printed at London by *G. Eld* for *I. Barnes*, dwelling in the long Walke
neere Christ-Church. 1619.

RAT CATCHERS

ONCE AGAIN, THE cat's place in society was enhanced by a public health disaster. In the early 1700s a sinister visitor began to spread across Europe from central Asia. It was the brown rat, larger than the black rat which was already familiar, more vicious, more cunning, and like its predecessor a carrier of the plague. Plague broke out in Germany in 1707 and in France in 1720. By 1730 shipborne brown rats had carried the plague to England, where it proceeded to drive the black rat to virtual extinction. It was time to welcome the cat again on board ship, in dockyards and harbours, and in city streets.

> **CAT FACT:**
> In wild conditions, small species of cat can live between 10–15 years, while big cats may live between 20–25 years if they are very lucky.

The eighteenth century was to be the age of the Enlightenment when superstition gave way, at least among the educated classes, to reason and cats were among the beneficiaries. In France, country houses were provided with an eighteenth century version of the cat flap (itself said to have been invented by the British scientist Sir Isaac Newton around 1700) which enabled the household cats to come and go as they pleased. Cats began to appear in paintings of Dutch interiors. The cat's popularity in high society was echoed in more humble homes, where it was allowed to move from the outhouse into the warmth of the kitchen.

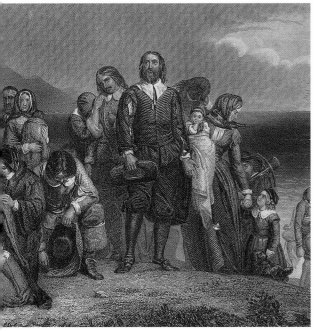

At this time, the cities of Europe and North America – particularly those with Atlantic seaports – were growing at an alarming rate. Building did not keep pace with population growth, and the cities became overcrowded, disease-ridden and filthy. Household scraps – and worse – were thrown into the street, where they would occasionally be shovelled into heaps to await, with luck, collection and disposal. Rats and mice moved in to feast on this waste, and cats were able to follow, winning both easy pickings and human approval. The cat's long night of persecution was over.

Top left
Cats' work on the
Mayflower saved them
from persecution in the
United States.

Bottom left
By the end of the
seventeenth century the
preoccupation with
witchcraft was receding.

Myth and Folklore

I T IS NOT ONLY in connection with witches that cats have, over the centuries and in many different cultures, attracted a body of folklore and superstition. Even today, for example, new mothers are often warned not to let a cat sleep in the same room as a baby for fear that it will smother the child or 'suck its breath', or that the child will choke on the cat's fur.

ADAM, EVE AND LILITH

THE ORIGIN OF this superstition seems to go back to an ancient Hebrew folk tale. According to this, Adam had a wife before Eve whose name was Lilith. She refused to submit to Adam and was therefore banished from the garden of Eden, after which she haunted the earth as a demon. Sephardic Jews believed that Lilith took the form of a giant black cat named El Broosha, which sucked the blood of the newborn.

BUDDHIST BELIEFS

CATS HAD A QUITE different place in the beliefs of one branch of the Buddhist faith practised in southeast Asia. Here, it was thought that on the death of a person who had reached the highest levels of spirituality the soul entered the body of a cat. It remained there until the cat died, when the soul entered Paradise. This belief may be reflected in the appearance of a cat at the feet of some statues of the Buddha, despite the contradictory view of the cat in other Buddhist lore. The more benign view seems to have persisted into the twentieth century. When King Prajadhipok of Siam (now Thailand) was crowned in 1925, a cat took part in the coronation procession as representative of the former king, Rama VI.

Top
Temples, such as this one in Thailand, often feature cats at the feet of the Buddha.

Bottom
A young woman holding her black cat; superstition would argue that she would now die a spinster.

SIMPLE SUPERSTITIONS

AT A MORE HUMBLE level of society, cats have inspired a whole collection of superstitions. From the seventeenth to the nineteenth centuries it was a frequent custom in Britain to wall up the body of a cat – usually mercifully dead, but sometimes alive – in a newly built house, or to place one under the front doorstep, to bring good luck. The country folklore of England was full of cats' tales. It was said that a cat

born in May would bring snakes into the house. Another story was that cats that were sold never made good mousers; the best mousers were always gifts. Girls of marriageable age should take particular care with cats. A young woman who nursed a cat on her knee would never be married, and girls who were fond of cats would die old maids.

But it is as weather forecasters that cats have attracted the largest number of superstitions. These may be an echo of the association of cats with fertility in many ancient cultures, or of the supposed ability of witches and their cats to bring about weather catastrophes. The sayings themselves can be contradictory. For example, one piece of weather lore says that when cats wash their ears it is a sign of rain, but another from the north of England says just the opposite. When a British television programme conducted a survey among its cat-owning viewers to try to settle the matter, the results were inconclusive.

The imminence of rain is the topic of another pair of conflicting sayings. In a poem by Jonathan Swift, the author of *Gulliver's Travels*, he quotes folklore to the effect that when rain threatens cats stop playing and become still and thoughtful. Swift was born and

lived in Ireland, and perhaps this was on Irish observation. Elsewhere in the British Isles it is often believed that if a cat gets excited and unduly playful rain will soon follow.

SPECTRAL CATS

GIVEN CATS' TRADITIONAL association with night and the underworld, it is perhaps surprising that they do not figure more frequently in stories of ghosts. But whereas few districts are without tales of spectral dogs, spectral cats are rare. A feline ghost was, however, said to appear near Chetwynd Hall in Shropshire, England, until it and its ghostly owner were exorcised in the middle of the nineteenth century. The owner was a Madam Pigott who had died in childbirth some 70 years before. She would be seen on moonlit nights in the park of the Hall, sitting at the foot of a tree combing her baby's hair and accompanied by a black cat.

The story of another cat haunting comes from Ropley in Hampshire, England, where about a century ago an old woman often met a cat on the stairs of her cottage or found it sitting by her fire, when it would walk across the room and abruptly disappear. She was not frightened, she told a local historian, because she was convinced it was the ghost of her mother – adding, rather curiously, that she recognised it because it had her mother's way of walking.

> **CAT FACT:**
> The Aztecs of Central America used to worship a jaguar god. Killing a jaguar and wearing its entire skin was thought to bring amazing powers to the wearer.

Top
This woodcut from c.1600 depicts witches with their cats.

Bottom
The body language of cats is said to prognosticate the weather.

Popular Cats

DURING THE EIGHTEENTH century cats became increasingly popular in intellectual circles. This was the age of philosophy, and it seems likely that the cat, which so often seems to be self-contained and sitting in quiet contemplation, suited the personalities of philosophers better than the more extrovert dog. The French philosopher Montaigne even used the example of his cat to pose a philosophical problem.

> **CAT FACT:**
> Measuring up to 2.7 m (8 ft 9 in) in total length, the puma is still classed as one of the 'small cat' species, although it is larger than the cheetah, a big cat species.

LITERARY CAT-LOVERS

'WHEN I PLAY with my cat,' he wrote, 'who knows whether she is not amusing herself with me more than I with her?' The eighteenth century also saw the rise of the salon as the meeting place of the intelligentsia and this was a setting more suited to the placid cat than to the ebullient dog. It must be remembered that at this time dogs were essentially of the country life, hunting or herding.

English literary life in the eighteenth century was also full of cat lovers. Perhaps the best known was Dr Samuel Johnson, the poet, essayist and wit, whose love of his cat Hodge was recorded by his biographer James Boswell. 'I shall never forget,' wrote Boswell, 'the indulgence with which he treated Hodge, his cat;

Top
Dr Samuel Johnson, Boswell and Hodge depicted at home.

for whom he himself used to go out and buy oysters, lest the servants having that trouble should take a dislike to the poor creature. I recollect him one day scrambling up Dr Johnson's breast with much satisfaction, while my friend, smiling and half-whistling, rubbed down his back and pulled him by the tail; and when I observed he was a fine cat, saying, "Why yes, sir, but I have had cats whom I liked better than this"; and then, as if perceiving Hodge to be out of countenance, adding, "but he is a very fine cat, a very fine cat indeed."'

Hearing of a young gentleman 'of good family' who had been going round London shooting cats, Johnson, according to Boswell's account, 'bethought himself of his own favourite cat, and said, "But Hodge shan't be shot; no, no, Hodge shall not be shot."' Boswell himself, however, was no cat lover. He confessed that 'I am, unluckily, one of those who have an antipathy to a cat, so that I am uneasy when in the room with one; and I own, I frequently suffered a good deal from the presence of the same Hodge'.

HORACE WALPOLE AND THE ANGORAS

A LITERARY CONTEMPORARY of Samuel Johnson was Horace Walpole, the youngest son of the first British Prime Minister. He was the author of essays, novels, poetry and books on subjects as varied as painting and gardening, but he is best remembered today for his letters, which were printed in many volumes. He exchanged over 1,600 letters with the French literary hostess Marie du Deffand, who despite going blind ran one of the leading salons in Paris society.

She was a lover of Angora cats, and many of her letters dwell on the virtues and beauties of this breed. She offered a pair to Walpole, but it is not known whether he took up the offer. Walpole also reported to Mme du Deffand the unhappy death of Selima, a cat owned by his friend Thomas Gray, in a goldfish bowl. Selima's unfortunate ending was the subject of a famous poem by Gray.

DEVOTED COMPANIONS

HODGE, SELIMA, the Reverend Doctor John Langbourne and Mme du Deffand's Angoras were clearly thoroughly domesticated cats, so at least in intellectual circles the habit of keeping cats as home companions in the drawing-room rather than as mousers in the outhouses was well established by the middle of the eighteenth century. So too was an interest in different breeds. In 1756 the French naturalist Comte de Buffon illustrated five distinct breeds of cats, including the Angora, in his *Histoire Naturelle*. This was a few years before Mme du Deffand was writing to Walpole about her Angoras.

Some monied owners so loved their cats that they made provision for them in their wills. When John, second Duke of Montagu, died in 1749 he left part of his fortune to several of his cats. As he had no heirs and no close relatives, there was no one to dispute his will. The case of the French harpist Mlle Dupuy was less happy. When she left most of her property to her two cats, a long struggle in the courts ensued, resulting in the will being overturned.

CATS AND ENGLISHMEN

THE ENGLISH PHILOSOPHER Jeremy Bentham was one of the more eccentric eighteenth-century cat lovers. He owned many cats, each of which was given a human-sounding name with a suitable honorific, for example the Reverend Doctor John Langbourne. Arriving for dinner, Bentham's guests would be astonished to be ushered into a room where a number of cats sat at table, each being introduced in turn.

CAT FACT:
In Africa it used to be believed that a stone found in a lions stomach would bring protection from animals. Killing a lion was therefore very important to hunters.

Top
Angora cats were made fashionable in the eighteenth century by socialites such as Marie du Deffand.

Bottom
Portrait of the poet Gray, who eulogised his cat Selima.

Bottom right
The eccentric cat lover Jeremy Bentham.

Cats in Literature

THE FIRST CAT to appear in a leading role in Western literature was probably Puss in Boots (*Le Chat Botte*), who made his debut in a children's story first published in 1697 by the French writer Charles Perrault.

CAT FACT:
In one interesting and bizarre experiment at Chicago Zoo, cubs from a leopard and jaguar pairing (laguars and jeopards) were successfully bred with lions.

THE CHESHIRE CAT
LEWIS CARROLL, THE Oxford don and children's writer Lewis Carroll was the next significant contributor to the place of the cat in literature. In 1865 he published *Alice's Adventures in Wonderland*, featuring the famous Cheshire Cat whose smile showed a number of sharp teeth. Lewis Carroll seems to have softened his attitude to cats, for by 1871 when he published *Alice Through the Looking Glass*, the mother cat Dinah and her two kittens Snowdrop and Kitty, were far more loveable creatures. The hundreds of

Top right
'"We're all mad here," said the Cat. "I'm mad. You're mad."'
From Alice in Wonderland.

Top left
A turn-of-the-century, newspaper illustration of 'Le Chat Botté'.

Bottom
The more amiable Dinah and Alice, two of Lewis Carroll's later protagonists.

TRADITIONAL TALES
PERRAULT WAS ALSO the original author, or at any rate collector, of the stories of *Red Riding Hood*, *Bluebeard* and *The Sleeping Beauty*. All these stories were quickly translated into English and other European languages, and found a place in the continent's nurseries. About 150 years after *Puss in Boots* was first published, it became one of the basic stories used year after year in the British Christmas pantomime tradition.

letters Carroll wrote to his young Oxford friends, mostly small girls, around this time show that he was personally very fond of cats and needed no excuse to work them into the fantasy life that he presented to his correspondents. He wrote, for example, of welcoming stray cats into his rooms and allowing them to sleep between sheets of blotting-paper as blankets with a pen-wiper as a pillow. For their breakfast, he said he provided 'rat-tail jelly and buttered mice'.

C IS FOR CAT

AFTER 1871, WHEN compulsory primary education was introduced for all children in Britain, there was suddenly a huge demand for reading primers. To this day, most English-speaking children learning the alphabet find that C is for cat. Cats also appeared as lovable, cuddly creatures in the nursery rhymes which were, in the nineteenth century, children's first reading. It is from the mid-nineteenth century that such rhymes as 'Pussy cat, pussy cat, where have you been?' and 'Pussy cat, Pussy cat, wilt thou be mine?' can be dated. Earlier children's books showed dogs and farm animals, but not cats.

DICK WHITTINGTON

ONE OF THE STORIES revived for use in nineteenth century schools (and also in pantomime) was that of Dick Whittington and his cat, which had first appeared as a play, now lost, in 1605. It was very loosely based on the true story of Richard Whittington, who was three times Lord Mayor of London in the fifteenth century. In fact, the real Dick Whittington came from a wealthy country family which had made its money in the wool trade. The story presents him as a poor boy who walks to London with his cat to seek his fortune. After many adventures in which the cat brings him good luck, he marries his master's daughter and lives happily and prosperously ever after. Unfortunately, the 'cat' was in real life not an animal but a coal ship plying between Newcastle and London. It is said that in preparing an illustration for an early printed version

of the story an artist showed Whittington with his hand resting on a skull. This was thought to be unsympathetic, and a cat was substituted. But it seems that the whole story of a poor boy who makes good with the help of his cat, usually thought of by the British as being essentially about the money to be made in the city of London, also turns up in Persian, Scandinavian and Italian folklore.

In Britain, the story is now so familiar through children's book re-tellings and pantomime versions that its London setting and the reality of Dick's cat cannot be denied.

MACAVITY THE MYSTERY CAT

AMONG THE MOST famous twentieth century literary cats are those in T. S. Eliot's *Old Possum's Book of Practical Cats*, first published in 1939. Eliot's friends and admirers, used to grappling with his enigmatic and 'difficult' adult poetry, were astonished when this collection of charming and accessible verse appeared, but it immediately became enormously popular. It was reprinted nine times in 10 years, and was followed by an illustrated edition which was equally successful, as well as quickly finding a place in poetry anthologies for schools. Generations of children have now become familiar with the eccentricities of the arch-criminal 'Macavity the Mystery Cat', 'Skimbleshanks the Railway Cat' who haunts the night train and 'Bustopher Jones, the Cat About Town'.

> **CAT FACT:**
> The molar teeth of cats, known as carnassials, have become specialised for eating meat. They shear flesh like a pair of scissors as the cat uses the side of its mouth.

Above
The musical *Cats is one of the longest running West End shows, a testament to the popularity of the cat in the arts.*

Left
The older, and more wealthy, Dick Whittington with his cat.

Cats in Art

I T IS NOT hard to guess at the appeal of cats to an artist. First, there is the graceful form, capable of being shown in a variety of movements and poses each of which is a challenge to the brush or the pencil, the burin or the chisel. Secondly, there is the attraction of a creature which keeps so much of itself to itself, so that its inner life can only be guessed at or suggested by art. Finally, there is the range of situations – as hunter, domestic pet, conversation piece, or even mere decoration – in which the cat can be depicted.

CAT FACT:
There is a noticeable trend with the different subspecies of tiger for them to become progressively larger and paler the further north they live, as an adaptation to climate.

relatively free hand to indulge their fancies. Even at the height of the Roman Catholic persecution of cats, the fifteenth century Italian painter Pinturicchio could not resist introducing a white cat to fill what would have been an awkward space in his Visitation to the Virgin Mary.

When, in the eighteenth century, cats again became respectable, they began to figure in portraiture. French painters in particular were cat lovers, and the tradition continued in the nineteenth century, notably with Manet. Among English painters recording the Victorian life of the countryside, it became almost obligatory to include a cat in, for example, a cottage interior as a symbol of the happy home. It was possibly the care that a queen lavishes on her kittens that made cats seem such appropriate symbols of Victorian family life. In popular art, cats appeared on cushion covers, firescreens and samplers, and porcelain cats graced many a mantelpiece.

By the last years of the century, a new theme was beginning to creep in. Its originator was quite probably Theophile Steinlen, a Swiss painter who settled in Paris and began using cats in his posters advertising foods. This was a time when painters were discovering that commerce was a profitable patron, and the portrayal of cats became markedly more sentimental and anthropomorphic. They were represented as society women, flower-sellers, dancers, babies, dairymaids, domestic servants. The essential nature of the cat was lost under the cloak of sentimentality, a foretaste of what was to come in the twentieth century.

EARLY DEPICTIONS

THE ARTISTS AND craftsmen of Ancient Egypt explored many facets of the feline character, as hunter, goddess and even, sometimes, comedian. In The Cat-Book Poems, early Thai illustrators pursued some of the same themes, as did early Japanese ink and water-colourists and medieval monks in Europe. Cats also appear as incidental illustrations on the roof bosses and misericord seats of medieval churches and cathedrals, the work of craftsmen who were given a

Top
An archetypal, nineteenth-century representation of the cottage home includes the cat in the foreground symbolic of a warm, welcoming abode.

Bottom
Cats became a central feature in eighteenth-century French portraiture.

EDWARD LEAR

EDWARD LEAR, THE English artist, humourist and amiable eccentric who lived from 1812–88, veered between the two extremes in his portrayal of cats. On one hand, he was the author of the enjoyable but sentimental nonsense verse 'The Owl and the Pussycat'. On the other, he left behind a series of realistic but affectionate sketches of his own tabby, Foss. He was so devoted to Foss that when he retired to San Remo in Italy he had his home copied exactly so that Foss would not be disturbed by the move.

POPULAR SUBJECT

A FEATURE OF the late nineteenth century was an explosion of popular art in the form of advertisements, greetings cards, magazine illustrations and showcards, largely as a result of developments in colour printing. Advertising itself was also becoming more sophisticated, but it was concentrated largely on household products from soap to cocoa. What better way to suggest the pleasures of hearth and home than by using a cat?

But these were cats in human roles, and the image of the cat thus became degraded.

One painter who specialised in popular pictures of anthropomorphic cats, and yet combined this with a genuine love of the feline animal, was Louis Wain, who was born in 1860. In 1884 the *Illustrated London News* published the first of the pictures which were to make Wain, in the words of a *Punch* critic, 'the Hogarth of cat life'. Wain's cats, reproduced on countless picture postcards and in illustrated annuals, tended to wear spectacles and bow ties, walk on their hind legs, take afternoon tea and behave like members of the middle class.

Yet despite this, Wain was also capable of accurate and unsentimentalised cat portraits, and he was respected enough in the cat world to become the second President of the British National Cat Club. His progress, or rather regress, as a cat painter is of interest to students of mental illness, for as he slipped into insanity in his later years – he died in 1939 – his cats became more bizarre and frenetic, the cuddly pets of his successful years turning into frazzle-haired, threatening monsters.

Top
An nineteenth-century illustration by Edward Lear depicting the marriage between his owl and pussy cat.

Bottom right
Impressionists, such as Renoir here in Nude Boy with Cat, *continued to include the cat as a subject.*

Cats in Film and Theatre

THERE HAS BEEN no feline equivalent of Rin-Tin-Tin, Lassie, or other dog heroes of the silver screen. Nor is there ever likely to be, for the obvious reason that cats do not, on the whole, take kindly to training and performance. Their movements do, however, lend themselves to the art of the animator, and the best-known film cats have been in cartoons.

CARTOON CATS

THE FIRST CARTOON cat appeared in the 1920s in *Felix the Cat*, but perhaps the most famous film cat is Tom of *Tom and Jerry*, the creation of American animators, William Hanna and Joseph Barbera. The two men met at MGM's animation studios in Hollywood in 1937, and in 1939 produced *Puss Gets the Boot*, featuring a cat and a mouse. Tom and Jerry had been born, and went on to appear in over 200 films. Critics have seen overtones of cruelty and sadism in Tom and Jerry cartoons, and certainly no one would watch the films for accurate portrayals of cat behaviour, but they have given innocent amusement to generations of children. The same cannot be said of the X-rated *Fritz the Cat* of the 1960s. Another cat cartoon much enjoyed in its time was the 1948 short, *The Cat that Hated People*, about a New York cat that tires of city noise and rockets to the moon for some peace and quiet. But it finds the moon even noisier and is glad to return.

WALT DISNEY

WALT DISNEY HAS also contributed to cat filmography. The 1963 film *The Incredible Journey* was the story of a Bull Terrier, a Labrador and a Siamese cat, Tao, who travelled 400 km (250 miles) across Canada to rejoin their owners. *The Cat from Outer*

Nº 1482.

6ᵗʰ EDITION

ISSUED IN CONJUNCTION WITH THE "FELIX THE CAT" CARTOONS
APPEARING EXCLUSIVELY IN Pathé's "EVE & EVERYBODY'S FILM REVIEW."

FELIX KEPT ON WALKING

WORDS BY Eᵈ·E·BRYANT

MUSIC BY
Copyright. HUBERT·W·DAVID   Price 6ᵈ net

Lawrence Wright

Space, released in 1978, was about a mysterious but super-intelligent cat whose spaceship develops engine trouble, forcing it to land on earth. Probably the best-known Disney cat adventure is *The Aristocats*, which appeared in 1970. Duchess and her kittens Marie, Toulouse and Berlioz are up against their mistress's wicked butler who has overheard her making her will in favour of the cats. He abandons them, hoping to come into the fortune, but is foiled by Duchess and her family with the help of Thomas O'Malley, a good-hearted alley cat, and an assortment of other animals.

STARRING ROLES

REAL CATS HAVE made a number of appearances in films, but only in bit parts. A white Persian called Solomon played a slightly sinister role in the James Bond film *Diamonds are Forever*, and in *Breakfast at Tiffany's*, Audrey Hepburn shared her apartment with a 'cat with no name.' In *The Third Man*, a cat plays a more major role. In post-war Vienna, the criminal Harry Lime disappears, having faked his death, and is being sought not only by the military police but also by his old friend, played by Joseph Cotten. He is betrayed when his girlfriend's cat, having escaped from her apartment, sidles up to him in the darkness of the Vienna night.

Just as cats usually reach the cinema screen in cartoon form, they are represented on stage by humans dressed in cat costumes. (Backstage cats are another matter. There are many real-life versions of T. S. Eliot's 'Gus, the Theatre Cat'. London theatre cats have included Ambrose at the Drury Lane Theatre, Plug at the Adelphi and Bouncer at the Garrick). Puss in Boots and Dick Whittington's cat became established Christmas pantomime characters in the late nineteenth century and continue to be popular.

THEATRICAL CATS

UNTIL THE 1970s, the best-known representation of cats on stage was probably in Tchaikovsky's ballet *The Sleeping Beauty*, based on Charles Perrault's children's stories and first performed in St Petersburg in 1889. Its characters include Puss in Boots and a White Cat. The White Cat enters in the wedding procession, sitting on a cushion and washing herself. Puss in Boots is charmed by her and courts her in a pas-de-deux which is one of the highlights of the ballet. Tchaikovsky chose the oboe to imitate the cats' voices. *The Sleeping Beauty* was a critical flop when it was first staged, but after Tchaikovsky's death in 1893 it was recognised as a masterpiece of its kind and went on to have a profound influence on twentieth century ballet.

Cats – or rather singers representing cats – have even appeared in opera. In 1925 Ravel wrote a short one-act opera *L'Enfant et les Sortileges* (The Charmed Child) featuring a cat duet, a brilliant and realistic piece of orchestration.

Without doubt, the greatest feline triumph on the theatrical stage has been in the musical *Cats*, based on T. S. Eliot's *Old Possum's Book of Practical Cats* with music by Andrew Lloyd Webber. First staged in London in 1981, it appeared with great acclaim in the United States and has been played all over the world to delighted audiences. Eighteen years after its debut, it was still showing in London.

Opposite
Cats have appeared in eclectic roles and representations; from Tom and Felix the cartoon cats to screen protagonists.

This page
Greene's The Third Man (left), Puss-in-Boots (bottom left) and Cats (bottom right) – all feature the cat as star.

> **CAT FACT:**
> The first known man-eater was a lion. It is portrayed as a line drawing carved onto an Assyrian ivory panel dating from c. 800 BC.

Cats in the Twentieth Century

I N THE 1990S, the cat overtook the dog as Britain's most popular domestic pet to achieve a position it had held for some decades in the United States. For practical reasons, it is not hard to understand why. In most families today, the greatest pressure is on time. Whether both parents work, or a single parent is coping with conflicting demands, a pet that can be left at home all day or allowed to wander in and out at will has obvious advantages over one that has to be walked once or twice daily. Also, new houses and gardens tend to be smaller, and a cat can be kept quite satisfactorily even in a small apartment. Where children are concerned, cats are seen as 'safer' pets.

CAT FACT:
The largest species of cat is the Siberian tiger, which attains an average total length of 3.15 m (10 ft 5 in), and is 1.07 m (42 in) tall at the shoulder.

MEDIA ATTENTION

WHILE DOGS HAVE come in for some bad publicity in the twentieth century, cats have had a good press. British newspaper readers were absorbed for many weeks in 1997 by the question of the whereabouts of Humphrey, the former resident cat at the Prime Minister's official residence, 10 Downing Street. It was rumoured that Cherie Blair, the wife of the incoming Prime Minister, had taken objection to Humphrey and had him banished – or worse. Could it be that the British had elected a Prime Minister, Tony Blair, whose wife was a cat-hater? The nation held its breath until it was revealed that Humphrey was thought to have reached retirement age and the frail felid had been found a home in the suburbs, away from the hurly-burly of central London. Meanwhile, Mrs Blair felt bound to assure the nation, through the Downing Street press office, of her affection for cats.

An earlier Civil Service cat had even more long-lasting fame. His name was Peter, and he was the official cat at the London headquarters of the Home Office. Living on a grant of £6.50 per annum (twice what his predecessor had been paid), he was on the staff from 1949 until his death in 1964. Peter enjoyed the occasional outing on television, and his various exploits in the course of duty were fully reported in the papers.

Above
Cats' independence and ability to 'walk themselves' makes them a desirable pet in today's busy lifestyle.

Right
Humphrey, the Downing Street cat, poses for the cameras in 1997.

POPULAR PETS

UNFORTUNATELY FOR DOGS, the tide of public opinion has swung against them in recent years. Horror stories about dogs that turn on their owners' children, medical worries about infection from dogs' faeces, and bye-laws that require dogs to be kept on leads in so many places, and their droppings to be gathered up and disposed of, have all played a part in making the more placid, clean and independent cat a more desirable alternative.

COMMERCIAL STARS

CATS APPEARING ON television, whether in commercials or in shows such as the BBC's Blue Peter and NBC's Today, also attract a public following. Perhaps Britain's best-known television cat was Arthur, whose star turn for many years before he died, aged nearly 17, in 1976 was to scoop cat food out of the tin with his paw to show his keenness on the product. For some time it was a well-kept secret that Arthur was in fact a female originally called Samantha. The High Court action that arose over the question of Arthur's ownership would probably have been dismissed as a publicity stunt if he had been a human television star, but it was serious enough and deliberated upon with all the solemnity of which British justice is capable. Writers of fan letters to Arthur, of whom there were thousands, received a personal paw-signed reply by courtesy of the cat food manufacturers.

Arthur's 'trick' looked simple enough, but no doubt it took many hours to record it on film. Cats can be a camera crew's nightmare. In 1992 a crew needing about 30 minutes of film to illustrate various aspects of cats' behaviour for a video visited a cattery on what they expected to be a straightforward, simple job. In the end, they used 35 hours of tape before they had captured the images they wanted.

THE PADDINGTON STATION CAT

ANOTHER LONDON CAT caught the public's imagination in the early 1970s. This was Tiddles, a stray kitten who was found bedraggled and hungry at London's Paddington Station, adopted by the attendant at the ladies' lavatory, Miss June Wilson and installed comfortably in Miss Wilson's 'den'. After the story appeared in the papers, Tiddles received offers of a new home, and indeed one of these was taken up until he made it clear that he preferred the comforts and no doubt the superior hunting facilities of the station. After that he settled down, the happy recipient of fan letters, requests for photographs, tender enquiries from passengers and a deluge of presents each Christmas. In 1986, at the age of 16 and tipping the scales at 11.8 kg (26 lb), Tiddles was reported to be still enjoying life to the full.

Top
Sam, the Post Office cat, at home on a mail van.

Bottom
Perhaps advertising's most successful cat Arthur.

The Naming of Cats

THERE IS ONE question that every owner of a new cat has to face. It can cause family arguments and even sleepless nights. It is: What shall we call it? The naming of cats, as the poet T. S. Eliot wrote, is a difficult matter. So difficult a matter, indeed, that whole books have been written on the subject.

LITERARY NAMES

PERHAPS THE DIFFICULTY arises because in naming a cat (as in naming a baby) we make a public statement about ourselves. If we have literary pretensions, we might name a cat Hodge after Doctor Johnson, Blatherskite after Mark Twain or Grimalkin after Christina Rossetti. On the other hand, we might quail at the thought of calling for Blatherskite or Grimalkin up and down the street. Film buffs might like to commemorate Orangey, the feline star of *Breakfast at Tiffany's* (known as Cat in the film) and a number of other films of the 1950s and '60s, or Solomon, the cat in the James Bond films *You Only Live Twice* and *Diamonds are Forever*. If you have a taste for the more trivial aspects of political history you might choose Slippers after President Theodore Roosevelt's cat, Socks after Chelsea Clinton's black and white shorthair, or Humphrey, after the cat who ruled 10 Downing Street during Margaret Thatcher's and John Major's premiership. We might not want to seem so unimaginative as to call our cats Tiddles or Tom. Then again, a name that seems amusing or clever now might not seem so in 10 years' time. A cat's name is for life.

CAT FACT:

The tail of the African golden cat is highly valued by the pygmies of Cameroon. It is worn as a talisman for good luck while they hunt for elephants.

Top left
Solomon in You Only Live Twice.

Top right
Enjoying champagne, Orangey in Breakfast at Tiffany's.

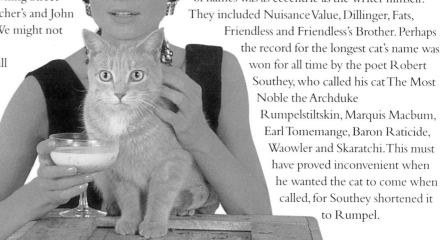

DISTINGUISHED TITLES

FLORENCE NIGHTINGALE NAMED her cats after distinguished public figures of her time, like Bismarck, Cavour, Gladstone and Disraeli. As she is said to have owned about 60 Persians at one time, finding names to add to this roll of honour must have been difficult.

Winston Churchill, perhaps not surprisingly in view of his patriotism, named the cat that sat out the London Blitz with him Nelson. Charles Dickens named his cat, less appropriately, William; it had to change to Williamina when it produced a litter of kittens. Another cat-loving author was Ernest Hemingway, who at one time had upwards of 50 cats at his home in Key West, Florida. His choice of names was as eccentric as the writer himself. They included Nuisance Value, Dillinger, Fats, Friendless and Friendless's Brother. Perhaps the record for the longest cat's name was won for all time by the poet Robert Southey, who called his cat The Most Noble the Archduke Rumpelstiltskin, Marquis Macbum, Earl Tomemange, Baron Raticide, Waowler and Skaratchi. This must have proved inconvenient when he wanted the cat to come when called, for Southey shortened it to Rumpel.

COMMON NAMES

THEN THERE ARE the traditional cat's names. Many of these seem, like children's names, to move in and out of fashion, but Mickey, Tiger (or Tigger), Charlie, Max (or Maxie) and Sam (or Sammy) seem to be hardy perennials. An American survey in 1994 found that the most popular cats' names in the United States were Smokey for males and Samantha for females, followed by Tiger and Misty respectively. But these commonplace names are not for owners who like a challenge or who think their cats need suitable honorifics. One owner in the latter category was the nineteenth century English philosopher Jeremy Bentham, whose cat was originally called Langbourne. In recognition of its good behaviour it was knighted as Sir John Langbourne and later in life it took Holy Orders and became the Reverend Sir John Langbourne, D. D.

DISTINCTIVE NAMES

TO TURN TO MORE practical matters, if you are going to allow your cat outside it will need a name that is distinctive, and that you can call outside without dying of shame if the neighbours hear you. If you have two cats, their names should be different in sound. These considerations apart, there are really no limits to the naming of cats, and there is the bonus that, unlike many children, cats will not be embarrassed by their names when they grow up.

Inspiration may, of course, come from the cat itself. One London family called their cat Biggles, after the fictional flying ace created by Captain W. E. Johns, because of its habit of launching itself through the air at anyone who sat in its favourite chair. The French owners of a mischievous kitten named it Non-non because that was what they always seemed to be saying to it. The neck colouring of a black and white tom earned it the name Vicar, and the owner of another mischievous kitten called it Crouton because, she said, it always seemed to be in the soup.

Top
Proving that he is still alive, Humphrey poses for the cameras.

Bottom left
This cat graced the pavement in Downing Street in 1939.

Early Cat Shows

THE WORLD OF CAT shows is a highly intense, highly competitive and extremely interesting one, and its fascination lies almost as much in observing the human participants as in admiring the feline ones.

THE FIRST SHOWS

THE FIRST CAT show on record was held in 1598 at St Giles Fair in Winchester, England. How the cats were judged, or by what criteria, is not known. In the United States, shows of farmers' Maine Coons were sometimes held in the nineteenth century as one of the attractions at county fairs. But the first cat show in the modern sense was held at Crystal Palace in south London in 1871.

Once owners started to breed cats for their appearance and trueness to type, it was natural that they should want to check their own efforts against those of others. The first British cat show was the brainchild of Harrison Weir, a writer, artist, and noted cat lover. He not only organised the show at what was then one of London's leading public venues, but he also wrote the standards by which the entries should be judged and was one of the three judges. Weir later incorporated his work into a standard manual for cat show organisers, *Our Cats*.

In this, he recalled that he had 'conceived the idea that it would be well to hold 'Cat Shows' so that the different breeds, colours, markings etc. might be more carefully attended to and the domestic cat sitting in front of the fire would then possess a beauty and an attractiveness to its owner unobserved and unknown because uncultivated before.' Weir had been distressed by the 'long ages of neglect, ill-treatment and absolute cruelty' that cats had suffered, and his main objective in organising the first show was the welfare of cats, not to provide an arena for the competitiveness of their owners. He was later to resign from the cat fancy over this issue.

The Crystal Palace show attracted thousands of cat lovers, many of whom returned to the provinces to organise their own shows on similar lines. From the start, most of these shows made a token attempt at democracy, instituting classes for ordinary domestic cats alongside those for the more exotic breeds. There were, at some shows, even classes for 'Cats Belonging to Working Men', with lower entry fees but also, unfortunately, lower prize monies. Money was never the object of showing a cat, however; then, as now, the amount was trivial. The attraction lay partly in competition and partly in the opportunity to exchange information and advice with like-minded owners. Even today, the element of showmanship at British shows is very muted.

CAT FANCY SPREADS

IN THE UNITED STATES, the first national cat show was held at Madison Square Gardens, New York – a venue equal in importance to London's Crystal Palace – in 1895, organised by an Englishman named James T. Hyde. As in Britain, it preceded the setting-up of a cat fancy organisation and was instrumental in inspiring fanciers to do so. Soon, cat shows had spread throughout the English-speaking world and were then taken up in continental Europe.

The development of cat shows and the mechanics of showing have diverged in different countries, partly because of geographical circumstances. For example, in Britain shows are normally one-day affairs because travelling distances are relatively small. In North America and continental Europe, shows tend to be larger and often last for two days. In continental Europe, many exhibitors travel to the major shows in other countries under the supervision of the FIFé.

BRITISH PARTICIPATION

SINCE 1902, RABIES, regulations enforcing six months' quarantine for animals brought into Britain have prevented the exchange of show cats between Britain and elsewhere, and so the British cat show world has been to some extent isolated. At the time of writing, abolition of the British quarantine regulations is being proposed. If this were to become law, it may be possible that the British cat fancy would play a fuller part in European cat affairs, including the opportunity to take part in such prestigious shows as that of the Cat-Club de Paris.

SHOWING ROUND THE WORLD

THE MAIN DIFFERENCE between shows in different countries is in the judging procedures. Broadly speaking, in North America, Japan and most European countries, judging takes place in a judging ring away from the pens where the cats are housed, and owners and other members of the public are allowed to watch. In Britain and most Commonwealth countries, the judges visit the pens and owners and others are excluded until judging is over. Neither system has any particular advantage, except perhaps that the North American system lends a little more public excitement to the proceedings, and indeed there is more razzmatazz about North American shows than at their more sober British counterparts.

> **CAT FACT:**
> The phenomenon of man-eating has been recorded in Asia and Africa. The cat species known to have turned man-eater are lion, tiger and leopard.

Opposite, top
Spectators admiring the cats at the 1871 Crystal Palace Cat Show.

Opposite, bottom
An 1871 illustration depicting the prize cats at the Crystal Palace cat show.

This page
These picture of the National Cat Club Show illustrate the extent to which shows have grown, with hundreds of exhibitors taking part.

The Cat Fancy

CLUBS AND ASSOCIATIONS of cat owners arose out of the interest that grew up in the nineteenth century in distinctive breeds of cats.

NINETEENTH CENTURY CLUBS

At first, the main interest was in Persians (now known officially in Britain as Longhairs), still the most popular breed in the cat fancy today. Owners found that by careful breeding they could improve the qualities of their cats in terms of stature, coat colour and general well-being.

This was a matter of observation, for the work of Gregor Mendel on heredity, although carried out in the middle of the nineteenth century, had not yet reached the scientific community, far less the general public. Breeders began to keep records of their matings through the generations, and gradually there became a need for some central body to regulate breed identification.

NATIONAL CAT CLUB

CAT SHOWS WERE already regular events when, in 1887, the National Cat Club was founded in London to promote the breeding of pedigree cats and organise shows. Its first President was the writer and artist Harrison Weir, who had organised Britain's first national cat show 16 years earlier, but he soon resigned because he felt that members were more interested in winning prizes than in his major aim of promoting the welfare of cats. He was replaced as President by the artist Louis Wain. But disagreement continued to dog

Top right
Portrait of Harrison Weir, who first introduced cat shows to Britian.

Top left
Persians are officially known in Britain as Longhairs.

the cat fancy. In 1898 an aristocratic breeder, Lady Marcus Beresford, founded a rival organisation, The Cat Club, said to include among its membership 'some of the most important people in the land'. Despite this, it foundered five years later but was followed by yet another group, the Cat Fanciers' Association.

CAT FANCY IS FOUNDED

AT LAST, A meeting was called in 1910 to try to unite the various British cat fancy interests, and the result was the establishment of the Governing Council of the Cat Fancy (GCCF). Its functions were (and are still) to act as the registration body for cats and cat pedigrees, to approve and classify cat breeds, to approve shows organised by constituent cat clubs, and generally to promote the welfare of cats. This arrangement allows for the overall supervision of breeding and registration while leaving some independence to the many regional and specialist breed cat clubs which, among other things, actually organise cat shows. Except for the annual Supreme Show, the biggest show in the British cat-showing calendar, which is organised by the GCCF, the GCCF only licences the shows and lays down the rules by which they are run.

In 1983 there was a further development on the British scene when the Cat Association of Britain (CA) was founded. This maintains a separate registry from the Governing Council and is more closely linked with the Fédération Internationale Féline d'Europe (FIFé), the major body governing the cat fancy in mainland western Europe.

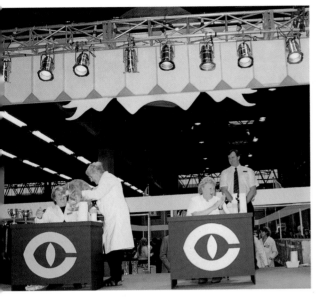

Although it might look at first sight as if the proliferation of American cat fancy organisations makes life needlessly difficult for American owners, there are some advantages. It is true that for a cat to be shown it must be registered with the particular association approving the show and must therefore live in that association's area. In practice, however, given a country the size of the United States this does not noticeably restrict access to shows, and in any case some of the larger shows, such as the annual gathering at Flushing, New York, are jointly sponsored by several associations. The upside is that the American system allows for a greater diversity of shows and a more liberal attitude to the acceptance of new breeds.

The cat fancy is well organised in most westernised countries. In Australia, as in the United States, the situation is complicated by the vast area, and each of the seven states has at least one cat fancy organisation. However, each recognises the others' registrations and show rules. New Zealand has only one organisation, the New Zealand Cat Fancy, with headquarters in Nelson. In Europe, the FIFé has member organisations in 12 countries and recognises only the registrations of those members.

AMERICAN ASSOCIATIONS

THE CAT FANCY in the United States has a more complex structure and history, partly for geographical reasons. The first organisation in the field was the American Cat Club, which opened its registry in 1896 but was later disbanded. The oldest United States organisation still in existence is the Cat Fanciers' Association (CFA), founded in 1906. There are also the American Cat Association, the American Cat Fanciers' Association, the Cat Fanciers' Federation, the Crown Cat Fanciers' Association, the National Cat Fanciers' Association, the International Cat Association and the United Cat Federation. Canada has its own Canadian Cat Association.

CAT FACT:
Man-eaters are usually female cats in search of easy prey to feed their cubs. Others are injured or sickly cats unable to catch their usual prey species.

CAT FACT:
The small incisor teeth of cats are used to remove skin from animals before eating begins. They are also used to nibble at parasites such as fleas and ticks in their fur.

Top
Steward takes cat from one judge to the next at the Supreme Show.

Bottom left
This Burmese kitten wins supreme exhibit at the Supreme cat show.

Showing Cats

I FYOU VENTURE on to this scene and intend to show cats of your own, you must expect to serve a long apprenticeship, learning the language and practices of the cat fancy, appreciating the high standards that are set and getting to grips with the subtleties of what is, after all, a highly specialised field

LEARNING ABOUT CAT FANCY

CAT SHOWS ARE also the places to go to find out about breeds and to study what peaks of perfection beautiful cats can attain, even if you do not intend to enter the lists yourself. It is always helpful to take along with you someone who knows something about the cat world and can show you the finer points that divide the winners from the rest – something that, in a hall full of excellent cats, you may not, as a beginner, be able to see for yourself. Most cat owners will be happy to talk about their exhibits, but you will find them more relaxed after the judging.

DIFFERENT SHOWS

CAT SHOWS ARE organised at a variety of different levels, from the informal shows of local cat clubs through individual breed shows to the big national events like Britain's National Cat Show, held each year in December, or the Empire Cat Show in New York, where literally thousands of cats can be seen. In Britain, cat shows, including even the National Cat Show, are one-day events, but in North America, Europe and elsewhere they often last for two days which means that overnight accommodation for both cats and owners must be arranged in advance. Only British-domiciled cats may be shown in Britain because of quarantine regulations, but elsewhere foreign exhibitors often travel abroad with their cats for the major shows.

Top
Learning the features that constitute a winning cat is a long process.

Bottom left
Owner holds her winning cat at this non-pedigree cat show.

Bottom right
Overhead view of the National Cat Show, the pens and sections can be clearly seen.

RULES AND REGULATIONS

ALL CAT SHOWS follow the same general rules of one or other of the cat fancy organisations; but the road to the highest honours is tightly structured. For example, in Britain, shows are licensed either by the Governing Council of the Cat Fancy (GCCF), the oldest cat fancy organisation in the world whose roots go back to 1871, or by the newer Cat Association of Britain (CAB), founded in 1983. At GCCF-licensed shows, judging takes place at the show pens in private, the results being announced when judging is over. The CAB follows the North American 'open ring' system in which the cats are brought to the judging hall to be judged, and the results announced in front of the exhibitors and spectators. Show practice in other countries follows slight variations in one of these two patterns.

THE GCCF

THE MAJOR DIFFERENCE between the two systems as far as the organisation of the show is concerned is that in the GCCF system, where the show pens are also the pens from which the cats are judged, strict anonymity is preserved. The only distinguishing mark allowed on the pen is a card

carrying the pen number. All the equipment that the owner brings – food and water bowl, litter tray and a blanket for the cat to rest on – must be white and the pen must be left undecorated. Unless this rule is followed, the cat will simply not be entered into the judging.

THE CAB

THIS STRICT ANONYMITY is not necessary in the CAB or North American (and most European countries') system, because the judge will not see the pen in which the cat spends the show day. Cats are transferred to special pens in the ring before judging. Consequently, the pens where they rest before judging, and where they return afterwards, may be highly decorated and the cats' owners may be identified. Many owners go to immense trouble to give their cats an attractive setting for the day, with drapes or curtains to tone with the cat's colouring, matching food bowls and litter trays, photographs of the cat's parents, and rosettes and ribbons celebrating past wins decorating the pen walls.

Top left
Outside Britain cats are taken to the show ring to be judged instead of from their cages.

Top right
In the United States contestants like to decorate their cats' pens.

Bottom left
A cat pen in Britain should conform to the rules which state that all items in the cage must be white with no name tags.

CHAMPIONSHIP LADDERS

IN BRITAIN, POTENTIAL Champion cats normally start their careers at sanction shows, where their owners can try them out for show behaviour and match them against the competition. From there they proceed up the ladder of full-scale Championship shows. Here, they have to receive three challenge certificates under three different judges at three different shows to be eligible to enter for a Championship. If they win three Champion challenge certificates, again under three different judges at three shows, they become Champions and can then be entered in the Grand Champion class. The Grand Champions are the aristocrats of the show ring, the cream of the feline world.

In mainland Europe, there is a similar system but cats can go on to another ladder of achievement to become International Champions and Grand Champions. In North America, details vary between the different cat fancy organisations, but there is no requirement that Champions should have qualified at different shows. The award of Grand Champion is based on the points gained at a number of shows, and it is therefore an elimination contest.

The structures described above are for entire (unneutered) cats, and of course the rewards for the breeders of winners, apart from the pleasure of owning a prize-winning cat, come either from fees paid for the service of a stud tom or from the sale of kittens whose sire or dam has Championship status. There is a similar but separate structure for neuters using the term Premier rather than Champion.

CAT FACT:
Cats have relatively few teeth compared with other carnivores. This is because they have such short muzzles. Most cat species have 16 upper and 14 lower teeth.

Top right
Children are encouraged to enter shows so that they can learn from more experienced owners.

Bottom left
This Persian has won best cat in show at the Madison Square Garden International Cat Show.

Bottom right
This Japanese Bobtail has won best of breed at Madison Square Garden.

EXEMPTION SHOWS

BELOW THE LEVEL of the sanction show, the bottom rung of the Championship or Premier ladder, are exemption shows which are less formal and more friendly but nevertheless highly competitive, and follow the same general rules. In North America, there are no exemption shows as such but informal shows are often held as part of county fairs or on other community occasions. Awards in these do not carry any significance for Championship status.

CHAMPIONSHIP SHOWS

CATS ENTERED FOR pedigree classes must have been registered as kittens with the appropriate organisation. There are also usually classes for non-pedigree cats which are particularly useful as a training ground for young owners whose pets are sometimes judged in a class of their own. The International Cat Association in the United States and the Cat Association of Britain allow the registration of non-pedigree cats which can then compete for Championship status under a variety of titles. These non-pedigree classes have seen the debut of many leading enthusiasts in the cat

fancy, and provide a valuable link between the specialised world of breeders and the ordinary cat-loving public. All cat fancy organisations regard the welfare of cats in general as equal in importance to their functions as pedigree registration bodies and controllers of the show world and for this reason welcome the participation of ordinary pet owners.

Details of forthcoming shows appear in the cat fancy press and can also be obtained from the sponsoring organisations. Better still, you could join a local cat club or breed association, which would make sure that you receive advance information. Membership is not usually conditional on owning a cat of the appropriate breed, but some shows are closed except to members of associations or affiliated bodies. Others welcome competitors from outside their membership, but they may not be eligible for the top prizes. The benefits of membership often include reduced entry fees and other concessions. For the beginner, there is also the bonus of mixing with experienced breeders and exhibitors and picking up a great deal of useful information and guidance.

HOW TO ENTER

THE FIRST STEP in entering a cat in a show is to send off (with a stamped addressed envelope) to the show secretary for a schedule and entry form. This will list the classes into which the show is to be organised and give the conditions for each class. For example, there may be classes for kittens and cats of specific ages, for neuters, for cats which have reached a particular stage in the Championship hierarchy and for cats which have not previously won an award. The schedule will also include the show rules such as a ban on exhibiting females within a stated period, usually two months, after kittening. For pedigree classes, the registration details of your cat will be needed. Make a note of the closing date for entries, which is usually some weeks, and may even be months in advance of the show, and check the rules of the show carefully.

Send off the entry form with the appropriate fee in good time. Organisers normally require a stamped addressed envelope for acknowledgement of your entry. This acknowledgement may include your entry number or other details, or you may receive these when you arrive at the show. If you have any queries, check with the show secretary before sending in the form.

Top
Shows allow owners and new competitors to exchange information about breeds.

Bottom
Breeders sometimes sell their pedigree kittens through cat shows.

PREPARATIONS

BEFORE THE SHOW date, you will usually (except for very local shows) receive various documents which you will need to take with you. The package may also include more show regulations; for example, it is sometimes a condition that the tips of the cat's claws should be trimmed for the show (but no show organisers will allow cats that have been de-clawed to

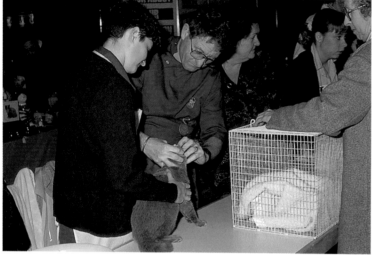

Top
Cat being vetted in to ensure that it is healthy.

Bottom right
Some cats dislike grooming and it is unfair to subject cats to showing if they do not like the process.

take part). You must also make sure that your cat's vaccinations are up to date and that you have the certificate or vet's card to prove it. Your cat's general health must be good enough to stand up to a veterinary inspection, for if it does not pass the 'vetting-in' procedure it will not be allowed in the hall. If any health problem should crop up at the last minute – a runny nose or discharging eyes, for example – you will have to withdraw your entry and let the show secretary know.

THE SHOW EXPERIENCE

THE EXPERIENCE OF showing is quite different for cats from that of dogs. The best show dogs are exhibitionists which enjoy the atmosphere of the show and the opportunity to show their paces in front of an audience. Much also depends on the ability of the owner to bring out the best in the dog. The situation in the cat show world is in sharp contrast. There, on the day of the show the cat stands on its own merits, and the owner's efforts have been put in beforehand. Experienced show cats are fairly phlegmatic about the whole thing, showing neither pleasure nor displeasure in the proceedings.

However, not every cat takes to the show world. Some dislike the bathing and intensive grooming that goes into the preparation. Others dislike the travel, and others again never take to the atmosphere of the show itself. There is no point in inflicting misery on these cats, which in any case will never win any awards because a stressed cat is not a cat in good condition. If you are still determined to show, the answer is to buy a kitten and train it for the show bench by getting it used to being handled by strangers, intensively groomed and travelling for long distances.

Alternatively, it is possible to obtain great enjoyment from the world of cat shows without ever exhibiting. Organising and staffing a show is a very labour-intensive process and there is always room for another spare pair of hands, even if only to staff the entrance and check tickets and exhibitors or to carry out backstage duties arranging the pens and preparing the hall.

ADMINISTRATION

THE KEY PERSONNEL at a show are the judges, stewards and clerks. Judges are always experts in one or more particular breeds, and will have been breeding and showing that breed successfully for several years. The process of qualifying as a judge varies between different associations. Some have written and practical

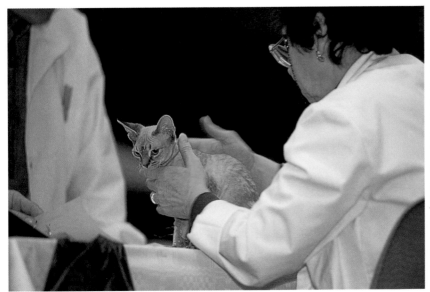

JUDGING

AFTER THE JUDGING of the individual classes, the show proceeds to its climax as the 'Best in Show', 'Best of Breed', 'Best of the Best' or similar titles are judged. This is a collective decision, made by three or five experienced judges who each examine the cats and then vote. Although they have the comfort of sharing the responsibility, these judges are faced with the task of

examinations together with interviews to assess the candidate's knowledge. Others rely on continuous assessment of a judge's work through years of training, perhaps first as a steward and then as a 'probationary' judge.

Judging at a show is highly demanding. The judge knows nothing of the cat on the bench except that it must have acquired the required minimum of points or certificates to be entered for a particular class. Cats arrive at the show bench anonymously and their owners are not identified. The judge has only a limited amount of time to inspect the cat and rank it against the others that have been seen. He or she will make notes and, when the judging of the whole class is over, compare the assessments before announcing the winner

choosing from among the show's top cats between which the differences in quality will be minimal.

Judges are assisted in their task by stewards and clerks. The steward is in charge of the judge's trolley which is moved from pen to pen. In Britain, the steward takes each cat out of its pen in turn and holds it on the trolley while the judge examines it. After each cat has been returned to its pen, the trolley and the steward's hands are disinfected. In North America and some European countries, the judge holds the cat up for examination. The clerk's job is to prepare the judge's book beforehand with the numbers of each entrant, note the judge's comments and award of points, and to act as a runner between the judge and the show secretary when the winners have been decided.

No owner or member of the public may speak to the judges before the competition is over, but then most judges are willing to discuss their assessments with owners and give advice for future shows.

Top
Cats should be accustomed to being handled from a young age if they are to be shown.

Bottom
Winner of best Burmese adult and best Burmese exhibit at the National Cat Club Show.

Show Standards

THE BASIC DOCUMENTS which govern the world of pedigree cats are the standards which cat fancy organisations in every country lay down for each breed which they recognise.

STANDARDS

STANDARDS DESCRIBE the general appearance of the breed, and then take each part of the anatomy in turn, prescribing certain features such as, for example, the slant of the eyes, the size of the ears or the length of the tail. The coat is also described in detail, noting its texture and quality, and coat colouring is defined. Some colour varieties require coat markings to be of a particular type and density, sometimes (as with tortoiseshell-and-whites, for example) the required proportions of different colours in the coat, and sometimes the positioning of the colouring, are stated. The standard also notes which eye colours are permitted, how the tail should be marked and the extent of colourpointing in appropriate breeds and varieties. Some standards also note faults, such as a squint in Siamese or a kinked tail in virtually all breeds.

Top right
Judge examining a cat's face, ensuring that its features are up to the breed's standard.

Top left
Profile of a lilac Burmese's head.

Bottom right
The breed standard can state the exact type of colouring and hair type that is required of a particular cat.

PERFECT STANDARDS

THE STANDARD IS, in fact, a description of a perfect specimen of a particular breed and colour variety for show purposes. There are of course no perfect specimens of any breed, but all the cats exhibited in a breed class at a major show will be very close to perfection. For this reason, it is always a good idea for a novice to go to shows in the company of an experienced fancier who can point out the subtleties of quality that lead to a judge's decision, and getting to know experienced fanciers is one of the advantages of joining a local cat club or association. It should be emphasised that the standard is not necessarily the description of a prize-winning cat, because other factors outside the standard could influence a judge's opinion. A cat might, for example, match the standard exactly but might not have a suitable temperament for showing, or it might have a health problem. To take an extreme example, a cat may bite the judge. With some but not all judges, this would disqualify it – and the judge has the last word.

THE THREE CS

THE MAIN PURPOSES of standards are to lay down physical criteria for breeders and exhibitors to work to and a guide for judges at shows. Generally speaking, what standards have to say about the ideal cat in each breed can be whittled down to the 'three C's': colour, coat and conformation.

A cat described as blue has to be blue within the standard's definition, although one breed's blue may not be the same as another's; there are, of course, no truly blue cats, and one standard might require bluish-grey and another bluish-white. As for coat, standards lay down the length and nature required. It would be no good exhibiting for show a short-haired Persian, if such a cat existed, or a British Shorthair without the dense coat which is one of the leading characteristics of the breed. Similarly, all cats of a specific breed have a similar body type; no Siamese is cobby, and no Russian Blue is svelte. Once these aspects of the cat are established, standards go into the finer points of each breed such as eye colour, markings, ear shape and so on.

ORGANISATION STANDARDS

EVERY ORGANISATION THAT provides registration services for pedigree cats writes its own standards, which often vary in detail from country to country and even, in the United States, from one organisation to another. It should be noted that the information given in the 'Breeds' section of this book is summarised, and for the fullest detail reference should be made to the standard of the organisation under whose sponsorship it is intended to show. In the United States and mainland Europe, this may involve consulting several organisations. This difficulty does not at present exist in Britain, where the cat fancy is isolated because of the quarantine law.

Intending exhibitors must make sure that they have the most up-to-date information, because from time to time standards are amended. Standards exist for all breeds to which a particular organisation has granted Preliminary recognition, and for some other breeds which are still being assessed for recognition; the latter, in particular, are liable to be amended as assessment proceeds. In extreme cases, a breed which has been assessed for recognition may be refused the final accolade, either because of worries about genetic abnormalities or because there are not enough purebred members of the breed (the usual requirement is 100) to ensure its continuation without excessive inbreeding. The cat fancy press keeps a close eye on changes in standards and on the admission of new breeds.

Top left
Judges will check a cat's colour, coat and conformation.

Top right
A Scottish Fold must have the typical, small, folded ears in order to conform to breed standard.

SHOW QUALITY

IF A PEDIGREE CAT does not meet its breed standard in every detail, this does not rob it of its pedigree; it simply means that the cat is unsuitable for showing because it will be in competition with specimens closer to the ideal; in cat fancy terms, the cat is not of 'show quality'. All breeders from time to time have the experience of kittens which fail the standard, and they are then faced with two possibilities. Either they can sell the kittens off, with or without a pedigree certificate and with or without the stipulation that they are neutered, as cats of 'pet' or 'household' quality (and this should be reflected in the price) or they can use them as breeding stock ('breeding quality') in the hope that imperfections in one generation might be corrected in the next. Whether this hope is justified depends on the nature of the fault, and this is why breeders have become intensely interested in genetics – one of the fascinating byways into which the cat fancy leads its followers.

AWARDING POINTS

THE BREED STANDARD is the show judge's basic guide, and as an experienced breeder he or she will know it off by heart. In theory, every pedigree cat at a show has the potential to score 100 points on its breed standard. The score of 100 points is broken down in different proportions depending on the breed, and the breakdown again varies between different organisations.

For example, in a specific breed up to 20 points might be awarded for the head, 15 for the eye size, shape and colour, 50 for the coat colour and condition and 15 for the body type or conformation. Of course, if any cat scored 100 points, that would be the end of the competition in that particular class for a year or two. In practice, although this schedule of points is enshrined in the show standards it is no more than a general guide to the judge as to the credit he should give for closeness to the standard for each feature. A judge who is minded to give two cats the same number of points for, say, the head will always, when it comes to the final assessment, favour the cat that he assesses to have the better overall condition and appearance.

> **CAT FACT:**
> The saying: 'there is more than one way to skin a cat' refers to the notion that a job can be regarded as done no matter how it is achieved.

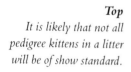

> *Top*
> *It is likely that not all pedigree kittens in a litter will be of show standard.*

The American Cat Fanciers' Association (not to be confused with the Cat Fanciers' Association which is also American) in the United States has a more prescriptive system, with points and even fractions of points awarded far more precisely. But even then, in the end, it tends to be the cat with the most pleasing overall features that wins.

JUDGING NON-PEDIGREE CLASSES

THE JUDGES FOR non-pedigree classes of what may be described, depending on the show organisers, as pet, household or domestic cats, or cats exhibited by children within a specific age range, naturally do not work to standards. The challenge of producing an all-purpose standard for family pets would surely defeat even the most diligent standards committees! In these classes, the judges are less intent on the finer points of breeding but are looking for handsome, healthy cats which are obviously loved and well cared for. No one should imagine, however, that these classes are a soft option. Competition is intense, standards are high, and as much care must go into preparing entrants for these as for the most exotic pedigree classes.

At the same time, judges are well aware of the reality that a family pet comes from a very different type of background to a pedigree cat in which its owner will have invested huge amounts of time and attention. The cat fancy values these non-pedigree competitions partly because they arouse interest in cat care in the general sense, but also because young competitors are part of the pool of cat lovers from which the more earnest pedigree competitors of the future will be drawn.

AMERICAN STANDARDS

IN THE UNITED STATES, show standards set out, in addition to the requirements for specific breeds and colour varieties, the general condition that is expected of cats exhibited for show. This is because American organisations have largely abandoned the process of 'vetting-in' cats at shows and rely on owners not to submit cats that fall below accepted standards of condition. In practice, no owner experienced in exhibiting would dream of entering a cat that was not physically in tip-top condition, but laying down these basic requirements provides a basis on which a judge can disqualify a cat deemed not to be fit to be shown.

CAT FACT:
Scientists are generally agreed that the main ancestors of domestic cats are African wild cats rather than European, with the possibility of crossbreeding with jungle and other wild cats.

Top
This young exhibitor's 15-month old tabby has won its pet class.

Getting Ready for the Show

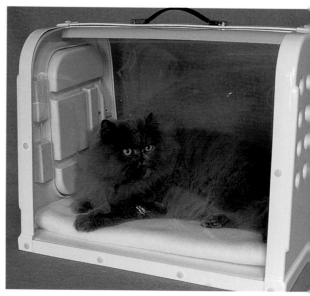

I DEALLY, PREPARING A cat for show should begin when it is a kitten. Shows involve a number of activities which cats dislike unless they are used to them, such as travelling long distances, remaining confined in a pen for long periods of time and being handled by strangers.

PREPARATION

THE SOONER A potential show cat gets accustomed to such things the better. Although a cat's temperament is not referred to in breed standards, it can be all-important at the show and is often the deciding factor when a judge has to choose between two cats of near equal show quality. Even a non-pedigree cat destined to be shown in 'pet' or children's classes will need to have these experiences if it is to look and behave its best on the day.

TRAINING FOR A SHOW CAREER

IT IS IMPORTANT, if your cat is going to do you justice, to make the experience of being shown pleasurable and to avoid causing any confusion. For example, if your cat associates being put in its travelling basket with a possibly painful and probably unpleasant visit to the vet, it is no good expecting it to react calmly when you basket it for the show. There are two ways round this problem. One is to 'swamp' the vet experiences with other more pleasurable ones, taking every opportunity to take your cat on increasingly long journeys in the basket with rewards

Top right
An excellent cat travelling container which is well-ventilated and easily cleaned.

Bottom
Cats should be trained to become accustomed to show pens.

at the end. Another is to buy for show purposes a carrier of a quite different design from the one you use for vet visits. You can then use this one for your 'dummy runs' and associate it with treats.

You will also need to accustom your cat to the show pen. Show pens come in a standard size and – in Britain, at any rate – design, and if you have your own at home you can train your cat by putting it in the pen for a short period each day, gradually increasing the length of time and making sure that there is a

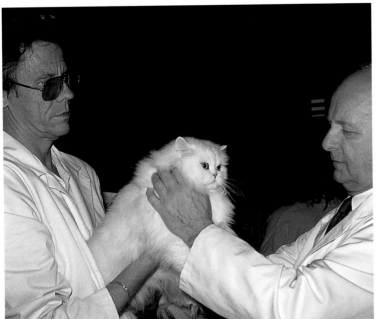

GENERAL SHOW PREPARATION
ALONGSIDE THE ELEMENT OF competition element in the cat fancy, the promotion of a healthy lifestyle for cats is one of its objectives and it is essential that cats entered for shows are in first class physical condition. This means paying close attention to the quality of the cat's diet, the general condition of its coat (as distinct from the special pre-show grooming described below) and the provision of exercise. In North America in particular, many pedigree show cats are confined to the house for understandable reasons, but this does mean that all

reward at the end of the session. Travelling baskets and carriers are unsuitable for this purpose because they are too small. As training proceeds, you can imitate show conditions by placing in the pen the regulation food and water bowls and litter tray and providing a blanket, so that your cat becomes familiar with these items of equipment.

Your cat will be handled at the show by people whose style of approach is professional and assured, unlike the everyday petting it will have known at home. In the ordinary way of a cat's life, the only handling of this kind it has experienced will have been at the vet's, so again you have to try to 'swamp' this with other occasions. If you plan your training programme with care, you can bring all these show conditions – time in the show pen, the travelling and the handling – together so that they become associated in your cat's mind. If possible, recruit friends and neighbours to act out the role of stranger so that the cat gets used to being handled by a variety of people.

You may find that, despite all your efforts, your cat simply does not take to this training. In this case, you must give up your hopes of a show career for that particular cat. There will be no awards for cats that arrive at the show already distressed and who continue to show signs of stress throughout the day.

kinds of stratagems have to be devised for exercise if they are not to become overweight. The ideal answer is to build as large an outdoor run as possible. Shorthairs and non-pedigree cats intended for show can be allowed more freedom, but it is difficult to maintain a longhair's coat in show condition if it is allowed to roam.

Serious preparation for the show should begin about four weeks before, but again it is wise to accustom the cat to intensive pre-show grooming by earlier rehearsals. This is also the time to make sure that your cat's vaccinations are up to date and that you have the relevant documentation, which you may be required to produce at the show, to hand. It is also worthwhile at this stage to have the vet inspect your cat, in the knowledge that you are entering it for a show.

Top
Cats should be introduced to a variety of strangers so that they are comfortable when handled at shows.

Bottom
Turkish Van in an outside run, these are an excellent idea for indoor cats.

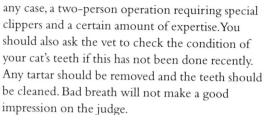

SHOW GROOMING

SHOW GROOMING IS more detailed, frequent and time-consuming than the ordinary routine for a domestic cat. The coat should first be combed with a fine-toothed comb, taking the opportunity at the same time to check for dandruff, parasites and the condition known as 'stud tail'. Then the coat should be brushed, preferably using a natural bristle brush. A longhair's ruff must be brushed up so as to make a frame for its face, and tangles on the legs and in the tail area must be teased out carefully. With shorthairs, use a pad of silk or soft chamois leather to give the coat a final gloss. All these grooming activities should be as gentle as possible, and accompanied by quiet, encouraging conversation, so that the cat will regard grooming as a pleasant occasion. Rex cats need especially careful treatment, as over-vigorous brushing may result in the appearance of bald patches; many experts advise the use of a short-bristled baby brush.

At an early stage – say 2–3 weeks before the show – you should check the condition of the claws. If they have not been kept short by the cat's own claw-sharpening activities and exercise, they should be clipped. Experienced owners often do this themselves, but if you have not done it before you should ask the vet. It is, in

any case, a two-person operation requiring special clippers and a certain amount of expertise. You should also ask the vet to check the condition of your cat's teeth if this has not been done recently. Any tartar should be removed and the teeth should be cleaned. Bad breath will not make a good impression on the judge.

Four or five days before the show the coat should be given a shampoo or, in the case of shorthairs, a bran bath. It will make your life easier if you have accustomed your cat to being bathed occasionally from an early age, although there are very few cats which ever learn to positively enjoy a bath. A kitten can have its first bath from the age of about six months.

BATHING THE CAT

BATHING A CAT, like trimming its claws, is best regarded as a two-person job – one to hold the cat and the other to do the bathing. The best bathtub for a cat is a large bowl on a kitchen work surface, with plenty of towelling round it as a good deal of splashing is almost inevitable. The water should be warm but not hand-hot, and can be tested with the elbow as with a baby's bath water. The shampoo should be either a brand formulated specifically for cats or a baby shampoo. On no account use normal adult hair shampoo.

Before the cat is bathed, any marks on the coat from paint, tar or other difficult substances should have been removed. The best method is to stand the cat alternately with its front paws and then its back paws in the water so that it retains some contact with

Top
Grooming involves a variety of stages, there are also many different types of brushes to choose from.

Bottom
Blue Persian being groomed in preparation for showing.

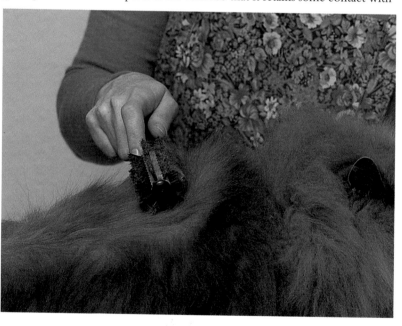

a firm, dry surface. Speed is of the essence. Moisten the coat all over and then rub in the shampoo, avoiding the eyes, ears, nose and mouth. Then quickly rinse twice to ensure that all the shampoo is removed, using a sprinkler if one is available. You should have warm towels at the ready to dry the cat at once, because cats are prone to chills. Some cats will tolerate the use of a hair-drier on a low (mild heat and quiet) setting, but do not persevere with this if it causes distress. After the bath, the cat should be groomed in the normal way and kept in the warm until the coat is thoroughly dry.

THE DRY BATH

FOR THE FAINT-HEARTED, and for the many owners of shorthairs who believe that bathing them is unnecessary, there are the alternatives of a dry shampoo or a bran bath. Special dry shampoos are available from pet shops, but many owners use unperfumed talcum powder, Fuller's earth (dry absorbent clay) or cornflour (corn starch). This again is a task for two people. The coat is 'opened' by light tail-to-head brushing and the chosen powder sprinkled and worked in gently with the fingers. It should be left for a few hours, during which the cat will lick and shake some of the powder out. The remainder must then be thoroughly brushed and combed out.

Show regulations invariably embargo any cat whose coat shows traces of cleaning substances, so dry shampooing should be done at least four days before the show. It is also prohibited to use any form of dye or other colouring agent to alter the natural colour of a cat's coat.

The procedure for a bran bath is similar. The bran used is the type fed to rabbits. It is warmed and then rubbed gently into the coat and left for a few hours before being thoroughly brushed out.

Talcum powder or its alternatives should not be used on dark-haired cats because any minute traces that remain could look like dandruff. There are many recipes for giving tone to a dark coat, ranging from the use of bay rum or cologne to rubbing with a solution of ammonia. Any of these could set up an allergic reaction and none should be tried without veterinary advice.

CAT FACT:
The wild cat populations on the Mediterranean islands are of the African species, which has been interpreted as the result of early human introduction as pets.

Top
Bathing should be introduced from an early age so that the cat is used to water.

Top right
Grooming longhairs should include powdering and brushing.

Bottom right
This Russian Blue is being bran-bathed.

GROOMING THE CAT

VARIOUS BRANDS OF grooming lotions are available from pet shops. The usual procedure is to put a few drops of these on an absorbent pad and work them in methodically from the shoulders to the tail, avoiding the head and finishing off with a gentle rub with a dry cloth.

With longhairs, removing any tangles by clipping them out must be avoided as the week of the show approaches. Signs of clipping will disqualify exhibits from British shows, and will certainly prejudice the judges elsewhere, although some United States associations admit to their shows cats whose coats have been clipped overall.

PREPARATIONS

IN THE FEW DAYS before the show, begin to collect all the equipment you will need to take with you on the day. Make sure that the travelling container is

clean, disinfected and provided with fresh bedding. You will need two or three warm blankets – one to line the show pen initially, with spares for accidents and emergencies. In Britain, these must be white and in plain weave; cellular blankets are not permitted; in many other countries they may be coloured, but consult the show regulations and, if in doubt, contact the show organisers for advice. You must also take food and water bowls and a litter tray.

In Britain, again, these must be white, but elsewhere they may match the blankets and other show pen fittings. You will be able to buy cat food and litter at the show, but it is advisable to take a supply of your cat's familiar brand. Many owners also take a supply of water from home, as cats will sometimes refuse to drink water from an unfamiliar source. You should also take some of your cat's favourite snacks, and a supply of plastic bags for used litter and other waste. In winter, pack a small hot water bottle which can be concealed in the blanket. Take one or two of your cat's toys, but in Britain these may not be placed in the show pen until judging is completed.

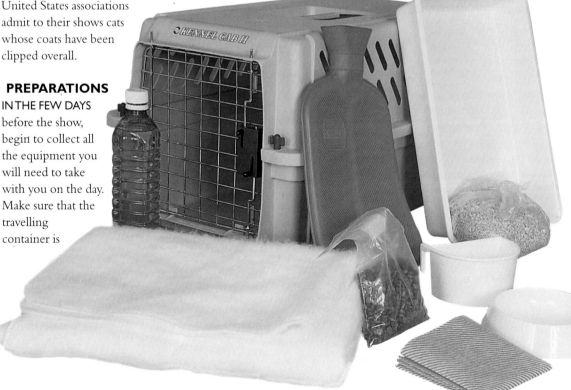

Bottom
Items that are required for a British cat show.

In North America and other countries where ring shows are the norm, you may also take coloured curtains, cushions and other items to decorate the show pen. Rosettes, ribbons and other awards from previous shows may be displayed, together with a board giving details of the cat and its owner. These items should also be made ready in advance to avoid a last-minute scramble on the morning of departure.

FINAL DETAILS

FINALLY, CHECK THE show rules again and make sure you have fulfilled all the conditions. Some rules require cats to wear a standard identification disc or label. If this involves wearing an unfamiliar ribbon or collar you should accustom your cat to it well before show day. Give your cat its final full grooming the night before the show, making sure that any powder you have used is brushed out. You will be allowed to use brush, comb and a cloth when you arrive at the show, but other grooming aids are normally prohibited.

On the morning of the show, you must make every effort to keep calm, since any sense of rush will be communicated to your cat. It is sensible to work to a timetable which you have prepared beforehand, working backwards from your time of arrival at the show. Leave plenty of time for settling the cat in its travelling container, after you have given it a quick check for runny eyes or nose or other signs of illness. If you have any doubts about your cat's health, the only course is to resign yourself to missing the show; there is no point in subjecting yourself and the cat to a long journey only to be rejected by the show management. You should, of course, ring the show hall to explain your absence.

CAT FACT:
The jaguar, of Central and South America, has a peculiar appetite for reptiles. It will readily kill and eat tortoises, turtles, snakes, lizards and even caimans.

Top right
A copy of a cat show schedule.

Bottom
It is a good idea to make a timetable so that you and the cat are not rushed on the day of the show.

Showing in America

EACH YEAR, ABOUT 400 major cat shows are organised in the United States under the rules of the major cat associations: the Cat Fanciers' Association (CFA), the American Cat Fanciers' Association (ACFA), the American Cat Association (ACA), the Cat Fanciers' Federation (CFF), the United Cat Federation (UCF), the American Cat Council (ACC) and The International Cat Association (TICA).

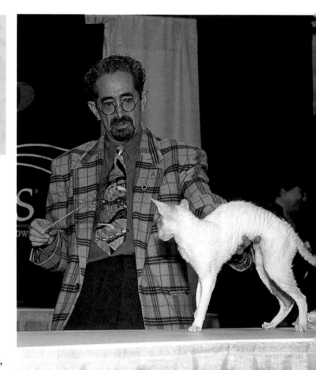

THE CAT FANCIERS' ASSOCIATION

OF THESE, THE Cat Fanciers' Association is the largest, with over 600 affiliated clubs in Canada and Japan as well as in the United States, and the American Cat Association is the oldest, established in 1898. Some United States associations are effectively regional; for example, the CFF operates mainly in the north-eastern states while the UCF is based in the south-west. There is also a separate Canadian Cat Association, which is the governing body for the cat fancy in Canada. In order for a cat to be exhibited under an association's rules, it is necessary for it to have been registered with that association.

OPEN RING SYSTEM

MOST SHOWING IN North America is on the 'open ring' system. The exhibits are brought in turn to the ring where the judge examines them and awards points according to the breed standard. Judging takes place, the results are announced in public, and the judge often adds a few general comments on the class winners as well as citing the points awarded. Unlike British judges, who receive only expenses, judges in North America are paid fees, and accordingly the qualifications are more stringent, involving examinations as well as practical experience and personal recommendation.

At any one show there may be several rings operating simultaneously, each ring being regarded as a separate competition and judged by a single judge. One or more of these rings may be for all breeds of cats within a certain age range (see below), while others may be restricted to longhairs or shorthairs. Thus it is possible for a cat to be judged in more than one ring at the same show and to collect more than one award which contributes to its show status. This makes it possible for American cats to accumulate their Championship or Premier honours faster than under the British system where only one title can be won at each show.

CATS' COMFORT

BECAUSE JUDGES DO not visit the main show hall where the cats are penned before judging, North American rules on the equipment and decoration of show pens are relaxed. Owners are allowed to decorate the pens with coloured draperies, advertisements and trophies of past successes, to use

Top
Judging at the Madison Square Garden.

Bottom
Longhaired winner of the Madison Square Garden cat show.

coloured bedding and to provide their cats with exotic toys and other comforts. Some owners even fit security devices and air conditioning to ensure their cats' safety and comfort during the show.

CATEGORIES OF CLASSES

IN SHOWS ORGANISED under the rules of the Cat Fanciers' Association, classes are designated as Championship, Pedigree and Non-championship. Championship classes are themselves divided into categories. The Novice class is for cats over eight months old competing in their first show as adults.

Cats which have achieved one award for best of class for breed, colour or sex can be entered for the Open class. Wins of four 'best of class' ribbons under three different judges qualifies an unneutered cat for the Championship class. From then on, progress to Grand Champion is by competition against rival Champions, points being awarded for each Champion defeated. This procedure, carried out in public, lends enormous excitement and tension to the climax of North American cat shows.

The Pedigree classes are for neutered pedigree cats and follow a similar pattern, leading to the award of Premier and Grand Premier ribbons.

Non-championship classes are for Kittens, 'Any Other Variety', Provisional Breeds, Miscellaneous and Household Pet cats. Kittens must be unneutered, not less than four months or more than eight months old on the day of the show and of registered pedigree. The 'Any Other Variety' (AOV) class is for unneutered cats or kittens 'the ancestry of which entitles it to Championship competition but which does not conform to the accepted show standard'. AOV winners may only receive awards in the AOV class and cannot progress to Premier or Championship classes.

The Provisional Breeds class is for cats (neutered or unneutered) or kittens of breeds which have as yet been awarded only Provisional status. The Miscellaneous class is for cats of breeds not yet accepted for Provisional status. Finally, the Household Pet class is for non-pedigree domestic kittens and cats (cats must be neutered).

Middle
Cats can win more than one category in the United States.

Bottom left
Owner showing her cat and its winning rosettes.

Bottom right
Kittens for sale at an American show.

> **CAT FACT:**
> The Cat in the Hat is an American literary character created by Dr Seuss. He appears in several books, teaching children the basics about reading and writing.

CAT FACT:
There are reports of a mysterious cat race in Scotland, known as the Kellas cat. It is now thought to be a cross between feral domestic and European wild cats.

ARRIVING AT A SHOW

ON ARRIVAL AT a show in North America, the procedure is to check in at reception and receive the cat's cage and catalogue number and a copy of the catalogue (sometimes provided in return for the entry fee but sometimes charged separately). Owners should check in the catalogue that their cats are entered into the correct classes and that the cats' names, parentage details, date of birth and the owner's name are printed correctly. Any errors should be reported at once to the show secretary.

In the reception area there will be a benching plan showing the layout of the show hall and the allocation of numbered pens. From this point on, the cat is regarded as 'benched' and subject to the show rules. Benching is carefully planned so that all of an individual owner's cats are benched in adjacent pens, but no two unneutered males may be placed next to each other. Owners may, as mentioned above, decorate their show pens provided that no decorations or other material protrude over the top of the pen.

THE SHOW

BEFORE THE COMPETITION in each ring, competitors' pen numbers are called over the public address system a maximum of three times. If there is no response they are then marked absent. On being called, competitors carry their cats to the ring and place them in the appropriately numbered cages. They must then go to the spectator area to await the judging. Competitors

'Vetting-in' is no longer a standard procedure at North American cat shows, associations relying on the good faith of their members in not bringing to the show cats with known infections. No cat is permitted to enter the show hall if it comes from a source where there has been any fungal or infectious disease during the previous 21 days. However, it is up to any exhibitor, show official or judge to report any cat with a suspected infection and ask for a veterinary inspection. If this confirms the suspicions, the cat concerned and any other cats from the same owner will be excluded from the show.

must not speak to the judge or make any comments on the exhibits in the judge's hearing.

Top
Vetting-in is not required in the United States; owners should ensure that their cats are healthy before entering them into a show.

Bottom
A decorated pen.

There may also be awards for the Best and Second Best Longhairs and Shorthairs, the Best and Second Best Kittens, and so on, and the judging may culminate in a 'Best of the Bests' award. For the beginner and the experienced exhibitor alike, this is the most valuable part of the show because the cats are presented to the audience by the judge, who comments on each winner. At some shows, winners of the 'Best' awards are penned afterwards in special cages in a separate part of the show hall, where their finer points can be compared by the audience. Now that judging is over, judges may be prepared to discuss their assessments, but they are not obliged to do so.

Owners are expected to keep their cats in the show pens until the show's closing time, but exceptions may be made for kittens and household pets. Show pens should be cleaned before owners leave, and all litter should be removed. On returning home, show cats should be watched carefully for a few days for signs of any infectious disease, and any symptoms should be reported to the show organizers. The final task is to apply to the appropriate cat fancy organization for the certificates of any awards that have been received.

Arrangements in the ring are supervized by the clerks. They are responsible for checking the entries against the catalogue, entering the judge's awards and drawing up a full record of each competition for the show secretary. A steward takes each cat in turn to the judge's table, where it is inspected and held up at arm's length for assessment. Any cat that bites, or that is judged to be behaving in a 'recalcitrant or threatening manner', will be disqualified and must be removed from the judging ring. It will not be eligible to appear in any other ring at that particular show.

Between each cat's turn, a steward disinfects the table and the judge disinfects his or her hands. When judging is completed, the results are announced and certificates, ribbons, and rosettes are distributed to the winners. These may be displayed on the show cage when the cat is returned to it. As in other countries, any cash prizes are merely nominal, but owners sometimes receive prizes such as magazine subscriptions, books on cats, diaries, and so on.

THE FINALS

WHEN ALL THE classes have been judged, the 'Finals' stage of the show is reached. The Best and Second Best Champion and the Best and Second Best Premier in Show will have been decided by the number of points awarded in the earlier judging.

Top
A Ragdoll on show, the table will be disinfected after each cat.

Bottom
Because of American rules this Cornish Rex is able to win best of breed and best cat in show.

Showing Cats around the World

THE CAT FANCY is an international movement with followers in most developed countries, although geographical distance and, in many countries, quarantine restrictions place limits on the extent of international showing. Nevertheless, many national cat fancy organizations maintain close contact with each other, especially over the recognition of breeds and the writing of breed standards.

THE CAT FANCY

THROUGH THE AUSPICES of this international network breeders are able to import and export

pedigree stock, a particularly valuable facility when, as occasionally happens, infectious diseases or other factors attack a country's stock of particular breeds, or when breeders want to establish a breed in a country where it is not recognized.

Each national organization has its own approach to the definition and recognition of breeds, partly accounted for by different national preferences and partly by the availability of stock. It is a general principle of the cat fancy that a breed cannot be recognized unless it has enough individual cats – typically, 100 – to create a viable gene pool and avoid excessive in-breeding.

SCANDINAVIA

THE SCANDINAVIAN COUNTRIES, Belgium, the Netherlands, France, and Germany were quick to develop cat associations and shows soon after Britain gave the lead in the late nineteenth century. In mainland Europe the free movement of pedigree cats

from one country to another has always been relatively unrestricted, subject only to proof of a rabies vaccination, and the larger shows in Germany, the Netherlands, and France have traditionally attracted large international entries. However, the two World Wars – in particular the Second World War – severely damaged the European cat fancy owing to the shortage of food, the spread of disease and the difficulty of maintaining the show structure in wartime conditions.

After the Second World War ended in 1945, increased international co-operation was seen as a

Top
Abyssinian being judged.

Bottom right
Continental Europe has traditionally attracted competitors from many countries.

is the largest cat organization in the world, representing over 150,000 breeders and exhibitors. The member countries' own affiliated clubs maintain their own breed registers, but they generally observe the breed standards and recognition agreed on by FIFé. The Fédération also regulates the introduction of new breeds, the management and regulation of the shows of affiliated associations, and the resolution of disputes and complaints. FIFé also has

ay to restore the fancy's fortunes. Since 1949 the Fédération Internationale Féline (FIFé) has provided a central organization for European cat associations, with representation from 12 mainland countries. FIFé

affiliated associations in many non-European countries. In addition to FIFé-affiliated associations, most European countries have at least one other association which operates a register and organizes shows, as well as clubs dedicated to the interests of specific breeds.

EUROPEAN MAINLAND

MANY EXHIBITORS IN Europe show their cats in a number of European mainland countries where, as in North America, major shows often last two days because of the traveling distances involved. One of the largest European shows is that of the Cat-Club de Paris, and the national shows in the Netherlands and Germany also attract large and comprehensive entries. The international aspect of these shows opens up the exciting prospect of an extended Championship system so that cats can become, on the basis of the awards received under a number of different judges, International Champions, and International Grand Champions, validated by FIFé.

> **CAT FACT:**
> The astrological or zodiac sign for Leo is the lion. The lion is significant because it symbolises strong leadership qualities combined with a self assured nature.

> **CAT FACT:**
> The lion has often been used as a symbol of strength in English history. King Richard I was known as the Lion Heart, and lions often appear on family crests.

Top
Showing in a variety of countries opens up the possibility of becoming an international champion.

Bottom
Germany attracts a large number of international entries.

Bottom right
The Cat Club de Paris is one of the largest show organizers.

In general, FIFé show rules follow those of other organizations on such questions as the anonymity of the exhibits to the judges, attention to health and hygiene and the award of ribbons, rosettes, and other trophies. Each European country, however, has its own requirements as to the health certification of imported cats and the granting of import licences. Trans-European exhibitors need to familiarize themselves with these well in advance of entering for a show, as some regulations stipulate periods of time prior to travel for certain vaccinations. No European countries other than Britain impose a period of quarantine, but all, except for Britain, require evidence of rabies vaccinations.

The usual procedure for shows on the European continent is a kind of hybrid of the British and North American systems. Cats are exhibited in the show hall where their owners may remain, but they are taken by stewards to a screened-off area or a separate smaller hall for judging in private. This means that the show pens may be decorated and that distinctive furnishings, blankets, and so on are allowed because the judges will not see them. Judges' comments are either written on cards attached to the pen or handed by a clerk to the exhibitors. Scandinavian shows, however, tend to follow the open ring system, where judging takes place in public in front of exhibitors and spectators, and judges explain their reasons for choosing the award-winning cats.

CANADA

THE CANADIAN CAT ASSOCIATION, based in Brampton, Ontario, is the all-Canadian registration association which operates mainly in south-eastern Canada and issues its publications in both French and English. In addition, three of the major United States cat fancy organizations – the Cat Fanciers' Association (CFA), the American Cat Fanciers' Association (ACFA), and The International Cat Association (TICA) – have affiliated clubs in Canada. As there are no quarantine regulations in either Canada or the United States, cats can travel freely between the two and there is a good deal of cross-border showing as well as two-way trade between breeders. Most Canadian shows are organized on the United States open ring pattern.

In Canada, there is an international Championship structure similar to that in Europe. Breeding in Canada tends to be overshadowed by activities in the United States, but Canada has the distinction of having introduced the Tonkinese breed to the cat fancy in the 1960s.

Top left
Unlike Britain the European continent cats are exhibited in the show hall so pens can be decorated.

Bottom
Outside Britain spectators are allowed to watch the cats being judged in the show ring.

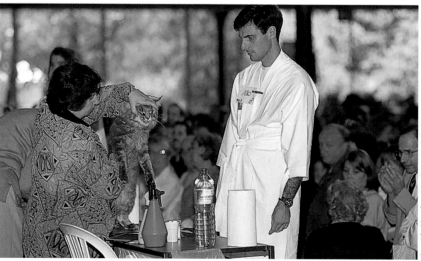

AUSTRALIA

AUSTRALIA HAS A number of cat associations, differentiated on a state basis and affiliated to the Sydney-based Co-ordinating Cat Council of Australia (CCC of A). The fancy is concentrated largely in the south-east. Australian cat shows are usually organized to rules similar to those of Britain's Governing Council of the Cat Fancy.

In addition to official events, less formal cat shows are often held as part of country fairs. There are no indigenous cats in Australia, and the first were taken there by settlers in the nineteenth century. The manifests of many British migrant ships from the middle of the century onwards list cats along with other essentials for farming such as seeds and tools, and no doubt these were joined by escaped ships' cats.

Top
Canadian cat shows are similar to those in the United States.

Bottom
Through shows in Japan the Japanese Bobtail was introduced to the West.

NEW ZEALAND

NEW ZEALAND ALSO has a thriving cat fancy (similarly based on imported stock) whose organization is the New Zealand Cat Fancy based in Nelson, which operates rules similar to those of the GCCF.

SOUTH AFRICA

SOUTH AFRICA WAS a relative latecomer to the pedigree cat world, but it now has its own breed clubs and registration body based on the GCCF.

JAPAN

THERE ARE VERY close links between the United States and Japanese cat fancies. The CFA, ACFA, and ITCA all have Japanese affiliated clubs which organize shows under their respective rules. It was through these links that, in the 1960s, the Japanese Bobtail was introduced to the western world, and the Japanese fancy, which is not subject to quarantine regulations, has benefited from liberal imports of breeding stock from the United States. Most shows in Japan are of the open ring type.

CAT FACT:
The fishing cat of eastern Asia is a small but heavily built animal. It has adapted for its semi-aquatic lifestyle by developing partially webbed toes to aid swimming.

Cat Behavior

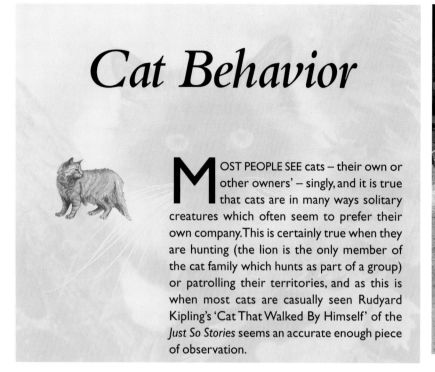

MOST PEOPLE SEE cats – their own or other owners' – singly, and it is true that cats are in many ways solitary creatures which often seem to prefer their own company. This is certainly true when they are hunting (the lion is the only member of the cat family which hunts as part of a group) or patrolling their territories, and as this is when most cats are casually seen Rudyard Kipling's 'Cat That Walked By Himself' of the *Just So Stories* seems an accurate enough piece of observation.

CAT FACT:
Cats tend to bolt their food down instinctively, because in the wild there might be any number of other predators waiting to steal their prey away from them.

THE SOCIAL LIFE OF CATS
DOMESTICATION, PROVIDING readily available food, shelter, and human company, tends to suggest the small cat's independence of to the rest of its species. But female feral cats live in mutually supportive groups of queens and kittens which sleep and play together, groom each other, and join in defending their chosen territory, and given the chance domestic cats will act out modified forms of this behavior.

Top left
These feral cats meet and socialize on common territory.

Top right
This feral queen moves her kittens to keep them safe from predators.

Bottom
These two cats greet each other in a friendly manner, they familiarize themselves with the other's smell.

TERRITORIAL RANGE
FERAL FEMALES OCCUPY fairly small ranges which contain individual feeding and sleeping places but also overlap with the ranges of other females. The area of overlap is the common ground where social contact can be made. Toms range more widely – a typical tom's territory is 10 times the size of the female's – and their territory may include a number of female ranges.

Queens are single parents. After mating, the tom wanders off or is driven away by the queen, who then settles down to face pregnancy and birth on her own. Six or seven weeks after a successful mating, she will begin to look for a suitable warm, sheltered, quiet, and private place to have her kittens. This is a period of great restlessness, and she may try and reject several places before making up her mind.

FERAL KITTENS
THE EASY AVAILABILITY of prey is an important factor, for once the kittens are born she will not want to leave them for more than a few minutes. The gestation period for cats is about nine weeks. As each kitten is born, the queen cleans it and eats the sac in which it is born, together with the umbilical cord and the placenta. For the next few weeks her life will be devoted to feeding, caring for and training her litter, although any weak or defective kittens may be ignored and allowed to die. Once she has recovered her strength after the birth, the queen may decide to move her family to new, clean quarters.

All this means that, in feral conditions, the basic family unit consists of mother and kittens. When the kittens reach sexual maturity at an average of six months, they go off to seek mates and the cycle begins again. Young toms begin a wide-ranging search, exercising their notorious promiscuity, while young females stay closer to home, but in their own ranges. Both males and females, however, enter into the social structure of their respective territories, based partly on their competition for mates and food.

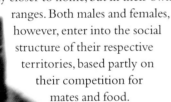

SOCIAL GROUPS

THE FEMALE HIERARCHY is based on the number of litters each queen has had, so that the dominant female will usually be the oldest cat still sexually active. In each social group some females will be from the same litter and will have maintained contact since birth, so the group is naturally cohesive. At the time of birth, the birthing queen achieves a kind of temporary seniority before taking her new place, once the kittens are weaned, in the social order. Sometimes another queen with a litter will help to clean newborn kittens, take part in their care and training and bring food for them.

A feral tom going out into the world has a much tougher time. He has literally to fight his way into a territory, taking on a number of challengers in fights which can be awesome to witness and are often damaging to be involved in. The typical feral tom with an eye missing, an ear torn or impressive facial scars is the product of these skirmishes, which may continue between the same two toms for several nights. After a series of fights, the new tom finds his place in the hierarchy, where he may face further fights if he wants to improve his status or challenge a rival for the chance to mate with a particular queen.

CAT FACT:
It is commonly known that brittle cooked chicken bones cause cats to choke. As cats are inclined to bolt their food this can happen with any bones, but not very often.

or most experienced tom that wins the queen. Female cats seem to have their own rules of taste unfathomable to the observer.

Once the queen has accepted a tom as a mate – a process which may take several hours if they are complete strangers – copulation is swift and decisive. The tom mounts the queen from the back, taking the scruff of her neck in his mouth. Once it is over, he makes his escape quickly to avoid attack, but after the queen's initial explosive reaction she will often accept the same tom again and again until he is exhausted. Alternatively, she may accept another mate or a whole series of mates until her oestrus is over. Equally, the tom may go off in search of other queens in oestrus.

LEADER OF THE PACK

THE PRIZES FOR being the dominant queen or tom at the head of the hierarchy include rights to the best sleeping places, the best birthing places in the case of queens, and the most promising hunting areas. Having resolved all these matters, the cats settle down in their respective groups in relative peace and friendliness until the next intruder comes along.

The social structure of feral cat life depends on sexual activity and does not allow for the infiltration of neutered or spayed outsiders. A strayed or dumped neutered domestic cat has no chance of finding a place in such a community and is condemned to a solitary existence and a good deal of harassment.

DOMESTIC ROUTINE

DOMESTIC CATS DO not have the opportunity for the social exchanges of the feral world, and if they have been neutered they do not have the sexual drive which is the underlying motive for cats' social behavior in the wild. But those allowed out at night often exhibit a modified form of social life. Groups of cats will assemble at a convenient spot such as a flat roof, usually outside any individual cat's home territory, and spend the night in companionable purring, grooming, or merely silent observation. Unless an intruder appears, they will be relatively quiet, with no sexual overtures or aggression. Towards the end of the night, the cats disperse to their own territories, evidently having enjoyed each other's company.

Similar behavior is seen in places such as animal sanctuaries where numbers of cats occupy a large enclosed space, and in urban feral colonies in such places as hospital grounds, railway sidings, and churchyards. Typically, the cats take up their positions

MATING PROCESS

THE OESTRUS CYCLE, or season, in queens occurs as few as two or three times, or as many as ten or more, each year; the lower figure is closer to the norm. In the wild, these cycles normally come in the first half of the year, dictated, it is thought, by the length of the day. Breeding queens kept indoors in artificial light can be sexually active at any time of year. In the first stage of the cycle, lasting up to ten days if the queen does not mate and ovulate and about half that time if she does, the ovaries produce female sex hormones which, combined with the stretching and treading movements known as lordosis and repeated calling, attract entire (unneutered) toms.

These gather close, spraying urine, scent-marking, and emitting courtship cries, and fighting among themselves for the right to claim the queen for their own. It is for her to make the choice, and if any tom is too forward he will be sent packing with blows and snarls. Young toms who have not yet learned the rules can be quite severely damaged in these encounters. But it is not always the dominant

Top
This female is in heat and demonstrates lordosis.

Bottom
An oriental tabby mates with a queen.

CAT FACT:
A domestic tabby from Texas, called Dusty, gave birth to an incredible 420 kittens between 1935–52.

tables are familiar with the apparently unlikely companionship that often develops between the resident cats, well fed from mice in the feedstuffs, and the horses.

The pivot of a domestic cat's social life is, of course, its owner and the rest of the family. Although it may appear to ignore them for much of the time, keeping its distance or sleeping, it is replicating within the limits of domestic life some of the behavior in feral colonies, especially its taste for quiet companionship and undemonstrative support. At the same time, perhaps because their natural development has been interrupted by domestication, home cats seem to need the continuation of kittenish play and tactile contact that their wild cousins grow out of. Perhaps the vet who suggested that domestic cats have never quite grown up was right.

in such a way as to define a personal space around themselves, but close enough for loose social contact. The space must be large enough for comfort, however. Like most mammals, cats react to overcrowding by becoming neurotic and aggressive. In such a situation, the weaker or less assertive members of the group will be bullied off the patch.

COMPANIONSHIP

DOMESTIC CATS ALSO often modify their behavior by seeking the company of dogs or other pets in the household, after initial caution, especially if they are introduced as kittens. (They do not take so kindly to animals introduced once they have established themselves). They may take part in mutual grooming sessions, snuggle up to each other for warmth, and play games together. The cat will greet its canine or other species friend with a vertical tail signal just as when two friendly cats meet. Owners of riding

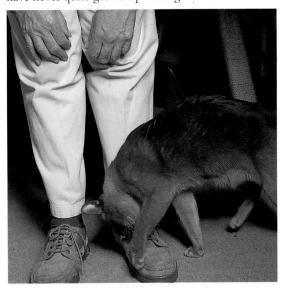

Top left
This kitten and dog have bonded.

Top right
In rubbing itself against its owner this cat marks him with its scent.

Bottom
Two kittens keep one another company while playing with this plant.

Genes and Heredity

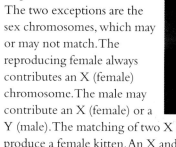

THE PHYSICAL CHARACTERISTICS of any individual cat – its body shape or conformation, the length and curliness of its coat, the color of its coat and 'points', its sex and so on – are determined by its genetic make-up or genotype, as biologists call it.

THE GENE POOL

WHEN AN EGG is fertilized by a sperm in the act of reproduction, each contributes a single set of genes to the genotype of the resultant offspring. These are carried in the chromosomes, the thread-like structures contained within living cells which are made up of molecules of DNA. Each chromosome contains an enormous number of genes, chemical compositions some of which play a part in determining the physical make-up (the phenotype) of the offspring. In the cat there are 38 chromosomes (eight fewer than in humans) in each cell, half of which come from each parent. As the mother and the father each has a different genotype and each contributes only half of the fertilized egg's chromosomes, the resulting kittens will have a selection of genes different from that of their parents but made up of elements of each.

FORMATION OF CHARACTERISTICS

WITH TWO EXCEPTIONS, the chromosomes line up in matched pairs that determine which particular physical and other characteristics of the parents are to be passed on to the kittens. The two exceptions are the sex chromosomes, which may or may not match. The reproducing female always contributes an X (female) chromosome. The male may contribute an X (female) or a Y (male). The matching of two X chromosomes will produce a female kitten. An X and a Y chromosome will produce a male. Y plus Y matches cannot occur because the Y chromosome cannot be contributed by the female. Thus it is always the father who determines the sex of the offspring, as it is in humans and virtually all other species of animal life.

The remaining matched chromosomes have genes arranged along them in a particular order so that genes related to a specific physical feature – length of hair, for example – are in pairs which are called alleles. Just one of the genes in each allele will be passed on to the kittens. If both the genes are identical – if both are genes for short hair, for example – then without question the kittens will have short hair. In that case the allele is said to be

Middle
Genotype determines all physical characteristics of a cat.

Bottom
These kittens are from the same litter but each has different genes, thus influencing their appearance.

homozygous for hair length. If one of the 'length of hair' genes is for short hair and the other for long hair, then the kittens will have short hair and the allele is heterozygous for hair length. To complete the range of choices, if the 'length of hair' genes are both for long hair (and are therefore also homozygous) the kittens will be long-haired.

DOMINANT AND RECESSIVE

THE SIGNIFICANT FEATURE of these three possibilities is the effect of the unmatched alleles: short hair plus long hair results in short hair. This is because the gene for short hair is said to be dominant and the gene for long hair recessive. Dominant genes always 'win' over recessive ones. If there is no dominant gene in the allele, as with the matched genes for long hair, then the recessive genes are free to pass on their characteristic to the kittens. As with the genes related to length of hair, so with genes covering other characteristics such as hair color, the shape of ears, and muzzle, general body conformation, length of tail, and so on. Some are dominant and others recessive, and all play their part in the dance of the genes which results in the make-up of a new creature.

If this were the end of the story, recessive characteristics such as long hair would become rarer as the generations passed, and would eventually become extinct. When the genes met in each succeeding generation, the recessive genes would be beaten every time. But although the

recessive gene may play no part in determining the hair length of a kitten of a particular mating, it is nevertheless passed on in the cells of that generation. If one of those kittens grows up to mate with a cat which also has the recessive gene for long hair, it is likely that some kittens with long hair will be the result. This explains why certain physical characteristics may disappear for a generation or more and then reappear.

HEREDITY

HEREDITY IS THE passing on of characteristics from one generation to the next – which is further complicated by two other factors. One is that although most genes are inherited quite independently of any others, like the gene for long hair, some are linked with others and tend to be inherited together. Tortoiseshell cats provide one example. The coat colors of cats are determined by their genotype, the color genes being part of the

make-up of the skin cells. As the genes for both red and black are found on X chromosomes, the female cats can carry the genes for orange (red) and black coloring, which together make up the tortoiseshell pattern.

Males can inherit either red or black, but not both, as they only inherit one X chromosome. As a result, almost all tortoiseshell cats are female, and the few males that are born are almost always sterile. The gene for orange (red) coat color is therefore said to be 'sex-linked.' There are other forms of linkage which do not involve the X or Y chromosomes, but which result in certain characteristics being inherited together. Examples of these are mentioned overleaf.

Top
The mother always passes on the Y chromosome and therefore cannot determine gender.

Middle
Tortoiseshells coat color is sex-linked.

Bottom
Although this tortoiseshell is different to the one pictured above, they will both be female.

In the beginning, all cats were short-haired tabbies. Over generations, mutant genes, or 'rogue genes' as they are sometimes called, have introduced all the variations away from short-haired tabbiness that make up the cat population. They have diluted colors, removed dark bands from the coat, introduced new kinds of markings, and accentuated certain colors at the expense of others. For example, all so-called blue (in fact, blue-grey) cats carry a gene which is a 'dilute' or mutation of black. Most mutant genes, but not all, are recessive, so they take a number of generations to establish themselves. But once they have happened, once the original genes have 'gone wrong', they do not put themselves right. They continue into succeeding generations.

When they affect more significant characteristics than hair color – body type, perhaps, or better resistance to temperature changes – they eventually become the basis of evolution. Although today's domestic tabby is similar to the African or European wild cat, it is not genetically identical. Even without the intervention of breeders over the past 100 years, the mechanics of survival have bred a different cat from the animal that, 5,000 years ago, first made its acquaintance with humans.

THE MUTANT GENE

THE SECOND COMPLICATING factor in heredity is mutation, but it is also mutation that accounts for the wide variety of body types, coat colors and lengths, and other physical characteristics that give pleasure to cat lovers and point to breeding programmes. Mutations take place when genes 'go wrong' – that is, they undergo changes in the process of being passed on from one generation to the next. If it were not for mutations, all the domestic cats in the world today would be like the African wild cat, the European wild cat, the Jungle cat and possibly Pallas's cat, although as a longhair, Pallas's Cat is itself a mutation.

CAT FACT:

A traditional way for diagnosing illness in a cat, which actually works, is to check its nose. If it is cold and noticeably wet, then it may have a chill, cold, or even cat flu.

Top
All cats descend from the shorthaired tabby.

Bottom
Although this classic tabby looks like the European wild cat genetically they are not identical.

EFFECTS OF MUTATION

SOME MUTANT GENES, like the 'dilute' black that produces blue cats, are so long established that their effects are hardly noticed. We accept that some cats are a blue-grey color just as we accept that others are tabby, and we do not stop to consider the multitude of genetic steps that have transmuted a tabby into a blue. But occasionally a mutant gene produces a spectacularly different and novel result. This is what has happened in the past few decades with the Scottish Fold (when a mutant gene produced laid-down ears), the Sphynx (an almost hairless cat) and the Rex (curly-coated) breeds. In nature, left to themselves, these mutations would have probably disappeared into the genetic pool and may well have died out, for all were chance events that happened to be noticed by people with connections in the cat breeding world. Consequently, selective breeding from the original mutations took place, and in each case a new breed was launched.

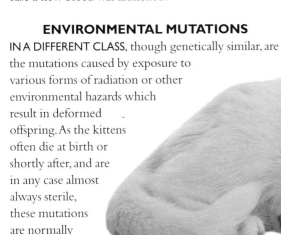

ENVIRONMENTAL MUTATIONS

IN A DIFFERENT CLASS, though genetically similar, are the mutations caused by exposure to various forms of radiation or other environmental hazards which result in deformed offspring. As the kittens often die at birth or shortly after, and are in any case almost always sterile, these mutations are normally canceled out.

Environmentally based mutations apart, there are a number of genetic defects that arise because the main effect of a gene carries with it an added liability. For example, the dominant white gene W which gives cats an all-white coat carries with it a linked tendency to deafness which is most prominent in blue-eyed whites but can also affect whites with orange or odd-colored eyes. The condition, a fault in the inner ear, begins shortly after the birth of a kitten and cannot be treated. The result is that the kitten fails to develop one of its essential survival senses and also grows up socially inept because it cannot respond to its mother's language. If it is female and subsequently bears kittens, things get worse. The deaf queen cannot respond to her kittens' cries, with the result that they are neglected. The only way to stop this cycle of deprivation is not to breed from deaf queens and to ensure that they are spayed.

Otherwise, the white gene may lie buried in the gene pool and come to the surface in subsequent generations. However, the common belief that all white cats are deaf is mistaken. It should be easy enough to check, if it were not for the fact that deaf cats can compensate by developing ultra-sensitivity in their paws so that while they may not hear you come into the room they can feel you through the vibrations in the floor.

Top left
This blue kitten's color is the result of a mutated black gene.

Middle left
The Scottish Fold's breed characteristic is the flat ears, a gene mutation.

Bottom Left
This cat may be deaf in the ear on the side of its blue eye.

death of the kittens in the womb, and even heterozygous matings sometimes result in lethal abnormalities. Altogether, the M gene is particularly unstable, as is evidenced by the fact that a litter of Manx kittens can include some with almost normal tails, some with bobtails and some with no tails at all. As one authority has commented, the congenital problems associated with the Manx 'would almost certainly disqualify it from recognition were it a modern development.' It is saved from this ignominy by the fact that it was apparently a spontaneous mutation dating back at least 300 years, not a breeder's invention, and became established because of the isolation of the Isle of Man where it occurred.

MUTATION PROBLEMS

ANOTHER GENE WITH an unfortunate side effect is the Siamese, which can carry a fault in the nerve connections between the eyes and the brain. This disturbs normal binocular vision, resulting in a blurred image and difficulty in judging distance. In an effort to correct this, some Siamese develop a squint, which is properly regarded as a fault in cat fancy circles. Squinting Siamese do, however, find their way into the pet market. Anyone who thinks of buying one should be aware that the cat will spend its whole life at a disadvantage.

Some individual genes are notoriously prone to problems. An example is the dominant gene M which produces the tailless or short-tailed Manx cat. Homozygous matings of Manx cats invariably result in the

PRODUCT OF ITS ENVIRONMENT?

THE GENES THAT determine the visible characteristics are only a few of the many thousands that govern other aspects of the physical cat. The rest make up what might be called the body's operating systems, many of them virtually automatic and unknowable but a few, such as those affecting taste, the inclination to

hunt, and the degree of aggression, observable in their effects by the human owner. But at this point the question of nature versus nurture enters the arena. It is a fact that a lazy, phlegmatic queen will not produce kittens

Top
The Siamese squint is the result of a gene mutation that creates blurred vision.

Bottom
Gene mutation in the Manx breed can cause severe deformities and often death for unborn kittens.

that turn out to be good mousers, and conversely that farm cats produce mousing champions generation after generation. The first few weeks of a kitten's life, possibly unrivaled outside the cat family for its intensity of teaching and learning, are without doubt critical here – but whether the hunting instinct is taught, in the genetic make-up, or a combination of the two, will never be known.

UNDERSTANDING GENETICS

CAT BREEDERS MAKE use of modern understanding of genetics in two ways. If they aim to breed 'true', that is to produce cats as close as possible to the ideal for the breed laid down in the standards of the various cat fancy organizations, they take care not to introduce any genetic variations into the breeding line if they can help it. Of course, they cannot always help it, because as has been explained recessive genes can spontaneously turn up several generations hence. The practice of registering cats with their history of registered parents, grandparents, and so on stretching back at least four generations is some kind of safeguard, but it is not foolproof. This is why breeders often have for sale kittens which are perfectly healthy but, for some reason of conformation or coat color, are not of show standard.

Then again, some breeders undertake breeding programmes in which mutant genes are combined and recombined to develop certain characteristics. Some of these efforts have resulted in 'new' breeds being admitted by registration bodies, while others have proved unsuccessful for a variety of reasons ranging from the 'new' breed not being distinctive enough to health threatening physical problems.

DESIGNER CATS OF THE FUTURE?

IN PRACTICE, THE relationship between cat fancy organizations and the veterinary profession tends to outlaw any attempt to produce 'designer cats' through genetic manipulation. Stories emerge from time to time about breeders who have successfully produced, for example, miniature cats along the lines of miniature dogs, but the extended procedures that cat fancy organizations use before admitting and recognizing new breeds are a bulwark against the worst excesses of selective breeding. After a century of experience, the cat fancy has built up a deep understanding of the nature of the domestic cat as a species and is constantly alert to the dangers of distorting its genetic nature beyond what is reasonable and right for the cat.

Top
The nurturing that farm kittens receive from birth makes them adept mousers.

Feline Terminology

THIS SECTION IS about the terms used by veterinarians and breeders in describing cats, distinguishing between types, breeds, and varieties, and laying down show standards. First, some definitions.

CAT FACT:
Cats are very sensitive to the smell of chlorine in water. This is why they would much rather drink from a dirty puddle or pond than from a bowl of clean tap water.

TYPE

THE TERM 'TYPE' covers the head and body features, including size, and shape, that characterize a breed. It is sometimes used more loosely to refer to a non-pedigree cat's resemblance to a breed. For example, it might be said of such a cat that it is 'a good specimen of the British Shorthair type'. This does not mean that it is actually a pedigree British shorthair, but merely that it shares the general conformation of that breed.

BREED

THE WORD 'BREED' describes a group of cats with common physical characteristics and registered ancestry going back several generations. It is by no means a precise term, because what is regarded as a breed in one country or in one decade may not be so regarded in another. While all cats in a specified breed will share some common physical features such as body type, they may vary in others such as coloring. Again, everyone understands what is meant by the Siamese or Abyssinian breed, but to the non-breeder the distinction between a Siamese and a Balinese looks fairly academic.

VARIETY

A 'VARIETY' IS a sub-division within a breed, usually distinguished by coloring but sometimes by other features. (In the Manx, for example, although only completely tailless cats are accepted for show, there are three varieties with varying degrees of vestigial tails, respectively called 'risers', 'stubbies' and 'longies'). A breed may consist of only one variety; an example is the Russian Blue, which in Britain and North America is recognized in only one color, although the New Zealand cat fancy accepts Russian Whites and Russian Blacks. In other breeds the number of varieties can be very large. About 60 varieties of Persian (in the UK, called Longhair) have been registered in Britain and North America, although not all varieties are recognized by both countries and in some cases one country's distinct breed can be another's variety or vice versa.

Top

This classic red tabby is a British Shorthair and could be described as being typical to type, for example he has a round face.

Bottom

An Abyssinian will have certain breed characteristics that will differentiate it from other breeds.

premium cat food or, one that will have to find its food where it can. When the kitten is born, genetics and indeed nature have finished their work.

BREED CLASSIFICATION

THIS POINT IS made because everything in this section is related to how humans, mainly as breeders but also as veterinarians, have classified cats according to certain characteristics. For example, it has been calculated that in terms of coat colors alone there are in excess of 2,000 possible permutations, given the genetic variables. If you multiply that across the number of breeds, and then across the other variables within each breed, the range of varieties of animal that could be genetically defined as a cat becomes astronomical, even allowing for the fact that some permutations would be genetically impossible or would result in unviable mutations. In practice, the cat fancy has taken an interest in only a tiny fraction of the possible variations, and the organization of the fancy is such that any potential new entrant into the privileged league is closely scrutinized and trialed before being granted admission.

The admission of a new breed does not imply the 'discovery' of a new kind of cat. Such discoveries are rare; there have been a handful in the 100 years' history of the cat fancy, mainly the result of genetic mutations. While this suggests that the world of feline genetics may still have further surprises up its sleeve, all it means when a 'new' breed or a 'new' color variety is recognized is that the authorities have voted to admit it. New or old, it is still only a cat, with a selection of the body types, coat lengths, coat colorings and so on which are genetically available to cats, and dominating the whole scenario is the fact that all domestic cats, from the humblest moggie to the finest Siamese, are members of one species, *Felis catus*.

The chromosomes of a kitten in the womb, half contributed by each parent, contain all the genetic information that will determine the sex and physical characteristics of the kitten as well as provide the operating systems for the functioning of its organs, senses, instincts, and so on. The kitten that is eventually born is a joint production of all these genes. Sometimes genes act independently and sometimes they act in groups which are called polygenes, but all work in concert to produce viable offspring which will continue the survival of the cat as a species and of that breeding line in particular. It is worth remembering that this is the only genetic imperative; it does not matter genetically whether the kitten is to be long-haired or short-haired, black or tabby, or tortoiseshell, a pretty cat or an ugly looking bruiser, a Championship cat, or an alley moggie, a stud cat, or a pampered pet, a cat fed on

Top
In Britain and North America this is the only color permitted for Russian Blues.

Bottom
Illustrations showing color range of cat fur.

Red	Chocolate	Blue	Cream	Black	Lilac	White

CAT FACT:
When domestic cats are used for breeding purposes the females are referred to as queens and the males are toms. A pregnant queen is said to be 'in kitten'.

SELECTIVE BREEDING

IT IS AN INTRIGUING thought that if humans had decided to domesticate the caracal, for example, as it is thought they came very close to doing in ancient Egypt and India for hunting purposes, you might now be reading about a wide variety of caracal types, selectively bred for hunting, retrieving, guarding the home, herding, and perhaps racing, probably in a large range of body and coat types.

As it turned out, the dog proved to be a more suitable animal for these purposes and it fell to three or four species of small wild cats to build a relationship with humans on a different basis. Despite what has

happened to them since, sometimes through the course of evolution and sometimes through human intervention, they are still primarily cats and only very secondarily creatures that conform with arbitrary human rules about how they should look.

CONFORMATION OR BODY TYPE

THE BASIC ATTRIBUTE of any cat is its conformation or type. This is a combination of its body size and shape, the proportion of its legs to its body, the length and shape of its tail, the shape of its head, and the appearance of its facial features. These factors are all determined by polygenes, groups of genes which act together in almost all cats to produce their major characteristic features. Generally, these polygenes stay together and the features they represent do not abruptly change between one generation and the next. They may, of course, be changed over generations by careful selective breeding programmes over a period of time to accentuate specific characteristics or suppress others.

There are a few exceptions to the general rule, such as the mutations that produced the Manx, the Japanese Bobtail, and the Scottish Fold and the rogue gene that occasionally produces cats with more than the usual five toes on each paw. These are all the effects of single mutant genes, whereas general type is determined by the group of genes, each small in its individual effect, which together produce a particular conformation. In general cats remain faithful to the body type inherent in the genetic make-up of their parents, and for this reason many breeders disapprove of crossbreeding as introducing complications into the normal genetic pathway. The proposal for recognition of crossbreeds is a cue for alarm bells to ring in the world of the cat fancy.

THE COBBY CAT

THERE ARE TWO basic body types. One is described as cobby, and is exemplified by the British Shorthair (known in mainland Europe as the European Shorthair) and the Persian (officially known in Britain as the Longhair). Features of the cobby type are a compact, sturdy body with a deep chest, broad shoulders and hind quarters, short legs and tail, and a short, round head. Within this broad definition there

Top left
Egyptians considered domesticating the caracal for hunting purposes.

Bottom
Manx cats are the result of one single mutant gene

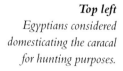

Oriental. The foreign or Oriental body is slender and lithe, the head narrow and wedge shaped and the legs long. Generally, the impression it gives is one of sleekness, sinuous movement, and relatively light weight.

Some biologists believe that the cobby type originated with the European wild Cat, *Felis silvestris*, whereas the foreign or Oriental type's ancestors were the African wild cat, *Felis libyca*, perhaps with an admixture of the jungle cat, *Felis chaus*, and Pallas's cat, *Felis manul*. But this is speculative, and interbreeding over the 5,000 years of the relationship between humans and cats – to say nothing of the interbreeding that took place before that relationship began – will have meant that the genetic pathways of the different contributing species have crossed and recrossed thousands of times.

s considerable scope for variations. For example, a round-headed cat may have a short or medium nose, small or medium ears, eyes set closer to or farther from the nose, and so on. Most moggies or alley cats are cobby. So too are the cats in typical children's picture books.

THE 'FOREIGN' CAT

AT THE OTHER extreme, for example the Siamese, is the so-called foreign type. In this context the word foreign has no geographical connotations; it simply means, in terms of the cat fancy, non-cobby. Extremes of the foreign type such as the Siamese are described as

CAT FACT:
The oldest domestic cat with a reliable birth date, was a male tabby with the highly original name of Puss. He died the day after his 36th birthday in England.

Top
This red and white Persian has a typical cobby look; a round face, compact body, and short legs.

Top right
The Siamese is the archetypal foreign cat. It is lithe and sleek .

Bottom
This Oriental tortie, has a light-weight appearance which is typical of foreign cats.

BOTH ENDS OF THE SCALE

THE TWO EXTREMES, cobby and foreign or Oriental, can be regarded as the opposite ends of a scale, with various intermediate types in between. The majority of pedigree breeds are in this intermediate category, and in this range the attribution of characteristics to a particular breed can be an inexact science. Some of the differences between North American and British breeding and show standards are due to the fact that the cat fancy organizations place a different emphasis on particular type characteristics in relation to the same breed and may accentuate cobby or foreign features.

This does not mean that one set of standards is 'better' or more true to breed than another; it is merely a matter of different national tastes, and sometimes a reflection of the history of a breed in one country or another. For example, in the Persian (UK Longhair) American breeders prefer a more compact, ultra-cobby body shape than the British, and this preference goes back to the early days of the breed in each country. Then again, within the same breed and even the same pedigree line there will sometimes be slight variations in body type, some so small as to be unnoticeable by the ordinary cat lover but sufficient to disqualify a cat for breeding or show purposes. A pedigree cat that does not meet show standards is still nevertheless a pedigree cat and a representative of its breed.

The terms classic or, in North America, typey are sometimes used to describe cats which conform exactly to the body type defined in the appropriate organization's standards. It is important to note, however, that show standards are not fixed for all time. The 'ideal' Siamese of 1900, which was markedly less sinuous than the modern version, would not stand a chance at a show today. Tastes have changed and breeding expertise has moved on, largely as a result of breeders' understanding of genetics.

COAT TYPE

THE SECOND MOST important distinguishing feature is the coat type. Broadly, cats are either short-haired like the British Shorthair or long-haired like the Persian. As was explained in the section on heredity, a cat's hair is 'naturally' short (or, as biologists would say, the hair of the 'wild type' is short), and long hair has been introduced over many centuries by a recessive gene. Once the long hair gene is present, the coat may develop over generations in 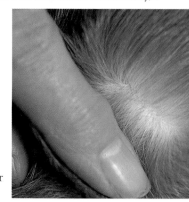 response to environmental conditions. This is what produced the shaggy coat of the Maine Coon, suited to the hard winters of the north-western United States. The range of hair the longest hairs in the coat, the guard hairs, between the British Shorthair and a show standard Persian is from about 1.75 in (4.5 cm) to about 6 in (15 cm).

Top
The guard hairs have been pulled back on this shorthair.

Bottom
The Maine Coon's coat has developed to protect the breed against the harsh winter climate of North America.

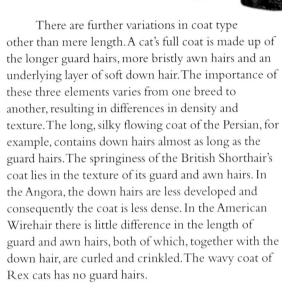

COLORS AND MARKINGS

WHEN YOU THINK of the solid color of the British Blue, the delicately shaded coat of a lavender or lilac Persian or the all-over cream, delicately set off by the points, of a Colorpoint Longhair, it is hard to remember that the basic coat color and pattern of all cats is brown tabby – irregular golden-brown markings laid over a lighter ground color. This coloring has an obvious advantage as camouflage and is common among wild mammals, including many members of the cat family such as the serval and the African wild cat.

There are about a dozen genes that, between them and in various combinations, govern the feline color spectrum. The genes responsible for the brown tabby coloring are, first, the agouti gene A, named after the rabbit sized rodent of that name found in Central America, and one or more of the T genes which produce various kinds of tabby patterns. These genes are present in the genotype of all cats, which means that all cats have within them the potential to be brown tabbies. The agouti gene is dominant to its counterpart, the mutant non-agouti gene A, which cancels out the tabby stripes.

The usual rules of heredity apply: any mating with one tabby parent will produce tabby kittens because of the presence of the dominant A gene, but two non-tabby parents, each contributing only A genes, will produce non-tabby kittens. But tabbiness and non-tabbiness are only relative terms. Even non-tabby kittens will have a tendency towards tabbiness, which often shows up in their early months only to disappear later, or may persist as 'ghost' markings faintly discernible in the adult coat. It seems that, in defiance of genetics, cats are reluctant to dispense with their natural tabbiness, which in the wild offers them protection against predators.

There are further variations in coat type other than mere length. A cat's full coat is made up of the longer guard hairs, more bristly awn hairs and an underlying layer of soft down hair. The importance of these three elements varies from one breed to another, resulting in differences in density and texture. The long, silky flowing coat of the Persian, for example, contains down hairs almost as long as the guard hairs. The springiness of the British Shorthair's coat lies in the texture of its guard and awn hairs. In the Angora, the down hairs are less developed and consequently the coat is less dense. In the American Wirehair there is little difference in the length of guard and awn hairs, both of which, together with the down hair, are curled and crinkled. The wavy coat of Rex cats has no guard hairs.

The ideal coat for a specific breed, as laid down in show standards, has been developed by selective breeding, in some cases over 100 years. But it must be remembered that even in the most favored breeds, the proportion of cats bred for show is small, which means that pedigree cats of any breed will include individuals whose coat type (as with the body type) is not what show judges would consider make good specimens of the breed.

CAT FACT:
A defining characteristic of all cats is that they are digitigrade. This means that they walk on their toes, which maximises the efficiency of their limbs for running.

Top left
This Cornish Rex does not have guard hairs.

Middle
This cream-colored British Shorthair displays ghost markings on its coat.

Bottom
A British Blue's coat contrasts greatly with its ancestor's, the tabby.

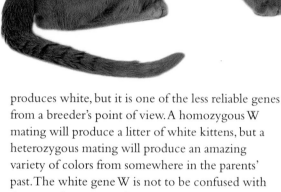

SELF (SOLID) COLORS

ONCE THE DOMINANCE of the agouti gene is removed, a combination of other genes comes into play. These produce colored coats in various shades – known in Britain as 'self' and in North America as 'solid' colors – according to the genetic mix.

One of the basic colors in cats is black, the result of the B gene which produces a black pigment, melanin, in the hairs. Mutations of the B gene can produce blue (in fact, blue-grey), chocolate brown, cinnamon (light brown), and lilac (UK) or lavender (North America).

The orange gene O produces red and, in its dilute version, cream. However, the non-agouti gene is not effective on the orange gene, so that the inherent tabby pattern tends to break through. This makes the breeding of self reds and creams difficult, tabby markings often appearing on the face, legs and tail. The dominant white gene W, which is a mutant,

produces white, but it is one of the less reliable genes from a breeder's point of view. A homozygous W mating will produce a litter of white kittens, but a heterozygous mating will produce an amazing variety of colors from somewhere in the parents' past. The white gene W is not to be confused with the gene that causes white spotting (see below), which is called S and which does not have the W gene's association with deafness.

These basic self or solid colors are only the beginning of the story. Other genes affect the distribution, the pattern and the relative strength of colors in the coat, the definition of the points (face, ears, paws, and tail) and what might be called 'special effects' such as shaded and tipped hairs.

TABBIES

THE MOST COMMON form of tabbiness is the classic or blotched tabby with clearly defined broad stripes on a lighter, greyish agouti ground. In a show classic tabby, judges look for evenly spaced bars on the legs and rings on the tail. The stripes on the neck and upper chest form 'necklaces', and lines run over the back of the head to meet the shoulder markings. On each of the cat's sides there should be a 'bullseye' consisting of one or

---

CAT FACT

Female cats will usually quite readily foster orphaned kittens or cubs, providing that they are smeared with her vaginal fluid so that they carry the correct scent.

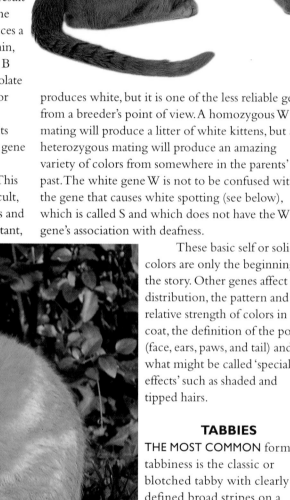

Top left
A solid, or self, black cat.

Top right
This solid Oriental's color is called lilac in Britain and lavender in North America.

Bottom
This red classic tabby illustrates the common broad stripes across the body.

Top
The markings on this mackerel tabby are typically closer together.

Bottom left
A spotted silver tabby shorthair.

Bottom right
Even at this young age the 'M' shape is clearly visible on this kitten's forehead.

CAT FACT:
The jaguarundi, of South America, is reckoned to be the least cat-like of cats. It is otter-like in shape and very good at swimming and climbing in its rainforest home.

more rings enclosing a light patch. As in all tabbies, the 'frown marks' on the forehead should form a distinct 'M' shape.

In mackerel tabbies the markings are narrower. They extend down the spine, where they are met with vertical stripes running down the sides of the body. As in the classic tabby, the bands of color on the legs should be evenly spaced and meet the body markings, with 'necklaces' at the neck and chest and a barred tail.

TABBY VARIETIES

IN THE SPOTTED tabby the mackerel stripes are broken up into areas reminiscent of spotted wild cat species such as the lynx and the pampas Cat. The spots are very difficult to maintain in breeding, kittens often reverting to mackerel stripes or to varying degrees of spots-and-stripes mixtures. Ideally, the spots should be round and evenly distributed, but in most spotted tabbies they are of varying shape, size and spacing. There is a line of spots (not always broken) along the spine, and bars on the legs and tail.

The ticked tabby (also called the Abyssinian tabby but not exclusive to that breed) has an all-over agouti coat but with tabby markings on the face and sometimes also on the legs and tail. The body hairs are ticked (flecked) with the ground and marking colors.

The basic color of the markings of all tabbies is black, the B gene being present in the genotype, but this is, by convention, always called brown and the term 'black tabby' is never used. Black can be modified by dilution genes to blue, chocolate brown, cinnamon, and lilac (lavender). The orange gene O is responsible for red and cream tabbies.

TORTOISESHELLS

THE BASIC TORTOISESHELL pattern, known as tortie in the cat fancy, is a random patchwork of black and orange which can be reminiscent of a jigsaw puzzle. As explained in the section on heredity, the tortoiseshell pattern is sex-linked and almost invariably restricted to females. The basic colors are subject to the usual range of variations, producing blue, chocolate, cinnamon, and lavender/lilac versions of the non-orange areas. Blue-cream and lavender-

(lilac-) cream cats are in fact tortoiseshells but are not recognized as such in some organizations and are classed on their own.

Tortoiseshells in which tabby markings replace the normal black patching are known in Britain as tortie-tabbies and in the United States as patched tabbies or torbies. They are blue, brown, or silver tabbies with patches of red or cream in the coat.

British and American practice differs on the desired mixture of colors in tortoiseshells. In Britain the preference is for small and intermingled areas whereas in the United States larger, separated patches are preferred. This preference is particularly marked in the respective show standards for blue-creams. But this is a case where show standards confound the breeder's best efforts, because the genetic difference between the two blue-cream patterns is minimal and producing one pattern or the other in a litter is virtually the luck of the draw.

SHADED OR TIPPED COLORS

CATS WITH SHADED or tipped coats owe their impressive coloring to the dominant I gene, which suppresses the pigment in the hairs. The result is that the hairs are colored at the ends, but the remainder of

Top
A non-pedigree tortie-tabby and white.

Bottom
This longhaired blue-cream is a tortoiseshell.

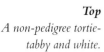

of each hair is white or cream. Tipped cats may be bred with long or short hair. The extent of the end colouring, or tipping, produces one of a variety of effects known as silver, golden, smoke or chinchilla, but all the variations tend to make casual observers do a double take. In a good specimen of the black smoke, for example, a cat that appears black when it is still, reveals when it moves, its underlying white. To watch this transformation take place can be a startling experience.

The lightest version of tipping is known as standard shell in North America and standard tipped in Britain. The main areas of tipping are on the back, flanks, head and tail, with less colour on the face and legs. When the tipping colour is red the coat is described as shell cameo or red chinchilla. Standard shell colouring is also seen in the chinchilla silver (black tipping over pure white) and chinchilla golden (black tipping over cream).

SHADED AND SMOKED

THE INTERMEDIATE tipped colouring is called shaded. If the basic colour is red over white, the cats are known as red shaded or shaded cameo. If the basic colour is black over pure white, the colouring is called shaded silver, which often occurs with the tipped effect in the tabby pattern. A version of shaded silver but with copper instead of green or hazel eyes is recognised in Britain but not in the United States. In the shaded golden, the colouring is black over cream.

Finally, there are the spectacular smokes, the most heavily tipped. The most common is black over pure white, but blue, chocolate brown red, cream, blue-cream, lilac and tortoiseshell smokes are also seen.

WHITE SPOTTING

WHITE SPOTTING MEANS the appearance of patches of white on coloured coats. It is caused not by the white gene W but by a dominant gene known as S. The extent of white spotting may vary from white 'gloves' on the paws or a dab of white on the nose or chest to an almost all-over white relieved only by patches of colour. The most striking example of white spotting is in the Turkish Van, which has auburn colouring only on its face, on the ears and at the tail. The Van pattern also occurs in Persians.

Smaller white areas on a coat of solid colour produce an effect known as bi-colour. The total area of white is normally between one-third and one-half. The tortoiseshell-and-white variety, where the white patches set off the black and red, is known as 'calico' in North America. The Japanese Bobtail is a bi-colour breed.

Top
This British Shorthair is black tipped, it carries the dominant I gene.

Bottom left
This beautiful coat is shaded silver coloured.

Bottom right
This archetypally coloured Turkish Van illustrates the auburn colouring on the ears and tail.

POINTS

A CAT'S 'POINTS' are the ears, nose, feet and tail. In cats with a pointed pattern coat, the basic coat colour is confined to the points, the rest of the body usually being pale cream, fawn or white.

The white may have a bluish, creamy or ivory tinge. Although precise colour requirements for pointed cats vary from one country to another, in general the colourpointing must match the basic body colour in show cats; for example, a blue point must have a bluish-white body.

COLOURPOINTING

THE SIAMESE IS the best-known example of colourpointing, but it occurs in a number of other breeds such as the Himalayan, a Siamese/Persian cross classed in North America as a Colourpoint Longhair. The colourpoint effect is related to the cat's body temperature. The lower temperature at the points encourages the production of pigment. This sensitivity is so marked in Siamese that in cool environments kittens develop stronger colouring, both on the body and at the points, than those reared in warmer climates. This effect is sometimes seen by comparing kittens born at different times of the year, although modern heating tends to compensate.

In pointed cats, the normal black colour appears as a dark sepia known to breeders as seal, and seal-pointed Siamese were the starting point for the variety. Blue, chocolate, lilac (known to some North American breeders as frost), red and cream are now also bred, together with tabby (in the United States known as the lynx) and tortie points.

EYES

THE COLOUR OF the iris is of great significance in the cat fancy and also influences the non-expert's perception of a cat's beauty. When kittens open their eyes at seven to 10 days, their eyes are always blue. The adult colour develops through kittenhood. The range of colour runs from deep orange through shades of amber and green to blue. Breed standards specify which colours are acceptable. These may vary between varieties in the same breed, but in

Right
A lilac point Siamese, this breed is the best example of colourpointing.

some breeds the colour requirement is specific. For example, in the Abyssinian, eye colour requirements are related to the body colour, whereas Siamese and Birmans must always have blue eyes, the deeper blue the better.

Odd eyes – one blue, one orange – often make strangers look twice, but the condition is quite common, especially but not exclusively in white cats and notably among Persians. As with blue-eyed whites, there is a tendency to deafness.

Eye shape as well as colour enters into breeding and showing. Broadly speaking, cobby types are required to have round eyes and foreign or Oriental types an almond shape. So too with the position of the eyes in relation to the nose. In cobby cats, eyes set well apart are preferred.

FACIAL CHARACTERISTICS

THE SHAPE AND prominence of the ears and their positioning on the head are laid down in show standards and are characteristic to specific breeds. In the Abyssinian, for example, the ears are large, pricked and pointed, contributing to the breed's typical alert, wide-awake expression. The Persian's ears, by contrast, are small with rounded tips, tilted forward

in the Siamese, or splendidly bushy as in the Maine Coon. Manx and Japanese Bobtail tails are either non-existent or vestigial, although surprisingly, considering how much the average cat uses its tail when climbing, this does not seem to inconvenience these breeds at all. In all breeds and countries, the cat fancy regards a kink in the tail as a fault. Siamese are particularly prone to kinks in the tail. There are many fanciful stories about how this fault arose in the breed's ancestry but the genetic basis of its true origin is not clear.

PAWS

SHOW STANDARDS REQUIRE the colour of the paw pads to be the same as that of the nose leather, which may be black or another colour (see above). Cats' paws are subject to two abnormalities, both caused by dominant genes, which are faults in the show world. A polydactyl cat may have six or seven toes, more commonly on the front paws. The second paw abnormality is split foot, a division in one or both front paws caused by a bone deformation. The polydactyl condition does not affect the cat's movements, but split foot makes climbing difficult or impossible.

and set wide apart to give the rounded contour of the head that is so prized among breeders of Persians. The ears of the Scottish Fold are unique among cats. They fold forwards to varying degrees ranging from small and tight to larger and looser. The fold can be seen in kittens but it only develops fully in the mature cat.

The size and shape of the nose and the colour of the nose pad or leather varies between breeds. The most extreme example of the short, snub nose is in the American standard for Persians, in which a pronounced stop or break between the nose and the forehead is favoured. This is taken to excess in the Peke-faced Persian, a breed that is not recognised in Britain because of the fancy's worries about breathing problems and other disorders associated with the very abbreviated nose.

At the other end of the scale, in terms of noses, is the Egyptian Mau, whose nose meets its forehead in a slight rise and is a very marked feature of the head as a whole. The required colour of nose pad for most breeds and varieties is black, but there are some variations. In Oriental Shorthairs, for example, brown nose leather is specified for the self (solid) brown, lavender for the lilac (lavender), blue for the Oriental blue and so on.

CATS' TAILS

A CAT'S TAIL is a balancing mechanism, part of its body language equipment and a draught excluder when it is asleep. It can be slim, long and whiplike, as

> **CAT FACT:**
> The rusty-spotted cat, which lives an arboreal life in southern India and Sri Lanka, is the smallest wild species. It has a maximum length of 71 cm (28 in).

Top
This blue-eyed Turkish Angora, like many blue-eyed whites, is also deaf.

Bottom
Japanese Bobtails are uninhibited climbers regardless of their lack of a tail.

Pedigree and Non-Pedigree

BY FAR THE majority of cats in the world, treasured pets as well as working animals such as farm cats, are non-pedigree or, to use the word used in Britain, moggies. Although they may lack the finer points of cat conformation in the eye of a breeder or a show judge, they are often handsome in their own right.

NON-PEDIGREE CATS

AS PETS, THEY have the advantage that having bred naturally – that is to say, usually accidentally – and almost certainly having strays at some point in their ancestry, they are likely to be healthy and hardy, any weaker specimens in the strain having been weeded out by the laws of survival. They are inclined to be less temperamental and more adaptable than pedigree cats, to be less demanding of attention, and to be less noisy and boisterous than some pedigree breeds. The ownership of a non-pedigree cat does not even prevent its owner from enjoying the pleasures of showing. Most cat shows have classes for what are usually called 'household cats' in which the prizes are awarded for good health, good nature and charm rather than adherence to strict standards.

THE MOGGIE

ALTHOUGH ESTIMATES ARE difficult, it has been suggested that well over 90 per cent of pet cats in the United States, Britain and comparable industrialised countries are non-pedigree. This may seem, as compared with the number of mongrel dogs, surprising. But it must be remembered that the breeding of dogs for specific purposes – sheepdogs, gundogs, racing dogs, hunting dogs, lapdogs – has been going on for hundreds of years. Interest in cat-breeding is not much more than a century old. Before then, a cat was simply a cat. Samuel Johnson would not have worried about what breed his beloved Hodge belonged to.

CATS ARE CLASSIFIED

ABOUT THE MIDDLE of the nineteenth century, cat owners began to take a more positive interest in their pets. Gregor Mendel had published his findings on heredity in

Top right
This non-pedigree tortie-white was a winner at a British Cat Show.

Top left
Farm cats, although working cats, still enjoy human company and make good pets.

Bottom
Many cats in the West will look similar to this non-pedigree.

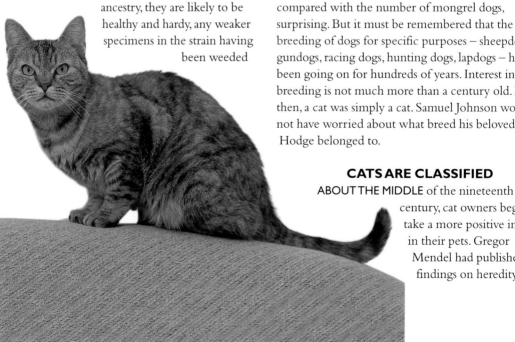

Skowhegan in Somerset County, Maine, for instance, the annual fair featured a contest for the title of 'Maine State Championship Coon Cat'.

SUBJECT OF STUDY

IN 1881 THE British biologist Sir George Mivart published the first authoritative and comprehensive book about the domestic cat. Mivart was a respected if controversial academic who had generally accepted Darwin's theory of evolution (which earned him excommunication from the Roman Catholic Church into which he had been born) but quibbled over some of the finer details. *The Cat* ran into many editions and profoundly influenced early cat fanciers on both sides of the Atlantic, largely by giving their interest scientific respectability.

The year 1892 saw the publication of a less academic book about cats which was for many years to be the Bible of the cat fancy world. This was *Our Cats* by Harrison Weir, who had organised the first British National Cat Show in 1871 and had become the first President of the National Cat Club. The full title of Our Cats gives an idea of its scope: *Our Cats and All About Them: Their Varieties, Habits and Management and for Show; the Standard of Excellence and Beauty Described and Pictured.* Harrison Weir gave breeders an agenda to work to, and the start of serious breeding for conformation, coat, colour and points can be dated from about this time.

1866, but they were not taken seriously by the scientific community until 1900 and it was long after that before their implications reached the public at large. What drove the nineteenth century cat fancy was a passion for classification, in line with the scientific spirit of the times. This was the passion that had taken Charles Darwin to the Galapagos Islands where he formulated his theory of evolution. Cat owners of the second half of the nineteenth century were increasingly reluctant to think that a cat was just a cat. They wanted to know what kind of cat, since there were clearly different kinds. At the same time, interest was growing in the ownership of an exotic cat as a status symbol, perhaps helped by the news that Queen Victoria had acquired a pair of blue Persians with which the royal household was greatly entranced.

STRIVING TO BE THE BEST

ANOTHER QUITE DIFFERENT impulse was also an influence. The nineteenth century was one in which competition was a significant force in many people's lives. State and county shows in North America and agricultural shows in Britain featured competitions for the best beasts, the best corn, the best fruit, the best herding dogs, the best carthorses and even the best farmers' babies. What could be more natural than that there should be competitions for the best cats? From about 1860, farmers in New England began to enter their Maine Coons – then basically farm cats – in local show competitions. At

Top left
This blue smoke Persian is similar in appearance to that which Queen Victoria would have owned.

Top right
Maine Coon cats were entered in American State competitions from the end of the nineteenth century.

Bottom
Author of the first comprehensive book on cats for cat-lovers, Harrison Weir.

THE PEDIGREE

WHAT, THEN, IS a pedigree cat? The answer depends to some extent on the country in which it lives. As has already been mentioned, the cat fancy organisations of different countries – and even within the same country in the case of the United States – are individualists in their recognition of breeds. But in general terms a pedigree cat is one whose ancestry in a recognised breed has been recorded and registered through at least four generations. Registration is the key function of the cat fancy organisations, and without it no cat is a pedigree animal.

Kittens are normally registered when they are about six weeks old. The registration document includes the date of birth, the description and breed, details of ancestry to the required number of generations, the names of the breeder and owner and of course the name of the kitten. This need not be the name by which it is commonly known. For example, the Nutwood breeding cattery may produce a litter of British Blue kittens, two of which are given the names Blue Haze and Blue Mist. The cattery is allowed to use its prefix (provided of course that it is a registered cattery), so the pedigree names of the kittens will be Nutwood Blue Haze and Nutwood Blue Mist. For all that, they may be known in the family as Tommy and Tiddles.

INDIVIDUAL BREEDS

THE HISTORY OF the cat fancy from the 1890s has been one of continuous refinement and re-assessment of breeds and varieties. For example, it was not until the 1950s that the Cat Fanciers' Association of America recognised Persians and Angoras as distinct breeds. Every decade has seen the recognition of 'new' breeds, either by the spontaneous discovery of variants such as the Scottish Fold or Devon Rex or by the introduction of new strains from abroad such as the Angora variation known in Britain as the Turkish Van, which was first brought to Britain from Turkey in 1955.

While many 'new' breeds have achieved show status, the fortunes of others have waxed and waned. For example, Angoras – Turkish Angoras in North America – faded from fashion in the western world from about 1900 until new breeding pairs were brought out of Turkey in the 1960s. The Maine Coon, although much loved by many American families, had to wait until the 1970s before it was recognised by the Cat Fanciers' Association of America and it was not until 1994 that it was given breed recognition in Britain.

Top
The Turkish Van is a relatively new breed in Britain.

Bottom
Although very popular in the United States Maine Coons did not receive breed recognition there until the 1970s.

BREED STANDARDS

TO KEEP THE registration process watertight, each change of owner must be recorded. An equal degree of rigour is imposed by cat fancy organisations on the acceptance of a new breed or variety. The aim is to ensure that the proposed breed is indeed different from any other,

that there are enough interested breeders to support it without excessive inbreeding and that a standard can be agreed. The process is generally similar in all countries although minor details vary.

When a proposal is made and accepted, the Preliminary stage of recognition begins. This usually lasts for about five years in the United States but may be longer or shorter in Britain. A breed standard is laid down, and specimens are assessed against these in non-competitive classes to see if the standard is stable and can be maintained or improved. If all goes well, the breed then passes to the Provisional stage, lasting one year in the United States but two or maybe more in Britain. At this stage cats may compete in shows, but not in Championship classes. Provided the breed continues to perform well, full recognition will follow and the breed becomes eligible for Championship status, the Olympics of the cat world.

BREED CLASSIFICATION

SOME NORTH AMERICAN organisations have a system of classifying breeds which is a useful general guide to the different categories. 'Natural' breeds are those which have an ancestry in the natural cat population, such as the British Shorthair and the Maine Coon. A kitten registered in these breeds must have ancestors all of that breed.

'Established' breeds are those which have originated in crosses between two or more natural breeds but any further back-crossings to the originals are not allowed. The Birman (Siamese/Angora cross) and the Burmese (Siamese/Oriental cross) are examples.

The third category is the 'hybrid', again created from a cross but in which further back-crossings are permitted in order to develop or improve the standard.

Finally there are the 'mutation' breeds such as the Rexes, in which crossing to the breed that produced the mutation is allowed.

Top
Although this British Shorthair appears to be a pedigree, it would have to be registered to qualify.

Bottom right
This Burmese is a Siamese/Oriental cross, an established breed.

Bottom left
An established breed such as the Birmans, is one that has been bred by humans.

Feral Cats

FERAL CATS ARE descended from domesticated cats which have rejected, or been rejected by, domestication. Some feral ancestors were strays abandoned by their owners. Others were ships' cats left behind on islands or (at least in legend) cats that survived shipwreck, although on islands uninhabited by cats they would have to have arranged to be shipwrecked in mixed pairs, which perhaps strains credulity. Feral colonies in the countryside are usually made up of the descendants of farm and estate cats. In towns and cities, movements of population and industry add to the feral count.

high proportion of ferals are black with white spotting on the chest, paws and nose, suggesting perhaps that this group of cats, living in a fairly restricted area with a high feral density, is more self-contained than most colonies.

WILD OR TAME?

EXCEPT PERHAPS IN colonies where ferals have had no contact with humans for many generations, as on some isolated islands, feral cats do not 'go back to nature'. They are *Felis catus*, not wild cats, and they retain distinctive behaviour patterns. This is perhaps because, unlike wild cats which are entirely dependant upon prey for food, ferals – at any rate in towns and cities – tend to congregate where more attractive and

COLOUR OF THE FERAL CAT

Top right
Eventually, through breeding, feral cats revert to tabbies.

Bottom right
In urban areas volunteers, such as this lady, feed feral cats which are friendly and behave as pets.

AFTER SEVERAL GENERATIONS of living wild ferals, however their ancestors started out, tend to revert to tabby coat patterns. Tabbiness is dominant and with uncontrolled breeding will eventually mask other colours. Surveys of ferals as far apart as Boston, Massachusetts and Hobart, Tasmania showed that the overwhelming majority of mature cats were blotched tabbies. It has been suggested that this may not be due to a process of reversion so much as that blotched tabbies, being closer to the original type, are better survivors. In central London however, a

easily found food is to be had. Thus they occupy the middle ground between the truly wild life and the cosy life of the domestic cat. Those with some kind of human contact with passers-by or regular visitors who feed them move in and out of a quasi-domestic lifestyle, signalling affection and greeting to their feeders as do pet cats to their owners but also, psychologically speaking, keeping their distance.

COLONY SIZES

IT IS IMPOSSIBLE to accurately estimate the number of feral cats in the world. One rough guess for Britain alone is 1.5 million. An area where food is plentiful and there is adequate space, such as a quayside or dockyard, can be home to hundreds of feral cats. A survey at Portsmouth Naval Dockyard in England found 200 feral cats occupying an area of 81 ha (210 acres). This would give each cat a tiny territory of about half a hectare compared with what a typical farm cat is used to, which is more like 10 ha (25 acres). However, the cats were by no means dependant on prey for their food. Within the dockyard were numerous waste bins and catering skips. In addition, food was provided, sometimes daily, by dockyard employees and the cats were not above begging from anglers fishing from the dockyard wall.

From small beginnings, a colony can grow phenomenally quickly, as becomes obvious when one remembers that an unspayed queen can have between 30 and 50 kittens in her breeding lifetime, while a tom can father a virtually infinite number of kittens. In the conditions in which many ferals live, by no means all – perhaps not even the majority – of the kittens will survive to sexual maturity; one study found the proportion of survivors to be one in eight. Even so, the population curve produced by those that do survive is still impressive.

Top
This farm cat may range over 210 acres still within its own territory.

Bottom
These urban cats have considerably less territory and often, as here, congregate around a food source.

PROTECTED SPECIES?

TO WHAT EXTENT feral cats should be controlled in urban areas is a matter of controversy. Some naturalists argue that they have by now achieved the status of wildlife and should be protected in the same

way as other species. Many animal lovers rightly react strongly to the trapping and gassing purges occasionally carried out by aggressive local authorities and pest control firms. These are in any case only a very temporary answer to the problem because, given any unoccupied territory on a likely feral site, new cats will quickly move in and before long a new colony will have been established. Yet it is true that feral colonies can be at least a nuisance and at worst a hazard to health and safety. Many premises such as flour mills and food processing plants where a few feral cats would once have been tolerated or even welcomed are now bound by food safety regulations to find other ways of keeping rodents out.

Apart from somehow discouraging people from dumping unwanted cats and kittens which are added to the feral pool, controlling the population growth seems the only answer. In Israel, where the feral population is thought to be about 250,000, there is a long-standing programme, going back 30 years, of feeding ferals weekly with food laced with drugs similar to those used in the human contraceptive pill. Despite the difficulty of ensuring that the right cats regularly turn up for their weekly feed, success is claimed for the scheme.

The alternative is a programme of mass neutering, a labour-intensive business because all the ferals have to be rounded up, looked after for a day or two after the operation and then returned to their

home territories. Again, because of the huge numbers involved, it would necessarily be a localised solution. In any case, such a programme could only be truly effective if there were some way of tag-marking the neutered cats.

FERAL REQUIREMENTS

THE TWO BASIC requirements of ferals, as of all cats, are shelter and food. Abandoned warehouses and factories, derelict farmhouses and barns, old allotment sheds, empty railway sites, deserted villages and abandoned slum areas all provide shelter and almost always, in the form of mice and birds, food. The central areas of cities, with their restaurants and well filled garbage bins, are the haunts of feral groups. The replacement of dustbins with plastic sacks has proved

a boon to urban feral cats. Not only can the plastic be easily torn with a well aimed claw to reveal the goodies inside, but the goodies are very unlikely these days to be sullied with

ash as they would have been in the past. The large wheeled bins used by many restaurants present more difficulty, but they are often left open or fail to close properly because they have been damaged, and moreover the space between the wheels provides shelter. As well as offering food, these areas are often littered with cardboard boxes which are a favourite form of shelter for homeless cats as they are for homeless people.

Top left

These feral cats hunt for food together.

Top right

This farmer encourages these feral farm cats to stay by feeding them, in return they hunt for mice.

Bottom

Cats can be scroungers and many city-dwellers will raid bins looking for scraps.

Another attraction of inner cities is that the night-time temperature tends to be a degree or two above that of the surrounding areas, a fact that in winter could mean the difference between comfort and hardship. Some fortunate feral colonies have established themselves in buildings such as hospitals and office and apartment blocks where there are both comfortable shelter in the basements among the hot water pipes and ducts and good pickings to be had from the waste bins outside.

INNER-CITY CATS

THE REDEVELOPMENT OF inner cities from the 1960s onwards and decline of the manufacturing industry in the 1980s added considerably to the urban feral population. Families were moved from terraced houses to high-rise flats where pets, if not actually forbidden, were considered to be impracticable. Many factories that had cats, fed by sympathetic employees, closed down, putting both employees and cats on the street. Industrial decline left large areas of major cities laid waste, either dotted with abandoned workshops and warehouses or reverting to urban scrubland. This was ideal territory for the development of feral colonies.

Urban ferals often gain regular support from kindly visitors, usually elderly ladies, who bring milk and canned food. This seems to be more a British than an American practice. Surveys of the food sources of urban ferals have shown that while in the

United States they live mainly on garbage, the British samples obtained twice as much food from human feeders than from raiding bins. Sometimes this support is on a more organised basis. Employees at the British Museum in London set up a committee of cat lovers on the staff to see that the large site's ferals were properly fed and had access to weatherproof shelter. The cleaners at a London publisher's office organised a rota to go in to work early to feed the ferals on an adjoining site, even travelling in at weekends. Office workers at a Lancaster factory who were in the habit of taking their lunchtime sandwiches outside to the canal bank on fine days found that they were being eyed wistfully from a distance by a number of local ferals. A few gave in to this silent approach, and before long they were feeding the cats on a regular basis.

Top left
This feral cat has found a home in this derelict building, sheltering it from the elements.

Top right
The British Museum, London, regularly feeds its population of feral cats and offers them shelter.

Bottom
This feral cat patrols its territory.

203

FACTORY FERALS

IN A SHEFFIELD steelworks, the outside shelters where the shop-floor workers took their 'snap' to get away from the noise were visited at the appropriate times by ferals, and this became a routine feature of the tea break. As the steelmen worked round-the-clock shifts, the ferals had the prospect of free food three times a day. In Britain, there have been instances of meetings between workers and management to sort out the future of factory ferals threatened by management policy. At the other extreme, some mental institutions and homes for elderly people give their ferals positive support because observing the passing cats is of therapeutic value to their patients.

PRECARIOUS EXISTENCE

THE MAJORITY OF feral cats, however, have to look after themselves, often in hostile environments. The feral life is a vulnerable one, and generally much shorter than that of the domestic cat. Few ferals survive beyond 10 years, the females living rather longer than the males. Most ferals are slightly smaller and lighter than domestics of a similar body type. This is probably due less to lack of food than to the fact that ferals have to spend more time hunting and keeping warm, so burning up energy that comfortable domestic cats conserve. The greatest single danger to ferals is from diseases such as respiratory viral infections ('cat flu') spreading unchecked through a colony which can have devastating effects. Less

serious but nevertheless debilitating health problems such as ringworm and intestinal worms are commonplace in the feral world.

Ferals are also, by virtue of their lifestyle, at greater risk from traffic and other accidents, falls, accidental poisoning, getting trapped in sewer pipes and similar hazards. Ferals have human enemies too. They become targets for mindless owners of air-rifles, shotguns and even, in some countries, handguns. They also face official opposition. In the heyday of the great British hunting estates, feral cats were routinely shot by gamekeepers as vermin because they were suspected of taking young game birds. One Dorset gamekeeper boasted that he had destroyed 300 cats in one year, luring them into traps by spreading valerian powder. Another keeper's wife made a cottage industry of making carriage rugs from catskins and found that tabbies made the most popular line.

Today, from time to time, local authorities and buildings managers worry about feral cats, usually on grounds of hygiene, and embark on programmes of live-trapping followed either by gassing or – more humanely – removal of the cats to an animal sanctuary.

ISLAND COLONIES

AMONG THE MOST interesting feral colonies are those on islands, some of which have been established for centuries and are of unknown origin. Others are more recent. The colony on the uninhabited Hebridean island of Shillay, off the north-west coat of Scotland, for example, dates

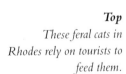

CAT FACT:
The tail is a very important feature for some species of cat. Those species which need to climb trees or pursue prey at speed, use their tail as a device for balancing.

Top
These feral cats in Rhodes rely on tourists to feed them.

Bottom
This Maltese alley cat scavenges the bins for food.

habitats, where the range of fauna is small, ferals soon assume a dominant position, feeding on the chicks of rare sea birds and even, on Galapagos, giant tortoises. If driven to it, they will disobey one of the basic dietary rules of cats and eat carrion.

back to 1942 when the population of the island's small fishing settlement left. Today, the cats live entirely independently except in the summer when Shillay is visited by an occasional fishing boat or group of birdwatchers.

Another interesting island colony is on tiny Marion Island in the southern Indian Ocean, close to the Antarctic Circle. It is hard to imagine a less hospitable habitat for cats. Marion Island is only about 500 km (300 miles) from the Antarctic pack ice. The average temperature over the year is only just above freezing and icy gales are the prevailing weather. Marion Island is a South African dependency, and in 1949 it was decided to import five cats to keep down the mice at the weather station there. By 1974 these five had grown to a colony of at least 500. Some observers estimated 2,000.

The scattered islands of the south Pacific are dotted with feral colonies, from the Galapagos Islands off the west coast of South America to the islands north of New Zealand. On some of these islands, including the Galapagos, cats were deliberately introduced, but on others the circumstances of their arrival are lost in the mists of time. Being volcanic, the terrain offers plenty of fissures and gullies for shelter. In such isolated

MYTH OR REALITY?

THE WIDE SPREAD of feral cat colonies through the south Pacific is perhaps the explanation of a conundrum that has puzzled anthropologists for many years. Despite the fact that there are no species of the cat family indigenous to Australia, the art and folklore of Australian aborigines include references to a Great Hunting Cat. It is known that the first aborigine settlers arrived in northern Australia about 50,000 years ago, having travelled across the islands of the western Pacific. It is possible that, whether deliberately or by accident, they brought cats with them, which they may have picked up on these islands. If this is so, either some disaster befell the cats or there were not enough of them to maintain a population. Whatever happened, it seems that long after they vanished they lived on in the folk memory of native Australians.

Top right
This feral cat in the distance is descended from the first cats introduced to the Galapagos Islands by man.

Bottom left
The jagged terrain of the Galapagos Islands offers caves which shelter the feral colonies.

Bottom right
The origins of this Australian feral cat are unknown; cats are not native to this continent.

205

Introduction to Cat Breeds

ALTHOUGH EVERYONE understands in general terms what is meant by, for example, a Siamese cat, the discussion of breeds is bedevilled by a number of factors. The first is that the number of breeds recognised by cat fancy organisations varies from country to country. The Governing Council of the Cat Fancy, Britain's major organisation, recognises about 100 breeds or variants. The number recognised in North America is about half that, but some of Britain's 'breeds' are mere colour varieties in North America.

have been given Provisional (that is, non-championship) status and others again have reached full recognition or Championship status. To achieve this, the breed must be at least 100 members strong, all bred to the standard. The same ladder of recognition applies to 'new' colour varieties within a breed.

Some breeders resent what they regard as the conservatism of the cat fancy, and certainly in the excitement of having developed a new variant and wanting to develop it at top speed the recognition process can be frustrating. But the laudable purposes of the proving period, which can last for several cat generations, are to ensure that it is a genuine new breed or variety, that there are enough interested breeders to support it, that enough specimens have been born to develop it further without undue inbreeding, that satisfactory show standards can be devised and, most importantly, that no genetic problems emerge in succeeding generations.

Thirdly, breeders' terminology sometimes varies between countries and even between organisations in the same country. For example, the cat known as a Colourpoint

RECOGNISED BREEDS

THE SECOND POINT is that the number of recognised breeds is not fixed for ever anywhere. At any one time, some 'new' breeds (which usually means new variants of existing recognised breeds, although it may also include spontaneous mutations such as the Sphynx) are going through a period in which they are under preliminary examination, when they may not be shown competitively, while others

Bottom right
Breeds such as the Turkish Angora can cause confusion as it is known in Britain as an Angora.

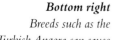

Longhair in Britain becomes the Himalayan in the United States, and the American breeder's Turkish Angora is the British fancy's Angora.

There are national variations in colour names too. The dark brown known in Britain as chocolate is sometimes called chestnut in North America, and North America's lavender is Britain's lilac. The standards by which ideal specimens of a particular breed are assessed is also variable. In the pages that follow, variations between British and American usage and practice are noted where appropriate.

The number of cats in particular breeds varies enormously. Some breeds, like the Siamese and Persian (officially called Longhair in Britain), are huge in number, seeming sometimes to dominate the show world. Others like the Sphynx or the Rex breeds are relatively tiny in population and are virtually unknown to cat lovers who do not frequent shows or read the cat fancy magazines. Generally speaking, the larger and longer a breed has been established, the more likely it is that any problems have been bred out, and anyone venturing into the pedigree world as a newcomer would be well advised to choose one of the older breeds.

The standard for each breed is a detailed description of each physical feature of the cat, based on the principle that 100 marks would be awarded to a perfect example of the breed or variety. In practical terms, a standard is more relevant to breeding than to showing, because although judges use it as a guide they are usually more concerned with an overall assessment of the cat as a member of its breed. A typical British standard might allocate 20 points to the head, 15 for the eyes, 15 for the body and 50 for the coat. In the United States, the distribution might be 30 for the head, including the eye size and shape, 10 for eye colour, 20 for the body, 10 for the coat quality, 20 for the coat colour and 5 each for balance and refinement. The allocation of points in both

countries may vary from one breed to another. For owners who plan to show their cats, it is imperative to study the relevant standard, know it by heart and use it constantly as a reference to the show-worthiness of the cat. Although all cats cannot be winners, there is no point at all in entering a cat that has no chance of success.

Many people, of course, enjoy owning pedigree cats without any intention of showing them or breeding from them. Breeders often have for sale kittens which, although of perfect pedigree and in every way satisfactory, they let go because for one reason or another they do not identify them as breeding or show material. These kittens are often sold as 'pet' or 'household' quality.

CAT FACT:
The stripes and blotches seen on cats' coats works as camouflage because it serves to break up their outline. If the stripes ran along the body they would not be effective.

Top
Longhairs are also known as Persians, which can add confusion to breed discussion.

Bottom
Cornish Rexes have a relatively small population when compared to other breeds, such as Persians.

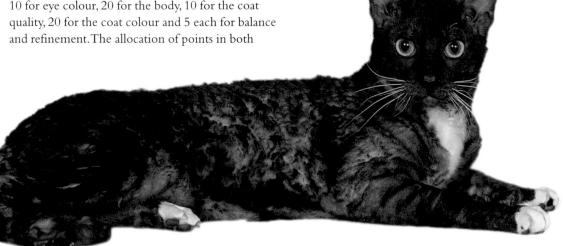

New Breeds

THE ESTABLISHMENT of 'new' cat breeds or varieties is rigidly controlled by the cat fancy organisations of each country. Recognition is not transferable from one country to another, which means that a breed established in the United States, for example, will have to go through the whole procedure again if it is to be accepted in Britain. Even then it may fail to achieve recognition. In any country, the fact that a breed has been recognised is no guarantee of a permanent place in the show world.

The history of the Peke-faced Persian has been dogged with problems. Its prominent jowls and snub nose give rise to breathing difficulties, and the wrinkled muzzle makes the tear ducts prone to blockage. The upper and lower teeth tend not to meet in an even bite, resulting in difficulties with feeding. All Persians are notoriously difficult to breed, but the Peke-faced variety is even more so. Apart from birthing problems, there is a high mortality rate – up to 50 per cent in the first six months – among the kittens because the formation of the mouth makes it hard and sometimes impossible for them to obtain milk from their mothers.

Given all this, it is hard to imagine how the breed ever got off the ground, and it is almost certain that it would fail to do so today. It has never been recognised in Britain, where the cat fancy and the veterinary profession have historically been resistant to breeds which might be regarded as 'novelties'. As it turns out, the Peke-faced Persian is also losing support in North America, perhaps because of the difficulty of maintaining a sufficiently large breeding stock. By the 1990s new registrations each year were down to single figures, and it looked as if the breed's days were numbered.

INTRODUCING NEW BREEDS

THE DIFFICULTIES AND controversies of introducing a new breed today are illustrated by the example of the Singapura, another breed not recognised in Britain or universally in the United States. The Singapura, billed as the

Top
All Persians, but in particular the Peke-faced Persians, have a high mortality rate.

Bottom
The dangers of inbreeding is one of the reasons that the Singapura has not been recognised in Britain.

THE PEKE-FACED PERSIAN

THESE POINTS ARE illustrated by the story of the Peke-faced Persian. The beginnings of the breed were in the 1930s, when occasional spontaneous mutations of the head type were observed in litters of red self (solid) and red tabby kittens in the United States. Its most obvious characteristics were a sharp indentation between the eyes and a snub nose, giving the kittens a resemblance to a Pekingese dog. It achieved recognition by the US Cat Fanciers' Association and the Canadian Cat Association, but not by all North American organisations.

world's smallest cat breed, is a ticked Abyssinian type said to have been discovered in 1974 among the street cats of Singapore. It is a very attractive cat and it is easy to understand the motives for establishing it as a breed in its own right. But doubt has been cast on whether it really did originate in the Singapore streets or whether the three cats imported to the United

States in 1974 were actually re-imports of small brown Abyssinians. The cat world enjoys a little occasional controversy, and there the matter rests. But as the breed's gene pool is so small, resting on only three ancestors, it is bound to be slow to develop without excessive inbreeding.

There have been many attempts to develop new breeds, in Britain, North America and elsewhere, by crossbreeding with the aim of producing a distinctive type. Many such attempts are doomed to failure, resulting in unacceptable abnormalities, insuperable health problems or sterility in the kittens which has put an end to further developments. This has been the fate of numerous breeding programmes aimed at producing a breed of 'toy' or 'miniature' cats.

There is no doubt, however, that the future of the cat fancy will hold some surprises. Leaving aside deliberate breeding programmes, there will undoubtedly be mutations like the Rex breeds and the Scottish Fold – nature's genuine surprises – still to emerge. These were spontaneous events which to a large extent relied on the presence of interested cat

lovers to observe and develop them. None of them occurred in the confines of a breeding cattery. Indeed, one of the parents of the first Cornish Rex was a feral tom living in a disued tin mine, and the other was a stray. The original Scottish Fold was a farm cat. All of which suggests that some of the most interesting developments in the cat world come from outside the fancy rather than within it.

CAT FACT:
The familiar terms 'mog', 'moggie' and 'moggy' used for mongrel domestic cats, actually originate as affectionate slang names for the cow in British dialect.

CAT FACT:
An old wives' tale says that 15 – 20 drops of gin on a cat's tongue will stimulate its appetite if it is persistently turning its nose up at some perfectly good food. Definitely not a safe idea to try on your cat!

Top left
The origins of the Singapura are in small, brown Abyssinians.

Top right
Natural genetic mutations, such as in the Rex, can create new breeds.

Bottom
The Scottish fold is the result of a natural genetic mutation.

Longhairs

IN THE CAT WORLD, 'longhair' is a difficult word. In North America, it is merely a general term defining a group of breeds all of which have long hair. In Britain, 'Longhair' is the name officially given to the breed known in North America and virtually everywhere else as Persian. (Nevertheless, most British owners and breeders use the term 'Persian' in everyday conversation.)

dealt with last, followed by the shorthairs. Each grouping includes breeds which are recognised in North America but not in Britain (such as the semi-longhaired Cymric) and others recognised as breeds in North America (such as the Himalayan) which are treated in Britain as colour varieties of other breeds. Classification is further complicated by the fact that not all colour varieties are accepted in all countries. These differences are noted where appropriate in the breed entries.

GROUPING THE LONGHAIRS

BRITISH CAT FANCY usage dates back to the foundation of the Governing Council of the Cat Fancy in 1910 which allocated a separate breed number to each Longhair colour. In North America, colours are generally listed as varieties of Persian, but confusingly, some varieties such as the Himalayan have their own breed identities.

NORTH AMERICA DIVIDES all domestic cats into only two breed groups, longhair and shorthair. Britain recognises seven groups: Longhair (i.e. Persian), Semi-longhair, British Shorthair, Foreign, Burmese, Oriental and Siamese. The Semi-longhairs are the Birman, Turkish Van, Maine Coon, Ragdoll and Norwegian Forest Cat, a rather mixed group united only by the fact that their hair is longer than that of shorthairs but not as long as Longhairs.

In the breeds entries that follow, the longhairs (American usage) are grouped together, with the semi-longhairs

ORIGIN OF LONGHAIRS

SHORT HAIR is the natural coat of the cat. The three recognised ancestors of the domestic cat, the European wild cat, the African wild cat and the jungle cat, are all shorthaired. Long hair is the consequence of a mutant gene way back in each long-haired cat's heredity. Some naturalists believe that the long-haired Persian derived from matings between one of the other ancestor species and Pallas's cat, also known as the steppe cat. This species was first identified by the German naturalist Peter Simon

Top

This Norwegian Forest Cat is a member of the semi-longhair group.

Bottom

Persians are known as Longhairs in Britain, however, a Longhair in North America would be considered just a generic term for all cats with a long coat.

Pallas in an area north of the Caspian Sea in the late eighteenth century. It has a longer coat than other wild species, giving it more protection from the cold climate of central Asia which is its natural habitat. According to Pallas, it commonly mated with domestic cats. From this observation arises the theory that this was the origin of the Persian coat. But this is mere speculation.

Longhairs of the Persian or Angora type were known in Europe as early as the sixteenth century and greatly prized by the Italian and French aristocracy. The two breed names were used indiscriminately together with others such as Chinese, Indian, Russian and Asiatic. Perhaps because they were quite distinct from short-haired working cats and because the ownership of one could imply the leisure or the staff to groom them, these cats gained great prestige among the wealthy.

In Britain, the seal was set on their desirability when Queen Victoria and her son Bertie, the future King Edward VII, became owners and fans. About the same time, the first Persians were taken to the United States where they attracted an even more enthusiastic following. Angoras, meanwhile, went out of favour and virtually disappeared from Britain and North America until they were revived (as Angoras in Britain and Turkish Angoras in North America) in the 1950s from native Turkish stock.

ORIGINS OF OTHER BREEDS

OTHER LONGHAIRS come from an entirely different genetic background.

The Maine Coon and the very similar Norwegian Forest Cat (both classed as Semi-longhairs in Britain) owe their magnificently dense coats not to putative matings in the Asiatic steppes but to environmental conditions in, respectively, the north-eastern states of the USA and the similarly harsh climate of Scandinavia.

Also included in the longhair section are the Somali, which is basically a long-haired Abyssinian and is included in the 'Foreign' section of British breeds; the Cymric, a long-haired Manx type not recognised in Britain; the Turkish Van and the Birman (classed in Britain as Semi-longhairs); the Balinese (classed in Britain as a variety of Siamese) and the Javanese. This last breed name can be a source of immense Anglo-American and indeed Euro-American confusion. The breed known in North America as the Javanese is, in fact, a tabby or tortoiseshell pointed Siamese. But the European FIFé uses the same name for the breed known in the United States as the Oriental Longhair.

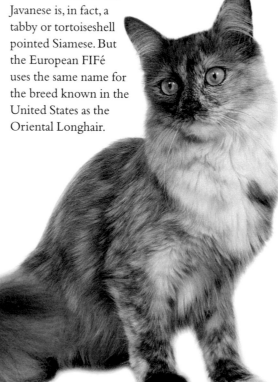

Top left
Most wild cats have shorthair, it is considered the original and natural coat type of all cats.

Top right
Pallas's Sand Cat is believed by some to have introduced the longhair gene to domestic cats.

Bottom
Turkish Angoras were highly desirable and fashionable cats in the sixteenth century.

Turkish Angora

BREED INFORMATION

NAME	Turkish Angora
OTHER NAMES	Angora
BODY SHAPE	Fine-boned
COLOUR VARIATIONS	All Longhair/Persian colours except (in US) chocolate, lilac and Himalayan pattern.

SIZE

COAT CARE

EXERCISE

THE ANGORA IS a breed over which there is a good deal of controversy and confusion, caused partly by its history and partly the naming of breeds. There are two quite distinct breeds which carry the Angora name, but they have common characteristics. For this reason they are dealt with together in this section.

ORIGINS OF THE BREED

THE BREED KNOWN in North America as the Turkish Angora is not recognised in Britain. It is a natural breed from the area of Ankara and still exists there in its original form in the local zoo.

The British Angora breed is a relatively recent invention, given Preliminary recognition in 1977, resulting from a scientific breeding programme without reference to Turkish Angora stock. It was recognised in the United States in 1988 as the Javanese or the Oriental Longhair. To complicate matters even further, some breeders insist that the only true Turkish Angora is a white one, and it is true that the Ankara zoo keeps only whites to ensure the purity of the breeding line. The distinctive Turkish Van presents yet another complication.

Top
A blue-cream Turkish Angora.

Bottom
To some breeders white is the only acceptable colour for Turkish Angoras.

A separate breed, it has a superficial resemblance to the Turkish Angora, and was once known in Britain as the Turkish Cat.

Angoras were among the first cats to reach Europe from the east, which they did in the sixteenth century together with Persians, and to begin with the two were bred indiscriminately. It is by no means clear whether Angoras and Persians share a common ancestry or whether the Angora is derived from accidental breeding with foreign or Oriental types.

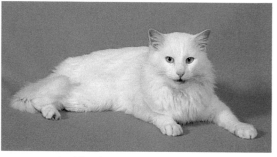

was recognised by the Cat Fanciers' Association in the United States. Other colours have since been bred, but white remains by far the most popular colour.

The manufactured British Angora was given recognition in 1977. It is similar to the Turkish Angora but more foreign in appearance, with a more sinuous body conformation and a more wedge-shaped face with larger ears.

Top left
One difference between Persians and Angoras is the shape of their faces.

Middle
The oriental influence in this chocolate coloured Turkish Angora is visible.

Bottom
Persians, such as this blue and white cat, were the most desirable breed at the turn of the century.

REVIVING THE BREED

GRADUALLY, PERSIANS TOOK the ascendant in Europe and the appearance of any Angora features in Persian cats was frowned upon. The result was that Angoras fell out of favour around 1900 and their numbers outside Turkey dwindled into extinction. There were two ways of trying to revive the breed in the west – either to go back to Turkey for original stock or, the British choice, to recreate the Angora by breeding from shorthairs of the oriental type carrying the longhair gene.

The American cat fancy chose the direct route. In 1962 an American breeder imported a pair of white Angoras – an odd-eyed male and an amber-eyed female – from the zoo in Ankara. A second pair was brought over in 1966 and these two pairs founded the revived breed in the United States. At first they were registered as Longhairs, but in 1968 a separate Angora breed was established and two years later it

> **CAT FACT:**
> The sand cat is one of the few cats which digs burrows. It does so because there is very little shelter from the baking sun to be found in the deserts where it lives.

213

CHARACTERISTICS

GRACE AND FLOWING movement are the hallmarks of the Angora. It is medium in size, with long but sturdy legs and small, neat paws. The coat is medium-length and fine, with a silky sheen and a tendency to waviness on the underparts. There is no fluffy undercoat, which makes the Angora easier to groom than a Persian. Angoras tend to moult rapidly and heavily in summer, replacing their coats with equal rapidity when autumn comes.

The ideal head is a wide, gently pointed wedge, with a straight, unstopped nose and large, pointed ears set high. In good show specimens the tips of the ears and the chin form a perfect triangle.

The tail is long, thin and gently tapering to a plume of silky hair at the end. The Angora often carries its tail horizontally over its back so that the tip almost touches the head.

White Angoras, despite their popularity, carry the same tendency to deafness as white Persians, especially if they are odd-eyed. All Persian (UK Longhair) coat colours are permitted, with the exception, in the United States, of chocolate, lilac and the Himalayan pattern.

TEMPERAMENT

ANGORAS ARE ALERT and intelligent, and respond well to play. They are adaptable and make loyal, affectionate pets, famous for their gentle nature. In the natural breed, litters are normally about four strong, but in the British version numbers tend to be higher. Kittens develop quickly, opening their eyes earlier than Persians and practising play routines as soon as they can move about. The adult coat is not fully developed until the cat is two years old, and may even take up to five years.

> **CAT FACT:**
> All cats are able to crouch surprisingly low and still move forward towards their quarry. Tigers even use the tip of their tail to distract their prey before they leap.

Top left
The wavy hair on this Angora's underside is typical of the breed.

Top right
This cat has a perfect triangle between ears and chin.

Bottom
The silky coat of Angora's make them easier to groom than Persians.

Left
Turkish Angoras are affectionate and amiable, making excellent pets.

Turkish Van

○○○○○○○○○○○○○○○○○○○○○○○○○○○○○○○

BREED INFORMATION

NAME	Turkish Van
OTHER NAMES	Turkish Cat
BODY SHAPE	Muscular
COLOUR VARIATIONS	Auburn and white. Also (US only) black, blue, torbie and tortie.

SIZE

COAT CARE

EXERCISE

CAT FACT:

True Manx cats, from the Isle of Man, should have a hollow where the tail would otherwise begin. It they have as much as a bump, then they are known as stumpies.

ORIGINS OF THE BREED

THE TURKISH VAN, which was originally known in Briain as the Turkish Cat, is classified as a Semi-longhair and in North America as a longhair. Although they share Turkish origins with Angoras, the two breeds are quite distinct, the Van having evolved separately because of geographical isolation. The Van is the more solid, heavy boned animal, although its markings lend it additional grace. It seems to have been purely a matter of chance that Laura Lushington discovered the breed's founding kittens in the area of Lake Van and so gave it its name. Apparently cats with the Van pattern are found quite widely in other areas of Turkey.

The Turkish Van was recognised by the UK's Governing Council of the Cat Fancy in 1969. The first Turkish Vans, from British stock, were imported into the United States in 1970 and in 1985 the breed received its first recognition by a North American organisation, the International Cat Association.

Top

The two Turkish Van kittens given to a British traveller in the 1950s represented the introduction of the breed to the UK.

Bottom

The Turkish Van is classified in Britain as a Semi-longhair, but in North America as a longhair.

VAN IS A LARGE LAKE, 128 km (80 miles) long by 64 km (40 miles) wide, high in the mountains of south-eastern Turkey close to the border with Iran. It is an inhospitable area, over 1,600 m (5,260 ft) above sea-level, lashed in winter by frequent icy storms. It was in a village on the shores of the lake that in 1955 an English traveller, Laura Lushington, came upon an unfamiliar breed of cat, a longhaired white with distinctive colouring on the head and tail. She was presented with a pair of kittens and took them home with her. Four years later, she returned for more. She had introduced the cat fancy to the Turkish Van.

CHARACTERISTICS

THE DISTINCTIVE FEATURE of the Turkish Van is its all-white coat relieved only by patches of colour on its head, on and below the ears but separated by a white blaze, and a full-brushed coloured tail which may have rings of darker red. The coat lacks a woolly undercoat, which makes it easier than Persians to groom. The Van pattern is caused by the white spotting gene S which is dominant, meaning that if either parent has the gene it will be passed on.

The Turkish Van is a medium sized, sturdily built cat, the male in particular having a muscular neck and shoulders. The legs are medium length and the feet small and round with good tufts. The coat, which is long, soft and silky with no downy undercoat, moults prodigiously in summer and it is in winter that this breed is seen at its handsome best. Show standards require a short, wedge shaped head with a long nose and large, upright ears close together and well tufted. The eyes should be large, and oval in shape. The nose leather and paw pads are pink.

Bottom
Auburn-coloured areas on the Turkish Van should be restricted to around the ears and on the tail.

CARE

OWNERS DESCRIBE THE Turkish Van as a loving and intelligent cat which is inclined to identify most closely with one person. Its appetite is surprisingly large for its size. Grooming is easy, combing two or three times a week being recommended with perhaps slightly more attention in the spring and summer moulting season. It is hardy and enjoys outdoor activity; a home with access to an enclosed garden, terrace or patio is ideal.

The term 'Van' is sometimes used to describe white cats of other breeds which have similar markings confined to the head and tail. This applies particularly to the American Shorthair and the Norwegian Forest Cat.

COLOUR VARIETIES

THE ORIGINAL VAN colour is white with red (called auburn) markings, which must match in the head and tail. In Britain, only the amber-eyed auburn is fully recognised, but white with cream markings is at the Preliminary stage. Either colour may show tabby markings. Eye colour may be blue, amber, or odd-eyed blue and amber. In the United States, black, blue, tortie and torbie coat colours are accepted.

The colour markings are present in kittens from birth, but as with the Angora it takes several years for the coat to reach its full luxuriant quality. Perhaps the most remarkable feature of the breed is its affinity, rare among cats, for water. In its natural habitat it is said to enjoy a daily swim in lakes or shallow rivers, and it is less reluctant than most cats to be given a bath.

Top left
Amber eyes are the preferred colour.

Top right
Markings can be seen on the heads of these three kittens.

Bottom
This tortoiseshell Turkish Van would be acceptable for showing in the United States.

Top
Unlike most other breeds the Turkish Van enjoys water and is an adept swimmer.

Bottom
The Turkish Van makes an excellent pet as it is friendly and affectionate.

219

Maine Coon

BREED INFORMATION	
NAME	Maine Coon
OTHER NAMES	Maine Coon Cat
BODY SHAPE	Muscular, rugged
COLOUR VARIATIONS	Self/solid, tabby, bi-colour, calico, tortoiseshell: tipped in white, black, blue, red and cream

IF ANY BREED IS entitled to be called the all-American cat, it is surely the Maine Coon. There are many legends about the origin of this natural and long-established American breed, some unlikely and some genetically impossible. They include, in the unlikely category, the story that Marie Antoinette, at the start of the French Revolution in 1789, planned to flee to the United States and sent on her possessions, including her Persian or Angora cats, in advance. These cats, the story goes, escaped and interbred with American domestic or feral cats and the Maine Coon was the result.

ORIGINS OF THE BREED

UNFORTUNATELY, THERE IS no evidence at all for this romantic tale or for the theory, which gave the breed its name, that the original Maine Coon kittens resulted from a liaison between a domestic cat and a raccoon. In any case, such a cross-species match is impossible. Slightly less unlikely is a mating between a domestic cat and the spotted wild bobcat, *Felis rufus*, which is found from southern Canada to central Mexico.

Yet another idea is that the first Maine Coons were in fact Norwegian Forest Cats which came to North America round about AD 1000 with the Viking explorers of Vinland. There is nothing to support this theory other than that it is quite likely that Leif Eriksson or his followers may have landed in Maine on their voyage to Vinland to the south. Yet again, a sea captain named Coon is said to have brought Angoras or Persians to North America in the early nineteenth century.

Disregarding the captain's name as a red herring, something like this is the most probable and simplest explanation for the Maine Coon: accidental crossbreeding between a domestic shorthair descended from one brought over by the early settlers and a later imported escaped longhair.

HARDY BREED

THE MYTHOLOGY OF the Maine Coon also extends to its size, with stories of cats of the past weighing up to 18 kg (40 lb). This, too, is unlikely, if only because life in the semi-wild is too harsh to permit a surplus of weight so far beyond the norm for the type, which is 5–7 kg (11–15 lb) and still makes the Maine Coon physically one of the largest breeds.

Left
Mythology states that Maine Coons are the descendents of breeding between domestic cats and the Bobcat.

Right
Maine Coons are hardy cats that have developed a thick coat to protect themselves from the continental winters.

Cosie having been named Best Cat at the first national cat show at Madison Square Garden in New York in 1895. Up to 40 years before that, however, Maine Coons often featured in shows of farmers' cats at country fairs. There are records of one such show, at Skowhegan in Somerset County, Maine, in 1861. Interestingly enough it was a Skowhegan breeder who played a leading part in the revival of the Maine Coon as a show breed in the 1950s, although by that time, of course, the Maine Coon was widely admired outside its native state. One Maine Coon achieved a mention in print very early on. In 1861 an American cat lover, F. R. Pierce of Maine, published his *Book of the Cat* in which he described a black and white Maine Coon named Captain Jenks of the Horse Marines which he and his brother owned.

What is certain, however, is that the Maine Coon had been a favourite farm and household cat for generations before it became a show cat. Its reputation for agility, bravery and toughness is well merited, and its independence and resourcefulness match the pioneer spirit of the society from which it sprang. The Maine Coon has adapted to survive in harsh winter conditions. Maine is the most north-easterly of the United States, on the border with Canada, with an average annual snowfall of 211 cm (83 in) and frosts for over seven months of the year, so it is not surprising that over the generations the Maine Coon developed a rugged coat and a solid build.

The stiff guard hairs on its back and flanks provide extra insulation, while the softer hair on its stomach forms a blanket for protection from snow and ice. The large feet, with tufts of hair between the paw pads, help the Maine Coon to cross ice and snow with assurance. The ears are large and, even by cat standards, unusually manoeuvrable to catch the sounds of distant prey or predators. This cat is a born survivor, and at least two centuries of its development in the semi-wild have ensured the weeding-out of unhealthy or unintelligent specimens.

Maine Coons were named Best Cat at the annual Boston Cat Show for three years in succession from 1897, but this early show glory was unfortunately not to last. An early American cat fancier, Frances Simpson, devoted a chapter to Maine Coons in her 1903 *Book of the Cat*, but the cat fancy quickly became seduced when Persians began to be imported from Britain in ever-increasing numbers, and by 1904 the Maine Coon had dropped out of the American show scene. Of course, Maine Coons continued to be the choice of farmers who wanted a robust working cat and families looking for a hardy pet, but it was left to a handful of breeders to keep the cat fancy interest going, which was an uphill struggle.

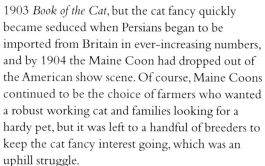

SHOW STEALERS

THE MAINE COON has a special place in the history of the United States cat fancy, a brown tabby called

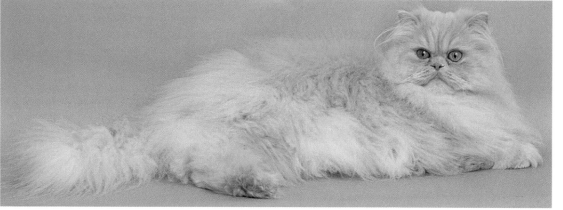

Top left
The Maine Coon is one of the largest breeds of cat.

Top right
These Maine Coon kittens are intelligent and healthy natural survivors and are thus regarded as all-American.

Bottom
Persians became more popular than Maine Coons early this century, leading to a decline in numbers.

PEDIGREE IS ESTABLISHED

IT WAS NOT UNTIL 1953 that the Central Maine Coon Cat Club, showing only Maine Coons and starting a record of pedigrees, was formed. From that time on, the breed's reputation slowly revived. In 1967 the first United States organisations recognised the breed, but it took until 1976 for the Cat Fanciers' Association to follow suit. The first Maine Coons were imported into Britain in 1983, but there was a fairly long wait before full British recognition followed in 1994. The breed also found favour during the 1980s in mainland Europe, particularly in Germany.

raccoon, the tree-dwelling mammal common across North and Central America, and no doubt played a part in the naming of the breed as well as giving rise to the raccoon ancestry myth.

The Maine Coon is a large, solid, rugged, muscular cat. Its smooth, shaggy coat is heavy but silky in texture, short on the face and shoulders but longer on the underparts and the hind legs, where it forms long 'breeches'. The body is long with a broad chest and level back, with strong legs set well apart, large, round, well-tufted paws, and a medium length plume-like tail. The head should be medium width, on a medium length powerful neck. The muzzle should be square and the chin firm, the cheekbones high and the nose medium length. The ears, set high on the head, are large and well-tufted, wide at the base and tapering to a point. The eyes should be large, slightly slanting and set well apart with a clear, alert look. Any pointedness of features or tendency to an undershot chin is a fault.

CHARACTERISTICS

NOT SURPRISINGLY IN a breed with such a long heritage, albeit much of it spent in obscurity, Maine Coons come in a vast range of colours and coat patterns – selfs (solids), tabbies, calicos, bi-colours, tortoiseshells, chinchillas, cameos and smokes, in white, black, blue, red and cream. The archetypal and original Maine Coon, however, and a show favourite still, is the classic (blotched) brown tabby. This and the plume-like tail are similar to the colouring of the

Top left
This robust cat, that had been shown by farmers since the nineteenth century, was not recognised officially until 1953.

Top right
The classic favourite is the brown tabby.

Bottom right
This cat express the typical look of the Maine Coon: it is alert-looking with slanted eyes and an intelligent appearance.

COLOUR VARIETIES

THERE ARE NO fewer than 25 acceptable colours, together with eight tabby colourings; in fact, Maine Coons come in all colours and patterns except for pointed colourings. The eyes may be green, gold or copper, with no relationship required between eye and coat colour. Whites (and only whites) may have blue or odd eyes. As with bi-coloured varieties of other breeds, American standards require that at least one-third of the body coat should be white, while the British standard is less demanding, though agreeing that the bib, stomach and all four paws must be white.

TEMPERAMENT

MAINE COONS make excellent household cats, being good natured, quiet, adaptable and fun-loving. They often adopt one particular member of the family as a favourite. As one would expect of cats with their backgrounds, they are champion hunters and really need access to the outside. Perhaps reflecting their semi-wild background, they are famous for choosing unusual places and positions for sleeping, and seem relatively impervious to cold conditions. Some are unusually adept with their paws, using them to play with water and even to eat.

CARE

GROOMING IS NOT particularly demanding, but the long hair on the stomach and chest tends to tangle. Maine Coons should be brushed and combed at least once a week, with any knots being gently teased out. The females usually have their litters – two or three is the most common number of kittens – without any problems.

Maine Coon kittens are deceptive. They look like rather disorganised balls of fluff, nothing at all like the solid, no-nonsense cats that they will grow into, reaching maturity at about the age of four years. The fluff will be replaced by the heavy, shaggy coat, the apparently uncoordinated body will develop into a compact, broad-chested form, the tail will lengthen and grow its long, flowing adult hair, and in tabbies the markings will become particularly strong.

CAT FACT:
Cat collars usually feature a section of elasticated fabric. This is so that the cat is able to release itself without being throttled, should it get caught in a tree.

Top
This endearing young kitten seems all ears and fur.

Bottom
Maine Coons are seemingly impervious to the elements.

Persian

BREED INFORMATION	
NAME	Persian
OTHER NAMES	Longhair
BODY SHAPE	Cobby
COLOUR VARIATIONS	Self/solid, tabby, tortoiseshell, bi-colour and tipped.

ALTHOUGH EVERYONE, on both sides of the Atlantic, knows what a Persian cat looks like and uses the term freely, in Britain Persians are classified for breeding and show purposes as Longhairs. This group includes some varieties such as Chinchillas which in North America are given separate breed names. The cats referred to in this section are what might be called 'regular' Persians, and varieties with other breed names are dealt with separately.

THE PERSIAN HAS a cobby build with short, thick legs, a round head, a short nose and large eyes. The tail is plume-like and the coat full and thick. Coat and eye colours are variable.

Top left
This Chinchilla queen and kittens would be classified as a Persian in Britain.

Bottom
Persians are the archetypal cobby cat, they have short legs and round features.

STATUS SYMBOL

FOR MOST PEOPLE, the Persian is the ultimate luxury lap-cat, associated with wealth and power. This is no doubt because the first Persians brought to Europe over 300 years ago by travellers to the East were often given as presents to noble patrons, so that the Persian became the cat of aristocracy. The Italian traveller Pietro della Valle (1586–1652) spent four years in Persia from 1617–21 and is credited with having brought the first Persian cats to Europe, although the earliest European reference to long-haired cats is dated 1520. In the account of his travels published after his death Pietro della Valle described the Persians' coat as 'soft as silk and so long that it forms ringlets in some parts and particularly under the throat'. The Persian quickly became a favourite in court circles on the mainland of Europe and spread through France to Britain, where they were known for a time as French cats.

It seems that at some point in the nineteenth century British breeders allowed or encouraged Angoras to infiltrate the breed. Although there are some differences between the two, they were classified and shown together as Longhairs. Subsequently, with the emphasis on the Persian, the Angora virtually died out until it was revived from Turkish stock in the 1950s.

EARLY PERSIANS

PERSIANS DOMINATED THE first British National Cat Show at Crystal Palace in south London in 1871. Blue was from the first the most favoured colour, although white and black were also prominent. 'Orange' (these days called red) was a development of

the early 1900s but was, as it remains, relatively rare. These early Persians would have been very different from the Persians of today, sharing with them only the long hair and general body type of the modern pedigree cat. The breed as we know it today is the product of highly skilled and selective breeding programmes, in response to a huge demand by enthusiasts all over the world and notably in the United States.

Soon after the first show, Persians made their way across the Atlantic to the United States and became established favourites there. By 1903 American breeders had their own standards for Persians, and national preferences in style began to emerge. The British cat fancy went for a less stocky

type, possibly closer to the original Persian conformation, while American breeders preferred a more compact build and worked to produce ever richer coats. These preferences still hold true today and are reflected in the subtly different Longhair (Persian) show standards of the British and American cat fancies. Most disagreement centres on the head. American breeders have produced extremely snub-nosed Persians which they refer to as 'the modern type.'

NATURAL SHOW-CATS

ONE KEY TO PERSIANS' popularity in the show world is their placid nature and ease of adjustment to new environments and experiences, which means that they are not temperamental on the show bench.

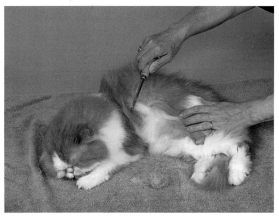

These qualities also make them good family pets, although they need daily grooming of up to an hour to keep the coat healthy and free of tangles. They also moult prodigiously. The long coat tends to collect the oily secretion sebum which builds up on the guard hairs and, especially in whites, causes staining. American Persian owners, who are perhaps braver than British ones, believe in frequent bathing to deal with this problem, but it can be at least alleviated by applying Fuller's Earth or unperfumed talcum powder, taking care to brush this well out afterwards.

CAT FACT:
Cheetahs end their chase after prey by tripping the animal over. They then suffocate the luckless animal by biting onto its windpipe until it is asphyxiated.

Top left
Blue Persians, such as this cat, were the favoured breed and colour in the late nineteenth century.

Bottom left
National preferences for certain characteristics influence how Persians are breed.

Bottom right
Persians require grooming on a daily basis, show-cats especially need a lot of time invested in them to keep their coats in excellent condition.

225

In general, a Persian should have a broad, round head with a short retrousse nose, full cheeks and small round-tipped ears set wide apart and tilting forward, low on the head with long ear tufts. The American preference is for a pronounced stop, or break, where the nose meets the forehead. The eyes should be large, round and set apart, with what the American standard calls a 'sweet' and the British a 'pleasing' expression. The neck should be short and thick, and the body cobby, solid and rounded, deep-chested and broad across the shoulders and hindquarters. The paws should be relatively large, rounded and with good tufts. The coat should be long, silky, flowing and shiny. Rich ruffs and deep frills on and between the front legs, throwing the head in relief, are especially prized. The tail should be short and carried behind, not above, the body.

CHARACTERISTICS

PERSIAN LITTERS ARE usually relatively small – two to three kittens – and although Persian queens are normally good mothers the kittens are often very delicate at birth, needing close attention for the first few weeks. The fine Persian coat begins to appear in kittens from the age of six weeks to two months, but does not develop fully until about two years. Self (US solid) kittens tend to show 'ghost' tabby markings in their first coat, but these disappear as the kittens mature.

SELFS (SOLIDS)

PERSIANS COME IN a wide variety of coat colours and patterns – over 60 – although not all of these are recognised for show. The first group consists of the self (US solid) colours:

black, white, blue, red, cream, chocolate (a medium to dark chocolate brown) and lilac (a pinkish dove-grey, called 'frost' by some American associations).

Top left
Persian kittens are particularly delicate at birth.

Bottom left
The long ear tufts can be seen on this silver tabby.

Top and bottom right
Both chocolate (top right) and lilac (bottom right) Persians have amber eyes.

Particular eye colours are associated with the coat colours. The eye colours specified for most self (solid) colours are brilliant copper or orange. However, whites may have deep blue, orange or copper, or one eye deep blue and one orange or copper. The latter are known as 'odd-eyed whites'.

GENETIC INFLUENCES

PERSIAN COAT COLOURS have waxed and waned in popularity. The whites were the first variety to be brought to Europe and became particularly popular in France. However, the dominant white gene W carries with it a liability to deafness, particularly in blue-eyed whites. This can appear in either or both ears and is caused by inner ear deformation. It becomes evident in kittens at 4–6 days old and is incurable, but with extra care to make sure that communication with the mother is maintained the kittens normally survive and learn to compensate with their other senses. However, the future life of such a kitten must be entirely indoors, and no further matings should be attempted

from queens who have borne deaf kittens or from the kittens themselves. A deaf queen is hampered as a mother by her inability to hear the distress cries of her litter, with the result that the kittens may be neglected. A deaf tom may pass the condition on.

BLACK AND WHITE

THE BLACK PERSIAN is almost as long-standing a variety as the white, and indeed appears in the breed list of the Governing Council of the Cat Fancy as breed number one. A pure black cat, with hairs jet black right down to the roots as required by the show standard is highly regarded. Most blacks carry a rusty tinge or flecks of white. The mature colour cannot be determined until the cat is about 18 months old, as many young cats with rusty or white hairs or faint tabby markings will lose them when they acquire their full adult coats.

CAT FACT:
The 'Catseye' reflectors seen glowing along the middle of roads at night were deliberately designed to copy the way a real cat's eyes will reflect a beam of light.

Top left
An odd-eyed white.

Top right
This solid black Persian is one of the most highly regarded cats.

Bottom left
Blue-eyed whites are likely to be deaf and should not be mated as the kittens will inherit the condition.

Top

*Persian blues are still the
favourite coloured
longhairs in Britain.*

Bottom

*This blue tabby has the
classic 'M' clearly marked
on its forehead.*

BLUE AND RED

BLUE PERSIANS ARE the most popular variety in
Britain, and until about 1960 were so in North
America too. Over the years, they have been much
painted and Blue Persian kittens are still favourite
subjects for greetings cards and chocolate boxes. They
are relatively easy to breed, as blue to blue matings
always produce a full litter of blue kittens whose
tabby markings, if any, usually fade as the cat matures.

Red Persians, by contrast, are notoriously
difficult to breed, at any rate to show standard, as the
tabby markings common in kittens tend to persist
into the adult coat. The standard requires a deep rich
red (in fact, orange) without markings or white hairs.
The red Persian is the source of the controversial
Peke-faced Persian.

OTHER COLOURS

CREAM IS THE DILUTE of the red gene O, and the first
cream Persians were produced by accidental crossings
of reds and blues. Cream Persians were rejected by the
British cat fancy for many years as unsatisfactory reds.

It was left to North American breeders to develop
this variety, and to this day there is a preference there
for a paler cream coat than in Britain. The colour of
choice has to be maintained by crossing to other
colour varieties, usually blues.

Chocolates and lilacs, warm-toned, evenly
coloured and entirely lacking in shading, markings
and white hair, complete the self (solid) Persian
picture in the British cat fancy. In the United States,
these two varieties are separately classed as
Himalayans or Kashmirs.

TABBIES

THE NEXT GROUP of Persians is the
tabbies, in blotched (also known as
classic), ticked, mackerel, spotted
and patched (tabby-tortie). A
well-marked 'M' on the
forehead is a requirement
in all varieties. In the
brown tabby the
ground colour is a rich

golden shade with jet black markings. The red contrasts rich red markings over a cream-red ground. The dramatic silver tabby has jet black markings over silver (clear light grey), the blue has blue markings over a bluish-white ground, and in the cream there are two contrasting shades of cream, the lighter underneath.

TORTOISESHELLS

TORTOISESHELL PERSIANS, derived originally from accidental matings between Persians and non-pedigree shorthaired tortoiseshells, have been popular on both sides of the Atlantic since the early days of the cat fancy. As almost all tortoiseshells are female, and the few males are almost invariably sterile, they are difficult varieties to breed as bi-colour males have

to be used in the breeding line. The blue tortoiseshell, known in Britain as the blue-cream Longhair, is a dilute form of the true tortoiseshell exclusive to females. The tortoiseshell-and-white, known in North America as the calico Persian because of its supposed resemblance to the printed cotton fabric, and once, for a similar reason, known in Britain as the chintz cat, is also an all-female variety. A dilute version, the blue tortoiseshell-and-white, can appear in the same litter. In the calico version, black, red and cream patches are interspersed with white, evenly distributed with a cream or white 'blaze' above the nose. In the American standard, the white should be concentrated on the legs, feet, chest and face.

BI-COLOURS

THE NEXT GROUP are the so-called bi-colours. Bi-colours should have white feet, legs, undersides, chest and muzzle, but not more than half of the coat, nor less than one-third, should be white. The white and the second colour should be symmetrical. Any self (solid) colour is accepted as the second colour in Britain; North American breeders are restricted to black, blue, red and cream.

TIPPED VARIETIES

FINALLY, THERE ARE the various tipped varieties, classified according to the extent of tipping on the individual hairs. The most heavily tipped are the smokes. These were well established in Britain in the early days of the cat fancy – records of smokes go back to 1893 – but they suffered mixed fortunes there, including the difficulty of maintaining breeding lines during the Second World War. Since the 1960s their numbers and popularity have been restored. In North America they have enjoyed continuous support ever since they were introduced.

In the smoke varieties, the coloured tipping, extending down the hairs to at least half their length, contrasts with the white undercoat which, in good examples, shows only when the cat moves. In repose, smokes should look solid coloured. They are recognised in black, blue, red (cameo), cream, blue-cream and smoke tortoiseshell.

In shaded varieties, the tipping extends to about one-quarter of the hair length on the back, flanks, legs and tail. Shaded silver (black tipping over pure white), shaded cameo (red tipping over pure white), shaded golden (brown tipping over cream, shaded tortoiseshell (tortoiseshell markings over pure white) and pewter (similar to the shaded silver but with orange or copper instead of green eyes) are recognised.

In chinchillas and shell cameos the tipping is at its lightest, only about one-eighth of the hair length. This, combined with the lighter undercoat, gives a shimmering, metallic effect to the coat.

In the chinchilla the tipping is black on pure white. In the golden chinchilla dark brown overlays cream. The shell cameo or red chinchilla has red tipping over pure white. There are also shell tortoiseshell, blue-cream cameo and cameo tabby varieties, in each case with the appropriate pattern over white.

CAT FACT:

Wild cats are regarded as some of the most difficult land animals to study and count, because of their secretive nocturnal ways and typically solitary nature.

Top
This tortoiseshell and white will invariably be female and sterile.

Bottom
A bi-coloured lilac and white Persian.

 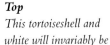

Colourpoint Longhair

○○○○○○○○○○○○○○○○○○○○○○○○○

BREED INFORMATION

NAME	Colourpoint Longhair
OTHER NAMES	Himalayan
BODY SHAPE	Cobby
COLOUR VARIATIONS	Seal point, chocolate point, blue point, lilac point, red point, cream point, tortiepoint, blue-cream point, lilac-cream point, tabby point and blue-cream tabby point. Also (US only) tortie-tabby points.

SIZE

COAT CARE

EXERCISE

CAT FACT:
Squints and crossed eyes are frequently seen in domestic cats. If these traits occurred in the wild, they would seriously disable the hunting prowess of the cat.

COLOURPOINT LONGHAIR is the British name for the breed that is still known in some North American cat fancy organisations as Himalayan or, in popular usage, Himmy. Until the mid-1980s all American cat fancy organisations regarded it as a separate breed for show purposes, whereas in Britain and elsewhere in the world it has always been shown as another class of Longhair or Persian.

CLASSIFICATION

THIS PRACTICE HAS now been adopted by the Cat Fanciers' Association and the American Cat Association. This almost certainly means that the days of the Himalayan's identification as a distinct breed are numbered, although breeders and owners will no doubt continue to use the term informally just as the British continue to refer to their 'official' Longhairs as Persians.

ORIGINS OF THE BREED

THE COLOURPOINT LONGHAIR is a man-made breed which results from crossing the shorthaired Siamese with the Persian to produce a longhaired Siamese type. The first crosses were made in the 1920s and early 1930s in Sweden and the United States by scientists interested in

genetic research rather than in cat breeding as such. The American experiments, conducted at Harvard Medical School, were with a Siamese queen and a black Persian tom and produced a litter of black shorthairs. Crossing a Siamese tom and a black Persian queen again produced black shorthairs, but matings between kittens from the two litters finally produced, in 1935, a longhair with Colourpoint markings. This was the first Himalayan or Colourpoint Longhair, named Debutante.

After these experiments, the geneticists seem to have lost interest, but their results had been noted by cat breeders in both North America and Europe. The name Himalayan, it is said, was coined by the early American enthusiasts, following the model of other animals such as goats, rabbits and fancy mice with similar colouring. Experimental breeders' clubs were founded in the United States, Canada and Britain but it was not until the late 1940s that extensive programmes of crossbreeding and back-crossing (breeding back to an original black Persian to enrich the genetic mix) began. Britain's Governing Council of the Cat Fancy recognised the breed as a variety of Longhair in 1955.

The Himalayan made its North American show debut at Calgary in Canada in 1957, and between 1958–61 the North American organisations one by one gave it recognition. The Colourpoint Longhair could be said to have 'arrived' in cat society when one was named Best Longhaired Kitten at one of London's premier shows in 1958.

CHARACTERISTICS

GENERALLY, THE HIMALAYAN has a cobby build and a round head with round eyes and long whiskers. The coat is Persian in type with Siamese markings. The eyes are always vivid blue. Breeders aim to produce the deepest eye colour that they can.

Show standards vary slightly between different countries and even, within the United States, between different organisations. But in general the requirement is for white or cream body coats, evenly coloured, with colour at the points – that is, at the

Top
In many organisations the Colourpoint Longhair would be shown in the Persian section.

Bottom
The first experiments that created this breed were with a black Persian and a Siamese.

face, ears, tail, legs and paws. The coat should be long, soft and silky, standing well away from the body, with a full ruff and a curtain of hair between the front legs. As with all Persian types, the coat requires frequent grooming. The body is deep-chested and massive across the shoulders and hindquarters, with short, sturdy legs. The paws should be large and round with good tufts. The tail should be short, full and carried low. Any tendency towards Siamese features, such as svelteness in the body or a long tail, is a fault.

The head is carried on a short, thick neck with a well-rounded face. There should be a definite break between the short nose and the forehead. The ears are well apart and set low on the head, small, rounded, tilted forward and with good tufts.

(sometimes called flame, with creamy-white body), cream point (creamy-white body), tortie point (fawn and red patched points with cream or ivory body), blue-cream point, lilac-cream point, tabby point (known in North America as lynx point), blue-cream tabby point and tortie point (US tortie lynx point). Some American organisations also recognise four tortie tabby points: seal, blue-cream, chocolate and lilac-cream.

Colourpoint Longhair kittens are born with a creamy-white coat which is fluffy but not yet long. The true Longhair coat does not appear until the kitten reaches maturity, but colouring at the points begins to show within a few days.

TEMPERAMENT

OWNERS SAY THAT Colourpoint Longhairs have all the temperamental virtues of Longhairs (Persians) such as placidity and adaptability, unlike Siamese which are inclined to be overly demanding of their owner's attention.

COLOUR VARIETIES

THE FOLLOWING COLOURS are accepted in Britain: seal point (with pale fawn to warm cream body), chocolate point (ivory body), blue point (bluish-white body), lilac point (magnolia body), red point

Top right
This kitten shows the characteristic body shape of the Colourpoint Longhair which is cobby.

Top left
The body colour of this breed should be white or cream.

Bottom left
This red point Longhair has blue eyes, the shade of which is extremely important to breeders.

Birman

```
○ ○ ○ ○ ○ ○ ○ ○ ○ ○ ○ ○ ○ ○ ○ ○ ○ ○ ○ ○ ○ ○ ○ ○ ○
```
BREED INFORMATION

NAME	Birman
OTHER NAMES	None
BODY SHAPE	Large-boned, muscular
COLOUR VARIATIONS	Seal point, blue point, chocolate point and lilac point. Also (UK only) tabby, tortie, and tortie-tabby.

SIZE

COAT CARE

EXERCISE

STRIKINGLY HANDSOME WITH its coloured mask and its pure white toes, the Birman is still a relatively uncommon breed, but it has its enthusiastic supporters in the British, mainland European and North American cat fancies and is equally welcome as a playful and well-disposed family cat.

LEGENDARY BREED

THERE ARE AT LEAST two legends connected with the Birman, the so-called Sacred Cat of Burma (which is not to be confused with the quite different shorthaired Burmese). One is long buried in history, the other about 100 years old.

    The older story goes back to the Middle Ages. In the ninth century AD, the countries of south-east Asia which are now Myanmar (Burma), Thailand and Cambodia were dotted with temple kingdoms under the control of the Khmer people. Each of these kingdoms was centred on a Buddhist temple: the major sites were at Ava and Pegu in Myanmar, Ayutthaya in Thailand, and Angkor in Cambodia. The kingdoms were under constant threat from Thai raiders who eventually wiped them out in the fifteenth century, although some of the temples were spared. Pure white cats lived in the temples and the

Top

The white socks of this Birman is a distinguishing feature that has been the subject of myths about the breed.

Buddhist belief was that they represented the souls of priests who had died. The cats had special status and were greatly pampered. Some accounts suggest that they were used to guard the temples against intruders, but Birmans have such a gentle, quiet nature that this seems unlikely.

SINH

THE STORY GOES that at the (unidentified) temple of Lao-Tsun there was an all-white cat with amber eyes named Sinh, the companion of the chief priest, Mun-Ha. One night, raiders broke into the temple and killed Mun-Ha while he was at prayer at the feet of the statue of a golden goddess with sapphire-blue eyes. Sinh at once jumped on Mun-Ha's body, and the old priest's soul passed into the cat. As he did so, Sinh's white coat was shaded with gold reflected from the statue, remaining white only where his feet rested on his holy master. His face, ears, tail and legs took on the colour of the earth, and his amber eyes turned sapphire blue. For seven days, the story goes on, Sinh lay beside Mun-Ha's body, guarding it and refusing to eat. Then Sinh himself died, carrying Mun-Ha's soul to paradise, and the temple's other 99 cats took on Sinh's new colouring. They are said to have circled round one of the young priests, indicating that he was Mun-Ha's choice of his successor.

This tradition passed into Buddhist belief, but the time came when the priests of Lao-Tsun fell out of favour. Late in the nineteenth century they were evicted from their temple. An Englishman and a Frenchman, Major Russell-Gordon and the explorer Auguste Pavie, helped the priests and their cats to travel across the border to Tibet and establish a new temple there. Some years later, in 1919, a pair of temple cats was sent to France as a token of gratitude. The tom died on the journey, but the pregnant queen, Sita, survived to become the founder of the Birman breed in Europe. Thus the Birman, according to these stories, is a natural breed.

ORIGINS OF THE BREED

SOME MORE SCEPTICAL breeders deride the romantic legend, although it seems exceptionally detailed to be a complete fiction, and say that Birmans were artificially produced in France in the 1920s by crossing Siamese with black and white longhairs. This theory is however confounded by the fact that Birmans invariably breed true, and there is no history in the breed of reversions to shorthaired kittens as would be expected if there were a history of crossbreeding. Yet another story is that the Birman is indeed the original temple cat, but the pregnant queen was smuggled out of the temple by a disloyal servant and sold to a French visitor. Whatever the truth of the matter, by the mid-1920s the breed, as Sacre de Birmanie, had become well established in France, where it was recognised in 1925, and later in Germany.

The standard still used for the Birman, written in France at this time, has since undergone only minor changes although there are small differences between European and American preferences. But the Second World War put an end to cat breeding in Europe, and when peace came there were only two individual Birmans surviving, at any rate in the west. Despite this, the breed recovered and by the early 1960s had crossed the English Channel to Britain.

The first Birmans to be imported into the United States arrived in 1959 from France. The breed was later strengthened by two cats brought from Cambodia by an American diplomat. This pair lent some credence to the 'Sacred Cat' story, as they were said to have come originally from a Tibetan temple and had the 'Sacred Cat' legend in their background. British recognition of the Birman (as a Semi-longhair) came in 1966, and the American cat fancy followed with longhair recognition the next year. The first Championship showing in the United States was at Madison Square Garden in New York that year.

DISTINCTIVE BREED

THE TWO DISTINCTIVE marks of the Birman are its deep blue eyes – the sapphire blue of the legend – and the pure white 'gloves' on all four paws. The white marking on the back paws ends in points extending up the back of the legs to a point just below the hocks, a marking known in North America as 'laces.' The white of the front paws end in an even line across the paw, with no extension up the legs. This is caused by the white spotting gene S. The white paws apart, the Birman's coat pattern is Colourpoint Longhair (US Himalayan) in style.

Top
A classic feature of the breed is blue eyes.

Bottom
As Birmans breed true it is unlikely that their origin lies in black and white Persians.

COLOUR VARIETIES

THE ORIGINAL BIRMAN colouring is the seal point, with a pale cream ground colour shading to fawn on the flanks and a lighter cream on the stomach and chest, and darker seal brown points except for the white gloves. The nose leather is dark seal brown and the paw pads are pink. A much-prized feature of this colouring is the faint golden 'halo' over the entire back, which is especially marked in adult males.

The blue point has a bluish-white body colour, warmer in tone on the stomach and chest, with deep blue points except for the gloves. American breeders favour a more glacial blue-white body colour and darker blue points than the British. The gloves should be pure white. The nose leather is slate grey and the paw pads pink.

Chocolate and lilac (lavender) points are also fully recognised in both North America and Britain. The chocolate point has an ivory ground colour with milk chocolate coloured points and pure white gloves.

CHARACTERISTICS

THE BIRMAN IS a large cat though less cobby than the Persian, with long, silky hair which tends to wave on the stomach and does not mat or tangle. There is a thick, heavy ruff at the neck, more marked in American-bred Birmans. The body should be medium-long but stocky, the legs sturdy and medium in length, and the paws round, firm and very large with the toes close together. The tail should be medium in length and bushy, and is often displayed as a plume. The broad, rounded head has a flat area in front of the ears, which are wide, rounded at the tips and spaced well apart. The nose is Roman and the cheeks are full. The eyes should be an almost round almond shape, and always deep blue. The body colour should be even, with the point colour confined to the face, ears, legs and tail. The white markings on the feet should be symmetrical.

Top left
American-bred Birmans tend to have a greater ruff at the neck than their European cousins.

Top right
A Birman's eyes should be almond shaped.

Bottom right
A blue point Birman, some breeders will only recognise this colour.

Top
A seal tabby Birman, one of the first colours to be recognised.

Bottom
Birmans are quiet and easy-going but should preferably be owned only by those with gardens as they enjoy the outdoors.

The nose leather and paws are pink. In the lilac (lavender) point the body is pure white and the points are a grey-pink, with pink nose leather and paws.

In addition to these, tabby, tortie and tortie-tabby points are also recognised in Britain. The breed can be regarded as still developing and further colourings and recognitions can be expected, although some Birman fanciers see seal and blue point colourings – the first to be recognised anywhere – as the only true Birmans.

CARE

BIRMANS ARE FAMOUSLY quiet, placid, gentle cats with great dignity and beauty. Their easy-going nature makes them good show cats unlikely to be fazed by the occasion. They enjoy the company of humans and other household pets and are playful though not boisterous. Although they are not great hunters and often not keen to venture outside, they dislike being too confined and should not be kept unless they can be offered plenty of space. This means that they will not enjoy confinement in a boarding cattery while their owners are on holiday, and if possible alternative arrangements should be made. The coat needs regular brushing and combing, but as it does not mat this is not an arduous task.

Unspayed females mature as early as seven months and become very restless in oestrus. Their keenness to mate is legendary. Birman litters normally number four or five kittens. These are born almost entirely white, but their colouring begins to develop faintly after a few days, at first on the ears and tail. The deep blue eye colour develops from a pale blue as the kittens mature.

Breeders in the United States have developed short-haired cats in the Birman pattern, which are known as Snowshoes or Silver Lace.

CAT FACT:
The Burmese King of Pegu and the Inca rulers, used to enjoy the gruesome spectacle of sending prisoners to their deaths by releasing them with big cats.

Balinese and Javanese

○○○○○○○○○○○○○○○○○○○○○○○○○○

BREED INFORMATION

NAME	Balinese
OTHER NAMES	In US, Javanese for certain colours (see below)
BODY SHAPE	Lithe, muscular
COLOUR VARIATIONS	UK: seal point, chocolate point, blue point, lilac, red point, cream point, tortie point, blue-cream point, lilac-cream point and tabby point. US (CFA): As Balinese, seal point, lavender point, chocolate point and blue point. Other colours recognised as Javanese.

SIZE

COAT CARE

EXERCISE

BREED NAMES CAN be deceptive. While the Turkish Angora and the Turkish Van can genuinely trace their ancestry to Turkey, there is absolutely no connection between the Balinese breed and the South East Asian island of Bali. The name is a breeder's invention.

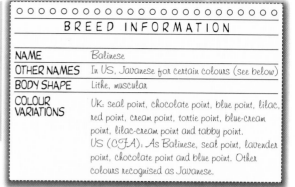

ORIGINS OF THE BREED

BASICALLY, THE BALINESE is a contradiction in terms to cat lovers who have not met one: a pure Siamese cat with a longhair coat. In genetic terms, it is a Siamese which is homozygous; its genotype includes two of the recessive longhair genes l, one from each parent. As a result, all matings from it will produce longhaired kittens. The origins of the breed go back to the 1940s when (whether by spontaneous mutation and sometimes as a consequence of a breeding programme is a matter of some dispute in the cat fancy) longhaired kittens began to appear in Siamese litters. As these would not meet Siamese show standards, breeders sold them off as pets and the cat fancy took no interest in them.

From about the mid-1950s, as a result of an increase in the numbers, breeders in the United States began to develop these long-haired oddities with the aim of establishing a separate breed. An essential first step in this procedure is to breed enough cats to the required standard to be able to maintain a programme without excessive inbreeding. The first deliberately bred Balinese

were produced in the United States in 1955 from a seal point longhair Siamese male and a blue point longhair Siamese female, both Siamese mutations, resulting in a litter of two blue point longhair kittens.

Independently of the Californian breeder of these, and at first unknown to her, a New York cattery was carrying on a similar breeding programme.

The breed's first designation was Longhaired Siamese, but it was the New York breeder, Helen Smith, who chose the name Balinese because the graceful movements of these cats reminded her of the dancers of the Indonesian island of Bali. The Balinese made its show debut at the Empire Cat Show in New York in 1961 as a Longhaired Siamese.

Top left
The name Balinese is a misnomer as the breed is not from Bali.

Top right
The Balinese is a long-haired Siamese (bottom), the faces of the two breeds are very similar, both are wedge shaped.

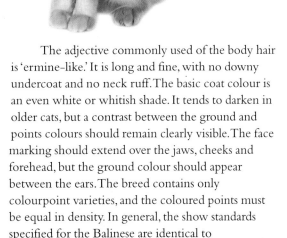

GAINING RECOGNITION

BETWEEN 1963–70, it was recognised (as the Balinese) by all the major cat fancy organisations in the United States. It was introduced to Britain in 1974 and full British recognition followed in the early 1980s, although American and British colour requirements differ.

CHARACTERISTICS

BALINESE ARE EXCEPTIONALLY graceful and beautiful cats, as would be expected given their Siamese origin, but their long coat softens both the lines and the colouring of their Siamese counterparts. The head is medium sized, wedge shaped and tapering in the Siamese fashion, although here again the effect is to some extent muted by the long coat. The nose and tips of the ears should form a perfect triangle. The nose is long and straight with no break between it and the forehead. The eyes, always deep vivid blue in all colour varieties, are almond shaped and slightly slanted towards the nose. They should be separated by at least an eye's width. The body is finely boned and dainty but well muscled, with a long, slender neck, long slim legs and small, oval paws. The tail, long and thin but well plumed, tapers to a point and is covered with fine, silky hair.

The adjective commonly used of the body hair is 'ermine-like.' It is long and fine, with no downy undercoat and no neck ruff. The basic coat colour is an even white or whitish shade. It tends to darken in older cats, but a contrast between the ground and points colours should remain clearly visible. The face marking should extend over the jaws, cheeks and forehead, but the ground colour should appear between the ears. The breed contains only colourpoint varieties, and the coloured points must be equal in density. In general, the show standards specified for the Balinese are identical to those for the Siamese with the exception, of course, of the long coat.

CAT FACT:
Wild cats often eat the intestines of their victims before any meat. This may be because they contain certain essential minerals and fats.

Top left
The colouring of Balinese is identical to that of the Siamese (top right).

Bottom
Like the Siamese the Balinese has blue eyes that slant down towards the nose.

COLOUR VARIETIES

THE RECOGNITION OF colour varieties differs between Britain and North America, and indeed between the Cat Fanciers' Association and other North American organisations. Taking the British Governing Council of the Cat Fancy first, Balinese are recognised in seal point (points deep seal brown over cream to fawn ground colour, seal nose leather and paw pads), chocolate point (points milk chocolate colour over ivory, cinnamon-pink nose leather and paw pads), blue point (points slate blue over white, slate blue nose leather and paw pads), lilac (points pinkish-grey over magnolia, nose leather and paw pads lavender-pink), red point (points delicate orange to red over creamy white, coral pink nose leather and paw pads) and cream point (points buff-cream over creamy white, coral pink nose leather and paw pads).

Britain also recognises tortie point (points patched with red and/or cream over ivory or cream, toning or pink nose leather and paw pads), blue-cream point (points blue patched with cream, slate blue or pink nose leather and paw pads), lilac-cream point (points frosty pinkish-grey intermingled with cream over magnolia, pink nose leather and paw pads) and tabby point. In the last-named, the point colour may be seal, chocolate, blue, red or lilac, with matching body colour, nose leather and paw pads.

NORTH AMERICAN RECOGNITION

THE US CAT FANCIERS' Association, following its definition of Siamese recognises as Balinese only four of these varieties: seal, lilac, chocolate and blue points, although others are recognised as Javanese. The other North American organisations recognise all the varieties accepted in Britain, except that in the lilac and lilac-cream point glacial white body colour is specified instead of magnolia, and in the lilac-cream the colours on the points should be patched rather than

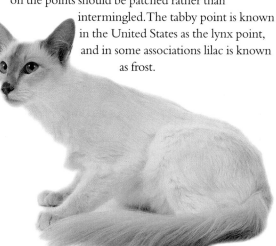

intermingled. The tabby point is known in the United States as the lynx point, and in some associations lilac is known as frost.

Top
Britain recognises more colour varieties than North America, such as the cream point.

Bottom left
The lilac point is recognised in North America and Britain.

TEMPERAMENT

BALINESE ARE QUIETER and less demanding than their Siamese forebears, but they are acrobatic, enjoy lively play, whether on their own or with their owners, and want to give and receive attention. They are definitely not cats for owners who intend to leave them alone for long periods or who cannot give them plenty of time. Grooming is easy, using a soft brush once or twice a week. As there is no downy undercoat the coat is silky, flat-lying and tends not to mat or tangle.

The kittens are born all-white and develop their markings at the points in the first few weeks.

Queens mature early, bearing typical litters of three to four, and are famed for their excellent standard of motherhood and tireless play with their kittens. As a result, the kittens develop quickly and early in life learn a considerable repertoire of

games and activities which can include, for example, the disrespectful treatment of curtains and upholstered furniture.

The US Cat Fanciers' Association and the Canadian Cat Association define the Balinese as a hybrid breed, which means that while most matings are Balinese to Balinese, producing all-Balinese kittens, out-crosses to the Siamese (and, in Britain but not North America, to Angoras) are still permitted to improve type. A breed introduced as relatively recently as the Balinese can be regarded as 'new', with the likelihood that further developments will take place as owners continue their breeding programmes.

Interestinglt one possible line of development concerns the Balinese to Siamese breeding programme. As explained above, Balinese to Balinese matings breed 'true', but Balinese to Siamese matings produce Siamese-type kittens with a fluffy coat but not as long as the Balinese. American cat fancy regulations prohibit the registration of these kittens as Siamese, as all Siamese registrations must have pure Siamese ancestry. These 'half-way house' cats are sometimes called 'short-haired Balinese', although this term has no official recognition. Their litters will in turn produce some longhaired Balinese kittens and some kittens with the intermediate fluffy coat. It remains to be seen whether an enterprising breeder will work on the intermediates to produce a new and acceptable breed.

If so, some opposition in the cat fancy can be expected from Siamese purists, many of whom already feel that the Balinese constitutes a threat to pure Siamese bloodlines.

THE JAVANESE

THE JAVANESE, LIKE the Balinese, has no geographical connection with the Indonesian island after which it is named. It is simply a breed name coined for use in North America to cover certain colourings of Balinese which are not recognised by the US Cat Fanciers' Association under that breed name. These include all of the colourings listed above except the four Siamese types, seal, blue, lilac (US frost) and chocolate points. In all respects except colour, the Javanese is a Balinese, with the same body type, coat and disposition, including a dislike of being left alone.

The distinction between the so-called Javanese and Balinese colourings is not needed in Britain, and indeed is not made since all colourings are permitted under the British show standards for Balinese. The position is complicated, however, by the fact that the European cat fancy organisation, FIFé, and its affiliated societies, have adopted the name Javanese for the breed known in North America as the Oriental Longhair, which is, in effect, a non-colourpointed Balinese.

Top
Balinese are less boisterous than Siamese.

Bottom
The Javanese is a Balinese whose colour is not accepted in North America, such as this cinnamon colour.

239

Cymric

```
○○○○○○○○○○○○○○○○○○○○○○○○○○○○○
   B R E E D   I N F O R M A T I O N
```

NAME	Cymric
OTHER NAMES	Longhaired Manx, Manx Longhair
BODY SHAPE	Rounded
COLOUR VARIATIONS	White, black, blue, red, cream, chinchilla, shaded silver, black smoke, blotched tabby, mackerel tabby, tortoiseshell, calico, dilute calico, blue-cream, bi-colour but not Himalayan pattern, chocolate or lilac.

SIZE

COAT CARE

EXERCISE

T HE CYMRIC (both c's are pronounced hard) is a fairly rare long-haired version of the tailless Manx breed and is recognised only in North America where it is also known as the Longhaired Manx or the Manx Longhair. Even there, only the Canadian Cat Association and some of the United States organisations accept it, and then only for show, not Championship, status. Cymric types have occurred in Manx litters in Britain, but it is not recognised there or in mainland Europe.

gene present in the Manx genotype was combined with the recessive longhair gene.

BREEDING THE CYMRIC

THE CANADIAN BREEDERS began mating Cymric to Cymric, but this led to lethal genetic abnormalities and it was clearly necessary to keep tailed or stumpy tailed Manxes in the breeding line to avoid too much crossing of tailless cats. As a result, numbers of tailed and stumpy kittens are born and reared to be sold as pets, but show Cymrics must be truly tailless.

Breeding is exceptionally difficult because, apart from the complications of keeping at least vestigially tailed cats in the line, stillbirths and kitten deaths are frequent (one quarter of all Cymric kittens fail to develop in the womb) and a measurable percentage of kittens suffer from spina bifida or other skeletal abnormalities. These problems no doubt

> **CAT FACT:**
> Habitat destruction has now replaced hunting as the primary cause of the demise of cat species, especially the big cats which require enormous hunting territories.

ORIGINS OF THE BREED

THE CYMRIC WAS named for a supposed Celtic connection. In fact, the only rather dubious Celtic link is the fact that some of the inhabitants of the Isle of Man and Wales are of Celtic descent and the Cymric, being a Manx mutation, is of distant Manx origin. Its immediate origin, on the other hand, is North American.

The first Cymric appeared in an otherwise normal litter of Manx kittens in Canada in the late 1960s. It was a mystery, but the Manx is notoriously difficult genetically, throwing up a variety of conformations and mutations which sometimes cause death in the womb and sometimes skeletal abnormalities. It was known that some Manx breeders had, in the 1940s and '50s, used Persians in their breeding programmes, but it seems that in the Canadian case the Cymric emerged from a mating involving seven or more generations of pure shorthaired Manx. Somehow, the dominant 'no tail'

Top right
The Cymric is a long-haired Manx.

Top left
The Cymric must be completely tailless for showing.

Bottom
Genetic abnormalities make breeding Cymrics complicated.

account for the slowness with which the breed has been taken up by the cat fancy, and indeed some veterinarians strongly disapprove of the continuation of Cymric breeding programmes which, they say, cause unnecessary suffering.

CHARACTERISTICS

THE SHOW STANDARD requires that the Cymric, as well as being tailless, to have the rounded look of the Manx, not unlike a rabbit, with long hind legs, a short back, and the rump consequently higher than the shoulders when the cat is standing. The gait of the Cymric and Manx is, incidentally, also rabbit-like.

Other requirements in the body are deep flanks, muscular thighs, and short, heavily boned forelegs set well apart. The feet are round and firm, with tufted toes. The head is large and round on a short, thick and well-muscled neck. The cheekbones are prominent and the nose is medium length, the eyes large, rounded and slightly slanted upwards towards the outer corners. The ears are prominent, wide at the base and tapering to tufted rounded tips, set slightly outward. The double coat is medium to long, with a thick 'cottony' undercoat which does not mat and a silky, glossy topcoat. Breeches and a ruff should be prominent.

The ideal show Cymric has a 'dimple' or hollow at the coccyx – the spine's last vertebra – where the tail should be, but the standards admit less perfect specimens, perhaps because perfection in this respect is so difficult to achieve. A slight rise at the coccyx is allowed provided it does not disturb the rounded appearance, and the absence of the 'dimple' is not regarded as a fault as long as the line is maintained.

COLOUR VARIETIES

PERHAPS SURPRISINGLY in view of the difficulties of breeding, a wide range of colour varieties has been developed in the Cymric. The following colourings are accepted: whites (blue, copper or odd-eyed white), blue, black, red, cream, chinchilla, shaded silver, black smoke, classic (blotched) and mackerel tabby in silver, red, blue and cream, tortoiseshell, calico, dilute calico, blue-cream, bi-colour and other colours and patterns excluding the Himalayan pattern, chocolate and lilac (lavender). The eye colour should be appropriate to the dominant colour of the coat.

CARE

THE CYMRIC IS QUIET, intelligent and affectionate but tends to be a one-person cat. Its coat does not mat easily and requires only a weekly combing to remove dead hairs. Like the Manx, its climbing skills do not seem to be inhibited by the lack of a tail. It does well as an indoor cat and does not show great enthusiasm for the outdoors provided activities and hunting substitutes are provided. As has been indicated above, breeding is difficult and best left to experienced breeders. Kittens with tails of varying lengths are sometimes available for sale as pets, but with all Cymric kittens expert veterinary inspection is essential before purchase in view of the breed's history of inherent genetic problems.

> **CAT FACT:**
> With dog-like paws, cheetahs hold onto prey with their mouths until death occurs. To manage this after a sprint they have enlarged airways to take in oxygen.

Top
The large thighs and round toes are visible in this cat.

Bottom
This Cymric has the characteristic round eyes and head of the breed.

Somali

```
○ ○ ○ ○ ○ ○ ○ ○ ○ ○ ○ ○ ○ ○ ○ ○ ○ ○ ○ ○ ○ ○ ○
```
BREED INFORMATION

NAME	Somali
OTHER NAMES	None
BODY SHAPE	Lithe and muscular
COLOUR VARIATIONS	Ruddy (UK: usual) and sorrel (formerly red). Also (US only) blue and fawn.

SIZE

COAT CARE

EXERCISE

THE SOMALI IS a long-haired Abyssinian. It is often characterised as a 'wild-looking cat' because of its shaggy coat and very full tail, but in fact it is a gentle and amiable breed. It has the ticked coat of the Abyssinian with bands of colour on each hair.

ORIGINS OF THE BREED

THE EARLY HISTORY of Somalis is similar to that of the Balinese. When occasional long-haired kittens were born to Abyssinians, breeders would neuter them and sell them off as pets. The longhairs were thought at first to have been the product of out-crosses to a long-haired breed, but it later emerged that for several generations certain breeding lines of Abyssinians had carried the recessive gene for long hair. Where this gene was present in both parents, long-haired kittens were the result.

PEDIGREE IS ESTABLISHED

THE FIRST WORK ON developing the Somali as a breed was done in Australia, where it was first shown in 1965, and in Canada, where a breeding line was established about the same time. In 1969 a breeder in New Jersey, Evelyn Mague, became interested, and she chose the breed name. The name Somali is a tribute to the breed's relationship with the Abyssinian but it is no more than that. In origin and develop-ment, the Somali has no African connection.

Top right
This blue Somali is a result of a naturally recessive gene for longhair found in the Abyssinian.

Top left and bottom right
The similarities between the Abyssinian (top left) and the Somali (bottom right) are clearly visible.

Championship status was awarded by the US Cat Fanciers' Association in 1978, and the other North American cat fancy organisations followed. The breed is now recognised in Britain in the foreign group, and on mainland Europe.

CHARACTERISTICS

THE SOMALI IS A medium sized cat with a body of the foreign type, but not extreme. It is lithe and graceful but well muscled. The back should be slightly arched. The legs are long and slim, with small, oval tufted paws. The tail is thick at the base and slightly tapering, with a full brush. The head is a slightly rounded wedge with no flat planes and all lines gently curving. There is a slight rise from the bridge of the nose to the forehead. The ears are set well apart towards the back of the head. They are large, alert, broad at the base and pointed, with good lynx-like tufts. The eyes are almond shaped, large, brilliant and expressive. Above each eye a short, dark vertical line like a pencil stroke goes from the upper lid towards the ear. This is the last remnant of tabbiness.

Gold or green are the required eye colours across all coat colour varieties. The coat is soft to the touch, full, silky and fine-textured but should be as dense as possible. The length is medium except over the shoulders, where it may be shorter. There should be a good ruff and breeches.

COLOUR VARIETIES

THE DIFFERENT NAMES given to Somali (and Abyssinian) colour varieties in Britain and North America can cause some confusion. The variety known as usual Somali in Britain is called ruddy in North America. The variety formerly known as red has now been renamed sorrel. Usual Somali and sorrel are the only two varieties with Championship status in Britain. In North America, blue and fawn are also accepted. In addition, breeders have produced silver and lilac (lavender) varieties.

In the usual (ruddy) Somali, the coat colour is orange-brown with each hair ticked with black, the darkest colour to be on the extreme outer tip. There is darker shading along the spine and tail, which ends in a black tip. The underside, inside of the legs and chest should be an even, ruddy colour without ticking. The ears are tipped black or dark brown. The toe tufts on all feet should be black or dark brown, with black between the toes extending up the back of the hind legs. Paw pads are black or brown, and the nose leather is brick red.

In the sorrel (red) variety, the body colour is a warm, glowing red – the deeper the better – and the ticking is chocolate brown. The ears and tail are tipped chocolate brown. The underside, insides of the legs and chest are reddish-brown with no ticking. Toe tufts are chocolate brown, paw pads pink and nose leather rosy-pink.

The blue variety has a warm, soft blue-grey body colour with slate blue ticking and an ivory undercoat. In the fawn variety, the body colour is warm rose-beige with light brown ticking.

CARE

THE SOMALI SHOULD only be kept in circumstances where it can be allowed out during the summer months but given warm shelter in the winter; the breed is noticeably disturbed by cold conditions. It is a cautious cat on first acquaintance but companion-able once it has settled down. The coat does not mat and only occasional grooming is necessary. Three or four kittens is the typical litter size. The kittens have very dark coats at first, and ticking does not appear until maturity at about 18 months.

Top left
A pair of red and blue Somali kittens.

Top right
Although Somalis have been described as having an untidy appearance, the oriental facial features gives this cat a majestic look.

Bottom
The typical ruddy coloured Somali.

Norwegian Forest Cat

BREED INFORMATION	
NAME	Norwegian Forest Cat
OTHER NAMES	Norsk Skaukatt
BODY SHAPE	Large, solid
COLOUR VARIATIONS	All colours and patterns except pointed patterns.

SIZE

COAT CARE

EXERCISE

ORIGINS OF THE BREED

ALTHOUGH THERE IS a superficial likeness between the Maine Coon and the Norwegian Forest Cat or Norsk Skaukatt, which no doubt gave rise to the tale

CAT FACT:
Big cats, especially lions, are thought of as proud; hence a pride of lions. They are never too proud though to pass up ready meals like a kill made by another predator.

Top left
Native to Scandinavia, the Norweigan Forest Cat has evolved to live in the harsh climate of the region.

Bottom
The coat of this breed protects the cat against the Arctic winters.

of the Maine Coon having been taken to North America by the Vikings, the Norwegian breed is natural to Scandinavia and the two breeds evolved entirely separately. But both have responded to similar climatic conditions, and they share a historical background as farm cats.

WELL-ADAPTED

THE NORWEGIAN FOREST CAT is a large, strong animal with a dense waterproof coat, even thicker than the Maine Coon's. The insulating undercoat is woolly, and the medium-long, glossy topcoat gives protection from rain and snow. The Forest Cat has finely tuned climbing and hunting skills and

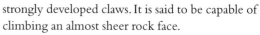

strongly developed claws. It is said to be capable of climbing an almost sheer rock face.

Intelligence, alertness and speed are combined with caution. Despite these rough, tough characteristics, however, the Forest Cat has a surprisingly dainty face, unlike the more severe and businesslike Maine Coon.

The Forest Cat has a long history in Norse folk tales. It appears in a Scandinavian version of Puss in Boots in which the villain is a troll. The Forest Cat, a female, knows that trolls die in sunlight and so, meeting the troll early in the night, she keeps him chatting until dawn comes. Other Norse stories tell of a sweet-faced, bushy tailed 'fairy cat' which lives in the mountains and can perform incredible feats of climbing.

PEDIGREE IS ESTABLISHED

THE FOREST CAT CAME out of the woodlands and farms into Norwegian breeding catteries in the 1930s, when a pedigree was established. But the Second World War brought development to a halt, and when the war ended the breed was almost extinct and the pedigree had been corrupted by breeding

with domestic cats. In the early 1970s serious efforts began in Norway, where the Forest Cat is prized as part of cultural tradition as well as for its own sake, to restore the breed, which in effect meant going back 40 years and making a fresh start. By 1977 the European cat fancy organisation, FIFé, had accepted the Forest Cat for Championship status. The breeder who masterminded the approach to FIFé was hailed in Norway as a national hero.

The Norwegian Forest Cat made its United States debut in 1979 and was given full recognition by the Cat Fanciers' Association in 1994.

Not all United States organisations have accepted it, however, perhaps not wanting to take attention away from the Maine Coon. The breed has Preliminary recognition in Britain as a Semi-longhair.

CHARACTERISTICS

SHOW STANDARDS REQUIRE a strong, muscular, well-built cat with a long body and long legs. The hind legs should be longer than the forelegs, the feet should stand wide, with heavy paws. The tail should be long and bushy and at least as long as the body. The head is triangular in shape and the nose is long, wide and straight with no break. The cheeks are full and the chin heavy. The ears are long, upright and pointed, set high on the head and well-tufted. The whiskers should be prominent and long, and the eyes large and almond shaped, set at a slight angle. The Norwegian Forest Cat has a double coat – a water-repellent silky topcoat and a tight woolly undercoat. A ruff round the neck and chest is prominent in the autumn and winter but disappears in summer.

COLOUR VARIETIES

ALL COLOURS AND PATTERNS, except pointed colourings, are accepted by those organisations which recognise the Norwegian Forest Cat. Many varieties have white on the chest and paws. Eye colour should be appropriate to the coat colour.

TEMPERAMENT

NORWEGIAN FOREST CATS are hardy, and the queens normally produce their litters with ease. The kittens begin to grow their adult coats at three to five months. The adult cats are playful, affectionate and extremely active. They should have access to the outside and are happiest in a large garden, the rougher the better. They are intelligent and easily become adept at skills such as opening door latches. Norwegian Forest Cats moult very heavily in spring and summer and need frequent brushing and combing then to prevent the formation of furballs.

Although Maine Coons and Norwegian Forest Cats are easily confused at first glance, there are in fact significant differences in type. The Forest Cat tends to have a bushier tail and its muzzle is more pointed. Its eyes are more slanted and the ears are less far apart.

Top left
In order to show a Norwegian Forest Cat it should be muscular with long legs.

Bottom
The coat and ruff around the neck moult during the summer.

Shorthairs

THE SHORTHAIR BREEDS are made up of two groups, broadly originating in the western and eastern hemispheres, together with a handful of entirely distinct shorthair breeds. British (European) and American Shorthairs are all basically similar in conformation or body type, and are descended predominantly from the European wild cat, *Felis silvestris.*

AMERICAN SHORTHAIRS

ALTHOUGH AMERICAN SHORTHAIRs have been developed by breeders to different standards from those in Britain and Europe, they share a common ancestry with their British and European cousins, having originally been brought to North America by settlers and sailors. The majority of non-pedigree domestic cats in European and North American homes are crossbred variations of these shorthairs, which have also traditionally supplied the feline farm workforce of Europe.

FOREIGN SHORTHAIRS

Top left
European and American Shorthairs have descended from the European wild cat.

Top right
The rare Havana Brown.

THE SECOND GROUP are known as Foreign and Oriental Shorthairs, dominated by the Siamese. In general usage, 'foreign' and 'Oriental' are fairly interchangeable terms, but in the cat fancy 'Oriental' is the word used in North America for some breeds in this group which are known to British breeders as 'foreign'. The matter is complicated because the breed groups of the Governing Council of the Cat

Fancy in Britain distinguish between 'foreign' breeds (the shorthairs are Russian Blue, Abyssinian, Rex, Korat and Tonkinese) and 'Orientals' (Oriental Shorthairs, Foreign White, Havana and Angora) while having separate groups for Burmese and Siamese. Summing up, in Britain at any rate the words 'foreign' and 'Oriental' may mean something different to a breeder from what they mean to you!

Siamese cats are genuinely cats whose breed originated in Siam (now Thailand), but they arrived in Europe and North America only in the mid-nineteenth century. Another important member of this group is the Abyssinian, whose right to its geographical name is rather more dubious. The sleek-coated Burmese is another shorthair, possibly related by ancestry to the Siamese but now a breed in its own right. The group also includes some

breeds derived from others such as the Exotic Shorthair and the Havana Brown, which now have a breed identity of their own.

OTHER BREEDS

AS WELL AS THESE two major shorthair groups, there are a number of other shorthair breeds which stand on their own. The tailless Manx, which came originally from the Isle of Man between Great Britain and Ireland, is

one of these. Others include the Scottish Fold with its ears folded forward due to a spontaneous mutation; the Japanese Bobtail, the native cat of Japan; the Egyptian Mau, said to be descended from the sacred cats of Ancient Egypt, and the misleadingly named Ocicat. The only thing linking these breeds is that they all happen to have short hair. The curly coated Rexes are included in this section, although really they are in a class of their own.

GROUPING THE SHORTHAIRS

IN THE BREEDS ENTRIES that follow, the British (European) and American Shorthairs are grouped together, followed by other western hemisphere shorthairs and then by the British-designated Foreigns, Burmese, Orientals and Siamese. As with longhairs, national cat fancy organisations do not always agree with each other on breed names,

permissible colour varieties or precise details of show standards. These differences are noted where appropriate in the breed entries. It should be borne in mind that the show standards and specifications for colour varieties are summarised to avoid repetition, and if exact details are required they should be obtained from the relevant cat fancy organisation in the appropriate country.

ORIGINS OF SHORTHAIRS

SHORT HAIR IS THE natural coat of the cat, derived from its wild ancestors, and the gene L for short hair is dominant. This means that in any large cat population there will be more shorthairs than longhairs, and most non-pedigree and feral cats are shorthairs. When longhairs were first seen in Europe in the seventeenth century their beauty and novelty overwhelmed cat lovers who had grown up with shorthairs. A similar story was repeated at the beginning of the twentieth century in the cat fancies of both Britain and North America, where for some years longhairs quite eclipsed the shorthair breeds. Even today, some cat lovers tend to look down on the standard shorthairs such

as the British (European) and American as mundane, considering them (to the annoyance of breeders who have spent years perfecting the breed types) little better than the alley cats to which they are distantly related. Questions of personal taste apart, the one overriding advantage of shorthaired cats is that, unless they are to be prepared for the show ring, they need far less grooming than longhairs. The range of shorthairs is wide, from the brisk, businesslike and generally laid back British (European) Shorthair to the svelte, elegant but demanding Siamese.

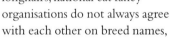

Top
The spotted Ocicat is a shorthaired cat.

Middle
A British Shorthaired silver classic tabby.

Bottom
Although some breeders disregard shorthairs in favour of Persians, this tabby illustrates that a short coat can be equally, if not more, beautiful.

CAT FACT:
The belly of a cat is its most vulnerable area. By rolling over and exposing its belly, a cat is therefore displaying a great deal of trust towards a person.

247

British (European) Shorthairs

○ ○	
BREED INFORMATION	
NAME	British/ European Shorthair US and UK: British Shorthair.
OTHER NAMES	Mainland Europe: European Shorthair
BODY SHAPE	Cobby
COLOUR VARIATIONS	Self/ solid black, blue, cream and white, tabby, tortoiseshell, bicolour, smokes and tipped.

SIZE

COAT CARE

EXERCISE

BRITISH AND EUROPEAN Shorthairs are identical breeds, and use of the alternative names depends entirely on where they are registered. The cat fancy in mainland Europe chooses the European Shorthair designation, although many Championship cats have British ancestry, at least in part. British and North American organisations refer to the British Shorthair.

and indeed there are breeders who consider the breed too 'ordinary' to deserve attention. The truth is, however, that as much attention has gone into perfecting the breed as into more exotic cats.

As the Romans advanced across Europe nearly 2,000 years ago, they brought cats with them to guard their food stores, and it is known that Roman settlers kept cats both as domestic companions and as vermin-destroyers. No doubt, during the Romans' 400-year occupation of north-western Europe and Britain, some of these domestic animals would have interbred with the European wild cat, which was widespread throughout western Europe, just as feral cats continue to do. It is thought that the 'classic' blotched tabby pattern seen in both non-pedigree domestic cats and in British Shorthairs may have resulted from a mutation of the striped tabby 'wild type' gene.

From matings between the Romans' domestic cats and the wild cat, the Shorthair, in something like the form we know it today but leaner and leggier, evolved with a wide range of colour variations. A fourteenth century writer, Bartholomew Glanvil, noted white, red and black cats, together with some 'spewed and speckled' at the points. No doubt some form of selective breeding took place among domesticated and farm cats. It would be noticed, for example, that a queen that was a good mouser passed on its hunting expertise to its kittens and so a line of good hunters could be established. It might be that the quiet, passive traits of the British Shorthair resulted from the selective breeding of quiet cats for the house. But these would be the efforts of individual owners; there was no organised cat fancy and there were no breed standards then.

ORIGINS OF THE BREED

EITHER WAY, THEY are all descended from the natural domestic cat of western Europe and related distantly to millions of family, farm and feral cats all over the continent, although they – or at any rate their owners – would not thank you for reminding them. If a child draws a cat, it produces something like the British Shorthair,

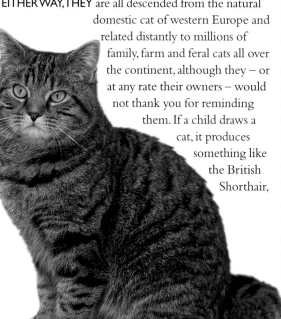

Top
Breeders have spent much time perfecting the look of the British Shorthair, such as this lilac point.

Bottom
Stripes can be clearly seen on this mackerel tabby.

BREED IS ESTABLISHED

THE 'FATHER' OF the British cat fancy, Harrison Weir, was responsible almost single-handedly for raising the humble British domestic cat to breed status. When he organised the first British cat show in 1871, British Shorthairs took pride of place, as they did in subsequent shows and again when Weir wrote his landmark book *Our Cats* in 1892. He was passionately concerned about the welfare of cats, and it was his hope that by emphasising the charm and qualities of the breed he would persuade owners of similar but less exalted shorthairs to care more for them, and that, in his own words, 'the domestic cat sitting in front of the fire would then possess a beauty and an attractiveness to its owner unobserved and unknown because uncultivated before.'

Weir later resigned from the Presidency of the National Cat Club which he had formed because he found that its members cared less for feline welfare than for the competitive spirit, but by that time, by creating the first show standard for the British Shorthair, he had brought the British cat out of obscurity into the limelight. At the time it was, after all, the only breed of which there were substantial numbers in the country.

Top
The British Shorthair has evolved from matings between the wild indigenous cat population in Britain with the domestic Roman pets.

Middle
Colourpoints, such as this blue point, and other colour variations, have existed for at least 500 years.

Bottom
British Shorthairs are related to both farm and feral cats.

Top

Persians' popularity endangered the population of British Shorthairs as fewer people wanted to breed this cat.

Bottom

This tortoiseshell's head shape and large eyes reveal the influence of Persians in the breed.

MAINTAINING THE BREED

WITHIN 20 YEARS, however, the situation had changed. The cat fancy became attracted more to Persians, which outnumbered entries at cat shows by four to one by the turn of the century. The British Shorthair had had its brief moment of glory centre stage but was now to spend several decades in the wings. Although it has recovered its position somewhat, the breed has not achieved anything like its former dominance despite the fervent efforts of enthusiastic breeders.

The result of the decline was a shortage of good quality British Shorthairs to maintain the breed, a situation exacerbated by the suspension of breeding activities during the Second World War. Afterwards, British breeders were forced to cross their Shorthair stock with Persians to perpetuate the breed. This produced complications in the show world, because as the British Shorthair was a natural breed the Governing Council of the Cat Fancy

would not accept Shorthair/Persian crosses. This problem was solved by setting up a supplementary register for the crosses. Cats were promoted from this to the main breed register only when three generations of Shorthair/Shorthair matings had 'purified' them. But all this did nothing for the bona fides of the breed, and for all that it is a true Briton a hint of Persian can still be seen in the shape of the head, unlike in the American Shorthair which does not have this episode in its history.

By the 1950s, it was reckoned that the British Shorthair was again respectable enough to take its place in polite cat show society, and the introduction of Persian blood came to an end.

AMERICAN RECOGNITION

ALTHOUGH, IN THE American Shorthair, North Americans have a similar though subtly different breed of their own developed from generations of all-American cats, the British Shorthair has its admirers there too. It was originally imported in the 1950s from Britain. By the late 1970s all the North American organisations had recognised the breed, though not in the entire range of colours accepted in Britain.

CARE

THE TYPICAL BRITISH Shorthair is quiet and even-tempered to the point of being phlegmatic. It is a good family cat and enjoys playing, but there are also times when it likes to be left to itself to think about things. It does not go in for living-room acrobatics like, for example, the Siamese, and its voice is quiet. British Shorthairs are notable for their intelligence, and this enables them to fit in easily with the daily pattern of the household – not objecting too much at being left alone, for example, provided there is a routine which will provide them with company and food at times they can predict. Grooming is easy and, show grooming apart, a weekly comb and check on the coat is sufficient. British Shorthair queens deliver easily, though litter sizes are unpredictable and may range from one to four or more. The kittens are usually healthy, sturdy, and keen to get on their feet and on with life.

SELFS (SOLIDS)

THE ORIGINAL ATTRACTION of the British Shorthair was in its self (US solid) versions at a time when self colours were relatively rare in other breeds. Pride of place in those days (and in the opinion of many fans of the breed still today) went to the British blue which was the first British Shorthair colour to achieve full recognition in North America. The colour is, in fact, bluish-grey, a shade which seems to emphasise the breed's solidity and sense of firm purpose. The show standard requires a solid light to medium blue with no white or silver-tipped hairs or tabby markings. (Some British blue kittens are born with slight tabby markings which fade over the first few months as the coat develops.) The nose leather and paw pads are blue, and the eyes brilliant copper or orange.

Top
This robust breed is physically strong and healthy.

Bottom right
The typical look of the British Shorthair is open and expressive.

CHARACTERISTICS

THE WORD FOR THE British Shorthair is 'massive.' Its solidity gives it a majestic, slightly aloof air, although in fact it is an ideal domestic companion. Nor is its appearance of strength deceptive. A background of generations of survival through all kinds of weather and living conditions has given the breed a legacy of exceptional hardiness, stamina and adaptability.

The body type of the British Shorthair is classic cobby. Broad-shouldered, muscular and powerful, it has a full, broad chest, strong, short legs and a level back. The paws are neat, well-rounded and firm. The tail is short, thick at the base and tapering to a round tip. The head is broad and round, on a short, solid neck especially notable in the male. The nose is straight, short and broad, without a stop, and the cheeks are well-developed. The ears are small and rounded, and set on the head so that the base of the inner ear is in line with the outer corner of the eye. The eyes are large round and level, and should have a wide-awake, expressive look.

CAT FACT:
A few cat species, including the lynx and Pallas's cat, are missing the first upper molar teeth, giving them a total of 28 teeth instead of the regulation 30.

BLACK

ALMOST AS STRIKING and popular is the British black. Its coat must be glossy jet black with no discolouration or white hairs. (Some kittens' coats have a rusty tinge for the first months, but this disappears when the adult coat grows.) Nose leather and paw pads should be black, and the eyes brilliant copper, orange or deep gold. Green eyes are a fairly common fault found in non-show specimens.

WHITES

SHOW STANDARD BRITISH whites may have deep sapphire blue, gold, copper, orange or odd eyes. Again, green eyes are common in non-show cats. Blue-eyed and odd-eyed whites are often deaf and should not be used for breeding. The coat should be pure white with no yellowish tinge, and the nose and paw pads pink.

CREAM

THE BRITISH CREAM completes the line-up of selfs (solids). The coat is a pale, even cream and there should be no tabby markings or white hairs. The nose leather and paw pads are pink and the eyes brilliant copper or orange. The coat standard is notoriously difficult to achieve, because many kittens retain tabby markings or are too dark. For this reason, creams were the last British Shorthairs to be recognised for competition.

TABBIES

BRITISH SHORTHAIRS TABBIES come in the three basic tabby patterns, classic (blotched), mackerel and spotted, all of which appear in a variety of colours: brown, red, silver, blue and cream. A good tabby should have clearly defined markings with the light and dark areas well contrasted. Many newcomers to the show world are so used to seeing the poorly defined coats of street tabbies that the brilliance of the contrast in good show specimens is a revelation, especially in the spectacular silver tabby.

Tabby is the basic colouring of the domestic cat, and all cats have tabby ancestors somewhere in their background. The tabby pattern's significance in the hierarchy of feline colouring is demonstrated by the frequency with which kittens of parents where the pattern has been conscientiously bred out are born with tabby markings which sometimes persist into the

adult coat. The aim of the breeder of tabbies is of course to accentuate tabbiness in succeeding generations, enhancing colour and contrast.

Top left
Black is one of the most popular colours.

Top right
This tabby has a beautiful, spotted coat with a stripped tail.

Opposite
On all of these three tabby cats the 'M' is clearly visible on the forehead.

ORIGINS OF THE TABBY

THE DICTIONARY TRACES the word 'tabby' to the Attabiya district of Baghdad, where in the seventeenth century a watered silk or taffeta, known in England as tabbisilk, was made. Old French had the word tabis for silk cloth. It is not hard to see how tabby cats reminded people of the patterns on watered silk. The hallmark of tabbies is the letter 'M' marking on the forehead (sometimes called frown marks) acquired, according to legend, when the prophet Mohammed fondled his cat Muezza. All tabbies have other similar head markings. These are unbroken lines running back from the outer corner of the eyes towards the back of the head and 'swirls' on the cheeks.

CLASSIC TABBY

IN THE CLASSIC (blotched) tabby, vertical lines over the back of the head extend to butterfly shaped shoulder markings, which ideally should contain well defined dots within the outline. Three parallel stripes, well separated by the ground colour, run down the spine to the base of the tail. On each flank a large blotch should be encircled by one or more unbroken rings, the size and form of these markings to be the same on both sides. There should be several unbroken necklaces on the neck and upper chest and a double row of 'buttons' (spots) from chest to stomach. The legs should be evenly barred with narrow bands of darker colour, called bracelets, and the tail should be evenly ringed. The silver classic tabby is the most popular of the tabby colours.

MACKEREL TABBY

IN THE MACKEREL tabby, there is an unbroken line running from the back of the head to the base of the tail. On the sides of the body narrow and clearly defined lines should run perpendicularly to the spine line. There should be several necklaces on the neck and upper chest and a double row of 'buttons' on the chest and stomach. The legs are evenly barred, the bracelets coming up to meet the body markings, and the tail is evenly ringed.

SPOTTED TABBY

THE MARKINGS IN the coat of the spotted tabby (sometimes known as the 'spottie') may vary in size and shape. They may be round, oval or rosette shaped, but should be numerous and evenly distributed, with none joining together to make a broken mackerel pattern. In the United States, preference is given to round spots. A line of spots runs the length of the back and there should be a double line of spots on the chest and stomach with spots or broken rings on the legs and tail.

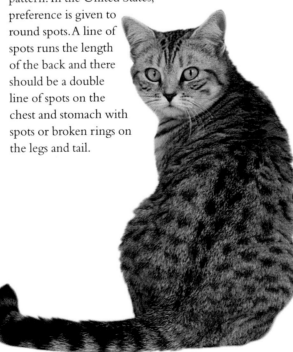

Bottom right
This tabby has perfectly distributed spots on its coat.

 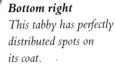

COLOUR VARIETIES

TABBIES ARE ACCEPTED in five colours: brown, red, blue, cream and silver. The brown colouring is a rich sable or coppery-brown ground colour with dense, jet black markings. The hind legs should be black from paw to heel. The paw pads are black and the nose leather brick red. The eyes are orange or deep yellow. In the red, the ground colour is rich red with dark red markings and red on the sides of the feet. Paw pads are deep red and the nose leather brick red. The eyes are deep orange or copper. The blue has deep blue markings over a bluish-fawn ground colour, blue or pink paw pads and nose leather, and deep yellow to copper eyes. Cream has a pale cream ground colour with darker cream markings, pink paw pads and nose leather, and gold or copper eyes. The silver tabbies are the most dramatically coloured, with dense, jet black markings over silver. The paw pads are black and the nose leather red or black. Eyes may be green or gold in Britain, but the United States standard requires brilliant gold, orange or hazel.

TORTOISESHELLS

THE TORTOISESHELL IS notoriously difficult to breed as the tortoiseshell gene is sex-linked and passes in the female line only. Male tortoiseshells are born, and one is on record as having fathered kittens, but the few that survive are normally sterile. Females must be mated to self (solid) colour toms, and the resultant litters may not contain any tortoiseshells, making breeding a chancy business.

The true tortoiseshell has a mixture of black, rich red and pale cream, in Britain evenly intermingled without definite patches of any one colour except for a short, narrow blaze on the face which is allowed. United States standards require a patched rather than intermingled look, the patches being clearly defined and well broken, and the blaze on the face, of red or cream, is quoted as 'desirable.' Paw pads and nose leather are pink or black. The eye colour is deep orange or copper (UK) or brilliant gold (US).

BLUE-CREAM

THE BLUE-CREAM shorthair is a dilute version of the tortoiseshell. The coat colour is blue with cream softly intermingled, with no tabby markings or white hairs or patches. Paw pads and nose leather are blue or pink and the eye colour copper, orange or gold (UK) or brilliant gold (US).

TORTIE-AND-WHITE

THE BRILLIANTLY COLOURED tortoiseshell-and-white is known in North America as the calico British Shorthair. It is boldly patched with black, cream and red on white with the patches equally balanced, clear and well defined. The pattern must cover the head, back, tail, legs and part of the flanks and there should be a blaze on the face. White is predominant on the underparts. Paw pads and nose leather are pink or black and the eyes brilliant copper or orange (UK) or brilliant gold (US).

Top
This red self Shorthair is an acceptable colour for showing.

Bottom
This tortoiseshell would have to be mated with a solid tom in order to have a litter, of which there may be no tortoiseshells.

BLUE TORTIE-AND-WHITE

THE BLUE TORTOISESHELL-and-white is called the dilute calico British Shorthair in North America. It has patches of blue and cream on white with white predominant on the underparts. Paw pads and nose leather are blue or pink, and eyes copper, orange or gold (UK) or brilliant gold (US).

In addition to the above, chocolate and lilac (lavender) tortoiseshells have preliminary recognition in Britain but not in North America.

BI-COLOURS

THE BI-COLOUR British Shorthair has even patches of red, blue, black or cream on a white ground colour. When this variety was introduced to the British show world in 1966, the standard required total symmetry of the colouring – an ideal which proved too demanding and so was softened five years later. The requirement now is for large patches of colour distributed evenly and as far as possible symmetrically on the head, body and tail, with not more than two-thirds of the cat coloured and not more than one-half white. There should be a white blaze on the face. There should be no tabby markings or white hairs in the colour patches. Paw pads and nose leather may be pink or in harmony with the main colour. The eyes should be brilliant copper or orange (UK) or brilliant gold, the more brilliant the better (US).

SMOKES

IN SMOKE VARIETIES the pigment in the guard hairs appears only on the outer three-quarters of the hair shaft, leaving the remainder white or silver and giving a shimmering effect in motion similar to that of Persian (Longhair) smokes. The pigmented colour may, in Britain, be any acceptable colour for British Shorthairs, including tortoiseshell combinations, but in the United States only black and blue smokes are acceptable. There should be no tabby markings or totally white or silver hairs. The paw pads and nose leather should accord with the coat colour, and the eyes should be copper, orange or deep gold (UK) or brilliant gold (US).

TIPPEDS

IN THE TIPPED colourings, the shaft of the guard hair is mainly white, with light tipping at the end in any of the solid colours: black, blue, red, cream, and (UK only) chocolate and lilac (lavender). The tipping should appear on the head, back, flanks, legs and tail, leaving the chin, stomach, chest and underside of the tail white. There should be no tabby markings but vestigial tail rings are allowed. Paw pads and nose leather should accord with the tipped colour. Eyes should be green in black-tipped cats and orange or copper in other colours.

Top
A black smoke is only one of two smokes acceptable in the United States.

Bottom
Bi-colours, such as this cream, were introduced to the show world in 1966.

American Shorthair

```
○○○○○○○○○○○○○○○○○○○○○○○○○○○○○○
    BREED INFORMATION
```

NAME	American Shorthair
OTHER NAMES	None
BODY SHAPE	Muscular, light-boned
COLOUR VARIATIONS	Self/solid olid black, blue, red, cream and white, tabby, tortoiseshell, calico, tipped, smokes and bi-colours.

SIZE

COAT CARE

EXERCISE

THE ORIGINS OF the American Shorthair are similar to those of its British and European cousins in that it is derived from the domestic cat. The only difference is that while Britain has had domestic cats for at least 1,000 years (and also had and still vestigially has a European wild cat population with which there was probably some interbreeding) the American cat has been established for only 400 years at most.

USEFUL BREED

IT MAY SEEM ODD that the native American Indians did not domesticate a member of the cat family. It is true that the native North American Felis species are large; the smallest, found in the southern United States, is the jaguarundi, which weighs up to 10 kg (22 lb). But there is evidence that the Ancient Egyptians tamed and to some extent domesticated the serval, which is almost twice as large. The answer is probably that farming, which might have benefited from the presence of cats to keep down vermin, was subservient in American Indian culture to hunting and fishing. Also, perhaps the unsettled life did not favour the keeping of cats. However, the fact that there is no domestic cat in American Indian social history seems to do away with the theory that the Maine Coon is descended from Norwegian Forest

Cats left behind on the North American continent by the Viking explorers. If semi-domesticated cats had indeed been left behind, they would surely have found their way to Indian settlements.

Bottom left
The Serval was domesticated by the Egyptians.

Right
The American Shorthair (bottom) and the Maine Coon (top) are both descended from the European cats introduced by colonisers.

So it was that the first domestic cats arrived in North America with European settlers and would have been joined from time to time by fresh arrivals with immigrants and escapes from ships. Some of these shorthairs then mated ferally with longhairs, that also were imported or had escaped, to found the Maine Coon breed.

From then on, shorthairs multiplied freely, earning their keep in the barn and grain stores and gradually finding acceptance in the kitchen. As pioneer families moved westwards, they took their cats with them, and so the domestic cat population spread across the continent. The conditions for survival, especially in the northern states in winter, were harsh and demanding. Although they lacked the insulating long hair of the Maine Coon, the shorthairs rivalled that breed in toughness. Their refined hunting skills, still evident in today's pedigree version, meant that they never went hungry. As in Britain and mainland Europe, shorthairs moved between domestic, farm and feral life, roaming and breeding freely and developing a range of colours and markings but tending generally towards tabbiness.

PEDIGREE IS ESTABLISHED

AMERICAN SHORTHAIRS WERE way down the line to the Maine Coons and the more picturesque, and, at that time, rare foreign breeds in the early days of the United States cat fancy, although there was a class for Shorthairs, under that name, at the first American cat show in 1895.

In those days, no pedigree was required for registration and the cat fancy was more open than it is today – although the spirit of the early days survives in the 'Household and Domestic cat' classes which are part of most cat shows.

It took a pair of Shorthairs imported from Britain to break new ground. Round about 1900 an American breeder named Jane Cathcart brought in an orange male tabby British Shorthair, inappropriately named Belle of Bradford, which became the first pedigree shorthair to be registered by the Cat Fanciers' Association. Miss Cathcart followed this with a second import, a male silver tabby named Pretty Correct.

Top
The American Shorthair has roots in both farming communities and domestic households.

Bottom
An orange male tabby was introduced from Britain to bring new blood into the American breed at the turn of the century.

THE FIRST AMERICAN SHORTHAIR

WHAT HAPPENED NEXT is something of a mystery, but in 1904 Miss Cathcart registered the first American-born Shorthair, Buster Brown, 'of unknown parentage.' She had evidently started on the practice which continued in the American cat fancy for some decades and is still permitted in some United States cat clubs today – the registration of non-pedigree cats and kittens as American Shorthairs provided they meet the standard. This practice was given the blessing of the Cat Fanciers' Association in 1971 when a non-pedigree cat was voted Best American Shorthair of the Year. By this time the breed, which had developed slowly until the 1950s, had become an established favourite on the American show scene. It is not recognised in Britain.

In the early years, the establishment of the new breed led to some dissension among American cat clubs as to what to call it. Originally designated as the Shorthair, it variously became the Domestic Shorthair and the American Domestic Shorthair until, in 1966, most clubs finally accepted the term American Shorthair.

than round as in the British standard. The neck is slimmer and more pronounced and the ears stand taller. The tail is generally longer and tapers more sharply than the British Shorthair's, and the legs are slightly longer.

CHARACTERISTICS

TYPICAL WEIGHTS FOR the American Shorthair are 6.5 kg (14 lb) for the male and 4.5 kg (10 lb) for the female. The Cat Fanciers' Association show standard describes it as a strong, well-built cat in which 'no part of the anatomy should be so exaggerated as to foster weakness'. It should be 'lithe enough to stalk its prey but powerful enough to make the kill easily', with 'legs long enough to cope with any terrain and heavy and muscular enough for high leaps'. The emphasis is on power, endurance and agility – the natural features that have made the Shorthair such a survivor.

Top
American Shorthairs are allowed to be registered even when their parentage has not been traced.

Middle
The American Shorthair is slightly less robust looking than its European cousin.

Bottom right
The American Shorthair is an athletic breed that is built for survival.

AMERICAN VARIETY

ALTHOUGH SERIOUS BREEDING began with British stock, the tastes of American breeders have taken the American Shorthair in a different direction, aided by interbreeding with native cats, and although the American breed is clearly related to the British or European Shorthair there are distinct differences in emphasis. The American Shorthair is more lightly built. It is more muscular but lighter boned, with a rather less 'rough and tough' appearance than its transatlantic cousin although it is no less bold in character. Its coat is short and hard, less plush than the British Shorthair's, and thickens in winter, perhaps reflecting conditions in the northern United States. The head is large, slightly longer than it is wide, rather

The body should be large to medium in size, lean, hard, athletic and powerful, designed for hunting, climbing and jumping. The chest and shoulders should be well-developed and the legs sturdy and medium in length. The paws are firm, full and rounded with heavy pads. The tail is medium-long, wide at the base and tapering to a blunt tip.

The head should be large, with a pleasant, full-cheeked face slightly longer than it is wide. The nose is medium in length and uniform in width with a gentle curve in profile. The muzzle is square with a firm, well-developed chin. The neck is medium-long, thick and muscular. The ears are medium in size but not too open at the base, set wide on the head with slightly rounded tips. The eyes are round and wide, set wide apart, giving the face a bright, alert look. Any tendency to fluffiness in the coat, to shortness of the nose in the Persian fashion, or to cobbiness in the British Shorthair style, is a show fault.

CARE

THE AMERICAN SHORTHAIR, like the British, is an ideal domestic cat, hardy, intelligent, affectionate and home-loving. It is an unfussy cat, ready to take life as it comes. It has a quiet voice and indeed, except when it enlivens its day with a bout of mock hunting, enjoys the quiet life. Only light grooming is required. It is a pity to confine indoors a cat so perfectly built for hunting, climbing and jumping, and if possible the American Shorthair should have access to a garden. American Shorthairs breed easily, four being the normal litter size. The queens are famously attentive and patient mothers. The kittens, which open their eyes at 9–10 days, are normally healthy and soon become adventurous and confident.

SOLID COLOURS

THE AMERICAN SHORTHAIR is accepted in black, blue, red, cream and white.

The black should be a dense, coal black, sound from the roots to the tips of the hairs, with no rusty tinge. The paw pads should be black or brown and the nose leather black. Eyes should be brilliant gold.

The blue should be an even tone of blue throughout, lighter shades being preferred, with the colour sound to the roots. The paw pads and nose leather should be blue and the eyes brilliant gold.

The red is a clear, deep, brilliant red without shading, markings or ticking. The lips and chin should be the same colour as the coat. The paw pads and nose leather are brick red and the eyes brilliant gold.

The cream has one even shade of buff-cream with no markings, sound to the roots, preference being given to lighter shades. The paw pads and nose leather are pink and the eyes brilliant gold. The white must be a pure glistening white, with pink paw pads and nose leather. The eyes may be deep blue, brilliant gold, or odd-eyed (one blue and one gold eye, the colours to be of equal depth).

Top
A typical American Shorthair's head is longer than it is wide.

Middle
The eyes of a solid black should be bright gold.

TABBIES

THE AMERICAN STANDARDS for classic (UK blotched) and mackerel tabby patterns are similar to those given for British Shorthairs , but there is no American equivalent of the spotted tabby in the American Shorthair.

SILVER CLASSIC

Top
The American Shorthair tabby has the same standards as the British Shorthair.

Bottom
A young blue and white calico Shorthair.

IF THE BRITISH BLUE is the pride of the British Shorthair breed, its equivalent in the American Shorthair is the silver classic tabby. It will be remembered that a silver tabby was the second British Shorthair to be imported in the early days. The standard requires dense black markings on a silver ground with the lips and chin pale, clear silver. The paw pads are black and the nose leather is brick red. Eyes may be green or hazel.

TABBY PATTERNS

THE REQUIREMENTS FOR the other recognised colours in the tabby patterns are as follows. The brown tabby has a brilliant coppery brown ground colour with dense black markings. The backs of the legs are black from paw to heel and the paw pads are black or brown. The nose leather is brick red and the eye colour brilliant gold. The red tabby's ground colour is red with deep, rich red markings. The paw pads and nose leather are brick red and the eyes brilliant gold. In the blue tabby, the ground colour is bluish-ivory with deep blue markings making a good contrast. There should be warm fawn overtones over all. The paw pads are rose, the nose leather old rose and the eyes brilliant gold. The ground colour of the cream tabby is very pale cream with buff or cream markings making a good contrast. The paw pads and nose leather are pink and the eyes brilliant gold.

Two other colour varieties complete the tabby range. The cameo tabby has an off-white ground colour with red markings, rose paw pads and nose leather and brilliant gold eyes. The patched tabby (torbie) is a silver, brown or blue classic or mackerel tabby with patches of red and/or cream, the tabby markings running through light and dark areas. If the American Shorthair were recognised in the Britain, this pattern would be known as tortie-tabby.

TORTOISESHELLS AND CALICOS

THE BASIC TORTOISESHELL standard requires black with well-defined patches of red and cream well broken on the body, legs and tail. A red or cream blaze on the face is desirable. The paw pads and nose leather are brick red and/or black, and the eyes brilliant gold.

The colouring known as tortoiseshell-and-white in Britain is called calico in North America. This requires white with unbrindled (clear-coloured) patches of black and red. White should be predominant on the underparts. The paw pads and nose leather are pink and the eyes brilliant gold. In the dilute calico, blue and cream replace black and red respectively.

The blue-cream is blue with well-defined and well-broken patches of cream on the body, legs and tail. The paw pads and nose leather are blue and/or pink, and the eyes brilliant gold.

TIPPEDS

THE CHINCHILLA IS one of the most striking colour varieties in the American Shorthair. Its undercoat is pure white, but black tipping on the back, flanks, head and tail give a characteristic sparkling silver look. The legs may also be lightly tipped. The chin, ear tufts, stomach and chest should be pure white. The paw pads are black and the nose leather brick red. The eye colour may be green or blue-green.

Shaded silver is a darker version of the chinchilla. The undercoat is white with a mantle of black tipping shading down from the sides, face and tail from dark on the ridge to white on the chin, chest, stomach, and under the tail. The legs should be the same tone as the face. The colours of the paw pads, nose leather and eyes are as for the chinchilla.

In the shell cameo, the tipping is similar to the chinchilla's but is red on a white undercoat. The paw pads and nose leather are rose pink and the eyes brilliant gold.

The shaded cameo or red shaded is similar to the shaded silver but with a mantle of red tipping heavier than in the shell cameo.

SMOKES

IN THE SMOKE patterns, the cat in repose should appear the colour of the tipping. In each variety, the undercoat is white and the tipping is deep. The colours permitted are black, blue, cameo (red smoke) and tortoiseshell. In each case the paw pads and nose leather colours are appropriate to the tipping (brick red or black in the tortoiseshell) and the eyes are gold.

BI-COLOURS

THE STANDARD BI-COLOUR is white with unbrindled patches of black, blue, red or cream. The paw pads and nose leather may be pink or in keeping with the solid colour.

In Van bi-colours (a term borrowed from the colouring of the Turkish Van) the colour is mainly confined to the head, legs and tail. The paw pads and nose leather may be pink or in keeping with the solid colour. The Van calico has patches of black and red on the head, legs and tail, and the Van blue-cream patches of blue and cream.

Top
The nose leather of this calico kitten is blue.

Bottom
This cameo tabby has the archetypal gold eye colour.

Chartreux

○ ○

BREED INFORMATION

NAME	Chartreux
OTHER NAMES	Chartreuse
BODY SHAPE	Cobby
COLOUR VARIATIONS	Grey-blue only.

SIZE

COAT CARE

EXERCISE

THE CHARTREUX OR Chartreuse, native to France, is not recognised in Britain and is regarded by many in the cat fancy as identical to the blue British Shorthair, although there are subtle differences in conformation. In North America and mainland Europe it is a recognised breed.

ORIGINS OF THE BREED

THE CHARTREUX IS said to be named after the Carthusian monastery, the Grande Chartreuse, founded in 1084 near Grenoble in south-eastern France. One story is that the cats were brought to the monastery by knights returning from the Crusades. Another is that a party of Carthusian monks travelled to the Cape of Good Hope in South Africa in the seventeenth century and brought a pair of cats back from there. In fact there is nothing except the breed name to connect the cats with the monastery, but the name has been attached to this breed since at least the sixteenth century, when it was already a familiar sight on the streets of France.

It was described by the French poet Joachim du Bellay in a letter written in 1558, and referred to in one of the earliest French dictionaries, published in 1723. There are frequent mentions of the Chartreux in eighteenth century French books of natural history. More recently, the French romantic novelist Colette, who was born in 1873, wrote lovingly of her own Chartreux.

An alternative explanation of the name has been suggested. This is that Pile de Chartreux was the name given to a kind of wool imported from Spain and that the word was transferred by association to the woolly-coated cat.

PEDIGREE IS ESTABLISHED

THE HISTORY OF THE Chartreux in the cat fancy begins in the late 1920s when two sisters named Leger moved from Paris to the island of Belle-Ile off the coast of Brittany. There they found a large population of blue-grey cats and began to breed from some of them. The first of the Leger sisters' Chartreux made its French show debut in 1931 in Paris, and one of the offspring of the first mating, named Mignonne, went on to win two prestigious prizes, the Belgian Challenge Cup and the Paris Prix d'Esthetics two years later.

Top left
In Britain the Chartreux is not recognised as a separate breed but would be described as a blue British Shorthair.

Top right
A view of the Carthusian monastery, the GrandeChartreuse, outside Grenoble, from the hills.

Bottom
A Chartreux at the monastery in France.

CHARACTERISTICS

THE BODY OF THE Chartreux is large, well-proportioned and robust, with large, muscular shoulders and a deep chest. The difference between the male and female size is emphasised, the male being much more massive. The tail should be moderately long, tapering to an oval tip. The coat may be longer than the American Shorthair's, the female's being silkier and thinner than the male's. It should be double-coated, dense, soft and a little woolly. The head is large and broad but not rounded. The nose is short and straight, with a slight stop allowed. The muzzle should be narrow in relation to the head, but not pointed. The cheeks are well-developed, the jaws powerful and the neck short and strong. The ears are small to medium, set high on the head with slightly rounded tips. The eyes should be large, round and expressive, coloured pale gold to orange, with the deeper tones preferred. The face as a whole should have a sweet, smiling expression.

COLOUR VARIETIES

THE COAT COLOUR MAY be any shade of grey-blue, with silver highlights at the tips, great importance being attached to evenness of tone. The paw pads are rose and the nose leather silver-grey.

TEMPERAMENT

THE CHARTREUX IS a cat with considerable presence. Owners say that it has many dog-like qualities. It is inclined to exercise in short bursts, will retrieve, and will defend its owner if it perceives a threat. Despite this, it is calm and gentle in play – especially, it is said, the male – and is easily trained. The kittens are hardy. Grooming need be no more than weekly.

The Chartreux fared no better during the Second World War than other European breeds and when it was over there were too few to maintain the breed without out-crossing. Crossings with Persians, British blues and Russian Blues were tried but failed to restore breed type. In the end breeders had to resort to painfully 'reconstructing' the Chartreux by mating the few remaining specimens with blue cats found on the streets. It was not until the late 1970s that the breed had been restored to something like its former standard, and further out-crosses were disallowed.

Meanwhile, in the United States, the development of the Chartreux had begun in 1970 with the importing of 10 cats from France. Three of these came, in fact, from the Leger cattery, where the sisters had maintained their interest in the breed for over 40 years. The similarity of the Chartreux to the British Blue dogged American breeders' attempts to get it recognised as a separate breed, but by 1990 most United States organisations had accepted it under its own name.

Top
Rumour says that Carthusian monks travelled to South Africa 200 years ago and brought back the breed to France.

Bottom
The colour can be any shade of grey-blue but must be even coloured.

Exotic Shorthair

○○○○○○○○○○○○○○○○○○○○○○○○○○○○○○

BREED INFORMATION

NAME	Exotic Shorthair
OTHER NAMES	Exotic
BODY SHAPE	Cobby
COLOUR VARIATIONS	All Longhair Persian and American Shorthair colours.

SIZE

COAT CARE

EXERCISE

THE EXOTIC SHORTHAIR is a relatively recent United States hybrid created by crossing American Shorthairs with Persians. It arose from attempts to bring a more Persian look to the breed, but there was no intention to create a new type. A similar exercise had been conducted in Britain after the Second World War when the shortage of British Shorthair stock led breeders to restore type by breeding to Persians. In Britain, once type had been regained the practice stopped.

ORIGINS OF THE BREED

AMERICAN BREEDERS' programmes seem to have been driven by two motives. One, according to some members of the United States cat fancy, was to meet the evident taste of show judges for the Persian look.

The second was to produce an 'easy care' Persian type, which had all the beauty and personality of the Persian but without the necessity for heavy grooming.

However, the result of the programme in the United States was resistance from breeders of American Shorthairs who wanted their breed kept true and were disturbed at the changes that seemed to be becoming permanent in the breed type. In short, breeders were showing as American Shorthairs, cats that were clearly not of that breed. The type was losing its hardness of coat in favour of a plusher texture, the eyes were becoming larger and rounder and the muzzle was foreshortened. There was also concern that some breeders had mated American Shorthairs to Burmese, which was thought to be genetically undesirable.

PEDIGREE IS ESTABLISHED

IN 1966 IT WAS decided to create a new breed name for the hybrids, the Exotic Shorthair, which would leave American Shorthairs free of mixed ancestry. The next year, the Exotic Shorthair was shown for the first time, and in 1969 a breed club was founded with the aim of achieving recognition. This followed in 1972. The Exotic Shorthair is the only hybrid cross recognised in the United States, and is rigidly controlled. The only crosses allowed for recognition are Persian to American Shorthair, Exotic to Exotic, or Persian to Exotic. The breed has provisional recognition in Britain.

CAT FACT:
By their co-operative hunting strategy, lions are better able to catch enough food, even though it has to be shared. They can kill animals as big as giraffes and buffaloes.

Top
The Exotic Shorthair is an American Shorthair/Persian cross.

Bottom
The breed has the distinct Persian look but does not need such intense grooming.

CHARACTERISTICS

THE EXOTIC SHORTHAIR is basically a short-haired Persian, though this description hardly gives credit to its unique appearance. It has the Persian's cobby build and distinctive head, but these features are curiously changed by the short, plush coat to establish a character of their own, perhaps best summed up by the breed's popular American nickname, 'the teddy bear cat'.

Generally, the Exotic Shorthair takes its standard from the Persian model, except for the coat. This is slightly longer but fuller than is usual in shorthairs, having the Persian's long down hairs. It is important that the coat should be even in length, with no ruff and no tufts on the ears or between the toes. It should be dense, soft and glossy, and stand out from the body. A flowing coat and ear or toe tufts are faults. All American Shorthair and Persian coat colours are permitted.

The body is medium to large, cobby, deep-chested and low on the legs, which should be short, thick and strong. The forelegs should be straight and the paws large, round and firm. The shoulders and rump should be massive, with a level back. The tail is short, but in proportion to the body, carried straight and low with a rounded tip.

The Exotic has a round, massive head, with a round face set on a short, thick neck. The nose is short and broad with a break. The cheeks are full and the chin full and well-developed. The ears are set far apart and low on the head, fitting its rounded contour. They are small, round-tipped, tilted forward and not unduly open at the base. The eyes are large, round, brilliant and full, and set well apart. Overall, the face should have a sweet expression.

TEMPERAMENT

THE TEMPERAMENT OF the Exotic Shorthair is docile and affectionate. It is playful but not destructive, intelligent, fond of home life with the family, and readily accepts other animals. It is not especially keen on exercise and will happily live an indoor life. Grooming is not as demanding as with the Persian, but regular combing is necessary to remove dead hairs.

Breeding the Exotic Shorthair is extremely difficult, and as a result the breed is relatively small in numbers. As Exotics are frequently bred back to Persians to maintain type, about half the kittens are longhairs. The difficulty is to know which kittens are which until the adult coat begins to grow. Litters usually number four.

> **CAT FACT:**
> Several of the species of cat have what are known as tear stripes. These are the black lines running from the eye to the cheek. They denote scent glands.

Top
This cat illustrates how the breed gets its nickname, the 'teddy bear cat'.

Bottom
There are normally four kittens in a litter, two of which are longhaired.

265

American Wirehair

○ ○

BREED INFORMATION

NAME	*American Wirehair*
OTHER NAMES	*None*
BODY SHAPE	*Cobby*
COLOUR VARIATIONS	*All American Shorthair colours.*

SIZE

COAT CARE

EXERCISE

THE AMERICAN WIREHAIR is the result of a spontaneous genetic mutation. In 1966 a litter of six kittens resulting from a farm cat mating was born on a farm in Verona, New York State. Five of the kittens had normal shorthair coats but one male had an unusually sparse but wiry red and white coat. This is a form of coat unknown elsewhere in the domestic cat world or even among wild *Felis* species, but similar to that of the Wire-haired Terrier – a likeness which accounts for the breed name.

ORIGINS OF THE BREED

The aberrant male, named Adam, and a female kitten from the same litter, Tip-Toe, were sold to a breeder who mated them at maturity.

From this mating there was a litter of four kittens, born in July 1967, of which two females were wire-haired red and whites. Only one of these, Amy, survived, but she produced a number of litters which included wire-haired kittens. They were distinguished at birth by crimped whiskers and hairs on the face and ears, giving them an extremely unkempt look.

Adam fathered two more litters with his wire-haired progeny, and a further litter with an unrelated farm shorthair belonging to a neighbour. This litter

included three wire-haired kittens, making it clear that the mutated gene in Adam's genotype was dominant. It was eventually given the identification Wh. It is not sex-linked. The ancestry of all American Wirehairs can be traced back to Adam.

UNIQUE COAT

THE BREEDER ORIGINALLY involved was interested in Rex cats and thought that the wire-hair might be another form of the Rex mutation. Samples of Adam's coat were sent to Britain for analysis by geneticists, who found that it was, in fact, a previously unknown coat type. The unique wire-haired effect is produced by the distinctive guard hairs. Instead of being smooth and tapered, they are crimped along their entire length and hooked at the end. The underlying down hairs are also twisted. Unlike the Rex coat, the Wirehair's is springy and rather coarse to the touch – and very similar to that of the Wire-haired Terrier.

Top left
This breed is only around 30 years old and results from an accidental genetic mutation.

Top right
American Wirehairs are born with crumpled whiskers.

Bottom
The coat is similar to that of a wire-haired terrier.

PEDIGREE IS ESTABLISHED

FROM THE SMALL stock of Wirehairs now available, all descended from Adam, a full-scale breeding programme began in the United States, with breeders in Canada and Germany also becoming interested. The coat, sparse in the original kittens, was developed to a consistency similar to that of sheep's wool. Selective breeding also bred out the longer legs and taller ears of the early specimens which were felt to be unattractive and too removed from the American Shorthair standard. Because the wire-hair gene Wh is dominant, it was relatively easy to out-cross Wirehairs to Shorthairs

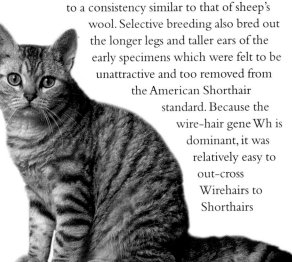

without losing the unique coat, but mating to longhairs was avoided. In the early days of the breeding programme, varying degrees of wiriness and springiness occurred in Wirehair litters, and the efforts of breeders were concentrated on stabilising the type so that the recognition process could go ahead. The American Wirehair was given championship status by the Cat Fanciers' Association in 1977, but is not recognised in Britain.

In the show standard, the overall wire effect and coarse, springy coat quality are considered more important than the crimping of the individual hairs. The medium length coat should be tightly curled into small ringlets rather than waves. Other hairs such as the whiskers and the hairs within the ears should be crimped, hooked or bent, giving an untidy appearance. Permitted coat colours are as for the American Shorthair.

CHARACTERISTICS

THE AMERICAN WIREHAIR'S body is medium to large with a level back and the shoulders and haunches the same width. The legs are medium in length but well-muscled and in proportion. The paws are oval and compact, and the tail should taper to a rounded tip. The head should be round with prominent cheekbones, a well-developed muzzle and chin and a slight whisker break. The nose should have a gentle curved profile. The eyes are large, round, bright and clear, with a slight upward tilt towards the ears and set well apart. The ears are medium sized, set well apart and rounded at the tips.

TEMPERAMENT

THE AMERICAN WIREHAIR'S somewhat urchin-like appearance is part of its charm and is matched by its nature. It is one of those cats which 'gets into everything' given half a chance. Wirehairs are only a few generations away from their farm cat ancestors and retain both an independent streak and an appetite for the hunt. Ideally, they should be allowed outdoors. They make their wishes abundantly clear in the home and tend to be impatient with other cats and interfering children. They need only light grooming. The queens are attentive mothers, bearing litters of three or four. The kittens are born with curly coats already in place and their whiskers and facial hairs all awry. They are robust and healthy, but there have been cases of kittens with respiratory and other problems born as a result of Wirehair to Wirehair matings.

> **CAT FACT:**
> Civets and genets are cat-like animals which are in fact the cats' closest living relatives. They differ only in having longer muzzles to accommodate far more teeth.

Top
Breeding this cat is relatively easy as the wirehair gene is dominant.

Bottom
The American Wirehair should have large, round eyes and medium sized ears.

Manx

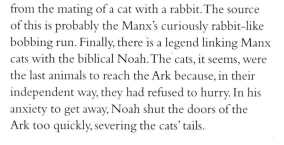

○○○○○○○○○○○○○○○○○○○○○○○○○○

BREED INFORMATION

NAME	Manx
OTHER NAMES	None
BODY SHAPE	Solid, short
COLOUR VARIATIONS	UK: All colours except colourpoint. US: All colours, except colourpoint, chocolate and lavender.

SIZE

COAT CARE

EXERCISE

THE TAILLESS MANX is another cat of legend – many legends, in fact. One story goes that in 1588, when the Spanish Armada was fleeing from the victorious English fleet round the north of Scotland and down the Irish Sea, a shipwreck off the Isle of Man enabled Spanish cats to swim ashore, where they established a colony. Unfortunately for this tale, there is no record of either a shipwreck off the Isle of Man or of tailless Spanish cats.

ORIGINS OF THE BREED

Another legend is that the Viking warriors who occupied the island in the early Middle Ages stole cats' tails as plumes for their helmets, and queens took to biting the tails off their kittens to avoid this ignominy. Yet another story traces the Manx cat back to Phoenician traders who sailed to the British Isles over 3,000 years ago.

Then there is the tale of an old tradition of the Celts, who preceded the Vikings on the Isle of Man, that anyone who trod on a cat's tail would be stung by a viper. An obliging Providence, the story goes on, caused cats to be born tailless to save Celts from this fate.

Among the biologically impossible ideas about the Manx cat's origin is that the first Manx resulted

from the mating of a cat with a rabbit. The source of this is probably the Manx's curiously rabbit-like bobbing run. Finally, there is a legend linking Manx cats with the biblical Noah. The cats, it seems, were the last animals to reach the Ark because, in their independent way, they had refused to hurry. In his anxiety to get away, Noah shut the doors of the Ark too quickly, severing the cats' tails.

PEDIGREE IS ESTABLISHED

GENETIC SCIENCE PROVIDES a more accurate if less romantic explanation. The Manx is the result of a dominant gene mutation which probably emerged on the island several centuries ago. The isolation of the Isle of Man – it was not until the late nineteenth century that it was developed as a holiday resort, and until then it was virtually a closed community – enabled the breed to flourish undisturbed. Records of tailless cats on the island go back to at least 1820. In the late nineteenth century the Manx was 'discovered' by the cat fancy, and a breed club was formed in Britain in 1901.

Left
The lack of a tail on the Manx breed has been a subject around which legends have been created.

Right
The omission of a tail is due to a genetic mutation which occurred at least 150 years ago.

King Edward VII was a Manx owner, and perhaps this encouraged interest in the breed. American cat fanciers started taking an interest in the 1930s, and the demand for breeding stock was so high that the Isle of Man Government feared for the breed's future on its native island. As a result, a government-funded breeding cattery was set up in 1960. It is still going, but is no longer owned by the government. On Man, the Manx cat is an important cultural symbol which has appeared on coins and stamps and is frequently seen in paintings, jewellery and ceramics for the tourist trade. It should be said, however, that the Isle of Man has no monopoly in tailless shorthairs. They are fairly frequently born to domestic cats, and exist too in some wild Felis species.

Travellers ranging from Marco Polo in the thirteenth century to the more reliable Charles Darwin in the nineteenth, reported seeing tailless cats in south-east Asia. A breed of tailless longhairs, the Cymric or Manx Longhair, also exists . But the tailless cats of the Isle of Man are the specific origin of the shorthair Manx breed.

The first Manx are believed to have been imported into the United States in 1933 and the breed is now recognised by all American organisations, as it is in Britain, though with some minor variations in show standards. The first Manx Grand Champion in the United States received its award in 1951.

BREEDING THE MANX

THE DOMINANT GENE M responsible for the Manx is unstable and unpredictable. As a result, Manx cats are notoriously difficult to breed. Homozygous matings, in which both parents carry the M gene, result in the death of all the kittens in the womb at an early stage of development. Consequently, the Manx can never be 'bred true', out-crossings to normal tailed shorthairs (in Britain) or tailed Manx (in Britain and North America) being frequently necessary to maintain the breed. Even heterozygous matings, in which only one parent carries the M gene, result in a high proportion of stillbirths and skeletal deformities including spina bifida.

The Manx can still cause controversy in the cat fancy. It has a band of devoted supporters, but on the other hand some veterinary opinion holds that its genetic problems are such that it would not achieve recognition if it were introduced today. While that may be true, it survived naturally on the Isle of Man long before the intervention of the cat fancy, possibly by frequent matings with normal tailed shorthairs on the island, and is by no means a breeders' invention.

Top
A tailless longhair is called a Cymric.

MANX TAIL

EVEN IF THEY OVERCOME the difficulty of producing live, healthy Manx kittens, breeders are faced with further problems. Manx litters may include kittens with vestigial tails of varying lengths, or with normal tails. These are distinguished by group names. The true Manx, known as the 'rumpy', is completely tailless and has a dimple where the tail should be. The 'rumpy-riser' or 'riser' (US) has a small number of vertebrae at the tail which can be felt or seen.

The 'stumpy' or 'stubby' (US) has a very short stumpy tail, often knobbly or kinked. The 'longy' has a medium-length tail, though still short in proportion to the cat's body.

Finally, there are fully-tailed Manx. In Britain only 'rumpies' may be shown, although 'stumpies' and 'risers' may be registered and used in breeding programmes. In the United States both 'rumpies' and 'rumpy-risers' may be shown. The occurrence of the tail variations are completely random. It is estimated that one-third of the kittens resulting even from 'rumpy' to 'rumpy' matings are tailed to some degree, and this proportion rises to one-half with 'rumpy' to tailed matings. The difficulties of breeders may be imagined.

CHARACTERISTICS

IN THE SHOW MANX, as indicated above, the absence of a tail (or, in the United States, the presence only of the 'rumpy-riser' knob) is the prime requirement. Apart from that, the medium sized body should be rounded and short backed with the hind legs longer than the fore legs. The flanks should be deep and the back should arch from shoulder to rump. The thighs are muscular. The head should be large and round with prominent cheekbones and a jowled look, with a strong chin. The nose is medium-long; the US show standard allows a gentle nose dip but the UK standard specifies no nose break. The whisker pads should be prominent. The ears are large, wide at the base and tapering, set on the top of the head. In the United States, rounded tips are preferred to the British choice of slightly pointed tips. The eyes are large round and full, set at an angle to the nose with the outer corners slightly higher than the inner corners.

THE COAT

THE MANX HAS A double coat – a thick, cottony undercoat and a glossy, hard topcoat which should not be too long, the whole effect being well-padded. In Britain, all colours and coat patterns except colourpoint are accepted. In the United States, the permitted colour range excludes chocolate and lilac (lavender). Eyes should harmonise with the coat colour; white Manx may be blue or orange eyed or odd-eyed (blue/orange).

TEMPERAMENT

IT WILL BE CLEAR from what has been said above that choosing a Manx kitten can be fraught with difficulties, and expert veterinary advice should be sought. Although Manx have a bobbing, rabbit-like gait when running, they should walk normally and when standing should adopt a cat-like stance and not rest on their hocks like rabbits. Provided there are no abnormalities, however, Manx kittens which would not be permitted at show because their tails are evident are perfectly delightful as pets.

Top left
This is a rumpy-riser as a small number of vertebrae are present forming the beginning of a tail.

Top right
To show a Manx it would have to have no remains of a tail.

Bottom
All colour varieties are accepted in Britain, except colourpoint.

CARE

MANX ARE LOYAL, affectionate, and quiet-voiced, chirping rather than mewing for attention. They are cautious on first acquaintance and have a tendency to be nervous if there is too much noise or if they are approached unexpectedly. Manx are easy to train, especially if this is in the care of one person, and will even defend their owners. They like to be part of the family and are not fond of being left alone, so they cannot be recommended for homes which are empty of people all day.

Surprisingly, in view of the importance of the tail in the movement and balance of most cats, the absence of a tail does not seem to inhibit the Manx's climbing and hunting ability, and it is an excellent and enthusiastic mouser. Manx should, for preference, have regular access to the outdoors.

Manx litters are between two and four kittens in size and may include kittens with a mixture of tail lengths or none. The kittens are delicate and need careful weaning. Death during the first few weeks, even in apparently healthy kittens, is not uncommon. But surviving kittens quickly develop a playfulness which persists into adult life.

> **CAT FACT:**
> Some pedigree cat breeds are so badly malformed in pursuit of 'perfection' that they can have serious breathing and eye problems.

Top
Manx make good pets in households where someone is present for most of the day.

Bottom left
Manx are adept hunters and would prefer access to a garden.

Bottom right
Healthy, surviving kittens are active and playful, they make endearing companions.

271

Japanese Bobtail

SIZE

COAT CARE

EXERCISE

○○○○○○○○○○○○○○○○○○○○○○○○○	
BREED INFORMATION	
NAME	Japanese Bobtail
OTHER NAMES	Mi-ke
BODY SHAPE	Slender
COLOUR VARIATIONS	Any colour except colourpoint and ticked.

THE JAPANESE BOBTAIL has been known as a domestic cat in Japan, Korea and China for at least 1,000 years. Its first mention in Japanese literature, in a manuscript written by the tutor to the Empress of Japan, dates from about the year 1,000. The Bobtail appears widely in Japanese paintings and other artefacts, and on the facade of the Gotokuji Temple in Tokyo there is a specimen with its paw raised, symbolising good luck.

ORIGINS OF THE BREED

Often beautifully marked, the Bobtail's outstanding feature is the curious tail structure which gives it its name. This is not, however, a hybrid or a mutation. The Japanese Bobtail is a natural breed. The shortened, rigid tail is due to a recessive gene and is maintained only by Bobtail to Bobtail matings. There are no genetic problems such as those associated with the Manx. The breed is recognised in North America but not in Britain. No out-crossing is allowed.

In Japan, the Bobtail is regarded as commonplace, although the white, red and black tri-colour – known as the tortie and white to the British cat fancy and as calico to Americans – is especially favoured. It is known in Japan as the Mi-Ke (pronounced mee-kay), meaning three-furred. The story is that the first cats to arrive in Japan from mainland south-east Asia were black, followed by white and then by orange (red). It is said that the Mi-Ke became such a favourite pet among the ladies of the Japanese court that the absence of the cat from mousing duties at silk farms threatened the silk industry. Consequently, in 1602 the Emperor ordered all cats to be sent back to the farms. Pictures and figures of the Mi-Ke are often used commercially as a welcoming symbol in shop windows.

Like other tortoiseshells, the traditional Mi-Ke Bobtail is almost invariably female. Natural male Bobtails are white with either red or black random markings, but other colour varieties have also been introduced.

BREED IS ESTABLISHED

INTEREST IN THE Bobtail outside Japan began when an American member of the occupying forces after the Second World War began to breed them. In 1963 American cat fanciers visiting a Japanese cat show

Top and bottom
The Japanese Bobtail is an ancient cat that dates back centuries.

Bottom
This breed was first introduced to the United States after the Second World War.

were very much impressed with the breed, which was new to them, and five years later the first Bobtails – a Mi-Ke female called Madame Butterfly and a red and white male called Richard – arrived in the United States. Their kittens established the breed in America. It was accepted for registration in 1969 and for Championship status in 1976.

CHARACTERISTICS

THE VESTIGIAL TAIL is usually about 5 cm (2 in) long, although if straightened out it would be about twice this length. Its crookedness is concealed by the hair, which grows outward all round to form a pom-pom.

Show standards require the Bobtail's body to be medium in size, long and lean but shapely and well muscled. The shoulders should be as wide as the rump. The legs are long, slender and high but not dainty or fragile in appearance. The hind legs are longer than the forelegs but are bent in repose so that the cat presents a level back, not raised at the rear. The tail is carried upright. The head should form an equilateral triangle between ear tips and chin, with gently curving cheeks, high cheekbones and a whisker break. The nose is long with a gentle dip at, or just below, eye level. The ears are large, upright and expressive, set well apart and appearing to tilt slightly forward. The eyes are large, oval, and slanted. They should appear wide and alert.

The Japanese Bobtail's coat is medium length, soft and silky with no undercoat, longer on the tail than elsewhere. Preference goes to the traditional Mi-Ke pattern: large patches of black and red on white, with white predominating. But any colour or pattern is allowed except for colourpoints and ticked tabby.

TEMPERAMENT

AS A NATURAL BREED with a long heritage, the Bobtail is hardy and has no inherent health problems. It has a quiet voice, but uses it a good deal in an extended language of chirps and miaows. Bobtails make affectionate pets, often greeting their owners with a wave of the paw. They do not like being confined and should have access to the outdoors including if possible the opportunity to swim, which they enjoy. Breeders say that although Bobtails will mix with other cats they prefer the company of their own breed. Grooming is easy because there is no undercoat to get tangled or knotted. A typical litter is four. The kittens are normally healthy and develop more quickly than in many other breeds.

Top
Bobtails should have a long nose and high cheek bones.

Bottom
Curled the tail is 5 cm long, unrolled it would reach 10 cm.

Scottish Fold

○○○○○○○○○○○○○○○○○○○○○○○○○○○
BREED INFORMATION

NAME	Scottish Fold
OTHER NAMES	None
BODY SHAPE	Cobby
COLOUR VARIATIONS	All colours except colourpoint, lilac and chocolate.

SIZE

COAT CARE

EXERCISE

THE FOLDED EARS which give the Scottish Fold its name result from a spontaneous mutation. There were stories in the nineteenth century about a folded-ear cat said to have been brought to Europe from China by a sailor, but no more was heard of it, and the Scottish Fold mutation appears unconnected.

ORIGINS OF THE BREED

IN 1961 A SHEPHERD on Tayside, Scotland, noticed that a kitten at the farm where he worked had ears which, instead of being pricked and upright, folded forward rather like those of a puppy. The white kitten,

Top
The origins of the Scottish Fold are found in farm cats.

Bottom
In North America Scottish Folds can out-cross with American Shorthairs to ensure the health of the breed.

named Susie, was of unknown origin, like most farm cats, and was otherwise unremarkable. Two years later she produced a litter which included two more folded-ear kittens. The shepherd, William Ross, bought one of these, named her Snooks and registered her. Together with his wife Mollie he created the foundation stock of the Scottish Fold breed. Test matings showed that the gene Fd which produce the folded-ear effect is dominant, so only one Scottish Fold parent is needed to carry it on.

Unfortunately, the breeding programme soon ran into difficulties. It was found that mating Folds to Folds resulted in a high proportion of thickened limbs and tails. At first, these were favoured features of the breed. Later it was realised that they were in fact skeletal abnormalities which affected the cats' movements. This, plus worries about the hygiene of the folded ears (stoutly denied by Fold breeders) and some problems of deafness, almost resulted in the abandonment of breeding. However, it was found that by mating Folds to British Shorthairs half the litter would be healthy Fold kittens without abnormalities – other than the desired one of folded ears.

BREED IS ESTABLISHED

BUT THE DIFFICULTIES had caused alarm bells to ring in the British cat world, and in the early 1970s the Governing Council of the Cat Fancy decided to stop registering Scottish Folds, thereby effectively banning the breed from British shows. (They are now accepted, however, by the rival Cat Association of Britain). Meanwhile, some of the original Scottish stock had been exported to the United States, where breeding began in 1974. A Fold female was mated to an Exotic Shorthair, resulting in three kittens of which one, Jed Callant, had folded ears. This was the first Scottish Fold to be registered with the Cat Fanciers' Association and shown in the United States. Today, the American Shorthair

COLOUR VARIETIES

WHERE THE BREED is recognised, all colours and patterns are accepted except chocolate, lilac (lavender) and colourpoint. Eye colour should be appropriate to the coat colour.

TEMPERAMENT

NO DOUBT BECAUSE of their background as working farm cats, Scottish Folds have a reputation for robust health and resistance to disease. They are also ferocious hunters, and should be given the opportunity to practise their skills. As pets, they tend to be 'one-person' cats.

is the only accepted breed to which Scottish Folds may be out-crossed. With this condition, the breed was accepted for registration in 1976 and awarded full Championship status in 1978.

CARE

LIGHT WEEKLY GROOMING is all that is necessary, but the ears should be checked weekly for mites. Dark brown wax is the usual sign of infestation, perhaps accompanied by persistent scratching of the ears. The condition is not serious – two out of three domestic cats suffer from it at some time in their lives – but it requires veterinary attention.

Typical Scottish Fold litters consist of three or four kittens. At first, folded-ear kittens are indistinguishable from normal-eared ones, but at three to four weeks the fold begins to show, the effect increasing as the kitten matures.

Bottom left
The Scottish Fold has an archetypal cobby body: round and thick set.

Top right
Tortoiseshells are accepted for showing.

Bottom right
Scottish Folds are adept mousers who love the outdoors.

CHARACTERISTICS

THE SCOTTISH FOLD'S body is medium sized, rounded and cobby, broad across the shoulders and the rump with a full, broad chest. It should be powerful and compact. The tail is less flexible than is usual in cats, but should be medium in length and thick at the base. The head is massive and round, set on a short, thick neck. The ears should be wide apart and show a definite fold line. The degree of fold may vary from a small, tight fold to a larger, looser one, but for show the tight fold is preferred, 'in a caplike fashion to expose a rounded cranium', to quote the American standard. The ears should be rounded at the tips. The nose is short and broad, with a gentle nose break. The cheeks should be full, with well-rounded whisker pads, and the chin full and well developed. The eyes are round, full and set wide apart. The Scottish Fold's coat should be thick, dense, short and soft.

Abyssinian

○ ○

BREED INFORMATION

NAME	Abyssinian
OTHER NAMES	None
BODY SHAPE	Lithe, muscular
COLOUR VARIATIONS	Usual (US ruddy), sorrel (US red), blue and fawn. Some other colours are recognised by individual organisations.

SIZE

COAT CARE

EXERCISE

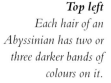

THE INSTANTLY RECOGNISABLE Abyssinian, with its unique ticked coat pattern, is one of the most popular cat breeds, both in the cat fancy and as a domestic pet. It is a natural breed which owes its distinctive coat pattern to the single dominant mutant gene Ta. This results in two, or preferably three, bands of dark ticking or colouring on each hair. Ideally the darker band is closest to the surface of the coat. The longhaired Somali is the only other breed with the Ta gene.

ORIGINS OF THE BREED

THE TRUTH ABOUT the origins of the Abyssinian is hard to establish. It is possible to see some similarities between Abyssinians and some of the cats depicted in Ancient Egyptian art, which gives credence to the theory that the breed is related by descent to the African wild cat, *Felis libyca*, and/or the jungle cat, *Felis chaus* through the Ancient Egyptian connection. This is strengthened by the historical ties between Egypt and Abyssinia (now called Ethiopia), which are linked by the Nile and were substantial trading partners and for long periods political allies in ancient times.

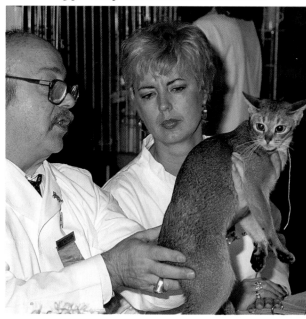

Others suspect the hand of the breeder in the creation of the modern Abyssinian which, they say, is descended by selective breeding from British Shorthairs. It is true that the Abyssinian's is a modified tabby pattern all but concealed in show specimens but sometimes visible in barring on the legs, tail and body of less perfect examples. The characteristic 'M' of the tabby is faintly visible on the forehead.

What is known for certain is that in 1868 a soldier returning from the British war with Abyssinia brought with him an Abyssinian-type cat named Zula. As far as is known, this was the Abyssinian's debut in Europe, but there the trail goes cold. There is no definite link between Zula and the breed that was first listed in Britain in 1882 as the Abyssinian. This was one of the many names by which it was first known, including the Russian, the Hare Cat, the Rabbit Cat,

Top left
Each hair of an Abyssinian has two or three darker bands of colours on it.

Top right
As it is a timid breed the Abyssinian does not make a good show cat.

Bottom
The cat in this Egyptian illustration is similar to the Abyssinian.

the Bunny Cat, the Cunny and the British Ticked. The last became the official British cat fancy's name for the breed in 1900, and so it remained for many years; perhaps this was an admission that, so far from being 'the Cat of the Gods' as claimed by some imaginative writers, the Abyssinian was really as British as the Tower of London. However, the facts are lost in the mists of the nineteenth century.

BREED IS ESTABLISHED

DESPITE THE SUSPICIONS about earlier out-crossings, the Abyssinian is regarded in the cat fancy as a natural breed, and that being so present day out-crossings are not permitted. The hare and rabbit names reflect the supposed similarity of the natural Abyssinian colouring to those creatures.

In 1909 the first Abyssinians reached the US from Britain and were shown at the Boston Cat Show. They were a male called Aluminium II and a female called Salt, which suggests that they were silvers. But American cat lovers were not impressed and it was

not until 1934 that serious breeding began with two new imports from Britain called Anthony and Ena.

The first American-born Abyssinian, named Addis Ababa, was born in 1935. Early reluctance then gave way to enthusiasm, and Abyssinians quickly became one of the most admired breeds in the American cat fancy. This history may well be accounted for by the fact that Abyssinians present a considerable challenge to breeders. Their coats are slow to mature and their litters are small and infrequent. As they tend to be shy with strangers they are not particularly well suited to the show ring. In Britain, the breed was brought close to extinction by food shortages during the Second World War, and by 1947 there were only four Abyssinians on the books of the Governing Council of the Cat Fancy. The breed had only just recovered when there was another blow – the outbreak of feline leukaemia virus in the 1960s and '70s which again almost wiped it out. Its recovery since then is a tribute to the determination of breeders and the popularity of the breed.

CAT FACT:
The whiskers on the face of a cat form a unique pattern which, in effect, gives each cat a 'fingerprint' from which it can be positively identified.

Top
This Abyssinian's coat resembles that of a rabbit, from which it gets its nickname the Bunny Cat.

Bottom
Where the Abyssinian's roots really lie is unknown: some breeders suspect British Shorthair tabbies.

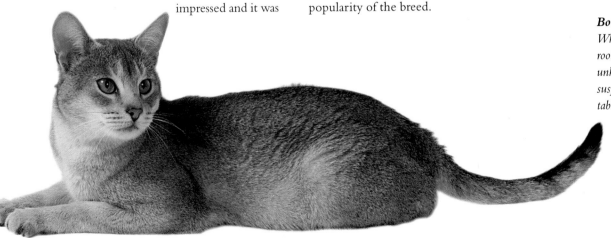

CHARACTERISTICS

THE ABYSSINIAN IS a medium sized cat, slender and lithe but solid and muscular, without the 'extreme' foreign body type of the Siamese.

The adult cat is regal in appearance and dignified in bearing, females usually being more active than males. The legs are slim and fine-boned, with small, oval paws. The Abyssinian's

characteristic pose when standing makes it look as if it is on tip-toe. The tail is thick at the base, tapering to the tip. North American and European standards show a slight difference in the requirements for the head. North American judges favour a shorter, more rounded profile than is seen in Europe. The ears are large, alert and pointed, broad at the base and with good tufts at the tips. The almond shaped eyes are set well apart and slanted. The coat is short but long enough for each hair to take two or three bands of ticking. It is fine and soft to the touch, dense and resilient. The ticking on the body should be even.

Top left

Although the Abyssinian is slender and lithe it does not have an oriental appearance.

Middle and bottom

These cats have the archetypal large ears of the breed.

COLOUR VARIETIES

THE PERMITTED COLOURS for the Abyssinian vary between countries and, in the United States, between cat fancy organisations, but usual (US ruddy), sorrel (US red), blue and fawn are recognised in both countries and all organisations at Championship status.

The usual (ruddy) coat is a rich orange-brown ticked with bands of black or dark brown and a paler undercoat. There is darker shading along the spine, but no ticking or other marking on the undersides of the body, chest or the insides of the legs. The paw pads are black or (US) dark brown, the colour extending between the toes and up the backs of the hind legs. The ears and tail should be tipped with the darker colour. The nose leather is brick red. Eyes may be gold, green or hazel, with as much richness and depth of colour as possible.

The sorrel (red) is a rich red ticked with chocolate brown and an apricot undercoat. The paw pads are pink with chocolate brown extending between the toes and up the backs of the hind legs. The nose leather is rosy-pink.

The blue is a warm, soft blue ticked with deeper blue and with a warm cream on the undersides of the body, chest and the inside of the legs. The tail is tipped with a deep shade of blue. Paw pads are blue with a deep shade of blue between the toes extending slightly beyond the paws. The nose leather is dark pink.

The North American standard for the fawn has a warm pinkish-buff ticked with deeper shades of pinkish-buff on a pale oatmeal undercoat. The British standard describes the coat colour as warm rose-beige ticked with light cocoa brown. Paw pads are pink with light cocoa brown (US deep pinkish-buff) between the toes. The nose leather is pink.

RECOGNITION OF COLOURS

LILAC (LAVENDER) (pale ivory ticked with frosty grey) and cream (pale cream ticked with darker cream) have preliminary recognition in Britain but have Championship status in some United States organisations. Britain has also given Preliminary status

to chocolate and to tortoiseshells in all colours, but these are not recognised in North America. All this is an indication that, as a breed, the Abyssinian can be considered still under development, and despite the fact that some purists declare that the only true Abyssinian is the usual (ruddy), further developments in colour varieties can be expected. The silver, which has been bred in black, sorrel, blue, chocolate, lilac and fawn, is an attractive group of varieties of which more will undoubtedly be seen. None is recognised in North America, but they have all begun to climb the ladder towards recognition in Britain.

TEMPERAMENT

ABYSSINIANS ARE VERY companionable cats, despite their regal bearing and their wariness of strangers. Unusually for cats, they respond well to training and can easily be taught to retrieve and play games provided they are treated as equals. Their ready acceptance of being walked on a leash makes them a popular choice of pet in those North American cities where loose cats are frowned upon.

CARE

THEY HAVE LIGHT, quiet voices and an apparently unlimited supply of energy. However, they do demand a lot of attention and if they are not given it readily they tend to force themselves on their owners' company. Many seem to prefer human to feline company, with the possible exception of kittens from the same litter, and Abyssinians are not suited to a household which is left empty for long periods. Grooming should be light but fairly frequent, at least once a week.

The queens are relatively quiet in oestrus compared with other breeds. Litters average about four kittens. The kittens tend to be large, with large heads, and deliveries can be difficult. Abyssinians are fiercely defensive mothers, but the litter needs to be watched carefully as the kittens are very quiet and may not cry if they wander away and get lost. They develop quickly and are fearless and playful from an early age, but the full Abyssinian coat does not develop until they are about 18 months old.

Top
To some breeders this silver-blue Abyssinian would not be acceptable as it is not ruddy coloured.

Bottom
Abyssininan kittens typically have large heads and, such as this one, are playful and active.

Egyptian Mau

○○○○○○○○○○○○○○○○○○○○○○○○○○○○

BREED INFORMATION

NAME	Egyptian Mau
OTHER NAMES	None
BODY SHAPE	Cobby but long
COLOUR VARIATIONS	Silver, bronze, smoke and pewter.

SIZE

COAT CARE

EXERCISE

THE SPOTTED EGYPTIAN Mau shares with the Abyssinian not only its build but also its supposed descent from the sacred cats of Egypt. There is a convincing link for the Mau which rests on the fact that it is the only natural breed of spotted domestic cat. Several wall-paintings in the temples of Thebes on the Nile, built around 1400 BC, show spotted cats taking part in duck-hunting expeditions, and it has been suggested that these cats were used to flush wildfowl out of their hiding places on the marshes or even (a less likely story) to retrieve game.

cat is occasionally found in spotted varieties, which points suggestively to *Felis libyca* as at least part of the origin of the Mau. Expert opinion is that somewhere between the dates represented by the artefacts mentioned above cats became fully domesticated in Egypt as economic and companion animals and were about to take on a role in Egyptian goddess worship. The foundations of the Mau breed can therefore be said to go back something like 3,500 years.

CAT FACT:
Hunting cats for fur and trophies has been re-allowed in some countries. Large fees are paid for the 'pleasure', which then ironically go into funding conservation.

ORIGINS OF THE BREED

AN EARLIER TOMB AT Thebes, dated about 1850–1650 BC, contained a glazed earthenware statuette of a spotted cat. The Egyptian Book of the Dead, the collection of 'spells' to ensure a safe passage into the after-life dating from about 1100 BC, includes more than one papyrus showing a spotted cat killing a snake or a serpent. Typically, the cat holds the snake down with one paw while wielding a knife with the other.

While other coat patterns, especially the striped tabby, are common in Egyptian art, the spotted cat appears often enough to make it clear that it was a well-known variety. The African wild

Top left
Myth states that the Egyptian Mau helped Ancient Egyptians to flush out fowl.

Top right
It has been suggested that the origins of the Mau lie with the Felis libyca as it also has a spotted coat.

The Mau (the word simply means cat) is now a common domesticated breed throughout north-eastern Africa and still a familiar street cat in Cairo. However, its history in the western cat fancy began in 1953. A Russian émigré breeder in Italy, Princess Natalie Troubetskoy, had admired two Maus, a spayed silver female and a smoke male called Gepa, which were pets at a Middle Eastern embassy in Rome. Through diplomatic channels, she obtained a silver Mau kitten named Baba which she brought from Cairo to her cattery in Rome, where it was first shown at the International Cat Show in 1955. Baba was mated with Gepa, the embassy tom, and the result was a litter of two males, Jo-Jo and Jude. Jude died, but Jo-Jo was mated with Baba and produced, among other kittens, a daughter, Lisa.

In 1956 Princess Troubetskoy took Jo-Jo, Lisa, and Baba to the United States, and these were the foundation of the breed in America. Indeed no further Maus have ever been imported, so every American Mau has one of these three cats in its ancestry. The same breeding line provided the foundation stock of the breed in Canada. From then on, the long struggle for breed recognition began, culminating in the Cat Fanciers' Association granting championship status in 1977, the last North American organisation to do so.

BREED IS ESTABLISHED

THE BREED'S HISTORY in Britain is rather different. The first Mau arrived there direct from Egypt in 1978, but the breed has not yet received recognition. Curiously, a different but broadly similar cat, now known as the Oriental Spotted Tabby, was originally called the Egyptian Mau in Britain, but this term was dropped in 1978 when the Oriental Spotted Tabby was recognised. This has a more Siamese appearance and, unlike the true Mau, is a breeders' creation (see Oriental Shorthairs,). Meanwhile the newer Mau seems to have all but vanished out of sight in the British cat fancy.

Because the development of the Egyptian Mau in the United States and Canada rested on only three cats, extensive out-crossings had to be made to extend the gene pool and this resulted in a loss of type. Although the Egyptian Mau is regarded as a natural breed, it is very different from the cats from which it was developed. In particular, breeders were concerned to civilise the original Mau, which was wild and unpredictable, vicious with other cats and highly disturbed by strange surroundings – definitely not good show material. In today's Maus, uneasiness with strangers and a dislike of change persist, although a generally quieter temperament has been bred in.

CAT FACT:
All cats have a vomero-nasal or Jacobson's organs, in the roofs of their mouths. This is what causes them to 'flehmen' when stimulated by pheromonal smells.

Top
An illustration of the festival of cats in Cairo, cats have been domesticated there for around 3,500 years.

Bottom
Maus tend to be timid around strangers and do not make good show cats.

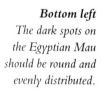

CHARACTERISTICS

THE DISTINCTIVE FEATURE of the Mau is its spotted coat, sharply contrasting with the ground colour. The dark spots should ideally be rounded and evenly distributed, although they are often random and run together to form broken stripes. The legs and tail are banded with the darker colour.

The Mau's body type is cobby but long, of medium size, graceful and muscular, similar in conformation to the Abyssinian. The overall impression is of an alert cat, vibrant with life and with a commanding presence. The hind legs are longer than the front, with small, dainty feet and round to oval paws. The medium-long tail is thick at the base and tapers slightly towards the tip. The head is a modified, slightly rounded wedge with gentle curves on the brow, cheek and profile. The ears are large and alert, set well apart and broad at the base with moderately pointed tips. The eyes are large, almond shaped, and slant slightly upwards towards the ears. The preferred eye colour for all coat colours is gooseberry green, but amber is acceptable. The coat should be lustrous, silky and fine, but dense and resilient to the touch. It should be medium in length, but long enough to show two or more well-separated bands of ticking.

The standard for the coat pattern requires good contrast between the spots and the ground colour. The 'M' mark on the forehead, sometimes called the scarab mark after the symbol that the Ancient Egyptians considered divine, should be distinct and prominent. Other lines extend between the ears and down the back of the neck and along the spine, ideally breaking into elongated spots. These should join at the haunches to form a stripe which

continues along the tail to the tip. There should be one or more necklaces on the upper chest, broken in the centre. The shoulder markings may be stripes or spots and the fore legs should be heavily barred. The hindquarters should carry bars on the thighs and back, and spots on the upper hind legs. The chest and stomach should have 'vest button' spots.

COLOUR VARIETIES

THERE ARE FOUR colour varieties in the Mau: silver, bronze, smoke and pewter. The silver has charcoal grey markings over the head, shoulders, outer legs, back and tail on a pale silver ground. The backs of the ears are greyish-pink and tipped with black. The upper throat area,

CAT FACT

Cheetah cubs up to three months old, are disguised to resemble the aggressive honey badger, with long grey hair. This deters potential predators from approaching them.

Bottom left
The dark spots on the Egyptian Mau should be round and evenly distributed.

Top right
Both ears and eyes should be large, this cat has the preferable eye colour, gooseberry green.

lightens to cream on the underparts, upper throat, chin and around the nose. The markings are charcoal or dark brown. The nose leather is brick red and the paw pads charcoal to dark brown in harmony with the markings.

TEMPERAMENT

THE MAU IS AN extremely active and agile cat which needs plenty of exercise and dislikes being left on its own. The ideal home has a large roofed outdoor run in the garden, with shelter from the sun and rain. An alternative is to train the cat to walk on a leash, which it accepts readily. In any event, the Mau should not be expected to live an entirely indoor life. It is very intelligent with a good memory and will teach itself tricks such as opening latched doors and windows. Maus tend to attach themselves to one person, to be possessive and to be wary of strangers. They are quiet-voiced, their usual articulation being a chirp.

CARE

ONLY LIGHT GROOMING is required to remove dead hairs, but it is in any case a pleasure to keep such a handsome coat looking its best, and the Mau enjoys the attention. It is said that, unusually, the male is as keen to play with and train the kittens as the female. The spotted coat shows up in kittens from birth.

chin and around the nose should be pale, clear silver. The nose leather is brick red and the paw pads are black, with black extending up the back of the hind legs. In the bronze, dark brown markings are laid over a light bronze ground colour which fades to a tawny buff on the flanks and a creamy ivory on the underparts. The upper throat, chin and around the nose are pale creamy white. The nose leather is brick red and the paw pads black or dark brown with the same colour extending up the back of the hind legs.

In the smoke, the markings are jet black on a pale, silvery white ground colour, the lightest being at the upper throat, chin and around the nose. The nose leather and paw pads are black. The pewter has black tipping on a pale fawn ground colour, this effect being achieved by bands of pale silver, beige and black on each hair. The ground colour

Top
This bronze coloured Mau reveals a tawny undercoat.

Bottom
The spots on this smoke coloured Mau are less obvious than on the lighter colours.

Ocicat

SIZE

COAT CARE

EXERCISE

THE OCICAT BEARS a superficial resemblance to the Egyptian Mau, but in fact it is a large, long-legged hybrid first produced in 1965 in the United States by one breeder, Virginia Daly.

ORIGINS OF THE BREED

First, a ruddy (UK usual) Abyssinian male was mated to a seal point Siamese female. A female kitten of the resulting litter was bred to a chocolate point Siamese, and one of the consequent kittens was a large ivory cat with bright golden spots. This first Ocicat was named Tonga. In the same year, a second litter from

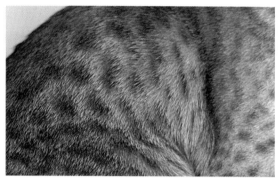

Tonga's parents also included an Ocicat. Until the mid-1990s, American Shorthairs as well as Abyssinians and Siamese were admitted to the pedigree.

A similarity is claimed to the cats of Ancient Egypt, but this is no more than fancy and the Ocicat is a breeder's creation whose Egyptian appearance is accidental. The name Ocicat, too, is misleading. There is no trace of the ocelot, *Felis pardalis*, in the breed's genetic make-up, although there is a passing resemblance in appearance which inspired the original American breeder to coin the name.

BREED IS ESTABLISHED

THE DEVELOPMENT OF the breed was a single-handed effort by Virginia Daly. She had initially hoped for the Cat Fanciers' Association's award of Provisional status in 1966, but for personal reasons which interrupted her breeding programme it was

not until 1986 that she achieved this goal. Full recognition followed the next year. The Ocicat's striking appearance proved an immediate hit with American cat lovers, and within four years over 1,750 Ocicats had been registered. The Ocicat did not reach Britain until the early 1990s but it is still a little-known novelty and is not recognised in the UK.

CHARACTERISTICS

THE OCICAT IS a large, athletic, exclusively spotted breed with a solid, long body. It is strong, muscular and powerful in appearance, evoking the jungle rather than the living-room. There should be no suggestion of bulkiness and the lines generally should be fine with a well-defined chest. When fully grown the female may weigh up to 5.5 kg (12 lb) and the male up to 7 kg (15 lb). The legs are long and the hindquarters should be slightly higher than the shoulders. The tail is long and

tapering, with a dark tip. The head is a modified wedge with a broad muzzle and strong chin. The eyes are large and almond shaped, angled slightly upwards towards the ears. They should be well spaced with more than the length of an eye between them. The ears are large, upstanding, wide at the base and curved at the tips.

The Ocicat's coat is smooth and glossy, tight and sleek. It is short, but long enough to display the bands of colour which are the breed's hallmark. Each hair should carry several of these bands, alternately

Left
The spots on this smoke coloured Mau are less obvious than on the lighter colours.

Right
The Ocicat has a spotted coat similar to the Egyptian Mau.

dark and light, and where the bands coalesce they form dark, thumbprint shaped spots on the lighter ground colour. These spots should be large, evenly distributed and well-defined.

gold spots, lavender (UK lilac) with darker lavender spots, and silver with black spots. The spots must be discrete and should not blend into a tabby pattern, although they may form bands on the legs and rings on the tail. Acceptable eye colours are copper, green, yellow, hazel or blue-green, but blue eyes are not permitted.

Top
This silver Ocicat has black spots.

Bottom left
Eyes should be round and almond shaped with a slight slant.

Bottom right
This Ocicat kitten is four months old and will already be active and strong.

TEMPERAMENT

THE OCICAT, SAY owners, is superbly healthy, intelligent, and playful with a gentle nature. It is tremendously sociable, tending to follow its owner around like a puppy. Also like a puppy, it is eager to please and will join in retrieving games, happily walk on a leash and respond to training. It does not enjoy its own company and is best kept in a home which is normally occupied all day. The Ocicat is a large cat which needs ample exercise, so secure access to the outdoors is essential.

COLOUR VARIETIES

THE ORIGINAL COLOURS were chestnut brown or light chocolate spots on a cream background, with golden-yellow eyes, but the following colours have now been added: blue with slate blue spots, golden with cinnamon spots, bronze with tarnished

CARE

GROOMING IS EASY, consisting of no more than an occasional brushing. The Ocicat's Abyssinian, Siamese and American Shorthair antecedents have not entirely disappeared from the pedigree, and litters may occasionally include non-spotted kittens. The kittens are robust and lively from an early age.

> **CAT FACT:**
> The canine teeth of cats are designed to puncture flesh and penetrate between neck vertebrae, forcing them apart to rupture the spinal cord and cause death.

Russian Blue

○○○○○○○○○○○○○○○○○○○○○○○○○○○○○○
BREED INFORMATION

NAME	Russian Blue
OTHER NAMES	None
BODY SHAPE	Medium, oriental
COLOUR VARIATIONS	Blue, black and white.

SIZE

COAT CARE

EXERCISE

THE RUSSIAN BLUE is an interesting natural breed combining distinctly Oriental looks with a dense, plush, upstanding coat tipped with silver.

ORIGINS OF THE BREED

IT IS SAID to have originated round the port of Archangel (now Arkhangelsk) in northern Russia, only about 200 km (124 miles) outside the Arctic Circle. This would certainly explain the heavy protective coat Russian Blues were brought out of

Archangel, so the story goes, by sailors visiting the busy White Sea port, though the period when this is supposed to have happened varies in different accounts from the days of the Vikings to the 1860s. The first Russian Blue was shown in Britain in 1880, when it was judged in a class with other shorthaired blues. At that time the breed went under a variety of names, including Archangel Cats, Maltese Blues, Spanish Blues and American Blues.

BREED IS ESTABLISHED

SERIOUS BREEDING SEEMS to have begun in Britain with the import from Archangel in 1900 of two kittens, Yula and Bayard. In 1912 the British cat fancy decided to distinguish British blues from what were called Foreign Shorthairs, of which the Russian was one. This term persisted until 1939, when Russian Blue finally became the official breed name although still classed among Foreign Shorthairs.

Like all British breeds, Russian Blues fared badly during the Second World War, and when the war was over British breeders began to cross with

British Blues and Siamese, to such effect that the Russian Blue show standard was rewritten. However, Russian Blue purists protested, and the decision was reversed in 1966 to return to the original Russian Blue type in which Siamese influence was deemed 'undesirable'. Meanwhile, Swedish breeders had started crossing a blue Finnish cat with blue point Siamese, producing a noticeably darker colouring. All these events influenced the British and European development of the breed and resulted in the European and American standards for Russian Blues being different in several details.

AMERICAN RECOGNITION

RUSSIAN BLUES (then known as Maltese) appeared in the United States in 1900 but it was not until the 1940s that the American cat fancy began to take a serious interest. About this time, the American breed name was changed to Russian Blue and the standards for the breed on either side of the Atlantic began to diverge. It took some time for the American cat fancy to appreciate the merits of the breed as distinct from the other blues – American Shorthair, British Shorthair, Exotic Shorthair, Korat and so on – in the lists, and it not until the late 1960s that the distinction became established.

Left

The oriental-looking Russian Blue has a dense coat that would have kept it warm in the Russian winters.

Right

If a Russian Blue appears too similar to the Siamese it would be unsuitable for show purposes.

CHARACTERISTICS

IN EUROPE OR North America, however, requirements for the coat, the breed's most outstanding feature, are the same. It is a double coat which should be very short, plush, silky and soft and stand out from the body owing to its density. The silver tipping on the guard hairs gives the coat a velvety sheen. In the Russian Blue's natural habitat the downy undercoat provides insulation while the shiny guard hairs repel water.

In general, the British standard tends more than the American towards the foreign or Oriental type. In Britain, the standards favour a long, lithe and graceful body, medium-boned, with long legs and small oval paws. The United States standard calls for fine bones and

CAT FACT:

In 1957 an excavation for building work in London yielded the remains of a cave lion, which had lived and died not long before the city began as a small settlement.

rounded paws. The British version has the ears set high on the head, which in America is a fault. In coat colour, too, the two standards differ, the British going for a darker hue. The nose leather and paw pads should be slate blue in Britain, but in North America the paw pads should be lavender-pink. Subtle preferences perhaps, but enough to indicate that the breed history has been different in each country.

Common requirements are that the tail should be long and tapering from a moderately thick base, the ears large, wide at the base and almost transparent without tufts, and the eyes a bright, vivid green. The whisker pads should be prominent.

COLOUR VARIETIES

GIVEN THE ATTRACTIONS of the Russian Blue's lustrous coat, it is not surprising that breeders have tried to apply this quality to other colours. Russian Blacks and Russian Whites have been bred, especially in Australia and New Zealand, and have Preliminary recognition in Britain.

CARE

RUSSIAN BLUES ARE affectionate cats, though they rarely express themselves vocally and then very quietly. Very hardy, easy to groom and fond of play, they make excellent pets for relatively quiet homes. Perhaps having folk memories of life in the sub-Arctic, they like nothing better than to sit in the warm, and they adapt well to the indoor life. The kittens, typically four in a litter, are born with fluffy coats and often show faint tabby markings until the mature coat grows. They are famously attentive parents.

Middle
These two Russian Blues demonstrate what affectionate cats and excellent parents they are.

Bottom
The British breeder prefers a darker coat and a slate coloured nose, whereas the North Americans favour lighter cats.

Korat

BREED INFORMATION

NAME	Korat
OTHER NAMES	None
BODY SHAPE	Semi-cobby
COLOUR VARIATIONS	Silver-blue.

SIZE

COAT CARE

EXERCISE

THE KORAT IS ANOTHER cat that comes with a long legendary history. A natural breed, it comes in only one coat colour, silver-blue.

ORIGINS OF THE BREED

IT ORIGINATED IN the Korat province of eastern Thailand, on the border with Laos. The Korat's Thai name is Si-siwat and it is in this guise that it appears

in *The Cat-Book Poems*, a Thai manuscript at least 300 years old and possibly older than 600, now held in the National Library in Bangkok. The poet describes the Korat's smooth hair, 'with roots like clouds and tips like silver' and its eyes 'like dewdrops on a lotus leaf'. The silver-tipped coat and vivid green eyes carried associations of good fortune. They were often presented to

brides as a token of a prosperous marriage, and were invited into the rice-fields in the hopes of rain and a good harvest, the mature Korat's eyes being the colour of young rice plants.

King Chulalongkorn of Siam, who reigned from 1868–1910, was very fond of cats and is said to have given the Korat its name after hearing the origin of an example he had particularly admired. In fact, Korats are, although rare, found throughout Thailand, not only in its easternmost province.

BREED IS ESTABLISHED

THE FIRST MENTION of the Korat in the west is in the records of the National Cat Show in London in 1896 where, described as a blue Siamese, it was exhibited by a traveller who had brought it back from Thailand. (Sadly, it was disqualified for being the wrong colour.) Nothing more is heard of the Korat until 1959, when a pair named Nara and Darra were imported directly from Thailand to the United States. Interest in the breed grew from there, and more Korats were imported, the gene pool at first being enlarged by out-crossing with blue point Siamese. (This practice has now been outlawed.)

In 1964 the Korat made its United States debut at the Empire Cat Club show, and by the next year there were enough owners to form a breed club with the aim of achieving recognition. Within five years this had been granted by all United States cat fancy organisations as well as in Canada, South Africa and Australia. The first Korats arrived in Britain in 1972 and British recognition in the Foreign group followed in 1975.

Breeding controls on the Korat, aimed at preserving the breed's integrity, are unusually strict. There must be no out-crossing, and every Korat's ancestry must be traceable back to Thailand. All imports are carefully documented.

CAT FACT:
The name 'leopard' may derive from an old notion that leopards were the result of crosses between lions (leo) and panthers (pard).

Top
This oriental cat can be traced back to at least 600 years.

Bottom
The Korat's eyes have been described as 'like dewdrops on a lotus leaf'.

CHARACTERISTICS

THE KORAT IS a semi-cobby, medium sized cat, supple and muscular, with a rounded back. The forelegs are slightly shorter than the hind legs and the paws are oval. Males should look powerful, and females smaller and dainty. The tail is medium in length, tapering to a rounded tip. The head is heart shaped with a semi-pointed muzzle, a strong chin and jaw, neither square nor pointed, and breadth between and across the eyes. The eyebrow ridges form the upper curves of the head, the cheeks gently curving down to the chin. There is a slight nose break, and the tip of the nose just above the leather has a downward curve. The ears are large, rounded at the tip and set high on the head to give an alert expression. They should be open at the base, with little hair inside the pinnae. The eyes, a brilliant green, should be large and luminous and set wide apart. They should be well-rounded when open but slightly slanted when closed.

The Korat's coat is single-layered, short to medium in length. It should be glossy and fine and lie close to the body. The silver tipping should be without shading, markings or white hairs, and should be most intense where the hair is shortest, especially on the backs of the ears, the nose and the paws. Paw pads and nose leather may be dark blue or lavender-pink.

TEMPERAMENT

KORATS MAKE AFFECTIONATE pets, enjoying being fondled and played with. They are quiet and gentle, moving slowly and cautiously. They dislike sudden loud noises, so are not a good choice for a home with young children or noisy dogs.

CARE

GROOMING IS MINIMAL. Korats seem unusually vulnerable to respiratory viral infections ('cat flu'). Litters are usually three or four but may be up to nine. The kittens are born with an untidy version of their adult coats, and often have amber eyes after the first weeks.

The perfection of the adult coat and the correct vivid green eye colour may take from 2–4 years to appear.

CAT FACT:
Cats do not have complete enclosed eye sockets like humans. In fact the brackets of their lower jaw protrude behind the eye ball when the mouth is closed.

Top
The Korat's coat should be silver tipped and sleek.

Bottom
Korats can take two to four years to acquire a perfect coat and amber eyes.

Burmese

```
○○○○○○○○○○○○○○○○○○○○○○○○○○○○
```

BREED INFORMATION

NAME	Burmese
OTHER NAMES	None
BODY SHAPE	Lithe, muscular
COLOUR VARIATIONS	US (CFA): Brown, blue, champagne and platinum. Elsewhere, also red, cream and tortoiseshells.

SIZE

COAT CARE

EXERCISE

Top
The Burmese was originally called a 'bad Siamese' when first introduced in the United States.

Bottom
From one cat brought back from south-east Asia a genetic study took place following the development of the breed.

FOR A CAT ONCE slandered as a 'bad Siamese', the Burmese has come a long way, although its progress as a breed has not been without controversy. A cat similar in looks to the modern Burmese is believed to have been fairly common in south-east Asia as long ago as the late Middle Ages, but the history of the breed as we know it does not begin until 1930.

ORIGINS OF THE BREED

IN THAT YEAR a retired US Navy psychiatrist, Joseph Thompson, returned to San Francisco from Burma (now Myanmar) with a solid-coloured walnut brown female cat called Wong Mau which he had kept on station as a pet. She was a handsome cat, but when Dr Thompson claimed that Wong Mau represented a new breed American cat fanciers were not impressed. It was merely, they said, a bad Siamese not worthy of attention except as a household cat.

Undaunted, Dr Thompson began a breeding programme. There was, of course, no other Burmese to mate with Wong Mau, so he crossed the female cat with a seal point Siamese, the best match he could find.

He then mated one of the kittens back to Wong Mau. The establishment of a new breed became Dr Thompson's retirement hobby, and he enlisted a handful of interested breeders and geneticists to help him. The result was that the Burmese became not only the first pedigree breed to be developed entirely in the United States but the first to be made the subject of detailed genetic study. After several generations, it turned out that a proportion of Wong Mau's descendants retained her all-over dark brown colouring. The others had either the Siamese colouring (pale bodies with dark points) or were dark with even darker points. (The latter colouring was later developed independently as the Tonkinese.)

BREED IS ESTABLISHED

IN 1934, DR THOMPSON set out to have the Burmese recognised as a new breed, but further difficulties lay ahead. Two years later, the Burmese was accepted for registration, but in 1938 its appearance at a San

Burmese were imported into Britain from the United States in 1948 and the breed was recognised there in 1952.

POPULAR BREED

BURMESE ALSO BECAME popular in mainland Europe and especially in Australia and New Zealand. Even now, however, the ability of the Burmese to arouse controversy has persisted. Some breeders consider the original sable (UK brown) variety to be the only true Burmese, but in Europe and Australasia other colours were soon being developed.

The blue, first shown in Britain in 1955, was the leader. Then followed lilac (lavender), cream, red, chocolate and tortoiseshells, not all recognised in every country. For a while, in the 1970s and 1980s, champagne (UK chocolate), blue and platinum (UK lilac) Burmese were registered as Malayans by the Cat Fanciers' Association although other American associations (and other countries) continued to regard them as Burmese. To complete the confusion, two styles of Burmese, the 'traditional' and the 'contemporary', exist side by side in the United States. The 'contemporary' look is short-nosed and generally flatter about the face, tending towards the Persian, with more prominent eyes.

Francisco show resulted in so many protests from Siamese breeders – then a large and powerful force within the United States cat fancy – that it was withdrawn. More trouble was to come. In 1947 the Cat Fanciers' Association, the United States' largest register, withdrew recognition from the Burmese because of the number of out-crosses to Siamese that were necessary to maintain the breed. This, they argued, meant that it could not breed true. Breeders of Burmese argued that the out-crosses were necessary because of the small number of true Burmese available; the only alternative was excessive inbreeding.

While Burmese remained on the registers of the other United States organisations, breeders worked to produce 'pure' Burmese with at least three generations of exclusively Burmese ancestry (some pedigrees can now show five or more). The programme included further imports from Burma. This paid off, and in 1957 the Cat Fanciers' Association restored recognition, initially in the sable (UK brown) variety only.

Meanwhile, the first brown

Top
Although some breeders only recognise the original brown colour, blue is one of the most popular colours.

Bottom
This cat has a 'contemporary' look, it has a flatter face and more prominent eyes resembling a Persian.

CHARACTERISTICS

THE BRITISH STANDARD for the Burmese describes it as a medium-sized cat with a muscular frame and a heavier build than its looks suggest. Adult males weigh up to about 5.4 kg (12 lb) and females up to about 3.6 kg (8 lb). The legs are long and slender, the hind legs slightly longer than the forelegs, with oval paws. The head tapers to a medium-blunt wedge from high cheekbones. Americans prefer a more rounded, cobby body type with a level back and round paws; the head should have a slight taper to a short, well-developed muzzle. The ears are medium in size, well pricked and alert and tilted slightly forward. The tips should be slightly rounded and the ears should be broad at the base. In the United States rounded eyes are preferred, whereas in Britain the top line should be more gently curved, giving a suggestion of the Oriental. The Burmese's eyes everywhere and in all colours (with the exception of the blue, see below) should be deep yellow or gold.

COLOUR VARIETIES

IN THE UNITED STATES, only sable (UK brown), blue, champagne (UK chocolate) and platinum (UK lilac) Burmese are recognised for competition by most organisations, although one (The International Cat Association) also recognises cinnamon (warm honey to orange), fawn (warm beige), red and four tortoiseshell varieties. The Cat Fanciers' Association regards reds, creams and the four tortoiseshells as a separate breed, Foreign Burmese. Outside the United States, all colours are generally accepted.

In the original brown (US sable) variety, the coat is a warm, rich deep brown, shading to a lighter hue on the underparts. The nose leather and paw pads are brown. The blue has a soft silver-grey coat shading to a lighter tone on the underparts. Ears, face and feet should have a silvery appearance. The nose leather is dark grey and the paw pads pinkish-grey. The blue is the only variety of Burmese in which a slight hint of green is permitted in the otherwise yellow or gold eye colour. As in all colour varieties, the coat is fine, sleek and glossy, short and close-lying.

The chocolate (US champagne) is a warm milk chocolate colour, described in the United States standard as 'a warm beige', shading to a paler tone underneath. Slightly darker shading on the points is permitted in Britain. The nose leather is brown, a darker shade being preferred in Britain, and the paw pads are pink to chocolate brown.

The lilac (US platinum) is a pale dove grey with slightly pinkish shading. The ears and mask are slightly darker in tone. The nose leather and paw pads are lavender-pink.

Top left
The Burmese is a medium-sized cat that disguises its heavy frame.

Top right
Although these two blue and brown cats both have green eyes, the Burmese can have any eye colour.

Bottom right
Some breeders regard tortoiseshells as a separate breed.

Top
*The Burmese is
an amiable and
adaptable cat.*

Bottom
*Kittens are born with a
pale coat that darkens
as they age, light-coloured
cats also darken as
they age.*

The other colour varieties are red (light tangerine), cream (rich cream), brown tortie (brown and red patches), blue tortie (blue and cream patches), chocolate tortie (chocolate and red patches) and lilac tortie (lilac and cream patches). In the red and cream, the nose leather and paw pads are pink. In the torties they should harmonise with the patched colours.

TEMPERAMENT

THE BURMESE IS AN exceptionally sweet natured cat, famed for its athletic prowess, equally at home in town or country and quick to settle down in new surroundings. But there are two caveats for intending owners. Burmese are intensely sociable and do not like being left alone. Fortunately, they enjoy each other's company and will spend hours playing kitten games, so two should be kept if the house is to be empty for any length of time. Burmese are good with children and dogs – but here again there is a word of warning. Some have a tendency to become jealous or angry if they are not getting what they feel is their due share of attention, so tact and diplomacy are necessary when handling other animals.

CARE

GROOMING IS EASY, involving only a light combing weekly. Burmese are noted for their longevity, a lifespan of up to 20 years being common.

The breed are model parents. A typical litter is five but can be up to 10, making a strong family unit in which the male often shares caring duties. The kittens quickly become active and playful. The kitten coat is pale, often almost white, and it is a few weeks before the adult colour begins to develop and can be distinguished. Kittens in Britain are normally healthy, but United States breeding lines have shown up a tendency to skeletal deficiencies, including dwarfism. Breeding for the 'contemporary' look in the United States has also produced an alarming number of cases of cleft palate, open skulls, misplaced eyes and detachment of the third eyelid, exposing the tear duct. The last condition, provided the kitten is otherwise healthy, can be surgically treated.

As Burmese age, the lighter-coloured coats tend to darken as a result of changes in circulation. In general, the main problem of old age in Burmese is putting on weight because their level of activity decreases, and on veterinary advice a change of diet may be necessary. If so, any change should be introduced slowly as, like older people, older cats tend to be conservative in their tastes.

CAT FACT:
The main problem now restricting breeding programs for endangered cats is lack of suitable habitat for release. Cold storage of genetic tissue has already begun.

Bombay

BREED INFORMATION

NAME	Bombay
OTHER NAMES	None
BODY SHAPE	Lithe, muscular
COLOUR VARIATIONS	Black.

SIZE

COAT CARE

EXERCISE

THE BOMBAY IS an exceptionally attractive shorthair hybrid breed first produced in the United States in 1958 by mating a black American Shorthair to a brown Burmese. All the kittens in the litter were black, but with the fine, silky, shiny coat of the Burmese.

ORIGINS OF THE BREED

THE BACKGROUND TO the 'invention' of the Bombay was the desire in the 1950s among breeders of Burmese to improve their cats' body type and coat colour. They therefore, against the rules, out-crossed their Burmese to black American Shorthairs, and some of the cats from these matings were later shown – and won prizes – in one or the other class. Such deceptions caused deep misgivings in the cat fancy, although in fact the prize-winning interlopers were very fine cats. A Kentucky breeder named Nikki Horner embarked on a deliberate breeding programme crossing Burmese and American Shorthairs, using Grand Champions of each breed for the first mating, with the aim of establishing a new breed and clearing up the confusion within the cat world.

PANTHER-CAT

A DESCRIPTION USED in the literature time and again of the Bombay (perhaps the original breeder's own) is 'the patent leather kid with new penny eyes'. The name Bombay was chosen because of the cats' supposed resemblance in miniature to the black panther (in fact, a very dark brown-black leopard) of western India, and Bombays are sometimes referred to as 'mini-panthers'. The name, which acknowledges the breed's eastern ancestry, is appropriate. With their black, shiny coats and, ideally, copper-coloured eyes, Bombays are certainly very striking and good to look at.

BREED IS ESTABLISHED

THE BREED DEVELOPED quickly because Bombays breed true – that is, mating Bombays to Bombays will produce a litter of Bombays because the black gene B is dominant, although 'brown Bombays' occasionally result from these matings. These pose a problem because they cannot be exhibited as Bombays, which can only be black. Most United States organisations insist that the browns should nevertheless be registered as Bombays and may be used in Bombay breeding programmes but cannot be shown. The International Cat Association, however, allows 'brown Bombays' to be shown as Burmese. This complex situation arises because, in order to improve stock, matings of Bombays back to American Shorthairs or Burmese are still permitted.

> ## CAT FACT:
> The marsupial cat from New Guinea and tiger cat from Tasmania are two species of marsupial which have evolved to fill the place of true cats in Australasia.

Top
The Bombay was bred to have a particularly attractive coat, one which was sleek and silky.

Bottom left
Bombays are compared to the black panther because of their coat type and colour.

In 1976, Bombays were accepted for Championship status by the Cat Fanciers' Association and at about the same time they also became an established breed in Canada. In Britain, they have preliminary recognition.

CHARACTERISTICS

IN JUDGING THE Bombay, the coat is of prime importance, other aspects being subordinate. It should be very short and close-lying with a satin-like texture and a shimmering patent leather sheen which is enhanced for showing by polishing with a silk cloth or soft chamois leather. In the mature cat the hairs must be jet black to the roots with no white hairs or patches. The body is medium in size and neither cobby nor rangy, the male being larger than the more dainty female. The legs and tail are of medium length and the tail should be straight. The head should be rounded, with no flat planes, and the face full with a good breadth between the eyes. There should be a short, well-developed muzzle and a visible nose break. The ears are medium in size, broad at the base with slightly rounded tips, set well apart on a rounded skull and tilting slightly forward. The eyes are round and set wide apart. The eye colour ranges from gold to deep copper, with the deeper colour preferred. Green eyes are a fault. The nose leather and paw pads are black.

TEMPERAMENT

IN TEMPERAMENT, Bombays combine the virtues of Burmese and American Shorthairs. They are hardy, affectionate and fairly quiet. However, they do inherit from their Burmese forebears a tendency to be possessive of their owners and jealous of other pets and children. They are not notably active cats and seem quite happy to live an indoor life provided they are not left alone for long periods, but they take quite well to being walked on a leash. Bombays seem to have extremely sensitive hearing. They prick their ears at the faintest sound, and react strongly to sudden loud noises.

CARE

GROOMING SHOULD BE carried out at least weekly with a fine-toothed comb. Typical Bombay litters consist of four or five kittens which are usually robust with appetites to match. The kitten coat often has rusty overtones before the jet black adult coat matures.

> **CAT FACT:**
> The papillae, or hooks on a cat's tongue, have a characteristic arrangement depending on its species. They also compensate for the lack of grinding molar teeth.

Top
For show purposes this cat should have a patent leather look to its coat.

Bottom
This cat has the archetypal eye colour of the breed, copper coloured.

295

Siamese

○○○○○○○○○○○○○○○○○○○○○○○○○○○○
BREED INFORMATION

NAME	Siamese
OTHER NAMES	Some colours are Colourpoint Shorthair
BODY SHAPE	Long, graceful
COLOUR VARIATIONS	Seal, blue, chocolate, lilac (US frost), red, tabby, cinnamon, caramel and fawn. In US (CFA) all except the first four are recognised as Colourpoint Shorthair.

SIZE

COAT CARE

EXERCISE

P OSSIBLY THE MOST popular breed among members of the cat fancy — certainly in Britain — and the one that most people can recognise instantly, the Siamese in its original form was a natural breed which has probably had more attention from breeders than any other. It has to be said, however, that some people find the sinuous, delicately-boned Siamese disturbing, even 'spooky', and cannot see the breed's fascination. Even Siamese fans agree that as a pet it is very demanding and jealous, and can in terms of temperament be a 'difficult' cat.

ORIGINS OF THE BREED

AS SO OFTEN with Asian breeds, there is a fair amount of fact, fancy and uncertainty in the history of the Siamese. It was the legendary Royal Cat of Siam (now Thailand), living in and even, it is said, guarding the royal palace by jumping down from the walls on intruders, and it was also a favourite temple cat. Illustrated manuscripts from Siam's ancient capital Ayutthaya, which flourished between 1351–1767, show a variety of cats including pale seal point Siamese. It has been suggested that these cats were carefully bred and selected for their beauty. At the same time, there is evidence that less prized cats of the Siamese type were common in the streets of Siam as early as the fourteenth century, interbreeding freely with other domestic and feral cats. In the eighteenth century there were also sightings by the German naturalist, Simon Pallas, of Siamese living freely in central Russia. Whether the Russian Siamese had been imported or were created by a Siamese gene mutation is not clear.

BREED IS ESTABLISHED

THE MODERN HISTORY of the Siamese begins in 1871, when the breed was featured – and illustrated in the catalogue – at the first British National Cat Show at Crystal Palace just outside London. What happened subsequently is not known, but the next significant year in the British history of the breed is 1884, when the British consul-general in the Siamese capital, Bangkok, Owen Gould, sent a pair of Siamese seal points to his family in England. He had been given these by the cat-loving King of Siam, King Chulalongkorn, so it may be that as they came from

Top

Cats similar to this seal point Siamese are documented in illustrated manuscripts that date back to the fourteenth century.

Bottom right

The kink in the Siamese tail was once desirable, now it is seen as a fault.

Bottom left

The Siamese is probably the most popular breed.

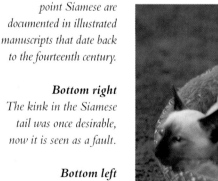

the royal breeding line they were superior to the Siamese of 1871. It seems that King Chulalongkorn, who ruled Siam from 1868–1910, was in the habit of presenting favoured visitors with gifts of Siamese cats from the royal cattery. Whatever the truth, the popularity of Siamese in the west took off from the mid-1880s onwards, and by 1892 the first show standard had been written.

This is interesting in three respects. First, it used the word 'svelte' to describe the Siamese, an adjective that has stuck to the breed ever since. Second, it made a point of saying that the Siamese was the very antithesis of the domestic shorthair in appearance. Third, the kink in the tail which is common in Siamese and is now regarded as a fault was, in those early days, an admired feature, together with the Siamese squint. There were even romantic (and quite absurd) explanations for

these features. The ladies of the Siamese court, it was said, stored their rings on their cats' tails, which developed a kink to stop the rings falling off. As for the squint, the story went that Siamese cats had been employed to guard the temples' most sacred possessions and had stared at them so fixedly that their eyes crossed.

Photographs of exhibition Siamese taken in the early years of the twentieth century show solidly built cats with more rounded, apple-shaped heads than those thought of as typically Siamese today. It is possible that these were in fact crosses between true Siamese and domestic cats, and that what was valued in the so-called Siamese of the time was the colourpoint pattern rather than the other characteristics of the breed.

FIRST SIAMESE IN BRITAIN

THE FIRST BRITISH Siamese champion was a cat called Wankee (which had a kinked tail) imported from Hong Kong and exhibited in 1896, and by 1902 the Siamese Cat Club of England had been founded. The breed was based entirely on the seal point – a pale cream body with deeper seal brown points. When a 'blue point' (possibly a Korat) was exhibited as a Siamese at a British cat show in 1896 it was disqualified by the National Cat Club President, the artist Louis Wain. There are still members of the cat fancy on both sides of the Atlantic who declare that seal points are the only true Siamese. Certainly they deserve to be regarded informally as the classic Siamese.

Top
Some breeders find the Siamese's conformation and demanding temperament mysterious and even frightening.

Left
A blue point Siamese, it is different in conformation and in coat colour from the Korat.

Cat Fancy in Britain four years later. Chocolate points (light ivory body with light tan points) first appeared in the 1930s. They were recognised in Britain in 1950 and in the United States in 1951. The fourth colour variety to be introduced was the lilac point (known in some United States organisations as the frost point), which arises from the combination of blue and chocolate genes. The lilac point's body is very white, with very light pinkish-grey points. It achieved recognition in the United States in the mid-1950s and in Britain in 1960.

FIRST SIAMESE IN THE UNITED STATES

IN THE UNITED STATES, the first record of a Siamese was in 1879. Early American Siamese seem to have been imported direct from Siam, some having been presented to visiting American breeders by the ever-generous King Chulalongkorn. But in the early 1900s Jane Cathcart, a famous American breeder, imported Siamese from France and Britain and bred from these. It was her breeding programme that put Siamese truly on the map of the American cat fancy. The Siamese Cat Society of America was founded in 1909. By the 1920s ownership of a Siamese had become a status symbol and the breed was in danger of becoming almost a fashion accessory. High demand led to overbreeding and a consequent decline in the type for some years.

CLASSIC SIAMESE COLOURS

THE GENES FOR THE four classic Siamese colours, seal, blue, chocolate and lilac (frost), are carried in the pure Siamese breeding line. To obtain Siamese in other colours it is necessary to out-cross Siamese to other breeds such as the British or American Shorthair and then back-cross to Siamese to retain both the colourpoint pattern and the Siamese body type. Here the British and most United States cat fancy organisations part company. In Britain, the fancy accepts red, cream, tortie and tabby (US lynx) points as Siamese. Most American organisations classify these varieties as a separate breed, Colourpoint Shorthairs, as they are in fact hybrids and not produced exclusively from the original Siamese bloodline.

COLOUR VARIETIES RECGONISED

THE SEAL POINT'S monopoly of the Siamese cat scene began to be challenged seriously in the 1920s, when blue points, with a bluish-white coat and deeper blue points, began to be shown. They were recognised in America by the Cat Fanciers' Association in 1932 and by the Governing Council of the

RED POINT SIAMESE

THE RED POINT Siamese, produced by crossing a seal point Siamese with a red tabby British Shorthair, was first seen in Britain in the 1930s, but it was not until the late 1940s that breeders began to develop this variety seriously. Its features are a creamy white body and warm orange-red points. The show standard specifies no tabby barring on the points, but in fact this variety is very difficult to breed without faint tabby marks. (The same applies to the cream point).

CAT FACT:
The ring-tailed cat from Mexico and toddy cat from Asia are actually a raccoon and civet which look similar to cats and are in fact distantly related to them.

Top left
The Siamese Cat Society of America was founded in 1909 raising the breed's popularity.

Top right
This lilac tabby point was bred by out-crossing to other breeds.

Bottom
This chocolate point Siamese is one of the breed's natural colours.

Recognition of the red point in Britain as a Siamese variety came in 1966. In the United States the Cat Fanciers' Association had, after protracted discussion, already in 1964 instituted the Colourpoint Shorthair as a new breed which included all Siamese colour varieties except for the four classic ones. As with many other breeds, the epidemic of feline leukaemia virus in the 1960s and '70s seemed likely for a time to threaten the future of the Siamese, but the breeding line mercifully recovered.

TABBY POINTS

TABBY POINTS ARE reputed to have been bred experimentally in Sweden in the 1920s, but no more was heard of these early examples. Officially speaking, the colour spectrum of the Siamese or Colourpoint Shorthair was widened in 1961 when a seal tabby point (US lynx point) made its show debut in Britain. Its background was a mating between a seal point Siamese and a domestic tabby. A tabby from that litter was mated to another seal point, and the result was a litter of six kittens of which four were seal tabby points including the one that was shown in 1961. Seal tabbies were followed by tabby points in the three other Siamese colours, and by tortie points. The latest admissions in Britain, in 1994, were cinnamon (milk chocolate points), caramel (light coffee-coloured points) and fawn points.

This completes the range of Siamese (Colourpoint Shorthairs) generally accepted by the cat fancy, but such is the enthusiasm of breeders for the Siamese look that many other colour varieties, so far unrecognised, have been developed. These have included silver tabby points and tipped varieties known in the United States as smokes and in Britain as shadow points.

> **CAT FACT:**
> Although cats can look remarkably similar, especially if they are from the same litter, their coats do actually vary considerably in detail when seen side by side.

Top
This red point Siamese is extremely hard to breed to show standards.

Bottom
Tabby points were only permitted as standard Siamese in the 1960s.

blue. A squint, regarded as the hallmark of the true Siamese in the breed's early days in the West, is now considered a fault.

The Siamese coat is short, fine and close-fitting on the skin, with a natural sheen. The colour varieties are defined by the colour on the points (the mask, ears, lower legs, feet and tail), which should be clearly set against a paler but complementary body colour which may be shaded slightly on the back and sides. The mask should cover the whole face but should not extend over the top of the head. The Siamese gene is sensitive to temperature, producing more pigment when the temperature is lower. This is what gives the breed its colour at the points, which are the cooler parts of the body, but it also means that the body colours of Siamese tend to darken in colder climates.

COLOUR SPECIFICATIONS

THE SPECIFICATION FOR the seal point Siamese is a warm cream body colour, slightly darker on the back and sides than on the stomach and chest. The points, nose leather and paw pads are deep seal brown. The chocolate point has an ivory body coat with milk chocolate coloured points. The nose leather and paw pads are cinnamon pink. The blue point's body colour is bluish-white with a warmer tone on the chest and stomach. The points, nose leather and paw pads are slate blue.

The lilac point has a magnolia body colour in Britain, glacial white in the United States, with pinkish-grey points, nose leather and paw pads.

The remaining Siamese (Colourpoint Shorthair) varieties are: red point (orange-red points over white); cream point (buff to light pinkish-cream over white); seal, chocolate, blue and lilac tortie points (points mottled with red and/or cream); blue- and lilac-cream points (points mottled with cream); seal, chocolate, blue, lilac, red, cream and blue-cream tabby points (tabby bars of the point colour); and torbie point (red and/or cream irregular patches over the tabby pattern on the points).

CHARACTERISTICS

THE CONFORMATION OF the Siamese looked for by British and North American show judges is similar. The body should be medium sized, dainty, long and svelte, strong and muscular but with fine bones. The line of the shoulders and hips should flow into that of the tubular body. The hind legs are slightly longer than the forelegs. The neck is long and slender and the paws are small, dainty and oval. The tail should be long, whip-like, thin and tapering to a fine point. A kinked tail is a fault.

The head is a long, tapering wedge, medium in size, the tips of the ears and the nose forming a perfect triangle. There should be no whisker break or dip in the nose. The ears are very large, pointed and wide at the base, continuing the lines of the wedge. The eyes, medium in size and almond shaped, should slant towards the nose, and in all varieties are vivid

Top left and right
The archetypal Siamese should have a svelte body, thin tail and a slender neck.

Bottom
The Siamese are boisterous and active cats.

strangers. Despite all this, they are affectionate cats which respond well to training, including training to walk on a leash.

CARE

TWICE-WEEKLY BRUSHING and an occasional polish with a chamois leather will keep the coat healthy and glossy.

Siamese are very fertile and females are often sexually mature from five months, signalling the oestrus cycle with loud, persistent wailing. They should not however be mated until at least nine months. They generally produce large litters – typically six – of strong, healthy kittens which are very quick to assert their individual personalities although they are inclined to be timid with humans. The kittens are born white with only the merest hint of colouring. In the early days, the eyes are the light blue of all kittens, but the vivid Siamese colour begins to appear at about eight weeks. The points begin to colour at about three weeks, but often the full colouring does not develop until about one year. After three years, the points and body sometimes gradually darken. As Siamese grow older and exercise less, they tend to put on weight, which increases the body temperature and again darkens the coat. Many Siamese live to 15 years and more.

TEMPERAMENT

THE SIAMESE IS NOT a cat to choose as a pet unless you are prepared to devote a good deal of time and attention to it. It has a boisterous temperament and this, combined with high intelligence, means that it can be a handful. The Siamese has a highly developed language with a variety of cries and calls for all occasions, and it uses this to get attention. For all its own loud vocalisation, it dislikes loud noises from others. The downside is that the Siamese tends to attach itself to one person and becomes jealous if that person pays attention to others, whether humans or animals. It dislikes being left alone and being ignored, and its highly sensitive nature renders it liable to mood swings makes its behaviour unpredictable. Many Siamese are distrustful of

Top
Siamese are very fertile breed; this queen demonstrates that she is in osterus by rolling on the ground.

Bottom
The coat of these Siamese kittens will start to darken at about three weeks.

Tonkinese

BREED INFORMATION	
NAME	Tonkinese
OTHER NAMES	None
BODY SHAPE	Lithe, muscular
COLOUR VARIATIONS	Natural mink, champagne mink, blue mink and platinum mink. Some organisations also recognise honey mink.

SIZE

COAT CARE

EXERCISE

CAT FACT:
The co-operative hunting technique practised by lions can be so effective that several prey are caught in the stampede panic, as they run head long into the lions.

THE TONKINESE, A hybrid produced by crossing a Siamese with a Burmese and familiarly known as the Tonk, has the distinction of being the first pedigree breed to originate in Canada, where development began in 1965 in Ontario. Cats of the Tonkinese type, from similar matings, had been produced in the 1930s during Dr Joseph Thompson's development of the Burmese, but these had been by-products of the breeding programme and were not followed up.

BREED IS ESTABLISHED

THE CANADIAN BREEDER of 1965, Margaret Conroy, was starting from scratch without knowledge of Dr Thompson's work. She was joined by a couple of United States breeders, and by 1974 she had achieved

recognition by the Canadian Cat Association. The Cat Fanciers' Association in the United States followed four years later, and championship status was awarded in 1984. Meanwhile, the Tonkinese had been recognised in Australia and Europe, including Britain where it has Preliminary status.

The original Tonkinese mating was of a seal point Siamese to a sable (UK brown) Burmese. This resulted in a full litter of Tonkinese kittens combining the dark coat of the Burmese with darker Siamese-type points. However, breeding Tonkinese to Tonkinese, which is now normal practice, produces kittens with Tonkinese, Siamese or Burmese colouring in a typical ratio of two Tonkinese to one other. Since the original acceptance of the Tonkinese, breeders have experimented with virtually the whole range of Siamese colours.

CHARACTERISTICS

THE BREED HAS TWO distinguishing features. One of which is the coat pattern, with coloured points, less clearly defined than in the Siamese, against a paler body colour. The other is the startling eye colour, ranging from aquamarine to turquoise, which is a constant requirement across all colour varieties.

The Tonkinese is cat of the Oriental type, medium in size and well-muscled, with long, slim legs. The hind legs are slightly longer than the forelegs. The paws are oval and dainty. The tail is long, thick at the base and tapering to a fine tip. The head is a modified wedge with a squarish muzzle and a slight rise from the bridge of the nose to the forehead. The

Top
One of the Tonkinese's defining characteristics is the coat pattern which should have coloured points but a darker body than the Siamese.

Bottom
Tonkinese have a variety of eye colours.

ears are medium in size, softly rounded at the tips, pricked slightly forward and set well apart. The eyes are almond shaped, slightly Oriental, and also set well apart.

The coat should be soft and close-lying with a natural sheen, recalling mink; hence the use of the word in the colour variety names. The mature coat has a rich, even body colour shading to a slightly lighter tone on the underparts.

Most United States organisations also accept honey mink, a warm, ruddy brown body colour with a slightly reddish cast. The points are a rich chocolate brown and the nose leather and paw pads mid-brown.

Some organisations also accept solid colourings in natural (brown), blue, champagne and platinum and more distinctly pointed versions of these colours.

TEMPERAMENT

THE MOST NOTABLE characteristic of the Tonkinese temperament is its adventurousness. It is one of those cats that are 'always into everything'. The ideal Tonkinese life contains plenty of activity to interest it and sharpen its wits. It is also extremely curious, and cannot be trusted with small pets such as birds and hamsters, even if they are safely caged. Owners say that the best way to deal with this very active cat is to keep two so that they occupy each other. Even so, they are not advisable pets for households where the furnishings and upholstery are expected to be kept 'just so'. The Tonkinese is an excellent show cat and an affectionate pet, but it needs continual human company and is possibly more suitable as a pet for families than for singles.

CARE

ONLY OCCASIONAL GROOMING is necessary. The kittens, typically four in a litter, are born paler in colour than their parents and gradually darken to maturity.

> **CAT FACT:**
> A study of lions in the Serengeti in Tanzania showed a surprising result: Some 81 per cent of the carcasses eaten by lions were kills scavenged from hyenas.

COLOUR VARIETIES

FOUR COLOURS ARE accepted by all organisations in North America. They are natural mink (the original colour), champagne (lilac) mink, blue mink and platinum (silver) mink. The natural mink is described as a rich, warm brown with dark chocolate points and brown nose leather and paw pads. Champagne mink is a warm, soft beige body colour with light brown points and cinnamon-pink nose leather and paw pads. Blue mink is a soft to medium blue-grey with blue-grey to slate points and blue-grey nose leather and paw pads. Platinum mink is a soft silver body colour with brighter silver points and pink nose leather and paw pads.

Top
The ears and eye shape of this Tonkinese reveal the oriental influence.

Middle
This lilac Tonkinese is one of the most accepted colours of the breed.

Bottom
The Tonkinese is an active and curious cat which enjoys shows.

303

Havana Brown

BREED INFORMATION

NAME	Havana Brown
OTHER NAMES	Havana
BODY SHAPE	Oriental
COLOUR VARIATIONS	Chestnut-brown.

SIZE

COAT CARE

EXERCISE

Top

The Havana Brown's origins, in the Siamese (bottom left), are clearly visible in the body shape and facial features.

Bottom right

Both American and British Havanas have mahogany-coloured, sleek coats.

A BREED KNOWN AS the Havana or Havana Brown is recognised by the cat fancies of Britain and North America.

ORIGINS OF THE BREED

Originating from the same breeding programme in the 1950s, subsequent developments on each side of the Atlantic have resulted in the emergence of two superficially similar but distinct breeds. In North America the Havana Brown is named as a breed in its own right. The British version is classified as a Foreign Shorthair.

In the early 1950s, two British breeders embarked on a programme aimed at producing a brown cat derived from a seal point Siamese and a black shorthair with seal point ancestry, each of which had the chocolate point gene in its genotype. The result was a solid brown kitten, first exhibited in 1953. Similar experiments took place in the United States, where the first Havana Brown kitten was born in the same year. The American strain was later strengthened by imports from Britain. The name 'Havana' was chosen as reminiscent of the brown rabbit breed or, according to another story, of Havana tobacco.

However, there is evidence of brown cats of the Siamese type having been shown in Britain as early as 1888, while in 1894 another brown cat, described as a 'Swiss Mountain Cat', was exhibited, and yet another, listed simply as 'Brown Cat', in 1930. These early examples of what came to be known as the Havana or Havana Brown were presumably the result of accidental matings between Siamese and other shorthairs carrying the chocolate brown gene. But these early brown cats seem to have disappeared without trace.

BREED IS ESTABLISHED

IN ITS REVIVED FORM, the breed was recognised in Britain in 1958 (originally as the Chestnut Brown Foreign, later changed to Havana), and in the United States, as the Havana Brown, in 1964. From then on, British and American breeding practice diverged. The British continued to back-cross the Havana to Siamese to avoid losing the foreign look they sought. The Americans prohibited Siamese crosses and developed the breed by mating Havana Brown consistently to Havana Brown. This has, however, limited the North American gene pool. Common to both versions is the gloriously rich and glossy mahogany coloured coat with brown whiskers and oval chartreuse eyes.

CHARACTERISTICS

THE BRITISH STANDARD for the Havana is as for the Oriental Shorthair. The cat is Siamese in type with a long, svelte, lithe and muscular body and a long, thin, tapering tail. The coat should be short, close-lying, glossy and fine, with no variation in tone from the roots of the hair to the tips and no tabby markings or white hairs. The nose leather is brown, the paw pads are pinkish-brown and the eyes are green, almond shaped

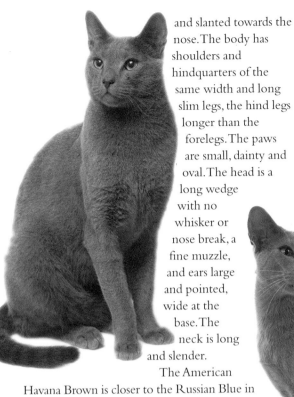

and slanted towards the nose. The body has shoulders and hindquarters of the same width and long slim legs, the hind legs longer than the forelegs. The paws are small, dainty and oval. The head is a long wedge with no whisker or nose break, a fine muzzle, and ears large and pointed, wide at the base. The neck is long and slender.

The American Havana Brown is closer to the Russian Blue in conformation, with a semi-cobby rather than muscular body and a shorter head. There should be a distinct nose and whisker break. The ears are large and tilted forward, with rounded tips. The tail is medium length and rather more firm and muscular than the British ideal.

Most American organisations also recognise the lavender Havana, bred by mating chocolate point Siamese to Russian Blue. In the lavender the coat is pinkish-grey and like the Brown should be solid throughout. The nose leather and paw pads are pink and the eyes chartreuse.

TEMPERAMENT

BOTH VERSIONS OF the Havana Brown are gentle, affectionate and have quiet voices. The American breed has a reputation for ceaseless activity in the house and needs to be provided with a large selection of playthings. It is noted for investigating objects with its paws rather than smelling them in the more usual feline way. The British Havana tends to be more vocal than its American cousin. In both breeds, the kittens are born with their adult colour although their large ears make them look rather unprepossessing until they achieve their mature proportions. Lavender Havana kittens will sometimes show faint tabby markings which fade as the coat matures.

CARE

BOTH BREEDS SHOULD be combed twice weekly and occasionally rubbed with a chamois cloth to help maintain the coat's sheen.

Top
The American Havana Brown is more similar in conformation to a Russian Blue, it is more cobby than its British cousin.

Middle
The Lavender Havana is recognised in North America.

Bottom
These Havana kittens have their adult colouring and like most kittens of the breed have oversized ears that they will grow into.

Oriental Shorthair

BREED INFORMATION

NAME	Oriental Shorthair
OTHER NAMES	None
BODY SHAPE	Long, graceful
COLOUR VARIATIONS	As for Siamese, but not pointed.

SIZE

COAT CARE

EXERCISE

BROADLY SPEAKING, Oriental Shorthairs are cats with the Siamese body shape but without the contrasting point colours that distinguish Siamese. Instead, they are coloured all over with self (solid) colours or bi-colour, tortoiseshell, tabby or tipped patterns. Similar cats are seen in Thailand as a result of accidental matings between street Siamese and other breeds, but the Oriental Shorthairs of the cat fancy are the result of deliberate breeding programmes. They are found in a wide variety of colours and patterns, not all of which are recognised by all cat fancy organisations. The history of the breed – or perhaps class would be a more appropriate word – is bound up with the politics of the cat fancy.

ORIGINS OF THE BREED

IN THE 1920s, the Siamese Cat Club of Britain was concerned to preserve the purity of the Siamese breed, while many breeders were trying to derive colour and pattern varieties from Siamese out-crossings. These efforts had produced, among other variations, self (US solid) coloured Siamese-type cats with yellow or green eyes. There were fears that the integrity of the Siamese breed would be weakened by these interlopers, and finally, in the late 1920s, the Siamese Cat Club decreed that only blue-eyed Siamese were eligible

Top
This Oriental Shorthair has a Siamese body but is solid in colour.

Bottom left
The eye colour of this lilac Oriental is different from the traditional Siamese blue.

Bottom right
Orientals do not have to be solid in colour, this is a solid ticked tabby.

for acceptance. This left the yellow-and green-eyed Siamese types without a place in the cat fancy.

Siamese types which fell outside the Siamese Cat Club's ruling were then known as Foreign Shorthairs, a term which survives in some European countries. But they fell out of favour, beaten in the popularity stakes by the 'pure' Siamese, in Britain, although some blue and black varieties seem to have had a limited following in Germany before the Second World War. Elsewhere, they virtually disappeared from view in the cat fancy until 1962. In the intervening period of war and post-war austerity, breeders had been hard put to maintain the more favoured breeds, let alone those in which few people seemed to have much interest.

BREED IS ESTABLISHED

HOWEVER, IN 1962 breeders in Britain, at first independently but later in concert, developed a hybrid breed of white, blue-eyed Siamese-type cats. These began to be seen in shows in the mid-1960s, but it was not until 1977 that the Governing Council of the Cat

genetically quite different Mau. Other breeders, inspired by the accidental mating of a chinchilla Persian to a chocolate point Siamese which resulted in a litter containing two shaded silver kittens, have developed a range of smoked and tipped types. Progress with these has been slow, however, because of breeding difficulties.

In Britain, the Governing Council of the Cat Fancy took the decision that the self-coloured Siamese-type shorthairs should be called Foreign Shorthairs and the patterned varieties should be called Oriental. Gradually, however, Britain is falling into line with North America, where all varieties are known as Oriental Shorthairs.

Top
This Oriental white has remarkably blue eyes.

Bottom
Cats, such as this chocolate Oriental spotted tabby, were bred in the late 1970s for their distinguished coat colouring.

Fancy gave them full Championship status in Britain under the name Foreign White. They were much admired from the first time they were shown in 1965, and an added attraction was that, unlike many white cats, they did not appear to be prone to deafness.

Meanwhile, some of the litters in the programme had included non-white kittens. These included the first British Havanas, which were originally registered as Chestnut Brown Foreign, and also a self lilac (US solid lavender). In Britain, the Foreign lilac was recognised in 1977. Since then, other colours found favour, including the Foreign black, Foreign cinnamon and Foreign caramel, a milk-coffee shade.

EARLY VARIETIES

SOME BREEDERS THEN took an interest in developing Siamese-type cats with tabby markings, recognised in 1978 as Oriental Spotted Tabbies. Originally, these had been known in Britain as Egyptian Maus, after the distinctive 'scarab' marking on their foreheads, but the name was changed to avoid confusion with the

Oriental Shorthairs first appeared in the United States from England and the Netherlands in the early 1970s. They achieved Championship status with the Cat Fanciers' Association in 1977 and may be said to have taken the American cat fancy by storm. In 1978 Oriental Shorthairs achieved seven Grand Champion awards, more 'best in show awards' and nomination among the CFA's 'top twenty cats'.

> **CAT FACT:**
> Big cats may mate up to 100 times a day. This is a strategy by the male to ensure that his sperm and not a rival's fertilise the eggs when ovulation occurs.

CHARACTERISTICS

ORIENTAL SHORTHAIRS are Siamese in type and the standards for the coat, body, head, tail and eyes are as for the Siamese. Some variations in eye colour are, however, allowed.

Top
These Oriental kittens, all from one litter, show the variety of coat colourings of the breed.

Bottom right
This Oriental blue would have been bred from either a Havana or a lilac Oriental.

Bottom left
The ideal nose and paw pad colour is illustrated in this Foreign white.

Oriental Shorthairs come in astonishing variety. There are over 50 colours, most of which are at various stages of recognition in Britain and the United States. The situation is confused, however, because whereas in Britain each colour variety is regarded as a separate breed, in the United States all are collectively shown and judged as Oriental Shorthairs. There is space to describe only a selection of the colour varieties here.

COLOUR VARIETIES

THE ORIGINS OF THE Oriental white (still known in Britain as the Foreign white) have been described above. It should be pure white overall, giving a porcelain effect, with no black hairs. The nose leather should be pale pink and the paw pads dark pink.

The eyes may be brilliant sapphire or china blue in Britain and green or blue in the United States. Odd eyes are not permitted.

The Oriental ebony (Oriental black in Britain) was developed in the 1970s by mating Havanas to seal point Siamese, but exclusively black to black matings are now required.

The black's coat must be overall jet black from the root to the tip of each hair. There must be no rusty tinge. The nose leather is black and the paw pads black or brown. The eyes are emerald green.

The Oriental blue appears in litters of Havanas and lilacs. The coat is a light to medium blue with no white patches or white hairs. The nose leather and paw pads are blue and the eyes green.

In the Oriental red, the coat is a rich, deep red without any of the tabby markings to which this colour variety is prone. The eyes may be copper to green, but green is preferred. The other self (solid) colours are cream, chocolate, caramel and fawn.

TIPPEDS AND SHADEDS

MATINGS OF SIAMESE to chinchilla Persians have produced a range of tipped, shaded and smoke patterned Oriental Shorthairs which come in virtually the entire range of colours and patterns. The standard for tipped varieties requires that the undercoat should be pure white, as should the chest and underparts. On the head, back, flanks and tail the coat should be lightly tipped with the contrasting colour to give a sparking sheen.

In shaded varieties the tipping should be heavier, giving the effect of a mantle of the contrasting colour overlying the white undercoat. In the smokes the tipping is heavier again so that in repose the cat appears to be of the tipped colour, the white undercoat being visible only when the cat is in motion. In all these varieties, preference is given to green as the eye colour.

TORTOISESHELL

FOUR VARIETIES OF tortoiseshell are generally recognised. The tortie has a black coat with clearly defined and well-broken patches of red and cream on the head, body, tail and legs. The blue (US blue-cream) tortie is blue with patches of cream, the chocolate tortie has patches of red and cream on the chocolate coat, and the lilac (US lavender-cream) is lilac-grey with patches of cream. Again, green eyes are preferred in all varieties.

TABBIES

CLASSIC, MACKEREL, SPOTTED and ticked tabbies are all accepted as Oriental Shorthairs. They include the brown tabby (US ebony tabby) with dense black markings on a warm coppery brown ground, the blue tabby (light to medium blue markings on beige), the chocolate tabby (US chestnut tabby; rich chocolate markings on bronze), the lilac tabby (US lavender tabby; deep lilac-grey markings on beige), the red tabby (deep, rich red markings on bright apricot), the cream tabby (deep cream on very pale cream), the silver tabby (black markings on silver) and the cameo tabby (red markings on off-white). In all varieties green eyes are preferred in the United States. In Britain, all eye shades from copper to green are permitted in the red and cream tabby.

TEMPERAMENT

ORIENTAL SHORTHAIRS ARE extremely active cats and in their eagerness to climb they can play havoc with curtains and soft furnishings. Like Siamese, they tend to be demanding of their owners' time and attention although they are less insistent and less vocal than Siamese. Their energy can sometimes lead them into mischief and they are experts at finding a way into the outside world. The ideal home is one with access to a roofed outside run. Like Siamese, Oriental Shorthairs dislike being left alone. Keeping two will solve this problem and will also help to defuse the cats' apparently boundless energy.

CARE

GROOMING IS CONFINED to an occasional combing and a rub with a chamois leather or silk cloth. Oriental Shorthairs develop early but should not be mated until they are about a year old. Litters are large, up to nine kittens being fairly common. Unlike Siamese, whose kittens darken progressively, Oriental Shorthair kittens are born with their adult colouring.

Top
This Oriental red has won both supreme exhibit and supreme kitten in Britain, to keep the coat in show condition it should be rubbed with a chamois leather.

Bottom
These two kittens have been born with their adult colouring: chocolate tabby and lilac tabby.

309

Rex Breeds

BREED INFORMATION

NAME	Cornish Rex
OTHER NAMES	German Rex
BODY SHAPE	Muscular
COLOUR VARIATIONS	As for American and British Shorthair.

NAME	Devon Rex
OTHER NAMES	None
BODY SHAPE	Muscular
COLOUR VARIATIONS	As for American and British Shorthair.

ALL REX CATS ARE curly coated, but the main breeds of Rex cats, Devon and Cornish or German, are quite distinct, alike only in having curly coats. Two different mutant genes are responsible for this characteristic in the breeds, although both are recessive. Rex genes are also distinct from the gene responsible for the American Wirehair.

ORIGINS OF THE BREED

NO DOUBT CURLY COATED cats have appeared from time to time in many places, but the first example on record was in Berlin in 1946. This was a black female feral cat found in the ruins of a war-damaged hospital. She was rescued, given the name Lammchen (Lambkin), and founded the breed known in continental Europe as the German Rex. It seems that Lammchen lived a quiet and undistinguished life as a household pet until, in 1951, she was discovered by a breeder and launched into stardom. She was mated to one of her sons, Fridolin. From this mating resulted a

number of German Rex kittens, including two which were exported to the United States in 1960. But meanwhile, other events had been taking place in the Rex world.

CORNISH REX

IN 1950 A CURLY haired kitten, to be named Kallibunker, was born to a farm cat on Bodmin Moor in Cornwall, England. The parents, a tortie-and-white domestic shorthair female and a ginger tom, both had normal coats, as did the other four kittens in the litter. Kallibunker's owner, Nina Ennismore, had been a rabbit-breeder and knew about the curled coat mutation in rabbits. She realised that Kallibunker must carry a similar mutation and so adopted the name Rex from the rabbit fancy. Mrs Ennismore was interested enough in Kallibunker's curious coat to seek the advice of a fellow rabbit-breeder who was an expert in genetics. The result was that, at maturity, Kallibunker was mated to his mother and produced a blue tabby male Rex, named Poldhu.

CORNISH REX REACHES UNITED STATES

THE FIRST CORNISH REXES to reach the United States were two of Kallibunker's descendants, who arrived there in 1957. They were a blue female and a red tabby male. The female had been mated to Poldhu and soon after arrival in America had a litter which included two blue-and-white kittens which were the founders of the Cornish Rex strain in the United States. The subsequent arrival of German Rexes

CAT FACT:
Cats need large territories to themselves because the prey they eat are predominantly herbivores, which need a lot of land to get enough foliage and grass.

Above
The ancestry of this red smoke Cornish Rex lies in a farm cat in Cornwall.

Right
This young black Cornish Rex displays its excellent hunting and killing skills with its

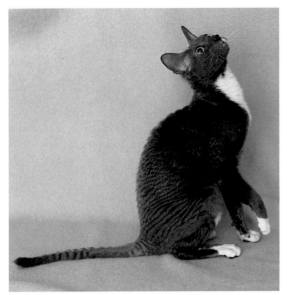

prompted a German to Cornish breeding programme, which showed that German and Cornish Rexes were genetically identical and could be mated to produce Rex kittens.

Meanwhile, another all-American Rex had turned up in the United States. In 1959 a breeder in Oregon found a black and white curly coated kitten in a normal litter. Subsequent research showed that this cat, named Kinky Marcella in honour of the 1930s hairdressing process, was genetically similar to the Cornish and German Rexes, but it seems that she did not figure in the establishment of the American German to Cornish Rex breeding lines. Nothing more was heard of her, nor of another Rex kitten reported in 1953 from Ohio. The 1957 imports founded the Cornish Rex breed in North America.

DEVON REX

THE DEVON REX originated in a separate (and, as it turned out, quite distinct) spontaneous mutation which occurred near Buckfastleigh in Devon, England, in 1960. This was the result of the mating of a 'rescued' tortie-and-white stray with a Rex-coated feral male which lived in a nearby abandoned tin mine. The resulting curly coated male kitten, Kirlee, was at first mated to a Cornish Rex in the belief that the two were genetically compatible, but this proved not to be so. The resulting kittens were all straight-haired. From then on, the Devon Rex was developed as a distinct breed – which it is – derived from Kirlee.

BREED IS ESTABLISHED

THE SPONTANEOUS APPEARANCE of these Rexes sparked off a great deal of interest in the cat fancy, and in 1962 an international society was founded to bring breeders together to promote the breeds (or rather, as it was thought at that time, the single breed). A German Rex Society was founded in 1967, followed two years later by a United States society devoted to the Rex.

Cornish and Devon Rexes were given Championship status as separate breeds in 1967 in the UK, and in North America by the Cat Fanciers' Association in 1979 when, for the first time, the two breeds were distinguished. Prior to that, Rex cats had been registered together in the United States as one breed. On mainland Europe both breeds are recognised, but the Cornish Rex is often known as the German Rex, reasonably enough since many of today's cats are derived from German breeding lines.

THE SI-REX

THE SI-REX is not a breed, but the unofficial name sometimes given to Devon or Cornish Rex cats with Siamese points to distinguish them from Rexes with other colour patterns. In the United States, Si-Rexes are officially known as Seal Point Rexes.

In these varieties, the only eye colour allowed for competition is Siamese blue.

Top
Unlike the Devon Rex, this blue and white Cornish Rex has no guard hairs.

Bottom left
This red silver Devon Rex is from a separate breed to the Cornish Rex.

Bottom right
A Si-Rex is the unofficial term for Devon or Cornish Rex cats that have Siamese points.

CAT FACT:
Lion cubs often exhibit spots and stripes. This may be a remnant of their common ancestry with tigers and leopards, since plain beige is a better camouflage for them.

NEW MUTATIONS

Top
The Devon Rex has a much coarser coat than the Cornish Rex.

Bottom left
The whiskers on the Cornish Rex should be curly and as this cat demonstrates the breed has large, rounded ears.

Bottom right
This lilac point Cornish Rex illustrates how every hair, including on the tail, should be curled on this breed.

CAT FACT:
Cats have a unique place in the minds of people. Throughout history humans have displayed emotions which oscillate between fear and affection, or hatred and love.

TWO INTERESTING POSTSCRIPTS to the Rex story come from the Netherlands and from Wyoming. In the 1980s yet another Rex mutation occurred in the Netherlands. This cat had a fairly coarse, bristly, wavy coat unlike the softer waves of the Cornish and Devon Rexes. Also unlike these, the Dutch Rex proved to have a dominant Rex gene and so was again genetically unrelated. It may be that in time this newcomer will join its curly coated cousins in the home and on the show bench. Meanwhile, 1987 saw the birth in Wyoming of a long-haired Rex, later named the Selkirk Rex.

CHARACTERISTICS

FOR THE MOMENT, however, the Cornish and Devon Rexes are generally fully recognised in the international cat fancy. They are quite distinct. The coat of the Cornish Rex has no guard hairs, and its awn hairs are almost impossible to distinguish from the down hairs. Consequently the coat has a plush feel, although it is in fact relatively thin.

The Devon Rex has a coarser coat, with all three hair types evident, although the guard hairs are barely detectable and some faulty specimens are virtually bald on the body. The Devon Rex's conformation is altogether more foreign and pixie-ish in appearance, distinguished by huge ears. In both breeds the effect of the gene for the curly coat is to restrict the growth of each hair to about half the normal shorthair length, a characteristic which also shows up in the whiskers and eyebrows, especially in the Devon Rex.

The Cornish Rex is a fine-boned and elegant cat, slender and standing high on long, straight legs. The paws are small, dainty and oval. The hair is short but dense and close-lying. Ideally, it should be curled on every part of the body including the tail and the legs right down to the paws. The whiskers are also

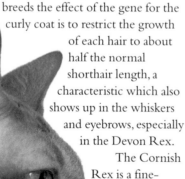

curly. The head is medium sized, with a flat skull and no nose break. The ears are large, high on the head, open at the base and rounded at the tips. The eyes are oval and medium in size. The tail is long, thin and tapering to a point.

The Devon Rex has a medium sized body, broad in the chest and standing on long, slim legs with a long, finely tapering tail. The hind legs are longer than the forelegs. The paws are small and oval. The hair is waved or curled on all parts of the body including the legs and tail. The whiskers and eyebrows tend to be brittle and are sometimes either absent or extremely short, but this is a fault. The head, set on a slender neck, is a rounded wedge, flat at the top, with rounded cheeks and nose and whisker breaks. The ears are very large, set low on the head, very wide at the base and with rounded tips. The eyes are large, oval, set wide and slightly slanted.

surprisingly large appetite. To cope with this, and to counter the effects of cold weather, some owners boost the intake of fat with dietary supplements. Rex litters average between three and six kittens, which are born with their curly coats already obvious. As soon as they are on their feet, they begin to demonstrate their curiosity and highly active temperament.

CAT FACT:
The 'cat and kittens' was a familiar name for a pewter wine or beer jug with a matching set of goblets in medieval English public ale houses.

COLOUR VARIETIES

THE GENES FOR curly coats are distinct from those for coat colour or length, and consequently any colour or pattern of Rexes, including white, can in theory be bred. All colours are accepted for competition. A particularly interesting and decorative version, originating in the United States, is the so-called Si-Rex, usually a Devon Rex with Siamese coloured points.

TEMPERAMENT

BOTH REX BREEDS have similar characteristics as house cats and make excellent pets. They are sociable, and in many ways dog-like, trotting everywhere after their owners and even wagging their tails with pleasure. Their long legs give them extreme agility and acrobatic skill. They are also able to move from repose to the chase extremely fast, which makes them efficient hunters. The inquisitiveness of Rexes is legendary. They are extremely vocal, with a notably loud purr.

CARE

REXES RARELY SHED their coats and so need little grooming. However, their coats are sparse and consequently Rexes need protection from extremes of heat and cold. They should not be allowed out in very cold or hot weather or kept in winter in unheated rooms. Stroking a Rex can be a surprise to the uninitiated because the coat is warm to the touch. In fact, the Rex's normal body temperature is a degree or so higher than in other cats. This gives them a higher metabolism and, as a result, a

Top
A chocolate and white Cornish Rex, one of the many colour varieties of the breed.

Middle
Rex kittens have curly coats from birth, as is visible on this young Devon Rex.

Bottom
Rex breeds are traditionally active, their kittens are inquisitive and playful.

313

Rare Breeds

T HE BREEDS DISCUSSED in this section are either relative newcomers to the cat fancy – so new, in many cases, that they have not yet begun the long climb to recognition – or are so rare that they are unlikely to be seen except at a specialist cat show or cattery. Some are experimental breeds which have still to prove their appeal or their veterinary respectability. Some critics regard the activities of experimental breeders with suspicion, alleging that they aim to create novelties rather than serving the wider interests of cats or the cat fancy. Certainly, some of these experimental breeding programmes result in many kittens which do not meet the breeders' requirements and so are released into the already overcrowded pet market. Yet some relatively recent breeders' creations have turned out to be robust and attractive breeds.

LONGHAIRS

Nebelung

○ ○

BREED INFORMATION

NAME	Nebelung
OTHER NAMES	Nebelung Blue
BODY SHAPE	Cobby
COLOUR VARIATIONS	Blue-grey.

SIZE

COAT CARE

EXERCISE

Bottom right
A Nebelung is a longhaired version of the Russian Blue shown here.

ORIGINS OF THE BREED

THE NEBELUNG IS sometimes called the Longhaired Russian Blue or the Nebelung Blue, which is as good a way as any of describing its appearance. But although Russian Blues have now been incorporated into the Nebelung's breeding programme, the original of this blue longhair was the spontaneous result of an accidental mating between two non-pedigree domestic shorthairs, a blue male and a black female, in Denver, Colorado in 1984. The firstborn was named Siegfried and for a time it seemed as if he would be a one-off and that nature was merely playing one of its tricks. But then another blue, this time a female, was born of the same parents, and a new breed was born. The blue gene, a dilute of black, is recessive, so that Nebelung to Nebelung matings always breed true.

CHARACTERISTICS

THE NEBELUNG IS a strikingly handsome cat with an alert stance and a businesslike expression. The body is long, lithe and slender with a fluffy tail carried erect. The head is a modified wedge, with ears set well apart, well pricked, well tufted, and wide at the base. The eyes are large, set well apart and slightly oval. The coat is medium-long with a dense undercoat, its colour similar to that of a Russian Blue. The eye colour is green. Curiously, the blue eyes of the kittens turn yellow before finally becoming green at maturity. Nebelungs are said to be robust and vigorous, needing only moderate grooming by longhair standards.

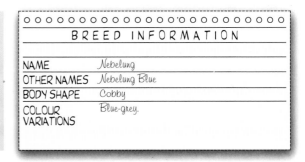

BREED INFORMATION

NAME	American Bobtail
OTHER NAMES	None
BODY SHAPE	Stocky
COLOUR VARIATIONS	Solid black, blue, red, cream and white, tabby, tortoiseshell, calico, tipped, smokes and bi-colours.

American Bobtail

THE AMERICAN BOBTAIL is totally unrelated to the Japanese Bobtail, and its stumpy tail, quite unlike the Japanese's pom-pom-like appendage, appears to be due to the Manx gene.

ORIGINS OF THE BREED

Its history begins with a semi-wild bobtailed male kitten found in a motel car park by an Iowa farmer, John Sanders, and his wife in the early 1970s. It was said to be the result of a mating between a bobcat and a domestic cat, but this was unlikely if not impossible. The Sanders took the brown spotted tabby, which they named Yodie, home with them, and there it mated accidentally with their own seal point Siamese, Mishi. There were several litters, which included a majority of normal-tailed kittens but a few with short tails. Some of these found homes in a barn on the farm, where they bred with a cream male barn cat with white Siamese-type markings. Some of the kittens of these matings were not only stumpy tailed but also carried white markings on their heads, legs, and tails.

At this point, one or two local breeders began to take an interest, and experimented in various ways with Himalayan and Birman crosses. The result of this was to introduce varying coat lengths, so that American Bobtails' coats can range from that of a semi-longhair to medium-short in length.

CHARACTERISTICS

IN 1990 TWO United States organizations, the Cat Fanciers' Association and The International Cat Association, accepted American Bobtails for registration, with all colours and patterns allowed, and it is likely that much more will be heard of this attractive and intriguing breed. It is not acknowledged in Britain or Europe. The American Bobtail is described as a short-tailed cobby longhair with a stocky body carried low to the ground. Ideally, the tail should be 2–4 in (2.5–10 cm) long and may either bend or curve to one side. The head is rounded, with full cheeks and ears set well apart. The eyes should be round, full, and alert.

The Manx gene is notoriously unstable, and American Bobtail kittens are frequently born with normal tails or with no tails at all in the Manx 'rumpy' style. The kittens are very playful from an early age and grow up to be sociable adults fond of human company. The semi-longhair coat needs to be groomed two or three times a week.

SIZE

COAT CARE

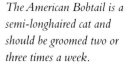

EXERCISE

The American Bobtail is a semi-longhaired cat and should be groomed two or three times a week.

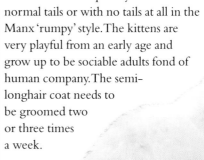

Ragdoll

○ ○

BREED INFORMATION

NAME	Ragdoll
OTHER NAMES	None
BODY SHAPE	Stocky
COLOUR VARIATIONS	Seal point, chocolate point, blue point, lilac (US frost) point, bi-colour and mitted.

SIZE

COAT CARE

EXERCISE

THE RAGDOLL OWES its name to the fact that it collapses in a limp heap, like a rag doll, when it is picked up. For a breed with a relatively short history – since 1965 – it has attracted a good deal of both mythology and controversy. The name, for one thing: any cat will flop in its owner's arms from time to time if it feels loved and secure, so the Ragdoll is by no means unique in that respect. Even more of a question mark must be raised over the story of the Ragdoll's origin.

ORIGINS OF THE BREED

THE SUPPOSEDLY 'LIMP' characteristic is said to be the effect of a road accident injury to the first Ragdoll's mother, a white Persian, which she passed on to her kittens. This is, of course, genetically impossible. No mutation – if that is what it is – could be passed on in such a way. But these circumstances are said to be the cause of other Ragdoll characteristics such as an immunity to, or at any rate high tolerance of, pain, their fearlessness, the apparent lack of the survival instinct and an exceptionally docile nature. It seems almost certain that these qualities are the result of highly selective breeding. Whatever the truth of the matter, the breed is derived from three kittens born to the white Persian road casualty, Josephine. One of these, Daddy War Bucks, was mated to a Birman and became the breed's foundation sire.

Top right
The Ragdoll is a large, longhaired cat with a bushy tail.

Top left
Ragdolls have descended from one white Persian but more resemble a Birman.

CHARACTERISTICS

THE RAGDOLL WAS developed in the mid-1960s by a Californian breeder, Ann Baker. Despite its deserved reputation for placidity, it is a large and impressive cat, stockily built with a heavy bone structure. Males weigh from 7–9 kg (15–20 lb) and females 4.5–7 kg (10–15 lb), and a typical male height is up to 45 cm (18 in) with a stride at full stretch of 91.5 cm (36 in). In general appearance the Ragdoll is similar to a Birman, and indeed, as noted above, there is Birman blood in its ancestry. It is broad across the shoulders and hindquarters, with a deep chest. The legs are medium in length and sturdy, with large, round, firm paws tufted between the toes. The tail is long and brushed, medium-thick at the base with a slight taper. The head

is large, with full cheeks and a rounded muzzle, on a short, thick neck. The ears should be medium sized, broad at the base, round-tipped, tilted forward and well-tufted. The eyes are large and oval, set well apart. The coat is semi-long, full and silky with a prominent ruff and long hair on the chest and stomach.

The Ragdoll has been recognised in the United States since the 1970s by all but one of the American organisations, and was given Preliminary status in Britain in 1992.

TEMPERAMENT

AN ASPECT OF the Ragdoll's nature is its unwillingness to fight or even protest. It is more likely to cower or hide. Its docile nature makes it good with children, although as it is infinitely patient children should be warned not to take advantage of this. Its non-combative nature makes it more suitable for indoor life. Grooming, particularly in summer when the Ragdoll moults heavily, is demanding. The dense coat tends to knot and tangle and should be combed out and then brushed frequently. The kittens are born white and do not achieve their full colour (or their mature size) for 2–3 years.

COLOUR VARIETIES

RAGDOLLS ARE BRED in four colourpoint colours as well as in bi-colour and mitted varieties. In the seal point, the body colour should be a pale fawn shading to pale cream on the underparts. The points are a deep seal brown. The nose leather is dark brown and the paw pads dark brown or black. The chocolate point has an ivory body coat with warm milk chocolate points and pink nose leather and paw pads. The blue point's body colour is grey-blue, shading to lighter blue on the underparts. The points are deep blue-grey, as are the nose leather and paw pads. The lilac (frost) point is an even milk white all over with frosty grey-pink points, lilac nose leather and coral pink paw pads.

The mitted variety is considered by some Ragdoll breeders to be the original and only acceptable version of the breed. This has a white chest, bib and chin, with a white stripe running from between the forelegs to base of the tail. There should be evenly matched white mittens on the front paws and 'boots' on the hind legs. The bi-colour extends the mitted effect to include the chest, stomach and legs. There should be a symmetrical inverted 'V' extending down the nose and over the muzzle to the chin to meet the white of the bib.

CAT FACT:
All cats are born in a semi-altricial condition, that is, they are dependent on their mothers, with closed eyes. A den is thus required while they are most vulnerable.

Top left
This Ragdoll has an archetypal appearance, it has large, round eyes and medium sized ears on a rotund head.

Top right
A bi-colour blue and white Ragdoll, one of the breed's many colour varieties.

Kashmir

```
○○○○○○○○○○○○○○○○○○○○○○○○○
        BREED INFORMATION
```

NAME	Kashmir
OTHER NAMES	Longhair/Persian. Known as Kashmir only by CCA and CCF
BODY SHAPE	Cobby
COLOUR VARIATIONS	Solid chocolate and lilac.

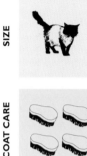

THE KASHMIR IS not a distinct breed, but a matter of nomenclature. It is included here because readers may be confused by finding it mentioned in the cat fancy literature. The Kashmir is simply the name given by the Canadian Cat Association and one United States organisation, the Cat Fanciers' Federation, to self (US solid) chocolate and lilac (US lavender) Longhairs (US Persians) classified as self-coloured Persians or Colourpoint Longhairs in Britain and generally as Himalayans in the United States. The show standard, where applicable, is as for the Colourpoint Longhair (US Himalayan).

Tiffany

```
○○○○○○○○○○○○○○○○○○○○○○○○○
        BREED INFORMATION
```

NAME	Tiffany
OTHER NAMES	Tiffanie
BODY SHAPE	Medium oriental
COLOUR VARIATIONS	Sable.

THE TIFFANY OR Tiffanie is not yet well enough established for there even to be agreement on the spelling of its name! A hybrid, it is essentially a Long-haired Burmese and is sometimes known by that name.

ORIGINS OF THE BREED

THE BREED'S HISTORY began in the early 1970s when North American breeders developed longhairs with the Burmese sable colour and the new breed (though unrecognised then as now in North America) was given the name Tiffany. Then, in 1981, the accidental mating of a Burmese and a Chinchilla in Britain produced a similar cat which was given the same name but with a different spelling because 'Tiffany' was already in the records of the Governing Council of the Cat Fancy as a breeder's prefix. Some doubts have been expressed about whether the American Tiffany and the British Tiffanie are the same breed, and certainly their bloodlines, which are unrelated, are different. This will have to be resolved before the breed achieves full recognition.

CHARACTERISTICS

THE HEAD HAS the look of the Burmese, rounded at the top with ears set well apart. The eyes are golden yellow. The coat is fine and silky, with a definite ruff around the neck and the tail hair distinctly longer than the body hair. The original Tiffany had the rich brown colour of the sable Burmese, though in a lighter tone. The Tiffanie received preliminary recognition in Britain in 1990.

BREED INFORMATION

NAME	Selkirk Rex
OTHER NAMES	Wyoming Rex
BODY SHAPE	Solid
COLOUR VARIATIONS	All colours.

Selkirk Rex

THE SELKIRK REX has been bred from the only known example of a long-haired cat carrying the Rex gene.

ORIGINS OF THE BREED

IT WAS BORN, a blue-cream and white female, in Wyoming in 1987 in a litter of normal kittens. When mated at maturity to a black Persian, it produced three curly coated kittens in its first litter of six. The gene producing Selkirk Rexes differs from the Devon and Cornish Rex genes in being dominant.

The breed has been developed by out-crossing to, among others, British, American and Exotic Shorthairs. It is accepted in all colours and patterns by some North American cat fancy organisations but is not acknowledged in Britain.

CHARACTERISTICS

THE SELKIRK REX is a medium to large cat, sturdily built with long, heavily boned legs. The paws are large and the tail is thick with a rounded tip. The head is round and full-cheeked, gently rounded at the top. The muzzle is short, with a pronounced nose stop. The medium sized pointed ears are set well apart, as are the eyes. The coat is soft, thick and medium long, with loose curls especially prominent around the neck and tail but also extending down the legs.

The Selkirk Rex is as yet extremely rare, but further development of the breed seems certain. It is a well-disposed cat which generally enjoys good health. Grooming is necessary at least twice a week.

SIZE

COAT CARE

EXERCISE

BREED INFORMATION

NAME	Siberian Cat
OTHER NAMES	Siberian Forest Cat
BODY SHAPE	Strongly-built
COLOUR VARIATIONS	Breed not yet fully developed.

Siberian Cat

THE SIBERIAN CAT, also known as the Siberian Forest Cat, is a member of that group of breeds – others are the Maine Coon and the Norwegian Forest Cat – built to withstand harsh conditions.

ORIGINS OF THE BREED

ALTHOUGH THEY ARE regarded in the fancy as a relatively new breed, long-haired Russian cats were in fact among the first exhibits at British shows at the end of the nineteenth century. Interest in them seems to have faded away, but it was revived when, in 1990, two American breeders, acting independently, between them imported 18 Siberian cats direct from Russia. The same year saw the arrival of the first Siberian Cat to be born on American soil.

CHARACTERISTICS

LARGE, MASSIVE AND strong are the key words for the Siberian. The tail is long and full, with a plume. The head is rounded with a strong, round muzzle and a slight muzzle break. The medium sized ears are round-tipped, and set wide and low on the head. The eyes should be large and round. The coat is glossy with oily guard hairs and a prominent ruff.

Siberians are said to be affectionate pets whose muscular physique, however, calls for ample outdoor exercise. Grooming is needed every 2–3 days. The kittens are slow to grow their adult coats.

SIZE

COAT CARE

EXERCISE

SHORTHAIRS

American Curl

SIZE

COAT CARE

EXERCISE

THE CURL IN THE name of the American Curl refers to its ears, which curve gently backwards as a result of a dominant mutation.

ORIGINS OF THE BREED

THE STORY BEGINS in 1981 when a longhaired black female stray kitten, to be named Shulasmith, wandered in off the street to the home of a Californian cat lover, Grace Ruga. Later that year, after an accidental mating, Shulasmith had a litter of four kittens, two of which turned out to have curled ears. Further litters produced similar results, and the establishment of a new breed was under way. Shulasmith and some of her kittens gave the American Curl its debut at a show in Palm Springs, California, in October 1983. Within three years The International Cat Association had given the Curl its first American recognition, and the Cat Fanciers' Association followed with Provisional recognition in 1991.

CHARACTERISTICS

THE EARS APART, moderation is the keynote of the Curl's conformation. The body and head are medium in size, with the tail in proportion to the body. The muzzle should be neither pointed nor square. The eyes are moderately large and oval, with a slight slant. The coat is medium-long and close-lying with a light undercoat and no ruff.

TEMPERAMENT

AT HOME, CURLS are said to be playful and adaptable, as moderate in their temperament as in their conformation. Only relatively light grooming is

required. The kittens are born with uncurled ears but within a few days curling begins, ending at about six weeks with the ears tightly wound. They then begin to loosen, reaching their adult state at four to six months, but the degree of final curling varies with individuals.

Top left
The curled ears of this breed are as a result of a genetic mutation, the degree of curliness varies between cats.

Top right
This American Curl has a medium-long coat, typical of the breed.

Burmilla

SIZE

COAT CARE

EXERCISE

The Burmilla's coat is short, close-lying and fine. Its tipping should be most dense along the spine and down the tail, fading down the flanks to disappear on the underparts. The tipped areas should be as free as possible of tabby markings, although these often appear faintly on the head, legs and tail. All colours except cinnamon and fawn are accepted in shell or shaded forms.

THE BURMILLA IS a tipped Burmese type, created in Britain as a result of a mating in 1981 between a chinchilla Longhair (Persian) male and a lilac Burmese female. The kittens were unprepossessing, but they grew into delightful black or brown tipped cats over a silver base coat.

ORIGINS OF THE BREED

THE BURMILLA WAS given its breed name, and a breed club was formed in 1985. Preliminary status was granted in Britain in 1990 in what is now called the Asian-Burmilla Group. The Burmilla is not recognised in the United States although it has been introduced there.

CHARACTERISTICS

THE BURMILLA has a semi-foreign body, medium in length and thickness with firm muscle and a straight, level back. The tail should be medium in length and thickness, tapering to a rounded tip. The head is a short wedge with a distinct nose break, gently rounded on top. The ears are medium to large, set well apart, round-tipped and inclined slightly forward. The eyes are full and set well apart.

TEMPERAMENT

BURMILLAS ARE EXQUISITELY beautiful cats which are rapidly gaining an enthusiastic following. They have inherited the affectionate nature of the Burmese, but also the dislike of being left alone. Grooming should be at least twice weekly. Burmilla kittens are born with pale coats, the tipping developing as they mature.

Top right
The Burmilla has a beautiful tipped coat, its base colour is silver.

Top left
This cat has a chocolate tipped coat.

Left
The coat on this black tipped Burmilla is short and fine.

California Spangled Cat

○○○○○○○○○○○○○○○○○○○○○○○○
BREED INFORMATION

NAME	California Spangled Cat
OTHER NAMES	None
BODY SHAPE	Muscular
COLOUR VARIATIONS	Silver, charcoal, bronze, gold, red, blue, brown and black.

SIZE

COAT CARE

EXERCISE

THE EXCLUSIVE AMERICAN department store Neiman-Marcus is famous for the expensive 'His and Hers' novelties it offers each year in its Christmas catalogue, ranging from twin aircraft to – 'His and Hers' cats. The Christmas offer for 1986 was the California Spangled Cat, a jungle-type cat for America's top people.

ORIGINS OF THE BREED

THE CALIFORNIA WAS the result of a ten-year breeding programme started in 1971 by a Hollywood scriptwriter and a leading cat geneticist. On the way it took in Angoras, Siamese, Manx and a number of non-pedigree domestic cats. The aim was to produce a spotted cat with all the characteristics of a wild cat but with the ability to adapt to indoor life. One objective was said to be to create a memorial to all the wild cats slaughtered over the years in the interests of the fur trade. Originally marketed at £775 ($1400), the California attracted the interest of moneyed cat fanciers but has yet to be recognised by any cat fancy organisation.

CHARACTERISTICS

THE CALIFORNIA IS a long, low-slung cat with a long, tubular but well-muscled body and strong legs. The tail is blunt-tipped. The head is medium in size with a slightly rounded forehead, wide and full-muzzled. The ears are medium in size, set high on the head, and the eyes medium-large, almond shaped and set wide. The coat is short and velvety, with spots covering the back and flanks. Markings continue on the legs in the form of bars, and the tail should have at least one dark ring.

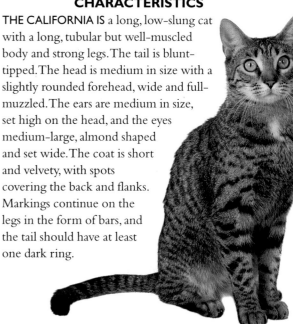

Californias have been bred in silver, charcoal, bronze, gold, red, blue, brown and black. Cat fanciers rich enough to own one, report that they are super-intelligent, even-tempered cats. Twice-weekly grooming is recommended. The kittens are born black and develop their markings as they grow.

Top right
Bred to appear similar to wild cats, a silver California Spangled Cat.

Top left
This gold spotted cat has the preferred blunted tail.

Bottom
Kittens are born black, this brown cat would have developed its markings with age.

BREED INFORMATION

NAME	Singapura
OTHER NAMES	None
BODY SHAPE	Small, muscular
COLOUR VARIATIONS	Ivory ticked with brown or white/tabby bicolour.

Singapura

THE SINGAPURA IS claimed to be the world's smallest breed of domestic cat, and it is a pity that such a charming ticked cat should be the subject of fierce controversy within the United States cat fancy.

ORIGINS OF THE BREED

THE STORY OF THE original breeders, which they later withdrew, was that they had found the original three Singapuras in 1974 wandering in the streets of Singapore, where the breed is a common alley and sewer cat. Doubters of this account say that the originals came from the streets of Houston, Texas. The Singapura is such an original and attractive cat that it hardly matters, except that the cat fancy tends to like a romantic story about a breed's origin.

Whether they originate in Singapore or Houston, Singapuras are well on their way to acceptance. Full Cat Fanciers' Association recognition was awarded in the United States in 1988, and since 1989 there have been a few exports to Britain, where the breed gained Preliminary recognition in 1997.

CHARACTERISTICS

THE SINGAPURA IS small, with distinctively large ears and an appealing, cute expression. Typical weights are from 1.8–2.7 kg (4–6 lb), but in Britain breeding for small size is discouraged as it is liable to cause kittening problems. The body is moderately stocky and muscular, with a slightly arched back, medium-long legs and small paws. The tail is medium-long and tapers to a blunt tip. The head is rounded, with a marked break between the cheeks and squarish muzzle.

The ears are large, wide at the base and cupped. The eyes are large, almond shaped and with a definite slant.

The coat is exceptionally short and close-lying, with an ivory ground colour on the back, flanks and the top of the head shading to creamy-white on the underparts. The hairs on the back, flanks and the top of the head should show at least two bands of dark brown ticking on the ivory ground colour, the tip of each hair being dark. Some barring is allowed on the legs. The nose leather is red and the paw pads dark brown. The eyes may be hazel, green or gold.

Clearly the Singapura's antecedents are feral, whether in Asia or North America, and this gives the breed its robustness although breeding is difficult because of the small gene pool.

TEMPERAMENT

SINGAPURAS ARE SAID to be friendly, inquisitive and busy, making excellent pets, although they take a little time to settle to new surroundings and new owners. They are best suited to an indoor life provided plenty of interesting activities are provided.

SIZE

COAT CARE

EXERCISE

Top
Breeders cannot agree on the origin of the Singapura, it is said to have been an alley cat both in Singapore and Houston.

Middle
The Singapura is the smallest breed of cat.

Bottom
These Singapura kittens are playful and curious.

Snowshoe

○○○○○○○○○○○○○○○○○○○○○○○○○○○○○

BREED INFORMATION

NAME	Snowshoe
OTHER NAMES	None
BODY SHAPE	Muscular and strong
COLOUR VARIATIONS	Seal point and blue point.

SIZE

COAT CARE

EXERCISE

THE SNOWSHOE, OTHERWISE known as 'Silver Laces', is a short-haired Birman type which has been developed since the late 1960s by a handful of American breeders.

ORIGINS OF THE BREED

IT WAS PRODUCED by crossing Siamese with American Shorthair bi-colours. The result is a colourpointed cat with white 'mittens', extended up the back of the legs to the point known in North America as 'laces', hence the alternative name. The breed was accepted for registration by the Cat Fanciers' Association in 1974 and for Championship status in 1983, but it is not recognised in Britain or by some other United States organisations.

The Snowshoe is a medium to large, muscular and powerful cat with a long back and a heavy build.

The legs are long and solid with rounded paws. The tail is medium in length, tapering slightly to the tip. The head should not look too Oriental. It should be a medium triangular wedge with a marked nose break. The ears should be large, well-pricked and pointed, broad at the base. The eyes are large and almond shaped, slanting upwards from nose to ear. Their colour is vivid blue. The coat is short, glossy and close-lying and should have a smooth, lustrous appearance. Seal point and blue point are the only colours permitted by the Cat Fanciers' Association, but other colours are bred both in the United States and in Britain, where the breed is not recognised. The Snowshoe has much of the temperament of the Siamese is vocal and demanding of the owner's attention. It is best kept indoors, but should not be left alone for any length of time.

Malayan

SIZE

COAT CARE

EXERCISE

THIS WAS THE term formerly used by the American Cat Fanciers' Association, dating back to 1960, for chocolate, platinum (lilac) and blue Burmese, which were regarded as constituting a separate breed. The CFA has now come into line with other organisations, however, and accepts them as Burmese.

Munchkin

```
○ ○ ○ ○ ○ ○ ○ ○ ○ ○ ○ ○ ○ ○ ○ ○ ○ ○ ○ ○ ○ ○ ○
       BREED INFORMATION
```

NAME	Munchkin
OTHER NAMES	None
BODY SHAPE	Miniature
COLOUR VARIATIONS	Breed not yet fully developed.

THE MUNCHKIN IS a relatively new breed, about 10 years old, with a huge question-mark over it.

ORIGINS OF THE BREED

Its outstanding feature is its abnormally short legs, allied to a generally miniaturised appearance which is not without its appeal. As the Munchkin has been refused registration by all those organisations to which its breeders have applied, no show standard has been laid down.

The worries of the cat fancy are twofold. First, it is suggested that the Munchkin's short legs may deny it the running, jumping and climbing activities which are every cat's right. Second, it is feared that the short legs may mask other genetic problems which would come to the fore with more intensive breeding.

SIZE

COAT CARE

EXERCISE

Opposite left
The Burmese was previously recognised by the CFA as a Malayan.

Left
This cat's short legs may restrict its jumping and climbing abilities.

Sphynx

○○○○○○○○○○○○○○○○○○○○○○○○○○○○

BREED INFORMATION

NAME	Sphynx
OTHER NAMES	Hairless Cat, Canadian Hairless Cat
BODY SHAPE	Fine and muscular
COLOUR VARIATIONS	All colours.

SIZE

COAT CARE

EXERCISE

THE SO-CALLED HAIRLESS Sphynx, also known as the Canadian Hairless Cat, is a spontaneous mutation that appeared in Ontario, Canada, in 1966. To most people, hairlessness is a denial of everything that cats are about, and it is true to say that, although a curiosity, the Sphynx has never caught on except with a tiny number of admirers.

ORIGINS OF THE BREED

IT IS INTERESTING, however, that the history of the Mexican Aztecs contains stories of a breed of hairless cats which in winter developed a slight growth of hair on the back and along the ridge of the tail. Some modern Sphynxes have the same characteristic. Given the emergence of the modern Sphynx in Ontario, and as the original prehistoric migration through the Americas was from north to south, perhaps it is not entirely fanciful to see the Sphynx as a relic of prehistory washed up on the tide of genetics.

The original modern Sphynx was just one of a litter born to a black and white domestic cat following an accidental mating with an unknown father. The hairlessness – so-called, because in fact the mature Sphynx has a very short downy coat which can be felt or seen only with difficulty, but no true eyebrows or whiskers – is caused by a recessive gene. The mutation changed not only the hair length but also the body type, so that the Sphynx does not merely look like a domestic cat without hair. It looks like an entirely different species. In cats with normal coats, the hair regulates body temperature, and the Sphynx's lack of hair causes it to sweat and also makes it warm to the touch. There is more obvious soft, short hair on the points and testicles.

Top
The Sphynx has an unusual body shape that does not resemble domestic cats. It has no whiskers and huge ears.

Opposite top
Domestic cats have been mated with the wild Geoffroy's Cat.

Opposite bottom
These Bengal kittens have descended from a domestic crossed with the wild leopard cat.

CHARACTERISTICS

THE SPHYNX'S BODY is long, fine and muscular, barrel-chested, with long, slim legs and small, dainty paws. The tail is long, thin and hard. The neck is long and supports a head which is slightly longer than it is wide. The ears appear disproportionately large, wide at the base and round-tipped. The eyes are deep-set and slanted. A number of colours are allowed but there are some exclusions according to the organisation with which the Sphynx is shown. The breed is recognised in the United States only by The International Cat Association. Its earlier recognition in Canada has been withdrawn, and it is not recognised in Britain. The cat fancies in the Netherlands and France recognise it.

TEMPERAMENT

SPHYNXES ARE SAID to be champion purrers but are not very affectionate as pets, resisting stroking and cuddling. They also dislike sharing their living space with other cats or domestic animals and so are suitable only for one-pet households. Sphynxes are essentially indoor cats as they have so little protection from adverse weather, and they do not like resting on cold surfaces. Their body temperature is a degree or two above the average for normal cats and they have voracious appetites to compensate for the heat loss. Sphynxes have a characteristic pose, when standing, of raising one foreleg. The kittens are born with a covering of fine down which they lose as they mature. Coat colours and patterns can sometimes be seen faintly in the adult down and on the underlying skin.

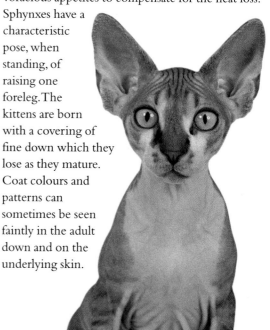

BREED INFORMATION

NAME	Safari Cat
OTHER NAMES	None
BODY SHAPE	Large and muscular
COLOUR VARIATIONS	Breed not yet fully developed.

Safari Cat

BREEDERS HAVE FROM time to time experimented with mating domestic cats to wild cat species. There is some logic in this since all domestic cats are derived from wild cats, but most of these experiments come to nothing.

ORIGINS OF THE BREED

ONE THAT HAS had limited success is the mating of domestic cats with Geoffroy's Cat, *Felis geoffroyi*, which is native to South America . This has produced offspring with the attractive ring-spotted coat of the wild parent, a unique pattern among domestic cats. The Safari Cat is, however, not acknowledged anywhere within the cat fancy and it remains a rare and interesting novelty.

 SIZE

 COAT CARE

 EXERCISE

BREED INFORMATION

NAME	Bengal
OTHER NAMES	None
BODY SHAPE	Large and muscular
COLOUR VARIATIONS	All colours.

Bengal

THE BENGAL IS another wild cat hybrid, resulting from crosses between the Egyptian Mau and the Leopard Cat (*Felis bengalensis*).

ORIGINS OF THE BREED

IT WAS DEVELOPED in the United States in the late 1970s. Its distinctive conformation combines a long muscular body with a relatively small head. Breeding is difficult as the male kittens are often sterile. Bengals received preliminary recognition in Britain in 1997.

 SIZE

 COAT CARE

 EXERCISE

Non-Pedigree Cats

ALTHOUGH THERE IS an enormous amount of pleasure to be obtained from the companionship of a fine pedigree cat, some of the most ardent cat lovers have never owned a pedigree cat in their lives, nor wanted to. Many beautiful, exquisitely patterned and good-natured cats, making decorative and delightful pets, owe their appearance and personality to the lottery of accidental mating rather than to the breeder's skill, and they lose no merit as domestic pets through not coming with a pedigree certificate.

NINE LIVES

IT IS A COMMON belief that non-pedigree cats are healthier than pedigree animals. The basis for this assumption is that pedigree cats are often inbred and that genetic flaws are thus passed on from one generation to the next. In fact, there is very little evidence for this belief, although of course breeds do vary in their susceptibility to disease and in their longevity. But in practice, diseases can spread as virulently through a population of cats sharing suburban gardens as they can through a breeding cattery, and defects can be passed on as easily through a non-pedigree breeding line as through a carefully planned breeding programme.

SHOWING NON-PEDIGREE CATS

Top left
This tabby-tortie white makes an excellent companion for the Persian kitten.

Top right
This beautiful cream longhair is a non-pedigree cat and could be shown.

PROUD OWNERS of non-pedigree cats are not precluded from exhibiting them, since most cat shows have classes for them (called Household, Pet or Domestic classes) in which each entrant is judged on its general merits rather than on standards laid down for a particular type. This means that non-pedigree cat owners can participate in the pleasure and education provided by showing almost as fully as breed fanciers. Preparing a pet cat for exhibition is an excellent way of encouraging children who may one day take a specialist interest in the cat fancy.

Against this, it must be said that the cats that hit the headlines in stories about feline longevity do tend to be non-pedigree pets, like the 31-year-old Smokey, a black and white female (with one remaining tooth but no other apparent medical problems) living in Gloucestershire who was declared in 1998 to be Britain's oldest cat. But the supposedly superior health of non-pedigree cats should not delude the owner of one into skipping the admittedly expensive requirements of vaccination against the common cat diseases . Nor should owners rely on the belief that non-pedigrees are necessarily more hardy. If they are allowed out, there should always be somewhere dry and warm where they can shelter from the weather if they cannot regain access to the house at will.

NON-PEDIGREE BACKGROUND

IT IS EXTREMELY unlikely that the parentage of a non-pedigree cat can be reliably traced, and to that extent taking one on is something of a gamble. However, if the basic rules of choosing a cat are followed this presents no real difficulty. The great advantage of non-pedigree cats is of course that they can be obtained at very small cost, and often at no cost at all.

What cannot be emphasised too strongly is that cats from whom it is not intended to breed (and it is pointless to breed non-pedigrees, of whom there are in any case far too many in the world, most sadly destined to be abandoned or destroyed) should be spayed or neutered at the appropriate time. For owners intending to exhibit their domestic cats this is essential, since classes for these cats at cat shows make it a requirement.

There is a compromise between taking on a cat with a completely unknown background and accepting the responsibility of a pedigree animal. All cat breeders have, from time to time, kittens for sale which, although of impeccable pedigree, are for some reason not suitable for show or breeding purposes. The fact that these are sometimes described as 'faulty' should not deter the potential buyer. The term is used in the cat fancy sense – that is, the kitten has the wrong colouring or perhaps a less than ideal conformation or coat quality, which makes it unsuitable to show or breed from. It does not mean that it is unhealthy or weak or in any way a poor specimen except in the very demanding terms of the show world. Such kittens are often sold relatively cheaply without a pedigree certificate (and are therefore, in the strict sense, 'non-pedigree') and on condition that, if this has not already been done, they will be neutered.

CAT FACT:
The triangular ear flaps of cats are called pinnae. The coarse hairs inside prevent foreign bodies from entering and may help filter the sound waves being collected.

Top
Non-pedigree cats tend to live longer than their pedigree cousins.

Bottom
Non-pedigree cats should be allowed access to a warm house and not forced to live outside permanently.

Opposite bottom
If you want to show your non-pedigree then it has to be spayed or neutered.

Wild Cats

ILD SPECIES OF the cat family are to be found in all the world's continents except Australasia and the Antarctic, although some islands such as the West Indies, Iceland, Greenland, the Falklands, Madagascar and New Guinea have no natural species. The 36 species of Felidae (which include the domestic cat, *Felis catus*) range in size from the tiger, which can weigh up to 350 kg (770 lb) to the tiny rusty-spotted cat at 1–2 kg (2–4.5 lb).

CHARACTERISTICS

LARGE OR SMALL, they have a number of characteristics in common. All are carnivores with a strong hunting instinct, honed into skills by their mothers from soon after birth. In all cat species, kittenhood or cubhood is a relatively short period of intense learning which begins as soon as the young are on their feet. Cats are sure-footed, with good balance and acute vision. Almost all are nocturnal by nature, and all have the mirror-like structure, the *tapetum lucidum*, backing the retina which results in the familiar 'cat's eye' effect and enhances their night vision. All have coats which camouflage them in their natural habitats, partly for protection but mainly to hide them from their prey. With only two exceptions, the cheetah, *Acinonyx jubatus*, and the fishing cat *Felis viverrina*, all cat species have retractable claws. An elastic ligament in

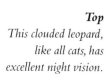

Top
This clouded leopard, like all cats, has excellent night vision.

Middle
Domestic and wild cats are both carnivores and have relatively short kittenhood or cubhood.

Bottom
The snow leopard is just one of the 36 species of Felidae.

the paw enables the cat to sheath its claws when stalking its prey, running or at rest, and to unsheath them for the kill or when climbing.

HUNTING INSTINCTS

THE CHEETAH IS again the exception when it comes to styles of hunting. It alone chases its prey, using its non-retractable claws to attain speeds of up to 100 km/h (63 mph) in bursts of up to a few hundred metres or yards. It is by far the fastest land animal. Most other cat species hunt by stealth, observing their victims, choosing the moment, creeping up on them and pouncing suddenly, or they lie concealed in wait for passing prey.

Only domestic cats seem to hunt for fun. This is probably because their natural instincts are thwarted by the provision of food by their owners. Generally, wild cat species hunt only when they need food. After a kill they gorge themselves, sometimes eating up to one-third of their body weight, enough to keep them going for several days while they find a secure and comfortable place to sleep. All cats are sound and prodigious sleepers, spending up to 18 hours a day asleep.

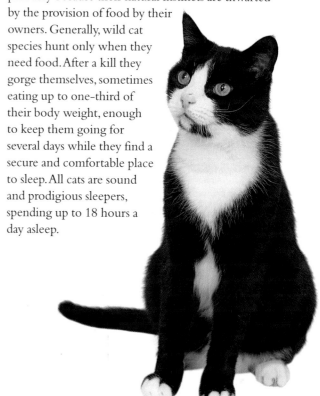

SOLITARY LIFE

MOST CAT SPECIES apart from lions are solitary by nature, males and females coming together only to mate. The lion again excepted, the males leave (or are driven off) after mating and the care of the young is left entirely to the females. These are famously attentive and caring mothers. The gestation period in wild cats varies between nine and 16 weeks, and litter sizes range from one or two in the ocelot up to six in other species, including the large cats.

VARIETY OF SPECIES

THE 36 CAT species are divided zoologically into five groups or genera. There are the five large cats classified as *Panthera*. The cheetah is in a genus of its own, *Acinonyx*, as is the clouded leopard, *Neofelis*. Then there are the four Lynx species, and the 25 species known as the small cats or *Felis*, which include the domestic cat.

A number of *Felidae* species are on the United Nations official list of endangered species and several more are giving naturalists cause for concern because of their declining numbers. In central Africa and India, big game hunting in the nineteenth century and the early part of the twentieth destroyed many thousands of animals, partly for sport and partly for the value of their fur. Many of the larger wild cats of North America suffered in the same way. Although some hunting continues despite conservation laws, a greater threat today is the destruction of the cat's natural habitats as land is cleared and towns and cities grow. This forces the wild cats into competition for food with other carnivores over smaller areas of land. There, they may become vulnerable to larger and more powerful rivals. Few people would think of the cheetah, for example, as a vulnerable creature, but a cheetah cub has only a one in 20 chance of surviving to adulthood because of attacks on their dens by lions and hyenas.

In South America, destruction of the Amazon rainforest similarly threatens the ultimate survival of tree cats such as the margay and the kodkod which do not adapt as easily as some other Felis species, such as the African wild cat, to new environments.

Top left
This fishing cat will spend most of its adult life alone, here it fishes on its own.

Top right
This Bengal tiger is one of the heaviest in the cat family.

Bottom
The lion is an exception to most cats as it hunts in a pride.

The Big Cats

FIVE BIG CATS – the jaguar, the lion, the leopard, the snow leopard and the tiger – are all members of the genus *Panthera*, while the clouded leopard belongs to the genus *Neofelis*. The big cats include the great roaring cats, given their powerful voices by a vibrating cartilage at the base of the tongue where smaller, quieter cats have a bone. There are two further distinctions between the *Panthera* and the other feline species.

THE BIG CATS lie with their front legs out in front, whereas the others tuck their front feet under them. Also, unlike the small cats, the *Panthera* do not bury or hide their faeces. All *Panthera* are powerful animals with, as adults, no real rivals in the animal kingdom except humans and occasionally each other if they find themselves in competition for food or, in the case of males of the same species, mates. Two of the big cats, the tiger and the snow leopard, however, are listed as endangered species and the clouded leopard is also under threat to a lesser extent.

__Whole page__
The five big cats are the tiger (top right), the leopard (centre right), the snow leopard (bottom right), the jaguar (centre left), and the lion (bottom left).

Jaguar

THE JAGUAR, *PANTHERA ONCA,* is the only one of the big cats native to the Americas. This single fact, together with its power and cunning, its hunting skill and its stealth, gave it supremacy over other wildlife, and it is not surprising that it came to symbolise qualities that humans envied. Both the Aztecs of Mexico and some South American Indian tribes used jaguar skins and images of the jaguar in their worship and ceremonies.

HABITAT

SOMETIMES CALLED the panther, the jaguar is found today in tropical forests and open country from southern Mexico southwards to Argentina. Until the 1940s there were still small colonies in Texas and Arizona. It is a good swimmer and prefers to live near water. Typical weights are from 40–135 kg (90–300 lb).

CAT FACT:
Sabre-teeth, for stabbing at prey, did in fact evolve independently in four separate animal groups, but their extinction suggests it was too specialised an adaptation to persist.

CHARACTERISTICS

THE JAGUAR'S COAT is usually yellow or tawny with dark spots forming rosettes and dark rings on the tail, but black panthers are also seen. The head is large, the body solid and compact and the legs short and powerful. Jaguars hunt large prey such as the tapir, the capybara or water hog, horses and cattle. They also take tortoises and river turtles, puncturing the shells with their strong canine teeth, and are reputed to even kill anacondas and other snakes.

After mating, the female makes a den close to water. The litter, typically of four, is born full-coated but the cubs do not achieve their adult colouring until about seven months. They stay with their mother until they are about two years old.

Top
This sub adult jaguar sharpens its claws on a log in Amazonia, Brazil.

Middle
Jaguars are fond of water, preferring to live nearby. This adult shows that he is an adept swimmer.

333

Lion

T HE LION, *PANTHERA LEO*, is the legendary 'king of the jungle', although in fact its natural habitat is open country and scrubland where its prey — typically zebras, giraffes and antelopes — is to be found and where the lion's tawny coat provides camouflage while hunting. Typical weights are between 135–225 kg (300–500 lb), but individuals have been reputed to weigh up to 340 kg (750 lb). Most, but not all, male lions have manes, the only cat to have this distinction between male and female. Lions, both males and females, are the only cats to have tufts at the tips of their tails.

CAT FACT:
Although the sabre-toothed cats are often referred to as tigers, they were not. All of the extant cat species, including tigers, come from a completely different line.

Top
Unlike other cats, lions prefer to live and hunt in their pride which can have up to 30 members.

Bottom
This adult male is king of the jungle.

THE PRIDE

LIONS ARE ALSO unique among all other wild cat species in choosing to live in stable sociable groups called prides. A pride is normally headed by one dominant male, who has sexual rights over the mature females, and may contain as few as six or as many as 30 individuals. These will include a number of mature females as well as immature males and females. At maturity, at about two years, the males will challenge for leadership of the pride or be driven off. They will then seek a new territory and form their own pride, or challenge for leadership of an existing one.

The authority of the male lion makes its mark on the pride as a whole. If the male is weak and fails to deter raids from other prides or from predators such as hyenas and leopards which attack the cubs, insecurity and tension rise among the females and they sometimes neglect their young, leading to a higher mortality rate among the cubs. A strong male, prepared to see off raiders, makes for a secure pride in which the females relax and share in looking after each other's young.

NATURAL HUNTERS

WHEN IT COMES to hunting for food, however, the females take the lead. The hunting is usually done in groups in the early evening. Typically, the hunters will circle round a herd of antelopes or giraffes before closing in for the kill, choosing a young or weak victim and isolating it from the herd. They will also work together by driving the quarry towards other members of the pride waiting in ambush. Killing is usually done with a blow from the forepaw to the neck or by jumping on the victim's haunches and breaking its back, then suffocating with a grip to the throat. The whole pride then shares the spoils, though not always, as is commonly believed, in strict hierarchical order — males, females and then cubs. Sometimes the male will take charge of the carcass

HABITAT

ONCE WIDESPREAD IN prehistoric times across southern Europe, Africa and southern Asia, the lion is now confined to Africa south of the Sahara and, in small numbers thought to be about 250, a subspecies exists in the Gir Forest in north-western India where a sanctuary was created in 1966. The past two centuries have seen its distribution diminish sharply. In the 1850s lions were common in central and northern India but by the 1890s they had become almost extinct owing to the activities of farmers and big game hunters. Lord Curzon, when Viceroy of India from 1898 to 1905, was responsible for securing the future of the colony in the Gir Forest, which was down to about a dozen individuals, by importing lions from Africa and prohibiting hunting in the forest.

Elsewhere, lions were given no such protection. The last Barbary lion – a particularly fine subspecies of the North African coast whose males had manes covering most of their bodies – was thought to have been shot in 1922. As recently as 1991 a lion colony which lived on the Atlantic coastal strip of Namibia was finally shot to extinction.

Although fearless and reputedly fierce in legend, lions are normally fairly phlegmatic and seek a quiet life among plentiful food supplies. They become bolder if they are hungry, but will usually keep out of the way of humans. Many stories were told in the past about man-eaters, but these were usually older lions too weak to join in the hunting of more agile creatures.

Top
Females are more dominant than males when hunting, although the whole pride share the kill.

Bottom
Lions roam over large territories in order to find sufficient food.

CAT FACT:
The cave lion was probably an outsized subspecies of today's lions. Adapted for a northerly European climate, it survived in the Balkans until only 9,000 years ago.

and choose his favourite pieces, but then the females and cubs can join in. For the cubs, competing for food over the body of the victim is an important aspect of training. The concept of sharing food is another example of the lion's different social code. For other cat species, sharing is anathema.

The food requirements of a pride of lions dictate that their territories are large, and it may be that only by working in concert can they keep up with the demand. If times are hard, lions will scavenge and even eat grass or insects. Unfortunately for the species, where farmland encroaches on lion habitats farm livestock provides easy pickings, with the result that raiders are shot.

BREEDING

LIONS ARE SAID to be capable of great sexual feats. One observer claimed to have witnessed over 100 copulations in 55 hours, each incident lasting about 21 seconds, between the same lion and lioness. The gestation period is 15–16 weeks, and the usual litter is up to four, but occasionally as many as seven, cubs. The female absents herself from the pride for the birth, making a den close to water, returning to the pride when the cubs are about three weeks old and able to walk. All the lactating females in the pride may then share indiscriminately in feeding the cubs and later training them to hunt. As with most of the big cats, mortality in cubs is high. It is estimated that only two-thirds of lion cubs survive the first few days, and only one-half reach one year old.

Leopard

THE TRUE LEOPARD, *Panthera pardus*, is the most widespread of the big cats.

HABITAT

IT IS FOUND across most of sub-Saharan Africa through Asia Minor to southern Asia, usually in forest and scrubland but also in semi-desert and swamp areas – an indication of the leopard's adaptability to a variety of habitats and prey. Prehistoric remains show that the leopard was once also widespread across Europe. It was then much larger than today's specimens, which weigh 30–90 kg (66–198 lb).

CHARACTERISTICS

THE LEOPARD HAS a pale brown ground coat, shading to white on the underparts, with rosette spots. Leopards living on the fringes of the desert weigh less and have lighter-coloured coats. The black leopard, in fact very dark brown, is a colour variant found in western India and often called the panther. The characteristic darker rosettes are faintly visible in the coat in certain light. Genetically, a black leopard is identical to one with normal colouring except for the presence of the recessive black gene.

Supporting its long, flexible body on relatively short but powerful legs, the leopard is the most agile of the big cats, scaling trees vertically with ease and often storing its prey in the branches when it has eaten all it can. Its closely positioned eyes provide perfect binocular vision for identifying and ranging prey, and it is said that a leopard can stalk its victim effectively in almost total darkness.

HUNTING

IT SLEEPS IN THE day and hunts from early evening through until dawn, taking a wide range of prey from antelopes to small rodents. The leopard's technique is to get as close as possible to its victim, relying on surprise and going for the kill with one bound. Leopards are capable of killing mammals three times heavier than themselves. Having killed, they set about their meal with great deliberation, first dragging the carcass to a place of safety – often a tree – where they can enjoy it without interference. They are clean eaters, taking care not to soil their coats with blood. If they have killed close to a supply of water, they take a drink in between bouts of eating. If not, they wander off after eating to find water before retiring to the trees to sleep off their meal.

The leopard leads a solitary life except after mating, when the male and female stay together for up to a year, and sometimes longer, after the cubs are born. Litters number between one and six, but many cubs die within a few days and are eaten by their mother. The male brings back food for the mother and cubs until she decides it is time to take the cubs out and train them to hunt. Then she drives the male away and completes their upbringing on her own.

Top

The leopard has perfect binocular vision which enables it to identify and range prey.

Top

Leopards are adept climbers and hide their kill in trees to prevent scavengers.

Bottom Left

This black leopard from Asia is genetically identical to the lighter spotted leopard.

Snow Leopard

THE LONG-HAIRED snow leopard, *Panthera uncia*, also known as the ounce, is another endangered species. The world population is estimated at about 5,000. It weighs in at between 45–70 kg (100–150 lb).

HABITAT

IT LIVES IN THE mountainous rocky terrain of the Himalayas and central Asia, staying on the snowfields and glaciers of the high ground up to 6,000 m (19,700 ft) in summer and retreating below the snowline in winter. In this environment food is scarce, and it is not surprising that the snow leopard finds a wide variety of prey, including pheasants, partridges, wild mountain sheep and goats, ibex, musk deer and even small rodents when other prey is scarce. Although it chooses habitats remote from humans, it will sometimes raid the livestock of a mountain farmer or nomad family.

CHARACTERISTICS

THE BACKGROUND COLOUR of the snow leopard's dense coat is lightish-grey, turning to yellow on the flanks and white on the underparts, with dark solid spots on the head, neck and legs and dark rosettes on the body. Thick tufts of hair between its toes act like snowshoes, enabling it to pad sure-footedly across a frozen landscape. Its extremely powerful hind legs, ending in huge paws, enable it to make vast leaps. The long, thick black-tipped tail is wrapped round the body when the snow leopard is sleeping, giving additional insulation. In winter, the snow leopard's coat thickens to keep out the bitter cold, but this has proved a mixed blessing for the preservation of the species as the winter fur was historically greatly sought after by hunters.

The snow leopard's cubs are born in summer, when they have a greater chance of survival. They are already full-coated at birth, and at about three months are ready to follow their mother down to lower ground for the winter. When they return to the mountains in the spring, they are ready to become independent.

Clouded Leopard

THE CLOUDED LEOPARD, *Neofelis nebulosa*, is smaller than the snow leopard with relatively short but powerfully built legs, weighing between 18–22 kg (40–49 lb). It is something of a mystery, having been known to Western zoologists only since the nineteenth century and probably always having existed, in recorded history, only in small numbers. It has not been studied in the wild, and almost all that is known of it comes from the observation of specimens in captivity.

HABITAT

THE CLOUDED LEOPARD lives in the forests, scrublands and mangrove swamps of southern and south-eastern Asia, lying in wait for its prey in the branches of a tree. It will take a wide variety of prey from rabbits to young buffaloes. Its hunting habits earned it the nineteenth century name of 'tree tiger'. Unusually among cats, its lifestyle does not seem to be particularly nocturnal, and it will hunt by day or night depending on whether it is hungry.

CHARACTERISTICS

THE CLOUDED LEOPARD'S coat is pale brown with large patches of greyish-brown often outlined in black. It is distinguished from the other big cats in two ways: by its unusually long upper canine teeth reminiscent of the prehistoric sabre-toothed tiger, which are used for holding prey and tearing meat from the bone, and by the fact that (like the cheetah) it is unable to roar.

The deforestation of its habitats poses an obvious threat to the clouded leopard, and it is believed to have become extinct in Taiwan. The population of Sumatra, where up to four-fifths of the forests have been destroyed since the start of the twentieth century, is also endangered.

Bottom left
This snow leopard roars, bearing its long canine teeth used for ripping flesh from its prey.

Bottom right
Unlike other large cats, the clouded leopard cannot roar.

> **CAT FACT:**
> It has been well established that cats use their tails for balancing while climbing, leaping and sprinting, but lynxes seem to manage very well without tails.

Tiger

THE TIGER, *PANTHERA TIGRIS*, weighs from 110–225 kg (250–500 lb) but sometimes reaches 320 kg (700 lb), rivalling and often exceeding the lion in size. It inhabits forests and jungles in southern and south-eastern Asia, north-eastern China and Siberia. With its orange-brown coat striped with black, ideal camouflage in a jungle environment, it is the only striped wild cat species. White tigers, with blue eyes, a white ground coat and light brown stripes – the result of a mutation – are occasionally seen.

HABITAT

THE TIGER IS a solitary hunter, usually at night. It is thought that the colder regions of Siberia and northern China were its original habitat, and this would explain why, although it has adjusted to the tropical jungle, it dislikes intense heat and makes for well-shaded hideouts in the heat of the day. It feeds on wolves, lynxes, young elephants, buffaloes and wild pigs, eating up to 27 kg (60 lb) of meat at a single sitting. The subspecies in northern habitats grow larger, have a longer coat and accumulate an insulating layer of up to 5 cm (2 in) of fat. Tigers are good swimmers and often take to the water to cool off, but they are reluctant to climb trees.

Tiger territories are determined by the males, which will allow females but not other males inside, but tigers change territories quite freely. The tiger's familiar prowling of its enclosure by in captivity echoes its behaviour in the wild, where it will sometimes cover hundreds of kilometres before deciding to scent its territory and settle for a while. One tiger, tagged with a radio device, was found to have covered 965 km (600 miles) in 22 days.

BREEDING

MATING IS PRECEDED by fierce fighting between two or more males, occasionally to the death, for the female on heat, with the female always accepting the winner. However, when mating is finished she drives the male off, often injuring it if it does not move fast enough. The typical tiger litter is two or three cubs, but may be up to seven, which take three years to mature. The tigress is a caring mother, teaching her cubs hunting skills until they are almost mature and able to fend for themselves. In their early months,

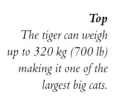

Top
The tiger can weigh up to 320 kg (700 lb) making it one of the largest big cats.

Bottom
A white Bengal tiger; this species is the only wild cat to be striped.

when they are vulnerable to attack, she moves her den frequently. They become independent at about 18 months. Tigers can live for 20–25 years in the wild.

ENDANGERED SPECIES

THE PAST 100 years have been disastrous for the world's tiger population. It is estimated that in 1900 there were more than 100,000. By the 1990s this number had shrunk to about 5,000. One by one, its habitats are reporting no sightings. On Bali, one of the islands of Indonesia, the last tiger was seen in the 1940s. Java, also in Indonesia, last saw a tiger round about 1980. Still in Indonesia, on Sumatra there are thought to be no more than 500 left.

There are about 50 tigers left in the whole of South China, and no more than 500 in Siberia. The Caspian tiger in central Asia is thought to have become extinct round about 1970. Hunting for sport, slaughtering for traditional medicines, the uprooting of the tiger's natural habitat and the use of insecticides have all played a part. So has the growth of cities. In Bangladesh, tigers could be found in the 1930s only a few miles away from centres of population, but growth has driven them southwards into the Sunderbans, the swampland of the Ganges delta, where there are thought to be only about 400 left.

Only in north-western India and Nepal has there been good news. Here, where there were about 40,000 tigers at the start of the twentieth century, there were fewer than 2,000 by 1970. They were Royal Bengal tigers, the most numerous subspecies of tiger in the world. In 1972 a conservation programme called Project Tiger was started, and by 1998 the numbers had recovered to about 4,600. But they are still vulnerable to poachers, and also to occasional understandable hunting by villagers living on the borders of the conservation areas whose families and livestock are attacked. Part of Project Tiger is the establishment of buffer zones between farmland and the tiger reserves in the hope of minimising contact between tigers and farmers.

Top
An adept swimmer, this Bengal Tiger takes a dip to cool off.

Bottom
Tigers have been hunted to extinction in some areas of the globe.

Cheetah

THE CHEETAH, *ACINONYX jubatus,* is in a genus of its own, distinguished by its permanently unsheathed claws. It is the only member of the genus Acinonyx. It is in a class of its own in other respects as well. Other cats, large and small, catch their prey by careful stalking and a final spring. The cheetah, by contrast, can keep up a moderately sustained chase, outrunning even the gazelle. With its claws constantly exposed, the cheetah is always in running mode and its long legs and long, narrow-waisted body are built for speed and rapid turning. This method of hunting affects the cheetah's whole personality. Attuned to the quick chase and kill, it does not have the patience of other big cats to lie in wait for its victim or pursue it stealthily. But the cheetah's reliance on speed becomes a disadvantage as it grows older. When it loses its agility, it loses its food. Cheetahs in the wild survive to only 5–7 years compared with 9–10 years for other big cats and about 13 for cheetahs kept in captivity.

and the widespread disappearance of the cheetah's habitat under the plough and cattle pasture has robbed it of its cover and its prey. Its favourite habitat is open country where its victims, grazing animals and in particular the Thompson's gazelle, are to be found. Its speed enables it to obtain its share of food in competition with the slower but more methodical lion and leopard, and with its muscular strength it can drag a Thompson's gazelle carcass many times its own weight back to the den to feed its cubs.

A cheetah has been timed over a 91.5 m (100 yd) course at 112 km/h (70 mph), but this was an exception. About 80 km/h (50 mph) is more usual, and such speeds can be maintained only over short distances. Even so, this enables the cheetah to outrun the fastest gazelle. Its rate of acceleration has been timed from rest to 64 km/h (40 mph) in two seconds, outperforming any sports car.

AMAZING SPECIES

THE CHEETAH, yellow-brown with dark spots, weighs between 30–50 kg (65–110 lb). It was once found from Africa through the Middle East to southern Asia, but numbers have dwindled. Only about 10,000 survive in Africa, some in national parks, while in the Middle East and Asia there are no more than 100.
Cheetah cubs are often killed in the den by hyenas and lions,

Top
Cheetahs run at 80 km/h (50 mph) on average, making them the fastest animal in the world.

Bottom Left
Cheetahs spend most of their time sleeping or resting, especially during the hottest parts of the day when they look for shade.

Bottom right
This cheetah's strength allow her to drag the prey back to her cubs.

Top

These cheetah in Namibia eat springbok while one keeps watch for hyena and lions.

Top right

It is unlikely that both of this cheetah's cubs will live.

Bottom

A mother teaches one of her cubs hunting techniques, they practice on a young Thompson's gazelle.

HABITAT

CHEETAHS REVERSE the usual territorial habits of the cat world. Females have larger territories than males, often up to 1,300 sq km (500 sq miles) compared with the males' 78 sq km (30 sq miles). Once the cubs have left the den, female cheetahs are solitary and avoid other females. Males, on the contrary, often form groups of between two and five which stay together for life. When males and females meet, there is a great deal of aggression, the males attacking the females and their cubs.

BREEDING

CHEETAH LITTERS are usually of between three and six cubs, but the mortality rate is high, mainly because of lion and hyena raids on the cubs' dens while the mother is out hunting at dawn or dusk. Only about one in 20 cubs reaches maturity. The first 12–15 months are periods of intensive learning as the mother shows her cubs how to kill and then how to hunt. Then, at about 15 months, there is a sudden rift in the family. The cubs leave home abruptly, never to return and never to even acknowledge their mothers or siblings if they see them again.

HUNTING SKILLS

THE CHEETAH'S HUNTING skills brought about a relationship with humankind which persisted from ancient times until fairly recently. The Ancient Egyptians tamed and trained cheetahs for hunting. The animal would be taken to the hunting-field in a low-sided cart, hooded, and kept on a leash while dogs flushed out the prey. When the prey was at a suitable distance, the cheetah would be released for the kill, finishing with a few gigantic bounds. The tradition of hunting with cheetahs was passed on to the ancient Persians and carried by them to India,

where it was kept up well into the twentieth century by Indian princes. Cheetahs were also once highly regarded as royal pets. Both Genghis Khan and Charlemagne are reputed to have kept them in their palace grounds, and as recently as the 1930s the Emperor of Abyssinia, Haile Selassie, was often photographed leading a cheetah on a chain.

> **CAT FACT:**
> The common names of wild cats can often be misleading: The mountain lion is not a lion, the snow leopard is not a true leopard and the bobcat is a lynx, for example.

Small Cats of Europe

MEMBERS OF THE *Felis* species are called small cats, although one, the puma, is as large as a leopard. Their distinguishing feature is the fact that they (and the cheetah and clouded leopard) cannot roar. In Panthera species, the voice-box and the skull are connected partly by cartilage, a tough elastic tissue which can vibrate to produce a full-throated roar. In the other cat species, the connection is entirely of bone and as a result only relatively weak cries can be produced.

Right

This Spanish lynx is a rare species and is on the United Nations' endangered species list.

Bottom left

The puma can reach the size of a leopard.

ONLY THREE SMALL cats are now found in the wild in Europe. They are the remnants of a larger feline population which included, up to 35 million years ago, the fearsome sabre-toothed cat and in far more recent times cave lions, leopards, jaguars, jungle cats, and a number of other unidentified feline species. Climatic change and hunting pressure exterminated some of these populations, while others moved out to warmer and less hostile environments. The three survivors are the Spanish lynx, the Northern lynx and the European wild cat.

Spanish Lynx

THE RAREST OF Europe's wild cats is the Spanish lynx, *Lynx pardinus,* which is on the United Nations' endangered species list. It is the third largest of the small cat species, weighing up to 13 kg (29 lb). The Spanish lynx, hunted almost to extinction, is now confined to a few remote mountainous areas of Spain and Portugal, and it was estimated in 1990 that there were no more than 200 individuals remaining in the wild.

CHARACTERISTICS

THE GROUND COLOUR of its coat is reddish-brown, with evenly distributed black spots. The tail is short and stubby. The ears are tufted and there is long hair on the cheeks, giving a bearded appearance. The Spanish lynx usually stalks its prey at walking pace, sometimes for considerable distances. Hares and rabbits provide its basic diet, but it will also catch birds, wildfowl and young deer.

Unusually, it appears that in the mating season the Spanish lynx female goes in search of a mate rather than the other way round as in other wild cat species. Although the young leave home at about one year old, they often do not breed for another two years. This is a factor in the slow restoration of a population which had been reduced by starvation or disease.

Northern Lynx

R ELATED TO, BUT generally larger than, the Spanish lynx is the Northern or Eurasian lynx, which is found in northern Europe and also in northern Asia. It weighs from 20–38 kg (44-84 lb). The Northern lynx has a grey or light brown dark-spotted coat, with prominent ear tufts and thick side-whiskers. It occupies snowy habitats, among others, and has large, well-padded paws which enable it to travel long distances on snowy ground. It was widespread in historical times across northern and central Europe and even, in prehistoric times, in Britain.

HABITAT

ONCE HUNTED FEROCIOUSLY, it has now recovered and in mainland Europe is found from Norway and Sweden (in both of which countries it is a protected species) to the Balkans and European Russia. A number of countries, including Switzerland, Finland, the Czech Republic, France and Italy have taken part in schemes to protect the lynx, either by regulating hunting or by releasing lynxes into habitats from which they had been driven out.

The lynx preys on hares, rabbits, small rodents, grouse, ducks, young deer and mountain sheep and is notorious as a particularly ferocious killer. Litters usually number two or three kittens, but the survival rate is low because the kittens are vulnerable to the hostile conditions in which the Northern lynx makes its home and to attacks from the lynx's main enemy, the wolf. In the wild, lynxes live to about 12.

> **CAT FACT:**
> Some cats, notably the lynx and caracal, have tufts at the end of their ears. Their function is not fully understood, though it may help with 'catching' sounds.

European Wild Cat

THE MOST WIDESPREAD is the European wild cat, *Felis silvestris*, which is found in all kinds of terrain and vegetation throughout mainland Europe from France to Poland, and in central and western Asia. There is also a population in Scotland, where it is a protected species, and the European wild cat is the only wild cat species now found in the wild in Britain.

CAT FACT:
The puma is the largest cat now extant in North America. It is taxonomically classed as a small cat species, but is easily the biggest of this group.

Top
The European wild cat is one of the most prolific species of wild cat.

Bottom left
In Scotland the European wild cat is an endangered species.

Middle
Similar to the domestic cat in appearance, the European wild cat is slightly heavier and stronger.

REVIVING THE SPECIES

WILD CATS HAD colonised Britain by two million years ago, and until the fifteenth century were common, although they do not appear to have extended to Ireland. Although it is generally agreed to be one of the ancestors of the domestic cat, the European wild cat's relationship with humans has been chequered, especially in western Europe. Hill farmers detested it because of its slaughter of poultry, lambs and goat kids. Gamekeepers shot it for attacking the nests of game birds. The result was a steady decline in the European wild cat population. The hunting estates of Scandinavia suffered particularly badly, while in Britain the eighteenth and nineteenth centuries saw the steady retreat of the European wild cat northwards. In 1811, a gamekeeper in the East Anglian county of Suffolk

recorded seven wild cats among his tally of vermin destroyed. By the 1850s the wild cat was not found south of the River Trent in the Midlands, and by the 1860s it was extinct in Wales. It was not until the beginning of the twentieth century that numbers revived, perhaps because of the abandonment of many hill farms and the break-up of many great hunting estates. By the 1930s the species was again flourishing across mainland Europe from France and Germany to Russia. In Britain it is confined to the Scottish Highlands, and even there is a rarity.

CHARACTERISTICS

THE EUROPEAN WILD cat is broadly similar in appearance to the domestic cat, but heavier, larger, more compact and much stronger. A black-striped tabby with a thick coat and a blunt, foreshortened tail, it weighs from 4–8 kg (9–17.5 lb), almost twice the weight of the typical domestic cat.

SOLITARY SPECIES

RECLUSIVE BY NATURE, the European wild cat chooses a solitary life in isolated habitats such as dense woods and rocky outcrops where it preys on hares, rodents and birds. It is rarely seen, and will disappear at once if it detects a human presence, even at a distance. However, it will visit remote farms for whatever food it can find if supplies are short or it is driven to lower ground by snow. No doubt it was such visits, many hundreds of years ago, that accounted for the assimilation of the species into the domestic cat's ancestry. This must have been a slow process, however. If captured and confined, the European wild cat remains fierce and shows no inclination to come to terms with humans, while matings between wild and domestic cats tend to produce untameable kittens. Such matings have, however, produced hybrid kittens which have been absorbed into the wild cat population.

BREEDING

MATING OCCURS IN the spring and the young, usually three or four to a litter, are born in early summer. The kittens are remarkably precocious. They make their first explorations from the den when they are only a few days old, and by seven days are exhibiting the aggressive tendencies of the adult cat, spitting and hissing if disturbed. This aggression is, in fact, defensive. Its object is to put the opponent off guard so that the cat can make its escape. Kittens learn this behaviour from their mother's reaction if any intruder threatens the security of the den.

The mother's training in hunting skills also begins early. At 6–7 weeks the kittens begin to pounce on their mother's waving tail, and soon afterwards they go out with her on their first expeditions, chasing leaves and insects. From then on they develop rapidly, and by five months are ready to leave the nest and live independent lives, equipped to survive the winter ahead. Their prey varies according to habitat, but small rodents provide the basis of their diet, supplemented by birds.

Some observers have suggested that male European wild cats are monogamous, returning to the same female year after year and even helping to provide food for the kittens. However, it is possible that this may be a reflection of the shortage of mates within a sparse population.

CAT FACT:
Cats instinctively attempt to move their food to a hiding place if they can. Leopards, among other species, will actually carry a kill into a tree for safe keeping.

Top
A fierce and aggressive animal, the wild cat hunts rodents and small animals.

Middle
The European wild cat is a solitary animal that inhabits woodland.

Bottom
Young wild cats begin hunting by pouncing on their mother's tail.

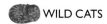

Small Cats of the Americas

CATS RELATED TO modern species are believed to have existed in the Americas for about 10 million years. Among the earliest examples in fossil records, dating from about 3 million years ago, are species similar to today's pampas cat, *Felis colocolo,* and the puma, *Felis concolor,* dating from about that time.

AT ABOUT THE same period, the jaguar and lion reached North America across the 'land bridge' from Asia, lions colonising the Americas as far south as Peru until climatic change defeated them. Fast-forwarding to about 100,000 years ago, fossils of species similar to the ocelot, the margay and the jaguarundi have been found in North America. From about then on, the small cats of the Americas seem to have pursued their own evolutionary path.

Top
Ancestors of this Margay have existed in the Americas for around three million years.

Bottom
This Andean Mountain cat lives at high altitudes in its natural habitat.

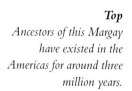

Kodkod

A NUMBER OF cats of the Americas are small forest-dwellers on the margins of the Amazon rainforest. The smallest of these Amazon species is the kodkod or huina, *Felis guigna*, at 2–3 kg (4–9 lb), which lives in the Andes foothills of Chile and Argentina.

CHARACTERISTICS

THE USUAL COLOURING is grey with dark spots on the body and dark lines running over the head and shoulders. The legs are also spotted and the tail is ringed. But variations from dark to yellowish-brown, bright brown and even black have been reported. The kodkod lives in deep forest and ventures out only at night to prey on small mammals and birds. It is virtually unknown even to zoologists, and almost all information about it comes from the observations of a Jesuit priest, Juan Ignacio Molina, who passed through the habitat over 200 years ago.

Pampas Cat

THE NOW RARE pampas cat, *Felis colocolo,* is a natural forest dweller despite its name, but has already moved out of the vanishing forest to the surrounding scrubland.

CHARACTERISTICS

IT WEIGHS 3.5–6.5 kg (8–14 lb), and its grey-brown coat with brown spots and bars and a ringed tail are well suited to its survival in its new habitat. Although rare, it is quite widespread, living in the scrubland of Chile, Argentina, Ecuador, Peru and Brazil, generally at fairly high altitudes. In Argentina it is a protected species. Despite its relatively small size, it is said to be fearless and aggressive. It feeds on small mammals, birds and domestic poultry.

Geoffroy's Cat

Tiger Cat

GEOFFROY'S CAT, *felis geoffroyi*, is a very similar species to the pampas cat. It was named after the 19th century French zoologist Etienne Geoffroy Saint-Hilaire who was one of the pioneers of zoological classification. He never travelled to South America, but identified Geoffroy's cat as a separate species from anatomical specimens he studied in his work as professor of zoology in Paris.

THE TALLY OF American small cats ends with the tiger cat, also known as the little spotted cat or oncilla, *Felis tigrina*, which is in the same weight range as Geoffroy's cat. The tiger cat lives in the forests of Central and northern South America, and is light brown with darker stripes and blotches.

Little is known about this species, which is believed to have become vulnerable to hunters and also to the deforestation of the Amazon basin.

CHARACTERISTICS

GEOFFROY'S CAT weighs only 2–3.5 kg (4–8 lb). It is a native of the lower wooded slopes and scrublands of Bolivia, Argentina, Chile, Uruguay and Brazil. The head is broad and short and the body elongated, with long legs and a long tail. Its colouring varies according to its habitat from grey to reddish brown with black spots and black bands on the face and head. This is another species with which attempts have been made to crossbreed with domestic cats, but with little success. One breeder reported that a Geoffroy's male killed all the domestic females it was introduced to.

Pregnant females appear to take particular care in choosing their birthing dens, which may be in undergrowth or on a rocky crevice. A typical litter numbers two or three. The kittens develop very quickly and at six weeks are fully mobile.

CAT FACT:
Before the intervention of humans, cats had not colonised most of the islands on the planet and they were completely absent from the Australasian continent.

Top left
This Geoffroy's Cat is a small, aggressive animal that can be found in several countries of South America.

Bottom left
Geoffroy's cat has a short, broad head on a long body.

Left
This unusual looking animal is the tiger cat of northern South America.

Puma

TAKING THE LARGEST of the American small cats first, the puma, Felis concolor, is one of the longest-established species. A larger form of the present species, probably exclusively a ground-hunter, existed in North America 3 million years ago.

CAT FACT
The caracal, a cat adapted for catching prey in the open desert, is so agile that it was once used by eastern princes for pigeon-catching sport contests.

Top
The puma has been the subject of several Native American myths.

Middle
The population of the puma has diminished due to hunting, fortunately it is now a protected species.

Right
This puma lives in rocky terrain, however as an adaptable cat it lives in varied habitats throughout the Americas.

HABITAT
TODAY'S PUMA inhabits areas as far north as Canada and as far south as the southern tip of South America, but is most common in the western United States and in Argentina. It was once widespread right across North America and greatly respected by North American Indians. The Pawnee tribe in southern Nebraska paid tribute to the puma by including it among the four beasts that guarded the Evening Star in their tribal myths. They believed it to be invincible, impossible to capture or kill. Early settlers in Virginia also reported seeing 'lions' on the prowl in the forests and hill country of the hinterland. These were undoubtedly pumas; it must be remembered that no one from Europe in the sixteenth century had ever seen a lion, which then existed in the Western world only in mythology.

RARE SPECIES
THE PUMA is now rare in most parts of North America, having paid the price for its ruthless attacks on the stock of the early pioneers. The first European settlers in North America brought with them livestock which was a welcome and easily obtained source of food. It needed only a few attacks by pumas – or even attacks attributed to them – to make the puma public enemy number one, and it was an easy target. The campaign to destroy the puma was prolonged and merciless, and faced with the settlers' onslaught, the pumas moved out to places which the white man and his gun had not reached. Numbers are, however, recovering in Florida's Everglades Park, where it is protected, and despite its disappearance from large tracts of North America the puma is still the most widely distributed wild cat in the New World.

Consequently, it has also been the most intensively studied. The key to its survival is probably that the puma is adaptable as to habitat, being equally at home in rocky terrain, on mountains, in open grassland and in the tropical rainforest.

CHARACTERISTICS
THE PUMA GOES under a variety of other names including panther, catamount, cougar, mountain devil, Mexican lion and mountain lion. Both 'puma' and 'cougar' come from South American Indian languages. The puma's average weight is from 46–60 kg (100–130 lb) although some South American males reach 113 kg (250 lb), which almost puts them in the

THE WANDERER

THE PUMA IS a great wanderer, often covering 40 km (25 miles) or more in a night's travelling, marking its territory with urine and tree-scratching as it goes. It is a cautious animal, avoiding other creatures except its prey and especially avoiding humans. Despite its size it is adept at concealing itself in natural cover. It kills by leaping on its prey, breaking the neck with a blow from a forepaw. It will then haul its victim, sometimes up to five times its own weight, to a place of safety before devouring it.

Unlike some other cats, the puma does not gorge on its prey. When it has eaten enough, it covers the carcass with leaves, goes off to sleep, and returns next day for another helping. It can take up to a week to devour the prey.

Puma litters number from one to four and occasionally up to six. The cubs are born with speckled coats and ringed markings on the tail, but the spots and rings disappear as they grow to maturity. They are usually driven off by their mothers when they are about 18 months old. A typical life span in the wild is 10–12 years; in captivity pumas can live up to 20 years.

big cat class. As might be expected of an animal with such a variety of habitats, there are wide colour variations. The main body colour, which is solid, ranges from light brown through silvery grey to black, with the underparts including the throat off-white. There are no markings on the coat. The length of the coat also varies according to habitat, being greater in more temperate regions.

The puma is renowned for its climbing and jumping abilities. It is said to be able to leap 12 m (40 ft) in a single bound. Although it is not equipped to roar, it produces loud purrs and screams like a much-amplified domestic cat. It is also, like many domestic cats, an obsessive self-groomer, licking its coat until it shines. The puma is as adaptable to food as it is to habitat. Its favourite food is deer, but analysis of the stomach contents of puma carcasses has revealed an amazing collection of prey, including deer, mules, cows, sheep, hares, horses, elks, moose, antelopes, beavers, porcupines, coyotes, martens, skunks, wild turkeys, birds, fish, lizards, grasshoppers and, in South America, anteaters. No doubt the puma's relatively large size and its active lifestyle account for the need to take in large quantities of protein fairly indiscriminately.

> **CAT FACT:**
> The cheetah, which can reach a total length of some 2.2 m (7.2 ft), is the smallest of the big cats. In fact it is somewhat smaller than the puma, one of the small cats.

Top left
The puma roams over great distances, in one night it can cover 40 km (25 miles).

Bottom
When this cub reaches about 18 months it will have to survive on its own.

Canadian Lynx

Ocelot

AFTER THE PUMA, the next small cat down in size is the Canadian lynx, *Lynx canadensis*. It was once thought to be the same species as the Northern lynx, and is very similar, but as it is around half the size of the other, at 8–10 kg (17.5–22 lb), scientific consensus is now that it is a separate species.

THE BEAUTY OF the ocelot, *Felis pardalis*, has been its downfall and put it on the list of endangered species.

HABITAT

NOTORIOUSLY fierce and bloodthirsty, the ocelot weighs between 11–16 kg (24–35 lb). A keen climber, it is closely related to the margay or tree ocelot (see below). Its preferred habitats are dense rainforest, bush country or marshland – in fact, almost anywhere but open, arid country. It tends to hunt at ground level at dawn or dusk, taking rodents, young deer, reptiles and birds, but takes to the trees to sleep.

CHARACTERISTICS

UNFORTUNATELY, ITS attractive coat has made it a favourite of the fur trade and the population, from the southern United States to Argentina, has suffered terribly. The coat is short, with a ground colour ranging from tawny yellow to reddish-grey. A pattern of black or dark spots runs along the flanks, with large circular black marks on the head, legs and feet. The cheeks are marked with black stripes, and the rounded ears are black with light spots. The tail is long and ringed with black.

Unlike most cats, ocelots often hunt in mixed-sex pairs, sometimes in daylight, communicating with each other vocally and by scent-marking, coming together to mate. A typical litter is two. The male ocelot helps feed the young in the early weeks, until he is driven off by the female.

HABITAT

THE CANADIAN LYNX is found throughout Canada and Alaska, sometimes moving down into the northern parts of the United States. In the past, the fur trade made huge depredations on the Canadian lynx population, but a more potent factor these days is the dependence of the Canadian lynx on snowshoe hares as the major part of its diet. This wild cat is not very adaptable, it seems, in its taste for prey, and a fall in the snowshoe hare population is inevitably followed the next year by a low conception rate and a high cub morality rate among lynxes.

Nevertheless, the Canadian lynxes appear to be in a stronger position than those in Europe.

Bottom right
The beautiful coat of this Venezuelan ocelot has meant that excessive hunting has placed the species in endanger of extinction.

Bottom left
The Canadian lynx population is more extensive than that of its European cousin.

Bobcat

CLOSELY RELATED TO the Canadian lynx, though smaller, the bob-tailed bobcat or bay lynx, *Lynx rufus,* has shown remarkable tenacity in holding its own against North American conditions and, of all North America's wild cats, has come closest to inspiring popular affection. Weighing 7–10 kg (15–22 lb), the bobcat still flourishes across a wide swathe of the continent from southern Canada to central Mexico.

HABITAT

IT IS A STURDY, heavily-built creature with tufted ears and side-whiskers, a stumpy white-tipped tail and a brown barred and spotted coat which takes on a reddish tinge in summer. Its favoured habitat is dry scrubland where it can hole up during the day, but adaptability is the key to its survival and wide distribution. At night, it emerges to prey mainly on hares and rabbits. Its typical hunting territory is between 13–26 sq km (5–10 sq miles), which it patrols in a businesslike fashion, stopping now and then to listen for the telltale sounds of rodents gnawing. Only in extreme hunger will the bobcat venture out of its hiding place before daylight begins to fade.

HUNTING

THE BOBCAT HAS no great turn of speed, and hares and rabbits can easily outpace it, so it takes up a position in a tree or on a rock and waits to drop on its victim. However, it is strong enough to take on a young deer and one observer reported watching a bobcat weighing about 9 kg (20 lb) stalk and kill a doe 10 times its own weight. Such audacity can occasionally land a bobcat in trouble. An attack on a fawn left for a moment by its mother can result in a fierce fight if the doe returns unexpectedly and surprises the predator with flailing hoofs. In winter, when food is short, the bobcat will approach towns and cities to prey on the suburban rat population, and will even take frogs, lizards and fish. In many respects, the bobcat mirrors the behaviour which led to the early domestication of wild cats, moving up where it can to take advantage of human settlement. It is a supreme example of feline adaptability, even prepared, if times are hard, to eat carrion.

BREEDING

BOBCATS ARE normally silent, but in the mating season from January to March they are capable of tearing the night apart with their courtship cries. Males often travel 50 km (30 miles) or more to find a mate, deserting her in typical feline fashion once the act is done. The mother finds the hollow of a tree, a sheltered rocky outcrop or a cave in which to have her litter, usually of two or three kittens but sometimes up to six. These normally leave home at the next mating season and, perhaps because of population pressure, will often travel over 160 km (100 miles) before finding their new territory.

Top and bottom left
The bobcat waits until dusk before emerging to prey upon rabbits and hares.

Bottom Right
This slow cat uses the height of a tree to gain an advantage when hunting.

Jaguarundi

THE JAGUARUNDI, *felis yagouarondi*, lives in lowland forest and bush from Texas south, through Central America, to Brazil and Paraguay.

CHARACTERISTICS

IT WEIGHS 5.5–10 kg (12–22 lb) and has a plain all-over coat except for its underparts. Some jaguarundi are brownish-grey and others more reddish, sometimes deep red, in tone. Some zoologists think that these colours appear at different stages in the mature individual's life; others say that the different colours appear randomly and that a variety of colourings can appear in a single litter. In the nineteenth century, when the jaguarundi was first observed, the grey and red forms were assumed to be two different species. The grey was named the jaguarundi and the red the eyra, both names derived from the Tupi Indian language. This distinction persisted until the late 1920s, when it was recognised that the difference was only a matter of coat colour. There are no spots or other markings on the coat.

The jaguarundi's head is unusually small and flattened, reminiscent of a weasel or an otter, and its body elongated but compact and powerful. Its short legs make it an excellent stalker, with a low silhouette as it moves through the bush and flattens itself before pouncing.

Top
The colour of the jaguarundi's coat can be red or grey but always solid.

Right
The jaguarundi has a face similar to a weasel but its short legs makes it an adept stalker.

HUNTING INSTINCTS

EVEN BY CAT standards, the jaguarundi is an exceptionally efficient hunter, negotiating dense undergrowth in silence and positioning itself perfectly for a swift kill. It hunts by day as well as night and tends to keep on the move rather than explore a well defined territory. In fact, it seems to have no great territorial sense at all, amiably sharing its hunting grounds with others, which suggests that the stalking instinct is dominant. It feeds mainly on small rodents, rabbits, young deer and guinea pigs, but is easily discouraged and does not enter into long pursuits. It will raid farms and villages for poultry if access is easy. Although basically a ground-dweller, it will take to the trees if chased, and can then demonstrate remarkable agility in leaping from branch to branch. The average jaguarundi litter is two or three. The kittens are often born with spots which fade as they mature.

In South America, jaguarundis have entered into a similar relationship with humankind as did the cats of Ancient Egypt. Some have allowed themselves to become domesticated in return for the run of the village barns and grain stores. This arrangement seems to suit their rather lethargic nature.

Margay

Andean Mountain Cat

THE MARGAY OR tree ocelot, Felis wiedii, also known as the long-tailed spotted cat, is found in the tropical forests and scrubland of Central and South America.

CHARACTERISTICS

IT IS AS ATTRACTIVE as the closely related ocelot but smaller at between 3–5 kg (6.5–11 lb). The coat is short, smooth and yellow-brown with white underparts, chest and neck. Dark markings similar to those of the ocelot run along the back and flanks, and the tail is ringed. The backs of the ears are dark with light spots. The legs and tail are long.

TREE-DWELLER

THE MARGAY SPENDS most of its life in the trees, living on birds and lizards, but it will descend for ground prey such as rodents, young deer and domestic poultry. The

margay is a secretive, elusive wild cat, well adapted to tucking itself away in the treetops until the night is old enough for it to emerge on a hunting expedition. It is particularly well suited to a life in the trees. Alone among cats, it is able to make the whole descent from a tree head first, thanks to the unusual flexibility of its hind legs which enables them to turn inwards to provide a secure grip on a tree trunk. This facility greatly extends the range of prey at the margay's disposal. The long tail also helps in managing the descent. The margay's attractiveness has led to its being one of the wild species that people have attempted to domesticate, but with very limited success as it does not take to confinement or domesticity.

THE SLOPES OF THE Andes from southern Peru to north-west Argentina are home to the Andean mountain cat, Felis jacobita, a medium sized 3.5–7 kg (8–15 lb) longhair. Sometimes called the mountain cat or Andean highland cat, it is a rare species about which little is known by zoologists. Anatomical evidence suggests that it may be a survival from an earlier phase in the development of the genus Felis, since it appears to have a double skull separated by a thin membrane. Its coat is brownish-grey with random brown or orange spots and a multi-ringed tail, with white underparts.

LITTLE-KNOWN SPECIES

THE ANDEAN MOUNTAIN cat lives on the edge of the snow line, between 3,000–5,000 m (10,000–16,500 ft), in treeless, rocky terrain and an inhospitable climate. It preys mainly on small rodents. Little more is known about its lifestyle and habits. The mountain cat is a distinct species, but the term is often used indiscriminately for the bobcat, lynx or puma.

CAT FACT:
Cave lions have been seen depicted in prehistoric cave paintings by Palaeolithic people. Humans undoubtedly played their part in their eventual extinction.

Top left
This Venezuelan Margay spends most of its life in trees.

Far left
The lynx is often wrongly called a mountain cat, this is, however, a separate species.

Left
The beautiful coat of this species is clearly visible, it has encouraged some breeders to try and domesticate the animal.

Small Cats of Asia

ASIA'S SMALL CATS range from species found widely right across the vast continent to cats confined to one small habitat – in the case of the Iriomote cat, to one single small Pacific island. Evidence of some of these species, such as the Chinese desert cat, exists only in the notebooks and drawings of naturalist explorers dating back, in some cases, to the nineteenth century and it is not known whether any specimens survive.

SMALL CATS, unlike big ones, are not so greatly admired and so do not attract so much attention from conservationists. Many of the smaller cats frequent habitats which are almost inaccessible to humans and are also markedly elusive.

Some Asian species are described in other sections. The caracal's territory, for example, spreads from Africa through Arabia to northern India. The African wild cat is found also in southern Asia. The territory of the European wild cat extends eastwards beyond the Ural Mountains, and the sand cat, usually associated with North Africa, also inhabits Asia Minor and the Caucasus.

Top
Leopard cats are nocturnal hunters, this cat has come out of his den in search of prey.

Bottom left
The jungle cat has adapted to a variety of habitats, this cat's coat camouflages the animal against the Indian jungle.

Leopard Cat

THE LEOPARD CAT, *Felis bengalensis*, is another widespread species in Asia. Fossilised remains of leopard cats dating back a million years have been found in several sites in Indonesia.

CHARACTERISTICS

THIS SMALL SPOTTED cat, sometimes known as the Bengal cat, typically weighs about 3–4 kg (6.5–9 lb) and is common in southern and south-eastern Asia from India to China, Japan and the Philippines. Cats in the southern part of the range tend to be smaller. The ground colour of its coat varies considerably from lightish grey to sandy brown, with darker spots arranged in rows on the body and legs, sometimes merging to form stripes, and conspicuous white markings round the eyes. The underparts are white.

HABITAT

FOR CHOICE, THE leopard cat lives in forest and scrubland, usually close to water, but it is adaptable and often chooses a habitat where it can raid human settlements for chickens, lambs and young goats. Its natural prey is hares, small rodents, reptiles, small deer, bats and squirrels. If necessary it will take to the trees in search of prey. It makes its den in hollow trees or rocky cavities and emerges to hunt at night.

Leopard cats are solitary except when they mate. A litter usually numbers two or three kittens, which remain in the den for the first four weeks.

The leopard cat is still a common species, but there are fears for its future because, with restrictions increasingly imposed on the hunting of other species, its pelt has become attractive to the fur trade. It is estimated that in three years during the 1980s nearly two million leopard cats were killed in China alone. In addition, leopard cats living close to human settlements are often killed because they prey on livestock.

Jungle Cat

THE JUNGLE CAT, *Felis chaus,* is associated with the finding of mummified remains in Egypt and with the origins of the domestic cat, but its true habitat is southern and south-eastern Asia, stretching westwards to the Caucasus and the eastern Mediterranean coast and northwards through Turkestan and Uzbekistan. In the east of its range its distribution overlaps with that of the African wild cat.

THE JUNGLE CAT is also known as the swamp cat and reed cat, but none of its common names should be taken to suggest a preference for either jungle or marshy environments. In fact, this species seems to thrive in a wide variety of habitats, and being an opportunist, the jungle cat often associates itself with human settlements, living on the fringes and taking advantage of the easy pickings that they provide. It combines fearlessness with a fox-like cunning and swift movement.

CHARACTERISTICS

THE JUNGLE CAT weighs from 7–16 kg (16–35 lb), specimens from central Asia being at the upper end of this range and those from south-east Asia at the lower. It is long-legged and short-tailed, with long, black-fringed, lynx-like ears. The coat is sandy brown, sometimes with a grey or red tinge, sometimes with very faint tabby markings on the body, legs and head, and the tail is ringed, with a blunt black tip. Black jungle cats have occasionally been reported.

Naturalists suggest that the jungle cat originated in the swamps and marshes of the river deltas in the Middle East, where it found its prey in thickets close to rivers and streams. It then spread eastwards, possibly under the pressure of population growth. In the process it discovered and adapted to new habitats, from dense woodland to high grassland. In India, it particularly favours the interior of sugar plantations.

HUNTING INSTINCT

THE JUNGLE CAT preys on rabbits, rats, mice, birds and reptiles and is a patient, painstaking stalker, ending the trail with a sudden burst of speed. Its territory may include a number of dens, often taken over from other creatures such as foxes or porcupines. It is less nocturnal than many other members of the cat family, hunting at first and last light.

The jungle cat's litter varies in size from three to seven. The kittens are born with distinct tabby stripes, which fade as the mature coat grows. They leave home at about five months, but it is another year before they reach full maturity.

The jungle cat is one of the hardiest and most widespread of the small cat species.

> **CAT FACT**
> Sabre-toothed cats comprised several species. They were also accompanied by another group of species with smaller canine teeth, called scimitar-toothed cats.

Top left
The white markings around the eyes of this leopard cat are clearly visible.

Top right
This jungle cat is a sandy brown colour; its preferred habitat is the interior of sugar plantations.

Bottom
This leopard cat is from Russia, the species has adapted to the cold climate.

Fishing Cat

SOUTHERN AND SOUTH-eastern Asia is also home to the fishing cat, *Felis viverrina*. Its size and weight vary widely, normally about 7 kg (15.5 lb) but sometimes up to 12 kg (26.5 lb). The fishing cat is usually found in marshes, swamps and reed beds and is specifically adapted for this kind of habitat.

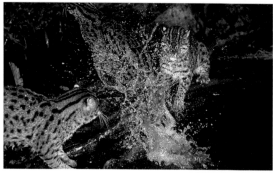

Top right
This grey fishing cat will use its claws as fishing hooks to spear fish.

Top left and middle
These three fishing cats hunt for their prey in this Thai swamp.

CHARACTERISTICS

Although many feline breeds and species, notably the Turkish Van among domestic breeds and the tiger among the big cats, will readily take to the water and will catch the odd fish if the opportunity is there, only the fishing cat finds most of its prey in the water. Its front paws are slightly webbed to aid swimming, and its claws do not retract fully. The claws –

Bottom right
A young cub

described by one observer as 'living fish-hooks' – are used to spear fish and scoop them out of the water, and to grasp muddy riverside banks. It has the infinite patience of the human angler and will wait on a bank or rock overlooking the water until its prey appears, occasionally venturing into the shallows if necessary. If supplies are plentiful, the fishing cat will live almost entirely on fish, but it will also catch reptiles, frogs, small mammals and birds. In Indian and Bangladeshi

villages it has a reputation in folklore for running off with young babies, and some instances of this have been reported.

The fishing cat is powerfully built, with a short, wide head, a long body, long legs and a fairly short tail. Its coat is light brown, sometimes with grey streaks, with dark spots in rows on the body. Dark lines run over the top of the head down the back of the neck. The underparts are white.

Pregnant females make a birthing den in reed beds, and after a gestation period of about eight weeks produce litters of two or three kittens. The kittens are weaned at about two months, and at nine months are fully grown. Fishing cats are killed for their skins in India and Pakistan, and in parts of India the species has suffered from the industrial pollution of waterways.

Pallas's Cat

PALLAS'S CAT, OR the manul, *Felis manul*, was widely distributed in prehistoric times throughout Asia and eastern Europe. It is now confined to an area of central Asia bordered by the Caspian Sea, Inner Mongolia and Tibet.

CHARACTERISTICS

IT IS EASILY distinguished among Asia's wild cats by its broad, flat head, with a low forehead, huge eyes, and ears set very low, giving it an owl-like appearance. The 'third eyelids' or haws are particularly well-developed, and it has been suggested that this is a defence against the dust storms promoted by the fierce winds across much of the species' range.

The manul's body is round and substantial, carried on short, stocky legs. The hair is long and dense, especially on the underparts. The tail is long and rather bushy, with four rings ending in a black tip. The coat colour is usually orange and grey, with black and white markings on the head, but depending on the habitat the ground colour of the coat ranges from yellowish grey to yellowish brown. The guard hairs are white-tipped, giving a silvery appearance. There are prominent dark markings on the cheeks and sometimes on the legs.

NATURALLY RECLUSIVE

PALLAS'S CAT WEIGHS from 3–5 kg (7–11 lb). Very reclusive, it is nocturnal and is rarely seen by humans but lives in rocky fissures and caves in country largely without vegetation. Its high-set eyes and low-set ears enable it to keep watch from behind rocks without exposing itself, waiting for the moment to attack its prey. In open country, it will crouch low to the earth and 'freeze' if it sees a likely victim, waiting for the moment to strike. Living in inhospitable environments with limited wildlife, Pallas's cat has to hunt diligently for its food and preys on a wide variety including rodents, reptiles and birds.

Pallas's cat can be extremely vocal, uttering a shrill cry when threatened and a dog-like yelp when seeking a mate. Litters number from four to six kittens.

INFLUENTIAL BREED

PALLAS'S CAT'S NAME commemorates one of the great pioneers of natural history exploration. Peter Simon Pallas was a German doctor who turned to the study of natural history and in 1768 was appointed to the Imperial Academy of Science in St Petersburg. Over the next 25 years, on instructions from Catherine the Great to survey the flora and fauna of her vast empire, he travelled extensively through southern and eastern Asia, and it was on one of these expeditions that he found and identified the manul. He also brought the first news to Europe of Siamese-patterned cats which he found in central Russia.

It has been suggested that Pallas's cat may have introduced the longhair gene into the ancestry of the domestic cat, but this is only speculation and generally dismissed by zoologists. It is true that the manul's coat is uniquely thick among wild cats, especially on the underparts, probably to provide insulation when it crouches or lies on the frozen earth of central Asia.

> **CAT FACT:**
> Scientists have had problems mapping the evolution of cats, partly because they tend to live in forested areas which almost negates the chances of fossilisation.

Bottom
The Pallas's cat has been compared to an owl because of its huge eyes and low ears.

Rusty-spotted Cat

THE RUSTY-SPOTTED cat, *Felis rubiginosa*, is the smallest cat species, weighing only 1–2 kg (2–4.5 lb).

Bottom
This rusty-spotted cat is from the forests of Sri Lanka.

CHARACTERISTICS

RUST-COLOURED WITH random shaded brown blotches on its back and legs, it has white underparts dotted with black spots. There are white and dark markings on the face, and four dark lines run over the top of the head and down the neck. The rusty-spotted cat lives in a variety of habitats – scrubland, forest, woodland and around waterways – mainly in southern India and Sri Lanka, but smaller, isolated colonies also exist in northern India. If its natural habitats are encroached upon it attaches itself to human settlements where it feeds on the rodent population, and it is said that kittens are easily domesticated and become playful, delightful pets.

Little else is known about the rusty-spotted cat, which it is suspected may be more widely distributed in India than is at present accepted.

Marbled Cat

THE MARBLED CAT, *Felis marmorata*, is a rare cat of the forests which has been seen from Nepal through Burma, Thailand and Malaysia to Indonesia. It spends most of its life, whether hunting or sleeping, in the trees where it preys on birds, reptiles and squirrels.

CHARACTERISTICS

ITS COLOURING is unusual, with irregular dark splotches and stripes over its body and legs and extending down its tail, on a light brown background. The tail is tipped with black. This 'marbling' is more definite and distinct than the pattern often described as 'marbled' in the cat fancy.

The marbled cat has a short, round head with unusually deep-set eyes for a cat. It is a very solid-looking cat with a powerful but well-covered body and a long, thick, blunt-tipped tail. In conformation and stance, especially when lying in repose, it closely resembles the leopard, although it is of course very much smaller. The coat is soft, thick and dense, especially on the underparts. The typical weight of a marbled cat is about 5.5 kg (12 lb).

Litters usually number three or four. The kittens are born without the characteristic marbled coat, but this is fully developed when they are about four months old.

Bay Cat

THE BAY CAT, *Felis badia*, is also known as the Borneo red cat. It is found only in the scrubland of Borneo.

CHARACTERISTICS

A SMALL CAT weighing only 2–3 kg (4.5–7 lb), its 'red cat' name is apt because its coat is a solid, fox-like reddish-brown, fading to reddish-white on the underparts. There are white markings on its face, and the long, whip-like tail has a white streak on its underside shading to all-over white at the end. Almost nothing is known about its favoured habitat, since sightings have been so rare, but it is likely that it prefers marshy or forest environments where there are rodents and nestlings to be preyed upon.

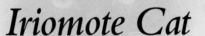

Iriomote Cat

IRIOMOTE IS A tiny mountainous island in the Pacific, about 200 km (125 miles) off the east coast of Taiwan at the southern end of the Ryukyu Islands. The Iriomote cat, *Felis iriomotensis*, was identified only in 1967, when there were thought to be fewer than 100 in existence. Its status as a distinct species was at first doubted, but fossil remains since discovered on an adjacent island suggest that the Iriomote cat has existed as a separate species for as long as two million years.

CHARACTERISTICS

THE SIZE OF A domestic cat, weighing about 5.5 kg (12 lb). The body is long, on short sturdy legs, with a fairly short ringed tail. The coat is medium brown, with dark spots which lead some zoologists to suggest that it is a subspecies of the leopard cat. Others have noted a resemblance to the South American kodkod, which has led to speculation about an evolutionary link. The answer is more likely, however, to be that similar species evolving in similar habitats and climates inevitably take on the same characteristics. The Iriomote cat's head and neck are barred with dark stripes.

> **CAT FACT:**
> Having round pupils instead of elliptical or slit shaped pupils is indicative of a more diurnal hunting activity where eyes are not so sensitive to bright light.

> **CAT FACT:**
> Cats often have noticeably conspicuous tips to their tails. They act as markers to help young cats keep with them when moving through undergrowth or tall grasses.

Left
This Malaysian marbled cat resembles a small leopard.

Bottom left
The Temminck's golden cat is renowned for being aggressive and fearless

Middle
This flat-headed cat is rarely seen in the wild because of its limited numbers and its reclusive nature.

Bottom right
This Malaysian flat-headed cat has a low body and a thick coat.

Temminck's Golden Cat

TEMMINCK'S GOLDEN CAT, *Felis temminckii*, known also as the Asian or Asiatic golden cat, lives in the mountains and forests of the eastern Himalayas, extending south-eastwards to southern China. It is also found on the Indonesian island of Sumatra.

HABITAT

TEMMINCK'S GOLDEN CAT favours humid environments. It is fierce and fearless and attacks larger prey such as small deer, sheep, goats and even small water buffaloes. It is given various local names: in China it is known as the rock cat or the yellow leopard, in Myanmar (formerly Burma) as the fire cat, and in various parts of south-east Asia as the tiger cat. Although apparently related to the African golden cat, it seems to have developed separately in Asia and is larger than its African cousin.

CHARACTERISTICS

A REMARKABLY HANDSOME, long-legged and very long-tailed cat, its thick coat is a solid dark golden brown, sometimes shading to a dark grey, with white, black-edged face markings. Its short, round ears are black on the back, spotted with grey. A subspecies found in Burma and Tibet is more heavily marked with dark spots or stripes on the body, and black individuals have also been reported.

The species has been hunted in the past, but deforestation, especially in Nepal and Sumatra, now poses a greater threat.

Temminck's golden cat weighs from 12–14 kg (26.5–35 lb). Some cat experts claim that it is somewhere in the ancestry of the Siamese, but although there is something Oriental about the lines of the golden cat the theory has not been proved.

Conrad Temminck was a Dutch naturalist who lived from 1778–1858 and wrote one of the first comprehensive manuals of ornithology. He spent his early life in Sumatra (then part of the Dutch East Indies), where he identified the Asiatic golden cat, and later became director of the major Dutch natural history museum at Leiden.

Flat-headed Cat

THE FLAT-HEADED CAT, *Felis planiceps*, is another rarity, found only in Thailand, Borneo, Malaysia and Sumatra.

CHARACTERISTICS

IT IS INDEED flat-headed, with ears set far apart and a notably pointed muzzle. Its body is long and low, on short legs, with a short, thick tail. Weighing 5.5–8 kg (12–18 lb), it has a reddish-brown coat, sometimes tipped with grey or silvery white, with thick black markings across its face and brown-spotted underparts. The coat is thick and long.

The flat-headed cat favours environments close to water, and fish form a large part of its diet, supplemented by frogs and waterfowl.

While its claws are not as fully exposed as the fishing cat's, they retract only partially so that their tips remain visible, and this may be related to the flat-headed cat's adeptness at fishing.

Its limited and inaccessible habitat and its reclusive nature mean that little is known about this species in the wild, although a few individuals have been studied in captivity. Equally, little is known about its relative growth or decline as a species.

Chinese Desert Cat

IN 1889 HENRI, Prince of Orleans and a member of the family of pretenders to the French throne, set out on an expedition through Siberia and Tibet to Thailand, then known as Siam. The Tibetan authorities refused his party permission to visit the country, and he was forced to divert across the mountains to the Chinese province of Sichuan in the Yangtze basin. There, Prince Henri was shown two skins of the Chinese desert cat, *Felis bieti*, and he and scientists in the party wrote up a description of the species from these skins and from local reports. Almost all that is known of the Chinese desert cat is derived from this description.

HABITAT

THE CHINESE DESERT CAT apparently inhabits a relatively small area of mountainous western China up to an altitude of about 3,000 m (10,000 ft). It weighs about 5.5 kg (12 lb).

CHARACTERISTICS

DESCRIPTIONS OF ITS coat vary from brownish-red to yellowish-grey. It may be that since it lives in the mountains the colour varies according to the season. There are broken stripes of dark spots running vertically down the flanks, and similar markings on the cheeks. The tail is ringed and tipped with black. The pads are well-tufted and there are also short tufts of hair on the tips of the ears.

> **CAT FACT:**
> The hyoid is a small bone in the throat. In small cats it is ossified and held rigid. In big cats it is only partially ossified and flexible, enabling them to roar.

Bottom
This angry Chinese desert cat displays its ferocity by bearing its long, canine teeth.

Small Cats of Africa

Sand Cat

IT IS NOTICEABLE that Africa lacks the rich diversity of small cat species found in South America and south-east Asia, although the equatorial forests might be expected to provide equally rich habitats for tree-hunting species. The answer may lie in competition from other carnivores, notably the leopard and hyena. But if the typical small cat of South America and south-east Asia is the tree-hunter, that of Africa is the cat able to survive on the fringes of the desert, an environment which larger species would disdain.

THE DISTRIBUTION of the sand cat, *Felis margarita*, is unusual in that it is discrete and patchy. The largest population is in the western Sahara, with smaller groups in Egypt, southern Arabia, Turkestan and smallest of all in western Pakistan, where the species is considered endangered. What these areas have in common is that they are all arid, with either sandy or rocky terrain.

Above
The presence of the leopard on the African continent has signified that smaller cat species have been prohibited from flourishing.

Bottom
The small sand cat has a soft, thick, yellow-brown coat.

CHARACTERISTICS

THE SAND CAT, also known as the sand-dune cat, is small, weighing only about 2 kg (4.5 lb). It has a soft, thick coat, yellow-brown or grey-brown, darker across the back and off-white on the underparts. There are darker markings on the legs and the tail carries three rings with a black tip. The head is disproportionately large for the body, and squarish in shape with prominent ears set low and particularly prominent whiskers. The ears are an interesting feature. Not only are the pinnae or ear flaps unusually large, but the internal ear mechanism is also enlarged. It has been suggested that the two adaptations together make it easier for the sand cat to detect the slight sounds made by the desert creatures which are its prey. Another unusual feature of the sand cat is a generous growth of hair up to 2 cm (0.75 in) long forming mats covering its paw pads. These mats protect the pads from the scorching heat of the desert sand and prevent them from sinking into the loose surface.

THE YOUNG SAND CAT

PREGNANT FEMALES dig a burrow in the sand for their litters, which average four kittens but may be as many as eight. The kittens weigh only about 39g (1.4 oz) at birth, but by five weeks they are ready to explore beyond the burrow, rapidly displaying instinctive digging behaviour themselves. Kittens display faint tabby markings which disappear with the growth of the adult coat. They begin to leave the burrow for an independent life from about four months.

HARDY SPECIES

THE SAND CAT is one of the most remarkable examples of the ability of the cat family to survive in the face of huge difficulties. It is born into an inhospitable climate with scarce food resources. It has to live virtually in the open, vulnerable to snakes, wolves and vultures and with few places to hide. Despite the poor resources of its habitat, a mother has to find food for a large litter of kittens whose appetite, given their phenomenal growth rate during the first weeks, must be voracious.

Sand cats burrow into the sand to protect themselves from the heat of the sun during the day, and come out to hunt at dusk. Their low-slung ears enable them to track their prey while remaining inconspicuous even in a landscape with little shelter. Sand cats prey mainly on desert rodents such as jerboas but they also eats birds, lizards and locusts. Their digestive systems are adapted to a waterless habitat; they obtain the liquid they need from their prey and conserve it within their urinary systems.

The sand cat's zoological name, *Felis margarita*, commemorates the French general, Jean Auguste Margueritte, who was responsible in the 1850s and '60s for opening up the western Sahara and claiming it as part of the French Empire.

> **CAT FACT:**
> Of the 41 species of cat (including the domestic), all but two have 30 teeth. Their kittens and cubs however, have only 26 milk teeth.

Top
Native to arid areas, such as the Sahara, the sand cat spends the hottest part of the day buried in the sand.

Bottom
The sand cat can fall prey to wolves and snakes.

Caracal

AMONG AFRICA'S SMALL cats, the caracal, *Felis caracal*, is the largest. Also variously known as the desert lynx (although it does not live in the desert), the caracal lynx and the Persian lynx, it weighs between 16–20 kg (35–44 lb). There is considerable disparity between the sizes of males and females.

Top right
The coat colouring of reddish-brown with white underparts is visible on this South African caracal.

Top left
The pointed ears of the caracal are prominent.

Bottom left and right
Renowned for its ferocious temperament, the caracal is an indiscriminate predator.

HABITAT

THE CARACAL HAS a lynx-like short tail and pointed, tufted ears. It is widespread on grasslands throughout Africa, particularly in South Africa and Uganda. It also inhabits semi-desert and mountain areas, but not true desert or rainforest. The caracal is also found in Arabia, Afghanistan and north-western India.

CHARACTERISTICS

THE CARACAL'S SHORT coat is an overall reddish-brown with white on the chin, throat and underparts and dark markings on the muzzle but no spots on the coat. It is an extremely muscular cat with a good turn of speed and highly developed jumping and climbing skills. Except when mating, it lives a completely solitary life in clearly defined hunting territories, moving by night and hunting by day. Notoriously fierce and predatory, caracals will kill far more prey than they need for food, apparently for the pleasure of killing, and can devastate farm stock. This indiscriminate killing, more typical of wolves and foxes, is unusual in the feline world, most of whose species are concerned only to hunt for their immediate needs.

In the wild, caracals attack lizards, rabbits, birds, antelopes and goats and have even been observed to take on eagles. They catch birds which have just taken off by jumping up and striking out with their paws. The caracal is equally at home in the trees as on the ground and often, like the leopard, drags its kill up a tree to eat at leisure.

BREEDING

ALTHOUGH THEY DO not live in family groups like lions, caracals do appear to have some structure in their social life, at any rate in the mating season which can occur at any time of the year. A female in oestrus will attract a number of males to her territory and they will mate with her one by one in order of dominance, the oldest and largest male first. They then depart to find another willing female elsewhere. The pregnant female finds a sheltered birthing den among rocks or in a hollow and after a gestation period of about 11 weeks gives birth to her litter, usually of two or three, but sometimes up to five, cubs.

The cubhood of the caracal is remarkably short and, by feline standards, unsettled. When they are about four weeks old the mother and cubs leave the birthing den and take up a nomadic life, moving each day to a new refuge in long grass and thickets. From about six months cubs are able to leave the mother and find their own hunting territory, which may be up to 100 km (62 miles) away. The caracal lives for 9–10 years in the wild, but up to twice as long in captivity.

African Wild Cat

THE COMMONEST AFRICAN small cat species is the African wild cat, *Felis libyca*. Whether this is a distinct species from the European wild cat, *Felis silvestris*, has long been a matter of dispute among naturalists, but contemporary opinion seems to favour the distinction. The European form is generally heavier, its coat pattern is generally tabbier and the colour darker, perhaps reflecting the climate of its habitat, the distribution patterns are different and, perhaps most convincingly, the two forms differ considerably in temperament. The European is a more secretive creature, avoiding contact with humans unless driven by extreme hunger, whereas the African seems positively to seek out human settlements – if only because of the food opportunities they afford. Certainly, however, both species share in the ancestry of the domestic cat.

HABITAT

THE AFRICAN WILD cat is found almost everywhere in Africa except in a tract of West Africa corresponding roughly with the basins of the Congo and Niger rivers. It is also common across southern Asia from Arabia to India and, in slightly variant forms, on some Mediterranean islands and in places along the northern shores of the Mediterranean.

CHARACTERISTICS

THE AFRICAN WILD cat weighs 5–6 KG (11–13 lb) and has a lean, muscular body with long legs and a thin but well-furred tail with three ring markings ending in a black tip. The ears are rounded with no

tufts, and when the cat is on the prowl they take on a swept-back appearance as they are pricked for maximum effectiveness. The coat colour ranges from pale grey to greyish-brown, a pale sandy fawn being the most common. The tabby markings on the body become more pronounced on the legs, appearing as brown rings.

TAMEABLE SPECIES

IN ITS NATURAL habitat, the African wild cat preys on a wide range of small creatures such as rodents, snakes, lizards, birds and even insects. But its long relationship with humankind began with its discovery that settlements in Ancient Egypt, with their fields and stores of grain, provided a rich harvest of easily caught small rodents. From then on, the relationship developed into one of mutual appreciation. The African wild cat is not as reclusive as its European cousin, and in particular not so resistant to human company. Whereas the kittens of the European wild cat are born, and remain, wild and untameable, those of the African take easily to domestication. Even today, the African wild cat lives in harmony with farmers in many an Egyptian settlement.

The gestation period for the African wild cat can be as short as eight weeks. Three or four is a typical litter size, and the kittens are mature at one year.

CAT FACT:
Smilodon, a sabre-toothed prehistoric cat, is known from some 2,000 fossilised skeletons, because it used to hunt prey stuck in dangerous tar pits.

Top
This African wild cat kitten defends its nest, it is, however, tameable.

Bottom
This ubiquitous African cat has a lean, muscular body.

Serval

THE SERVAL, *Felis serval*, is found throughout Africa except in the deserts, but is most common in central Africa. Observations suggest that its distribution is gradually shrinking, especially in North Africa where it is regarded as endangered.

CHARACTERISTICS

WEIGHING BETWEEN 13.5–18 kg (30–40 lb), it finds its favoured habitats in forests near rivers where it can lie in wait in dense undergrowth for small antelope and birds such as guinea-fowl. However, it has adapted well to living near human settlements and is a notorious raider of poultry runs and farmyards. Partly because of this, and partly because of its attractive coat, the serval is hunted extensively.

It is a graceful, elegant animal with a slender, agile build, long legs, a short tail, and large ears pricked attentively forward. Uniquely in the cat family, the front legs are longer than the hind legs, giving it a characteristic bounding movement in the chase. Its coat is generally orange-brown, shading to white on the underparts, but servals living at higher altitudes tend to have paler, yellowish-buff coats. Indeed, this difference in coats is so marked that at one time naturalists considered that the animals with paler colours were a separate species which they called the servaline, but this theory is now discredited. The ground colour in all servals is overlaid with black markings which vary in intensity, size and shape, again apparently depending on habitat.

Servals in forested areas have smaller, discrete black spots, while those living in grassland have markings which merge to form stripes on the neck, back and flanks. The markings form rings or bars on the legs, and the ringed tail ends in a black tip. Some black or partially black examples have been reported, especially in more temperate, wetter regions such as the Kenya highlands.

HUNTING INSTINCTS

THE SERVAL IS skilled at both stalking and ambush, and uses both methods to find its prey. It is said that its large ears are adept at detecting the sounds made by mole rats, one of its favourite victims, underground, which are then dug out. Servals have a habit of standing still, listening intently with their ears directed to a suspected source of food. Other prey includes birds, young antelopes, lizards, birds and frogs. The end of the day is the serval's favourite time for hunting, punctuated by a longish period of sleep in the middle of the day and a shorter one at dead of night.

Servals have a reputation for viciousness, but perhaps this has been fostered as an excuse for hunting them. They are certainly extremely vocal with hisses and spits if their food is threatened or they are cornered. On the other hand, there are accounts of servals that have been successfully domesticated.

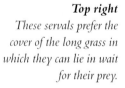

Top right
These servals prefer the cover of the long grass in which they can lie in wait for their prey.

Top left
The serval is a graceful cat with a slender build.

Bottom
Typical behaviour of the serval is to sit and listen intently for prey.

their birth weight within 10–11 days. They leave to establish their own territories at about one year old, being driven out of the nest by their mothers if they show no inclination to move for themselves. This is a testing time for the young serval, which often has to make several attempts to establish a territory before it finds one where it is not encroaching on a rival's. Serval territories are not large, but they are fiercely defended.

The serval is a superb athlete. It is said to be able to jump up to three metres (10 feet) into a tree. It has a good turn of speed over short distances, and can also climb and, if necessary, swim. Its main enemy, apart from humans, is the leopard which, unless surprised, it can usually escape by swift footwork.

BREEDING

MALE AND FEMALE servals come together only in the February to April period when they mate. The pregnant serval will find the burrow or den of another creature and take it over, driving out the resident if necessary, or make a nest of dry leaves at the foot of a tree. Two or three is the normal litter size. The kittens are small but chubby, and double

> **CAT FACT:**
> Lions, tigers, leopards and jaguars all have circular eye pupils. They all hunt during the day as well as night, to take full advantage of opportunities.

Top
This serval is hissing, a typical reaction to danger in this vocal species.

Bottom
These two serval will stay with the mother until they are one year old when they leave to establish their own territories.

African Golden Cat

Top
The head is petite but attractively shaped giving the animal an amiable appearance.

Bottom right
This beautiful and mystical creature forms part of the local African folklore.

Bottom left
The African golden cat often inhabits the same territory as the leopard, resulting in them competing for food.

THE AFRICAN GOLDEN cat, *Felis aurata*, is a cat of western and central equatorial Africa from the west coast of Senegal eastwards to the forests of Kenya. It is an extremely beautiful creature, normally coloured golden brown, with a suggestion of a double sized and handsome domestic shorthair. Not surprisingly, it has a place in the folklore of the tribes which share its habitat. Its skins were once reserved for the robes of native chieftains, and carrying its tail as a lucky charm was supposed by pygmy tribes in the Cameroons to ensure success in elephant-hunting.

HABITAT

THE AFRICAN GOLDEN cat is closely related to the Asian golden cat, *Felis temmincki*, although their habitats are at the extremes of Africa and south-east Asia respectively. It has been suggested that, perhaps a million or more years ago, they were a single species inhabiting a swathe of Africa and Asia along the Equator, and that climatic change produced the arid conditions of the Middle East and so divided them. Certainly they both choose similar forested habitats.

CHARACTERISTICS

WEIGHING UP TO 5–12 kg (11-26 lb), the African golden cat varies in both the ground colour and the degree of marking on its coat. Some have hardly any visible markings except on the legs and tail, while others are densely spotted over the entire body. Some have a dark line running down the back and tail, while in others the tail is ringed.

The ground colour ranges from a true golden red to silvery grey. The African golden cat is compact and gives an impression of strength and muscular power. It is long-legged with large paws. The head is relatively small and the ears are rounded. It is equally at home on the ground or in trees but tends to take to the trees to sleep.

HUNTING INSTINCT

THE AFRICAN GOLDEN cat's favoured habitat happens to coincide with that of the leopard, which brings the two species into competition for prey and can lead to fierce confrontation. But while the golden cat will take a young antelope if the chance comes along, it is more likely to prey on rodents and birds. It also raids farms for poultry.

Solitary and reclusive, the African golden cat has been little studied in the wild. It apparently has a relatively long gestation period, up to 11 weeks, after which a litter of one or two kittens is born. These develop quickly and begin to play hunting games under their mother's supervision at about three weeks. They are mature at about 18 months.

Black-footed Cat

THE BLACK-FOOTED cat, *Felis nigripes*, is the smallest African member of the cat family, males typically weighing less than 2 kg (4.5 lb), and females no more than 1.5 kg (3.25 lb). It has an extremely restricted distribution, being found only in the semi-desert and grassland of south-west Africa, mainly on the Kalahari Desert.

CHARCTERISTICS

THE BLACK-FOOTED cat gets its name from the barred markings on its legs which deepen to black on its feet. Its ground body colour is light yellowish-brown, with rows of dark spots which merge across the neck and shoulders to form stripes and turn to bars on the legs. The tail is ringed and black-tipped.

Black-footed cats, living in open country, seem aware of their vulnerability to other carnivores. If threatened, they make great displays of defiance, but they tend to avoid danger by 'squatting' in other creatures' secure homes to make their dens. The burrows of spring hares and even the nests of termites are often taken over for this purpose.

BREEDING

THE SEXUAL LIFE of the species needs to be precisely timed. Females are in oestrus for only 5–10 hours (compared with 6–10 days in a domestic cat and up to 14 days in cheetahs), which means that a male must be very close for mating to take place. Females are therefore very vocal during oestrus, and their cries are said to carry over remarkable distances. As with most cats, the male disappears after mating, and in about nine weeks a litter of one or two kittens is born. As they are tiny, they are extremely vulnerable to predators, and kittenhood is a time of tension for both generations. The mother removes her kittens from the nest as soon as possible and takes them with her on hunting forays, hiding them under grasses and shrub. The kittens can purr from birth, and in the early weeks the purrs of mother and young provide continuous assurance that all is well. If threatened while the mother is absent, the kittens 'freeze' until her purring reassures them. By six weeks, they are starting to hunt and catch their own food, but they are relatively late – over one year and sometimes up to 18 months – before they leave the mother and go out to fend for themselves.

LEGENDARY SPECIES

THE BLACK-FOOTED cat has acquired a curious and incredible legendary status which seems to arise from the hearsay of just one observer, a South African government official in Bechuanaland, E. E. Cronje Wilmot. He reported that the cat attacked sheep by leaping on their backs, fastening onto their necks and hanging there until the jugular vein was pierced. This is unlikely enough, but Wilmot went on to say that local tribesmen reported black-footed cats as killing giraffes in the same way.

CAT FACT:
The cat is responsible for the extinction of many mammals and birds over the past 300 years, but only because people introduced them to foreign locations.

CAT FACT:
Female cats, like other mammals, feed their young with milk secreted from mammae. Some cat species have two pairs, others have four pairs.

Bottom right
The black markings on the legs of this cat, after which the species is named, are visible on this cat.

Bottom left
The black-footed cat inhabits semi-arid regions on the margins of the Kalahari Desert.

Useful Addresses

CAT FANCY ORGANISATIONS

AUSTRALIA
Co-ordinating Cat Council of Australia (CCC of A)
GPO Box 4317
Sydney NSW 2001

Feline Association of South Australia (FASA)
PO Box 104, Stirling
South Australia 5152

BRITAIN
Cat Association of Britain (CAB)
Mill House
Letcombe Regis
Wantage
Oxfordshire OX12 9JD

Governing Council of the Cat Fancy (GCCF)
4–6 Penel Orlieu, Bridgwater
Somerset TA6 3PG

CANADA
Canadian Cat Association (CCA)
52 Dean Street, Brampton
Ontario L6W 1M6

EUROPE
Fédération International Féline (FIFé)
23 Doerhavelaan
Eindhoven 5644 BB
Netherlands.

NEW ZEALAND
New Zealand Cat Fancy (NZCF)
PO Box 3167
Richmond, Nelson

SOUTH AFRICA
Governing Council of the Associated Cat Clubs of South Africa
45 Edison Drive
Meadowridge 7800

USA
American Cat Association (ACA)
8101 Katherine Avenue
Panorama City CA 91402

American Cat Fanciers' Association (ACFA)
PO Box 203
Point Lookout MO 65726

Cat Fanciers' Association (CFA)
PO Box 1005
Manasquan
NJ 08736

Cat Fanciers' Federation (CFF)
PO Box 661
Gratis OH 45330

The International Cat Association (TICA)
PO Box 2684
Harlingen TX 78551

United Cat Federation (UCF)
6621 Thornwood Street
San Diego CA 92111

ANIMAL WELFARE ORGANISATIONS

American Humane Association
5351 South Roslyn Street
Englewood CO 80111, USA

Canadian Society for the Prevention of Cruelty to Animals
5214 Jean-Talon Street West
Montreal
Quebec H4P 1X4,
Canada

Royal Society for the Prevention of Cruelty to Animals
The Manor House
Horsham
West Sussex RH12 1HG, UK

Scottish Society for the Prevention of Cruelty to Animals
19 Melville Street
Edinburgh EH3 7PL, Scotland

MAGAZINES AND PERIODICALS

BRITAIN
Cats Magazine
Our Dogs Publishing Co Ltd
5 James Leigh Street, Manchester
M1 5NF

Cat World
Avalon Court
Star Road, Partridge Green
West Sussex RH13 8RY

All About Cats
27 Lark Ave
Moormede
Staines, Middx
TW18 4RX

Show Cats
Avalon Court
Star Road, Partridge Green
West Sussex RH13 8RY

The Cat
Cats Protection League
17 Kings Road
Horsham
West Sussex RH13 5PN

USA
Cats, PO Box 290037
Port Orange FL 32129

Cat Fanciers' Almanac
PO Box 1005
Manasquan NJ 08736

Cat World International
PO Box 35635
Phoenix AZ 85069

ADVICE SERVICES

American Feline Society
41 Union Square West
New York City NY 10003, USA

American Humane Association
5351 South Roslyn Street
Englewood CO 80111, USA

Feline Advisory Bureau
235 Upper Richmond Road
London SW15 6SN, UK

Pedigree Petfoods Education Centre
Stanhope House
Stanhope Place
London W2 2HH, UK

CAT MUSEUMS

Katzen Museum
Baselstrasse 101
4125 Riehen/Basel
Switzerland

Musee du Chat
Rue d'Eglise
70880 Ainvelle, France

SHELTERING AND RE-HOMING

Cats Protection League
17 King's Road, Horsham
West Sussex RH13 5PN, UK

Wood Green Animal Shelters
King's Bush Farm
London Road, Godmanchester
Cambridgeshire PE18 8LJ, UK

The Dogs' Home
4 Battersea Park Road
London SW8 4AA, UK

Animal Welfare Trust
Tyler's Way, Watford
Herts WD2 8HQ, UK

Blue Cross Animals' Hospital
Hugh Street
London SW1V 1QQ, UK

Celia Hammond Animal Trust
High Street
Wadhurst
East Sussex TN15 6AG, UK

Delta Society
321 Burnett Avenue South
Third Floor
Renton
Washington 98055, USA

Identicat Scotland
14 Thistle Street
Cowdenbeath
Fife KY4 8NF, Scotland

San Francisco Society for the Prevention of Cruelty to Animals
2500 East 16th Street
San Francisco CA 94103, USA

Voluntary Animal Welfare Society
53 Braeside Avenue
Patcham
Brighton BN1 8RL, UK

Lost and found
National Petwatch
PO Box 16, Brighouse
West Yorkshire HD6 1DS, UK

Petsearch UK
851 Old Lode Lane
Solihull
West Midlands, UK

Selected Bibliography

Roberta Altman, *The Quintessential Cat* (Blandford 1994)

Dr John Bradshaw, *The True Nature of the Cat* (Boxtree 1993)

David Burn and Chris Bell, *Cats* (Brockhampton 1997)

Jill Caravan, *An Identification Guide to Cat Breeds* (Quintet 1991)

Dr Bruce Fogle, *The Encyclopedia of the Cat* (Dorling Kindersley 1997)

Desmond Morris, *Cat World* (Ebury Press 1996)

Peter Neville and Claire Bessant, *The Perfect Kitten* (Hamlyn 1997)

Grace Pond and Ivor Raleigh, *A Standard Guide to Cat Breeds* (Macmillan 1979)

Angela Sayer, *The Complete Book of the Cat* (Octopus 1984)

Marcus Schneck and Jill Caravan, *Cat Facts* (Quarto 1990)

Anna and Michael Sproule, *The Complete Cat* (Prion 1988)

Roger Tabor, *Understanding Cats* (David & Charles 1995)

Roger Tabor, *The Wildlife of the Domestic Cat* (Arrow 1984)

Meredith D. Wilson, *Encyclopedia of American Cat Breeds* (TFH Publications, regularly updated)

Michael Wright and Sally Walters, *The Book of the Cat* (Pan 1981)

Glossary

Abyssinian tabby
See ticked tabby.

Acinonyx
The genus of Felidae which includes only one species, the cheetah.

Adolescent
In British showing, a cat between 9–15 months old.

Agouti
The ground colour between a tabby's stripes.

Alleles
Pairs of genes that produce alternative physical characteristics (e.g. the longhair/shorthair genes).

Alley cat
A non-pedigree cat.

Amino-acids
Organic compounds which are the component molecules of proteins.

Animal protein
Body-building constituents of the diet derived from meat, fish and animal products such as milk.

Animal shelter
An organisation which looks after strays and other homeless pets and finds new homes for them.

Antibodies
Substances produced in the blood which neutralise or destroy bacterial infections.

Awn hairs
The secondary hairs in a cat's coat which are bristly with thickened tips.

Back-crossing
Mating a cat to one of its parents.

Bacteria
Micro-organisms, some of which produce disease.

Barred markings
Dark stripes.

Bi-colour
A patched coat of white and one other colour.

Bile
Fluid in the digestive system which aids the digestion of fats.

Bite
The meeting of upper and lower teeth when the mouth is closed.

Blaze
Marking in the centre of the forehead.

Blotched tabby
See classic tabby.

Boarding cattery
establishment where cats are cared for in the absence of their owners.

Body language
Movements of parts of the body which convey meaning.

Booster
The injection of a vaccine to maintain immunisation against disease given by a previous dose.

Break
A change in direction of the nose, also called the stop.

Breeches
long hair on the upper part of the hind legs.

Breed
A group of cats with common ancestry and similar physical characteristics.

Calico
US term for tortoiseshell and white.

Canine teeth
Sharp, pointed teeth at the front of the mouth, two in the upper jaw and two in the lower.

Carnassial teeth
Teeth at the extreme sides of the jaw.

Carnivore
Meat-eating animal.

Cat fancy
Organisations of pedigree cat breeders, exhibitors and owners.

'Cat flu'
Common term for feline upper respiratory virus infections.

Catnip (*Nepeta cataria*)
A herb whose scent is attractive to cats.

Cell
The basic structural unit of all living things.

Cerebellum
The area of the brain which controls movement and balance.

Championship status
The second highest level of awards at a show.

'Chintz cat'
Term formerly used in Britain for the tortoiseshell and white cat.

Cholesterol
A chemical occurring naturally in the body which is converted by sunlight to vitamin D.

Chromosomes
Thread-like structures within living cells which carry molecules of DNA and control heredity.

Classic
Conforming entirely with the body type defined in breed standards.

Classic tabby
A cat with clearly defined broad stripes on a lighter agouti ground.

Cobby
Short and compact.

Coccyx
The last vertebra of the spine.

Colourpointing
Having a deeper shade of the body colour on the ears, nose, feet and tail.

Conformation
Body type, size and shape; also known as type.

Congenital
Inherited or resulting from abnormal development in the womb.

Crossbreeding
The mating of cats of two different breeds.

Declawing
The surgical removal of a cat's claws.

Digitigrade
Walking on tip-toe.

Dilute gene
A gene which results in a paler coloured coat.

Dinictis
A group of prehistoric carnivores from which the Felidae evolved.

Displacement activity
An activity carried on to distract the sufferer's attention at a time of stress.

DNA
Abbreviation for deoxyribonucleic acid, which is contained in chromosomes and is responsible for the transmission of hereditary characteristics from one generation to the next.

Domestic class
A class for household pets at a show.

Dominant gene
A gene which passes on a physical characteristic even if it is in the genotype of only one parent.

Down hair
The short, soft hair forming the undercoat.

Entire
Not neutered.

Fault
A departure from the breed standard resulting in the loss of points at a show.

Felidae
The order of mammals consisting of the genera *Panthera, Acinonyx, Neofelis* and *Felis*.

Felis
The genus known as the small cats.

Femur
The upper bone of the hind leg.

Feral
Living wild but descended from domestic cats.

Flanks
The sides of the body.

Flehmen behaviour
A grimacing expression, where the cat tests airborne chemicals using the Jacobson's organ.

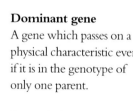

Follicle
The point on the skin from which a hair grows.

Foreign
Fine-boned and elegant, also known as Oriental.

Frills
Long hair growing from the chest between the front legs.

Frost
US term for a pinkish dove grey also known as lilac or lavender.

Gene
A unit of heredity which determines an organism's physical characteristics, growth and function.

Gene pool
The extent of genetic variety in a given group of cats, especially a single breed.

Genotype
The set of genes inherited from both parents.

Gloves
Markings on the paws.

Guard hairs the long, bristly hairs making up the outercoat.

Hairball a mass of compressed hair which has been ingested, sometimes called a furball.

Haw
The third eyelid.

Heredity
The process by which physical and other characteristics are passed on from one generation to the next.

Hertz (Hz)
The unit of sound frequency, measured in cycles per second.

Heterozygous
Having two different alleles for a particular characteristic, one from each parent.

Himmy
Himalayan.

Hocks
The joint on a cat's hind legs corresponding to the ankle in humans.

Home range
The inner area of a cat's territory.

Homozygous
Having identical alleles from each parent for a particular characteristic.

Household quality
Term used by breeders for pedigree kittens which are not of sufficient quality to be shown or used as breeding stock.

Humerus
The upper bones of the front legs.

Hunting range
The outer area of a cat's territory where it will hunt but not settle.

Hybrid breed
A breed originally produced by crossing two other breeds.

Inbreeding
The mating of parents to offspring or of siblings.

Incisors
The teeth between the canines, six in each jaw.

Jacobson's organ
Also known as the vomero-nasal organ; found at the back of the mouth and sensitive to airborne chemicals. Responsible for a combined 'taste-smell' sense.

Jugular vein
Vein in the neck that returns blood to the heart from the head.

Junior
British show term for cats over 15 months but under two years old.

Laces
Markings extending from the paws up the back legs almost to the hocks.

Ligament
Fibrous tissue forming part of the joints in the body.

Litter
(1) The kittens born to a queen at one episode of labour (2) Material used to line a tray into which cats can defecate and urinate indoors.

Lordosis
The crouched position in which a queen presents herself to indicate that she is ready for intercourse.

Lynx (coat colour)
US term for tabby point.

Mackerel tabby
Coat pattern with narrow stripes extending down the spine and flanks.

Marbled
Coat pattern with irregular dark blotches and stripes on a lighter ground.

Marsupial
A mammal that is born immature and continues its development in the pouch of the mother.

Mask
The dark-coloured parts of the face.

Melanin
The pigment which colours the hair and skin.

Membrane
Thin body tissue.

Metabolism
The chemical processes in an organism which control growth and functions.

Miacid
A prehistoric tree-dwelling creature.

Mitted
With white markings on the front and hind paws.

Moggie
An affectionate British term for a non-pedigree cat; also moggy.

Moult
To shed hair.

Mucous membrane
A membrane coated with fluid that lines passages in the body that are open to the air.

Muscular
Term applied to breeds such as the Rex breeds whose body form falls between cobby and lithe in type.

Mutation
A change in a gene which results in a change in hereditary characteristics between two generations, also known as a rogue gene.

Muzzle
The nose and jaws.

Natural breed
A breed that has evolved on its own without human intervention.

Necklaces
Stripes encircling the chest and upper neck.

Neutered
Castrated or spayed.

Nocturnal
Active by night.

Non-pedigree
One or both parents unknown or unregistered.

Nose leather
See nose pad.

Nose pad
The hardened skin surrounding the nostrils.

Nurture
The training of young by their parents.

Nutrient
Substance that contributes to the growth, development and maintenance of a living creature.

Odd-eyed
With one eye of one colour and the other of another colour.

Oestrus
The period in which a queen can be successfully mated, also known as calling or being on heat.

Olfactory
Related to the sense of smell.

Oriental
See foreign.

Out-crosses
Deliberate crosses with another breed.

Ovulate
To release eggs during oestrus.

Pack animal
An animal that lives in a social group which has a leader.

Panthera
The genus of Felidae which consists of the six large cat species.

Parasite
A creature that lives on or inside another and feeds off its host's tissues.

Patched tabby
US term for tortie-tabby.

Pedigree certificate
A document issued by a cat registration organisation stating the ancestry of the cat and accepting it as a pedigree cat.

Pet quality
Another breeder's term for household quality.

Pinna
The ear flap (plural = pinnae).

Placenta
The organ connecting the unborn kitten to the lining of the mother's womb through which it receives oxygen and nutrients; discharged as the afterbirth.

Plantigrade
Walking on the soles of the feet.

Points
The head, ears, feet and tail.

Polydactyl
Having more than five toes

Predatory
Habitually hunting and killing other animals for food.

Polygenes
Groups of genes that act together to produce hereditary characteristics.

Preliminary recognition
The stage in the recognition of a breed where specimens may be exhibited but are not eligible for competition.

Protein
Chemical compounds associated with the growth and maintenance of the body.

Provisional recognition
The stage in the recognition of a breed where specimens may compete in shows, but not in championship classes.

Quarantine kennels
Boarding catteries in certain countries where cats are kept in isolation for a period to ensure that they are free from rabies and other infections.

Receptor
A nerve ending that receives information through the sense organs and transmits it to the brain; also called sensors.

Recessive gene
A gene that will pass on a characteristic only if another identical gene appears in the allele.

Recognition
The acceptance by a cat fancy organisation of a breed or colour variety.

Reflex action
An automatic response to a stimulus; for example, a cat's purr.

Registration
Recording the details of a pedigree kitten's birth and ancestry with an official registration body.

Ringed (tail)
Marked with circular rings extending round the tail.

Ring-spotted
Marked with spots grouped in rings.

Ringworm
A fungal infection resulting in circular patches of inflamed and flaking skin.

Rosette
Spots arranged in a circular pattern enclosing a patch of the basic coat colour.

Ruff
Long hair round the neck.

Sabre-toothed cat
A prehistoric carnivore distinguished by its long curved upper canine teeth, also known as *Smilodon*.

Scapula
Shoulder blade.

Sebaceous glands
Organs in the skin secreting an oily substance known as sebum which lubricates the hair and gives protection against bacterial infection.

Self (colour)
British term for a coat of a single colour, known in North America as solid.

Semi-longhair
British term for breeds of cats which have hair longer than shorthairs but shorter than longhairs.

Senior
Term used in British show circles for cats over two years old.

Sex-linked
A characteristic such as the tortoiseshell coat which is associated more with one sex than another.

Shaded
Coat which shows a gradual variation in colour from one part of the body to another.

Shock
Collapse caused by a failure of circulation or severe lowering of the blood pressure.

Small intestine
The part of the digestive system where the breakdown of food into nutrients and waste matter takes place.

Smoke
Coat colouring in which the roots of the hair are pale and the remainder coloured.

Snub nose
A nose which is fore-shortened and turned up.

Solid (colour)
US term for a coat of a single colour, known in Britain as self.

Spayed
Neutered, of a female.

Spina bifida
A congenital abnormality of the spine formation which results in paralysis.

Split foot
Division of the front paws as a result of a bone deformation.

Spontaneous mutation
An alteration for unknown reasons in genetic makeup between one generation and the next.

Spotted tabby
Tabby in which the stripes are broken into discrete spots.

Spottie
Popular term for the spotted tabby.

Standard
The specification laid down by a cat fancy organisation for an ideal specimen of a certain breed.

Standard shell
US term for light tipping, mainly on the head and body.

Standard tipped
British term for standard shell.

Stocky
Thick-set.

Stud tail
A greasy condition at the base of the tail caused by over-active sebaceous glands.

Subspecies
A division within a species with slightly different characteristics, usually caused by the isolation of its members.

Tabby
With a striped, blotched or spotted coat.

Tabby-tortie
A tortoiseshell with tabby markings.

Tapetum lucidum
The reflecting layer at the back of the cat's eye whose function is to increase the intensity of vision.

Territory
The area within which a cat lives and hunts.

Ticked
Colouring at the tips of the coat hairs which gives a flecked effect.

Ticked tabby
Coat with tabby markings on the face, legs and tail and a ticked effect on the body.

Tipped
All-over colouring of the ends of the coat hairs.

Torbie
Tabby tortoiseshell, known in North America as patched tabby and in Britain also as tortie-tabby.

Tortie
Tortoiseshell.

Tortie-tabby
See torbie.

Tortoiseshell
Patched coat pattern usually made up of black and orange but also seen in other mixtures of colours.

Type
See conformation.

Typey
US term to describe a cat which conforms exactly with the body type defined in the breed standard.

Umbilical cord
The tube connecting a kitten to its mother before and during birth which supplies oxygen and nutrients and carries away waste products.

Undercoat
The layer of the coat consisting of down hairs.

Valerian
(*Valeriana officinalis*) Also known as allheal, a plant whose scent is attractive to cats.

Variety
A division within a breed, usually related to colour.

Vertebral column
Spinal column.

Vestibular apparatus
An organ in the cat's inner ear which enables it to manoeuvre so that if the cat falls it will land on its feet.

Vestigial
A non-functioning remnant of an organ.

Vetting-in
Inspection of cats on arrival at a show by a veterinarian.

Veteran
A term in British show circles for a cat over seven years old.

Viral epidemic
Widespread infectious disease spread by an organism which reproduces within the body.

Weaned
Having had the diet changed from mother's milk to solid food.

Whisker break
See break.

White spotting
Random patches of white on a coloured coat varying from small spots to large white areas.

Wild type
The basic form of a species; in the cat, the wild type is the short-haired brown striped tabby.

Zoonoses
Infections and diseases that can be transmitted to humans from other animals

Picture Credits and Acknowledgements

With thanks to Karen Villabona for valuable editorial assistance.

The publishers would like to point out that veterinary practice differs from country to country and that local medical advice should always be sought.

Anatomical Illustrations by Suzie Green: 12 (tl), 12 (bl), 13 (b), 14 (tr), 14 (bl), 15 (bl), 16 (bl), 20 (tl), 22 (bl), 22 (tl), 30 (tr), 109 (bl), 185 (b) and **General Illustrations** by Jennifer Kenna and Helen Courtney courtesy of Foundry Arts 1999

All pictures are courtesy of Marc Henrie except:

AKG: 126 (t), 139 (br), 141 (t),

Ardea: 205 (tr), Ferrero-Labat: 40 (t), 332 (cr), 336 (tr), 340 (br), 341 (b), 341 (tr), 343 (t), 343 (br), Clem Haagner: 68 (tl), 122 (b), 336 (br), 340 (t), 364 (t), 365 (b), John Daniels: 84 (tl), 242 (tl), 332 (br), P. J. Green: 120 (bl), Kenneth W. Fink: 120 (br), 338 (b), 346 (t), 354 (t), 370 (bl), P. Morris: 123 (tl), 211 (tr), 330 (t), 347 (bl), François Gohier: 127 (b), 330 (bl), 331 (tr), 334 (b), 336 (cl), 340 (bl), 347 (tl), 348 (tl), 348 (tr), 348 (b), 349 (t), 349 (b), 351 (t), 351 (br), 351 (bl), 353 (b), 366 (tl), Peter Stein: 186 (tl), 364 (bl), Yann Arthus-Bertrand: 195 (br), 272 (b), 282 (bl), 334 (t), Jean Paul Ferrero: 205 (br), 342 (br), 342 (t), 344 (tl), 347 (br), Ian Beames: 205 (tl), 352 (t), 354 (br), Stefan Meyers: 211 (tl), 344 (tr), M. Watson: 246 (tl), 249 (t), 332 (bl), 337 (l), 337 (r), 339 (b), 339 (t), 343 (bl), 344 (br), 350 (br), 121 (l), 366 (tr), 367 (t), J. M. Labat: 275 (tl), Chuck McDonald: 332 (t), Nick Gordon: 333 (tl), 333 (tr), 333 (br), 346 (b), 352 (b), 353 (tl), Wardene Weisser: 333 (bl), 336 (bl), Caroline Weaver: 335 (b), Martin W. Grosnick: 336 (tl), 362 (tl), Joanna Van Gruisen: 338 (t), 354 (bl), Adrian Warren: 341 (tl), Dennis Avon: 345 (tl), Chris Martin Bahr: 358, Alan Weaving: 365 (t), Richard Waver: 368 (t), Chris Harvey: 369 (r), 369 (l),

Bridgeman Art Library: 138 (r), 280 (tl),

Cogis: Dr/Cogis: 38 (t), 65 (bl), Schwartz/Cogis: 17 (tl), 23 (b), 42 (t), 94 (tr), 151 (tl), 156 (tr), 170 (bl), 266 (b), 269 (b), 271 (br), 283 (b), 335 (t), Vedie/Cogis: 17 (b), Lanceau/Cogis: 26 (t), 151 (br), 152 (bl), 166 (b), 170 (t), 173 (t), 243 (tr), 245 (tr), 245 (tl), 256 (t), 257 (b), 258 (bl), 261 (b), 273 (t), 282 (br), 325, 382,

Hermeline/Cogis: 46 (tr), 147 (tr), 171 (br), 172 (b), 266 (tr), 267 (t), 279 (b), 320 (b), 320 (tl), 320 (tr), Gissey/Cogis: 47 (b), 332 (cl), 342 (bl), Varin/Cogis: 102 (bl), 366 (b), 367 (b), Francais/Cogis: 149 (br), 151 (tr), 152 (br), 153 (t), 153 (b), 166 (t), 167 (bl), 167 (br), 167 (tl), 167 (c), 173 (b), 208 (l), 243 (tl), 257 (t), 260 (bl), 260 (br), 261 (t), 267 (b), 280 (tr), 371, Bernie/Cogis: 155 (t), 178 (br), Vidal/Cogis: 168 (b), 168 (t), 171 (t), 172 (t), Alexis/Cogis: 170 (br), Excalibur/Cogis: 171 (bl), 258 (t), 258 (br), 259 (b), 259 (c), 259 (t), 260 (t), 266 (tl), 276 (tr), 281 (b), 282 (t), 283 (t), Labat/Cogis: 274 (b), Lili/Cogis: 331 (b), 364 (br),

Dorling Kindersley: 240 (tl), 240 (b), 241 (b),

Giraudon: 124 (bl),

Mary Evans: 122 (tr), 124 (t), 126 (b), 127 (t), 128 (t), 129 (t), 129 (b), 131 (tl), 131 (tr), 131 (br), 131 (bl), 133 (t), 134, 135 (bl), 136 (t), 136 (br), 139 (t), 140 (bl), 141 (bl), 146 (b), 146 (t), 148 (r), 197 (br), 281 (t),

Paul Dawson: 11 (br),

Pictorial Press: 140 (br), 140 (t), 145 (br), 376 (t),

Still Pictures: Roland Seitre /Still Pictures: 21 (t), 121 (r), 123 (bl), 294 (bl), 331 (tl), 345 (b), 355 (b), 356 (tl), 356 (tr), 356 (bl), 356 (br), 357 (t), 357 (b), 359, 360 (t), 360 (bl), 360 (br), 361, Peter Weimann: 350 (t), 363 (b), Habicht-Unep: 350 (bl), Klein/Hubert/Still Pictures: 353 (tr), Javier Eichaker/Still Pictures: 362 (tr), 362 (b), 363 (t),

The Kobal Collection: 144 (t), 144 (b),

Topham Picture Point: 6, 124 (br), 125 (bl), 128 (b), 130 (t), 130 (b), 132 (t), 135 (br), 136 (bl), 137 (r), 137 (l), 138 (l), 139 (bl), 141 (br), 142 (t), 143 (t), 143 (b), 145 (t), 145 (bl), 202 (tl), 203 (tr), 204 (t), 204 (b), 205 (bl), 240 (tr), 241 (t), 262 (tr), 263 (t), 305 (b).

Every effort has been made to contact the copyright holders and we apologise in advance for any ommissions. We will be pleased to insert appropriate acknowledgements in subsequent editions of this publication.

Index